Instructor's Manual to Accompany

■ Introduction to ■

PSYCHOLOGY

Exploration and Application

Seventh Edition

Dennis Coon

Santa Barbara City College

Prepared by

Saundra K. Ciccarelli

Gulf Coast Community College
Panama City, Florida

WEST PUBLISHING COMPANY

Minneapolis/St. Paul   New York   Los Angeles   San Francisco

WEST'S COMMITMENT TO THE ENVIRONMENT

In 1906, West Publishing Company began recycling materials left over from the production of books. This began a tradition of efficient and responsible use of resources. Today, up to 95% of our legal books and 70% of our college texts and school texts are printed on recycled, acid-free stock. West also recycles nearly 22 million pounds of scrap paper annually—the equivalent of 181,717 trees. Since the 1960s, West has devised ways to capture and recycle waste inks, solvents, oils, and vapors created in the printing process. We also recycle plastics of all kinds, wood, glass, corrugated cardboard, and batteries, and have eliminated the use of Styrofoam book packaging. We at West are proud of the longevity and the scope of our commitment to the environment.

Production, Prepress, Printing and Binding by West Publishing Company.

 TEXT IS PRINTED ON 10% POST CONSUMER RECYCLED PAPER  PRINTED WITH SOY INK™

CONTENTS

Introduction

Instructional Materials

Chapter 1   Psychology: The Search for Understanding

Chapter 2   Research Methods and Critical Thinking

Chapter 3   The Brain, Biology, and Behavior

Chapter 4   Sensation and Reality

INTRODUCTION TO THE INSTRUCTOR'S MANUAL

The purpose of this manual is to support the unique features of Dennis Coon's *Introduction to Psychology: Exploration and Application*, Seventh Edition, and to facilitate its use. Provided in the manual for each chapter are learning objectives, demonstrations, discussion topics, motivators, classroom exercises, cultural enrichment exercises, supplemental lectures, and suggestions for further reading and films. There are also reading tests, references for the teaching of psychology, a list of resource materials, and crossword puzzles containing important vocabulary words for each chapter. The comments that follow will acquaint you with the text, its study guides and ancillaries, the test bank, and the contents of this manual.

■ THE TEXT

The content and format of the text reflect a combination of goals. First and foremost, the text is written for students, not for instructors. It attempts to make the reader a voluntary participant in learning, rather than a passive and inattentive captive. To achieve this goal, chapters are structured around a unique study/reading format. Also, each chapter includes a section on practical applications of psychological principles. It is hoped that the extra effort taken to show students how to apply psychology gives the text an unusual degree of relevancy and impact.

Organization The text consists of 22 topical chapters (condensed from 26 chapters in the sixth edition), an appendix on careers in psychology, a statistics appendix, a glossary, references, and an index. In the latter part of the first chapter, various study skills are presented to students, including the SQ3R method. This section is a key to the rest of the text and should be assigned. In addition to giving students a good start and some helpful suggestions, it explains the chapter format and shows how it is designed to foster active learning.

Overall, the ordering of chapters and units was dictated by two concerns. Generally the organization reflects an underlying relationship among topics. But additionally, topics are ordered to balance high interest subjects with drier material. The chapters are quite independent and can be rearranged to suit the needs of various course outlines.

Each of the 22 chapters in the text is considerably shorter than a traditional chapter. (Their apparent length is deceptive due to the in-chapter quizzes, or *Learning Checks*.) Chapters were kept short so that each could be read in a single session with full attention and concentration. In a typical semester course the pace would be one to two chapters per week; in a quarter course, two per week. Either arrangement will produce a complete and well-paced course.

Instructors teaching semester courses who would like more rigor or breadth may want to assign an ancillary selection of readings (see list of readers under "Helpful Resources for Teaching Introductory Psychology"). However, the *Explorations* sections that conclude each chapter are intended to serve as in-text "readings" to round out coverage. In most instances, no outside assignments will be necessary for a complete introductory course.

Format Perhaps the most distinctive aspect of the text is the chapter format, which guides students through an active reading and information-processing experience. Each chapter begins with an attention-arousing *Chapter Preview* of very high-interest material. Each *Chapter Preview* is accompanied by a chapter outline, *In This Chapter*, and by a short list of *Survey Questions*. Both of these features are designed to augment the survey portion of an SQ3R reading approach, but they are no substitute for an actual chapter survey. Students should, therefore, be encouraged to study all topic headings in a chapter and to read the *Chapter Summary* before they begin reading.

Guide Questions establish a feeling of dialogue and anticipate student questions. *Learning Checks* (brief self-quizzes) are also interspersed throughout the text. *Learning Checks* offer immediate feedback and a chance to do some recitation while reading. A new feature of this edition is the inclusion of a critical thinking question in each *Learning Check*. Most students will find them helpful enough to use them voluntarily. However, students might be further encouraged if you include some Learning Check questions on quizzes or tests and announce in class that you plan to do so. A new **running glossary** has also been added to enhance the text's pedagogy.

Another feature of each chapter is the inclusion of several *Highlights* in each chapter. These discuss current issues of interest. For this edition nineteen new or substantially revised *Highlights* have been added. Each *Highlight* has been carefully integrated into the test to facilitate reading.

After core topics have been covered, each chapter has an *Applications* section that discusses explicit applications of psychological principles. Alternatively, the *Applications* sections offer added information of high personal relevance or practicality. The information presented in *Applications* is designed to meet the real needs of students and to bring psychology to life.

There is a constant tension in introductory courses between the need to present core concepts and a desire to make students aware of controversies, emerging research, and intriguing but nonessential topics. It is the author's view that after students have understood the main ideas of a chapter, they will be ready and willing to explore more widely. Accordingly, each chapter concludes with a *Exploration* designed to provide highly stimulating information.

In general, *Explorations* cover high-interest material of a controversial nature, frontier areas in psychology, contemporary issues, or topics almost sure to launch classroom discussion. Most *Explorations* are brief and of such interest that they should draw little protest from students. Because they are clearly identified by a colored background, *Explorations* are easy to delete from reading assignments whenever desired.

A detailed, point-by-point *Chapter Summary* provides a concise synopsis of all major topics in the chapter. The *Chapter Summary* is organized around the survey questions which were posed at the beginning of the chapter.

Each chapter concludes with a series of *Questions for Discussion*. Most of these questions were written to promote divergent thought and to spotlight issues that do not have simple answers. They should work equally well either in discussion groups or as a way to encourage participation in large lecture settings. Additionally, the queries can be used, in almost every case, as essay questions-- especially where creative thinking is desired.

The seventh edition contains some improvements in chapter design, strengthened contributions to the development of critical thinking skills, and more information on human diversity and cultural differences. Eight former chapters have been combined into four new chapters to enable a more streamlined presentation of closely-related topics.

Design features have been included to make the text more accessible to students. *Highlights* are placed exactly where students should pause and read them, improving the information flow in the chapter. Figures and table references are marked with small geometric shapes so that students can find their place when they return to reading. A section titled *A Look Ahead* provides a transition from general text to the *Applications* and *Explorations* sections that conclude each chapter. *Survey Questions* from the beginning of the chapter are repeated in the *Chapter Summary*. These questions structure the summary to help students review and remember main points.

Critical thinking is promoted by the SQ3R method. Many of the *Guide Questions* that are used to introduce topics in the text act as models of critical thinking. In this edition the revised *Exploration* for Chapter 1 specifically discusses critical thinking skills. This leads into Chapter 2, "Research Methods and Critical Thinking," which is actually a short course in critical thinking. Chapter 9, "Cognition and Creativity," also focuses on thinking skills. In addition, several *Explorations* critically evaluate controversial topics. Throughout the text many *Highlights* present topics that students should approach with healthy skepticism.

This edition includes additional discussions of **human diversity**, including differences in race, ethnicity, culture, gender, abilities, sexual orientation, and age. The purpose is to discourage stereotyping, prejudice, discrimination, and intolerance. Students are encouraged to appreciate social, physical, and cultural differences and to accept them as a natural part of being human.

■ ANCILLARY MATERIALS

The following is a listing of supplements to accompany the Seventh Edition of *Introduction to Psychology: Exploration and Application*. The number of ancillaries has become so large that it requires a separate document to give detailed information about their contents. West Publishing Company has prepared a *Guide to Instructional Materials* that gives a description of the content of each supplement and discussion of how it can be used. All supplements are keyed to the textbook. The *Guide* will assist the user in making the most effective use of these materials.

The ancillary materials are categorized here for easy identification. Some may appear in two categories because of the type of materials they contain.

A.   Study Guides

The *Study Guide* by Dennis Coon structures learning by providing a list of key terms and concepts, a programmed review, a practice test, and a crossword puzzle for each chapter. An integrated exercise is included for each chapter, challenging students to apply what they know.

The *Mastery Study Guide* by Tom Bond provides a thorough review. It includes a list of important terms and people, learning objectives, two tests ("Do You Know" and "Can You Apply"), and a fill-in-the-blank review for each chapter.

B.   Audiovisual Materials

The *Discovering Psychology* video series, produced by WGBH Boston in conjunction with the American Psychological Association, consists of 26 half-hour videotapes on topics covering the entire introductory psychology course. Each program contrasts historical perspectives with recent findings to encourage critical thinking. Excellent computer animations and documentary footage of classic experiments help students understand psychological concepts and relate them to their own experience.

Images of Psychology Videodiscs, a two-disc set, uses laser technology to present still-frame art, charts and tables, animated sequences, motion video sequences, and on-screen quizzes. These materials may be accessed instantly, in any order, by entering a frame number. Companion software for Macintosh computers (and compatibles) allows an instructor to prepare an entire laser-disc lecture, via hypercard stacks, and save it for future use. An *Instructor's Manual* by Lonnie Yandell lists and annotates all frames and video segments, describes their contents, and gives suggestions for their use.

Transparency Acetates contain over 140 tables, graphs, charts, and drawings.

C.   Computer Software

A variety of computer software has been assembled for the seventh edition. Test-generating materials include a computerized textbook *Westest 3.1* that organizes the test items like a desktop, using window displays.

Mind Scope software, created by Robert W. Hendersen, consists of twenty computerized exercises. They are designed to help students discover and analyze aspects of their own behavior. It runs on the IBM (or compatible) microcomputer.

Microguide is a computerized study guide available for both Macintosh and IBM PC's and compatibles.

Psychware was developed by Robert S. Slotnick and the staff of the New York Institute of Technology. There are tutorials, simulations, and experiments for use on Apple PC's.

D.   Print Materials

The seventh edition contains print materials that are new as well as some that are familiar to the user.

The *Test Bank* has been updated and reorganized by Laura Sidorowicz and Sid Hochman of Nassau Community College and contains approximately 4000 multiple choice items. The items are organized to correspond to the learning objectives, are page-referenced and classified according to type. These items also appear in *Westest 3.1.*

A separate packet of student data and *Worksheets* for all the exercises and crossword puzzles found in the *Instructor's Manual* is provided for easy duplication.

Cross-Cultural Perspectives in Introductory Psychology, Second Edition, is a collection of original articles written by William F. Price and Rich Crapo. It provides a multi-cultural view of human behavior and gives students an opportunity to place their own cultural practices in perspective.

The *Developmental/ESL Reader's Guide* is a 120-page booklet suitable for developmental and/or ESL students. It serves as a guide to reading the textbook and contains explanations of idioms, historical and cultural allusions, and unfamiliar vocabulary. All terms and phrases are page-referenced and followed by a concise definition.

The College Survival Guide, Third Edition, by Bruce Rowe is designed to help students to succeed in college. It contains tips on financing an education, time management, preparing for exams, and much more. It is most useful to first-year, re-entering, and non-native students.

A *Guide to Instructional Materials*, prepared by David Filak, integrates all the instructional materials that accompany the textbook. It coordinates learning objectives, *Test Bank* items, transparencies, cross-cultural readings, software, laser disc frames, and videotape segments. This is the first place to look to find out what materials apply to any particular chapter in the text.

■ THE INSTRUCTOR'S MANUAL

This *Instructor's Manual* provides resources that can enrich the experiences of the student and make it easier for the instructor to provide the variety that successful teaching requires. Since students come to psychology with varied backgrounds and learning styles, a single mode of presentation cannot adequately meet their needs. This manual provides, for each chapter, ideas for fruitful discussion, classroom exercises, and supplementary lecture material. There are also suggestions for films and readings. The behavioral objectives provide the instructor and students with a detailed outline of each chapter.

Behavioral Objectives The objectives follow the organization of the chapters and state in concrete terms what students should know when they have learned the material presented in the textbook. The objectives not only communicate to the students what they should learn from reading the text, but also serve as a way to review for tests since they clearly identify the important points in each chapter.

An instructor should provide students with a copy of the objectives for each chapter that is assigned for reading. If the students are tested for the chapter, the test questions should be based on the objectives.

Demonstrations, Dramatizations, and Discussion Involving the students in the classroom activity increases motivation and enhances learning. The activities presented in this section are intended to promote learning and enthusiasm for the course. They can provide the substance for a change of pace in the classroom routine and serve as demonstrations of how psychologists observe behavior. Most are simple demonstrations or discussions, requiring little preparation or equipment. In every instance, it is important to tie in the activity with the material being studied in the course, and the relevance of conclusions arrived at should be underlined for maximum benefit to the students. It should never be assumed that the students will make the connections on their own or that they are self-evident.

One-Minute Motivators Sometimes an instructor needs an idea to spark some discussion or provide a change of pace during a class session. These demonstrations, examples, props, or challenges can be introduced at appropriate times in a presentation. Used judiciously, they can add an extra dimension to the classroom activity.

Classroom Exercises There are one or more classroom exercises developed for each chapter in the text. These exercises are more elaborate than those found in the Demonstrations section. Each of the exercises has a rationale, an explanation of the purpose and procedure, a specific set of directions for carrying out the exercise, data sheets and worksheets for collecting information, and some points for discussion after the exercise is completed.

The data sheets and worksheets that are needed by the students to complete the exercises are contained in this manual. They may be duplicated and distributed for student use. Moreover, West Publishing Company has made these available in a separate packet as well. No longer do you have to try to make a good copy from the book. Using the separate sheets should guarantee good copies and ease of duplication.

Some of the exercises can be done in one session in the classroom. Others may take more than one class period and may require some work outside the classroom. Most of the exercises require students to work in groups, which should help to promote student interaction. It is important to change the groupings for each activity so that students will get to know each other and will not get into a rut.

Broadening Our Cultural Horizons This section provides some ideas for developing the students' awareness of cultural diversity. Differences among individuals and groups can be explored in the context of a psychology class. Instructors should take advantage of the cultural diversity found in most classrooms and communities. Opportunities should be provided for students to share their own experiences and to learn about others. An introduction to psychology class is a good place for students to grow in their understanding and appreciation of diversity.

Supplemental Lectures A significant feature of this manual is one or more supplemental lectures provided for each chapter. In each case, the lecture is related to the material in the chapter but is not simply a repetition of what the text contains. Each lecture is unique. It presents either a different point of view or new and relevant information on a topic that can be found in the text.

In most of the lectures, the ideas have been developed by the late Michael Sosulski from years of teaching, discussing, studying, and thinking about the topics. There are no handy references to which an instructor can turn for more information. For this reason, most of the lectures have been developed in detail to give the basic ideas some substance. It should be possible for teachers and students to review the material provided and discuss the implications, drawing whatever conclusions seem appropriate. It is probably more important to grapple with new and interesting ideas than to come up with some single conclusion on which everyone can agree.

Suggestions for Further Reading A list of additional readings is provided for each chapter in the text. Some care has been taken to find reading material that is accessible to students and in-teresting to read. Some of these could be assigned as enrichment for the class. Assignments to review articles or books for credit or extra credit could be made from this list. Some of the items are classic and should be introduced to serious students of psychology. Other readings are simply informative and/or entertaining.

Film Suggestions Films are suggested for each chapter. No attempt has been made to provide a complete list. These are simply some suggestions of films that have been found by instructors to be helpful in class. Every teacher of introductory psychology will have personal favorites and could add to the list provided. An additional source of audio-visual materials that has not been tapped for this edition of the manual is the growing supply of videotapes. The number and quality of these is increasing and should provide instructors with a rich new source of material to supplement classroom instruction.

Appendix E is an up-to-date listing of film sources. You can write for catalogs or have students send for them as a class assignment. Students who are writing major papers should be required to list some audiovisual materials as resources which they consulted.

■ APPENDICES

Appendices A and B provide two reading tests. Because of the complexity and scope of the introductory course in psychology, students need to read and collect information on their own as well as comprehend the text and participate in classroom activities. Since comprehension may be a problem for some students, an instructor may administer a reading test early in the term so that (s)he and the students may become aware of their problems, and remediation can be provided, if necessary.

Also, in the appendices are guidelines for *Leading Productive Discussions*, some *Helpful Resources for Teaching Introductory Psychology*, *Film Sources*, *Crossword Puzzles*, *Crossword Puzzle Solutions* and a listing of available *Transparencies*.

The puzzles provided in *The Study Guide* are for students to use for review. The puzzles in Appendix F of this manual, however, are not accessible to the students, and you have control of the solutions, so you can use these in any way that fits in with your program. They can serve as exercises, be part of an exam, can be assigned for homework, or may be used for extra credit assignments. They provide another interesting way for students to read and review a chapter. The solutions are provided in Appendix G.

Each puzzle in this manual contains between twenty and thirty-one terms and significant names. Challenge your students to read the chapters and find the solutions to each one. Individual copies of each puzzle are provided in the packet of worksheets for easy duplication.

Appendix H contains a master list of *Transparencies* for the seventh edition.

■ ACKNOWLEDGMENTS

The preparer of this Instructor's Manual wishes to acknowledge her deep indebtedness to the late Michael Sosulski, whose hard work and creativity in preparing previous editions of this manual contributed enormously to its value as a teaching resource. Thanks also go to Jeffery Strickland, a student at Gulf Coast Community College, who assisted in the preparation of the crossword puzzles for this edition of the Instructor's Manual.

CHAPTER 1

Psychology: The Search For Understanding

■ BEHAVIORAL OBJECTIVES

The student should be able to:

1. List two reasons for studying psychology.
2. Define psychology.
3. Describe what behavior is and differentiate overt from covert behavior.
4. Explain empirical evidence and give an example of it.
5. Identify the point at which psychology became a science and what sets it apart from other fields.
6. Give two reasons why the study of some topics in psychology is difficult.
7. Explain what the anthropomorphic fallacy is and how it can lead to problems in psychological research. Explain why and how animals are used in research and define the term "animal model" in the discussion. List two ways in which psychological research may benefit animals.
8. List and explain the four goals of psychology and its ultimate goal, including why the word "control" has a special meaning for psychologists which is distinct from the everyday meaning of the word.
9. Explain the sentence "Psychology has a long past but a short history."
10. Describe the school of psychology known as structuralism including:
    a. where and when it was established
    b. who established it (the "father" of psychology)
    c. the focus of its study
    d. the research method and its drawback
    e. its goal
11. Describe the functionalist school of psychology including:
    a. its founder
    b. its goal
    c. major interests
    d. impact on modern psychology
12. Describe behaviorism (S-R psychology) including:
    a. its founder
    b. why its founder could not accept structuralism or functionalism
    c. its emphasis
    d. Skinner's contribution
    e. role of cognitive behaviorism
    e. therapeutic outgrowth

13. Characterize the representation of the sexes in early psychology and explain the reason for the discrepancy. State the ratio of the sexes receiving doctorates in psychology today. Name the first woman to receive her doctorate in psychology.

14. Describe the Gestalt school of psychology including:
   a. what the word "Gestalt" means
   b. who founded it
   c. its goal
   d. its slogan
   e. areas of interest

15. Describe the psychodynamic school of psychology including:
   a. who founded it
   b. point of departure
   c. four contributions to psychology
   d. method of psychotherapy
   e. psychodynamic psychology today

16. Describe the humanistic school of psychology including:
   a. how its approach differs from psychoanalytic and behavioristic thought
   b. who its major representatives are
   c. position on "free will" (as contrasted with determinism)
   d. psychological needs
   e. interest in an objective, behavioral science
   f. subjective factors
   g. concept of self-actualization

17. Describe the eclectic approach.

18. List and briefly describe the five major perspectives in modern psychology (especially cognitive and biopsychological).

19. Explain how understanding human diversity may help us better understand ourselves and the behavior of others.

20. Characterize the differences in training, emphasis and/or expertise among psychologists, psychiatrists, psychoanalysts, counselors, and psychiatric social workers.

21. List the three points in the professional code for psychologists established by the APA.

22. Identify the largest areas of specialization among psychologists. Name the major source of employment for psychologists.

23. Differentiate basic from applied research.

24. Describe each of the following areas of specialization in psychology:
   a. clinical psychology and counseling   g. biopsychology
   b. developmental   h. social
   c. learning   i. cultural
   d. personality   j. industrial
   e. sensation and perception   k. school
   f. comparative   l. experimental

25. Explain what SQ3R means, showing how the steps in this method can be applied to using Coon's textbook.

26. Name two keys to note-taking and tell how to effectively use notes.

27.   List five things you can do to make study habits more productive.

28.   List two possible reasons why people procrastinate, and describe three ways to combat procrastination.

29.   List seven ways to improve objective test performance.

30.   List four ways to improve performance on essay tests.

31.   Explain what critical thinking is by listing and then applying six questions which should be considered when evaluating information.

32.   Indicate the foundations and fallacies of each of the following pseudo-psychologies:

       a. palmistry
       b. phrenology
       c. graphology
       d. astrology

33.   List and explain the three reasons why pseudo-psychologies continue to thrive even though they have no scientific basis.

■ DEMONSTRATIONS, DRAMATIZATIONS, AND DISCUSSION

1.   **The short true-false quiz in Chapter 1 of the textbook can be useful in class.** Students are usually interested in why all of the answers are false, especially since most will have incorrectly answered many of the questions. It can be interesting to see if class members can provide explanations for their answers. Among other things, this will give you an idea of the degree of sophistication of students in that particular class. If students cannot provide adequate explanations, yours will help establish the breadth of your knowledge, and it can be an excellent way to give students a taste of the kinds of information found in later chapters.

       Briefly, here are the reasons all fourteen statements are false:

       1)   The peak rate of neural transmission is about 100 meters per second (225 miles per hour). Therefore it takes a pain message about one-fiftieth of a second to travel the distance from foot to head.

       2)   Persons sighted in one eye have been known to fly airplanes, and many drive cars. It's true that their depth perception is greatly reduced, but the remaining monocular cues are sufficient, with practice, to allow a person to get by.

       3)   The atmosphere can indeed refract and distort the sun or the moon when either is directly on the horizon. Sometimes this causes the sun to appear "squashed" or layered. However, the apparent magnification of the moon is a perceptual illusion caused by the abundance of depth cues present when the moon is low in the sky. More depth cues imply greater distance, and greater distance implies a larger object (assuming the size of the retinal image remains the same).

4)   This myth about hypnosis is often perpetuated by television dramas and movies. Hypnosis may, in fact, uncover additional previously unrecalled information. However, it also produces confabulations and pseudo-memories that cannot be distinguished from accurate recollections.

5)   EEG records make it clear that the brain remains quite active during sleep (especially during REM sleep). It would be more accurate to say that the <u>pattern</u> of activity, not its amount, shifts.

6)   Punishment suppresses responding; it does not reinforce new habits.

7)   It was once widely believed, even among psychologists, that all memories may be permanent. However, reanalysis of Wilder Penfield's brain experiments suggests that direct brain stimulation most often elicited pseudo-memories and dreamlike reveries rather than true memories. It is highly unlikely that all long-term memories are permanent. In addition, it is clear that much information is never transferred from STM to LTM, so it was never stored.

8)   Psychological research has clearly shown that intelligence and creativity are independent qualities; at any given level of intelligence, some people are more creative than others.

9)   It is true that a person facing a threatening situation (such as surgery) can increase stress by worrying excessively. However, to deal effectively with threat, a person must devise a system of coping strategies; for many people "worrying" is part of this process.

10)   Stress occurs any time an organism must adjust or adapt to external demands. Thus, stress accompanies many pleasurable activities, as well as those which are threatening or traumatic. The only way to be completely free of stress is to be dead.

11)   Heredity clearly has an effect on intelligence, but no reputable theorists, including the most ardent hereditarians, seriously believe that intelligence is entirely genetically determined.

12)   This is one of the classic myths about suicide. Most suicidal individuals give warning of their intentions, either directly or indirectly.

13)   Many students confuse schizophrenia with multiple personality--probably because the mistake is so often made in the popular media. The "split" in schizophrenia refers to disjunctions in thought, emotion, and action.

14)   Research on bystander apathy suggests that the more potential helpers present, the less likely it is that help will be given. When many helpers are present, no one feels

personally responsible for giving aid; that is, a diffusion of responsibility occurs.

2.   **The method of observation called introspection can be demonstrated in class by a simple exercise.** Students will readily see the problems inherent in this method. Ask students to identify the most basic taste sensations. With some help from you they will come up with the four basic ones: sweet, sour, salty, bitter. Now ask them to introspect by identifying the taste of water. They should identify which of the four basic tastes it resembles most closely--if not one, then perhaps a combination of two or more. Students will arrive at a variety of answers but mostly consternation because of the near impossibility of the task. The difficulty of using introspection as the only or major research method should be readily apparent.

3.   **At some point in coverage of the first chapter, you might want to bring up the subject of pop psychology, especially as it is represented in self-help books and commercial therapies.** As the <u>New York Times</u> News Service observed a few years ago:

> If you were to believe the current dogma, happiness is getting rid of your erroneous zones, looking out for No. 1, asserting yourself, taking charge of your life, and learning to love every minute of it. It is clearing your psyche by screaming, esting, rolfing, encountering, hallucinating, meditating, and levitating, tuning into your biorhythms, following your stars, getting in touch with your feelings, letting it all hang out, and teleporting yourself into an extrasensory universe.

In addition to providing a good contrast to academic psychology, pop psychology can lead into a discussion of empirical and non-empirical approaches. At the very least, the self-help books pale in comparison to Maslow's work on self-actualization. As Jonathan Freedman of Columbia University points out in the same article, "most of the advice in the pop psych books and therapies is dangerously egocentric. It teaches people just to look out for themselves. Yet, to be happy, you have to care, to take responsibility. Egocentric, narcissistic types don't form relationships very easily or maintain them very well.

4.   **Countering widespread student belief in astrology can be worth the class time and effort.** The inaccuracy of the system can be illustrated by use of the adjective check-list that follows. In class, have students check all of the adjectives that apply to their personalities (interpretation follows).

1) pioneering	*13) extroverted*	*25) honest*
2) enthusiastic	*14) generous*	*26) impulsive*
3) courageous	*15) authoritative*	*27) optimistic*
4) stable	*16) critical*	*28) ambitious*
5) stubborn	*17) exacting*	*29) hard-working*
6) organized	*18) intelligent*	*30) cautious*

7) *intellectual*	19) *harmonizing*	31) *original*
8) *adaptable*	20) *just*	32) *open-minded*
9) *clever*	21) *sociable*	33) *independent*
10) *sensitive*	22) *secretive*	34) *kind*
11) *nurturing*	23) *strong*	35) *sensitive*
12) *sympathetic*	24) *passionate*	36) *creative*

The adjectives in this list were compiled by William Balch from eleven astrology books. They represent the most frequently mentioned characteristics for each astrological "sign." After students have made their responses, identify the signs corresponding to each group of three adjectives. **They are: 1-3, Aries; 4-6, Taurus; 7-9, Gemini; 10-12, Cancer; 13-15, Leo; 16-18, Virgo; 19-21, Libra; 22-24, Scorpio ; 25-27, Sagittarius; 28-30, Capricorn; 31-33, Aquarius; 34-36, Pisces.** Next, call for a show of hands from those students who checked all three adjectives listed for "their sign." Follow this with a show of hands by students who checked all three adjectives for any other sign. You should, of course, get a roughly equal number of hands raised each time--showing that there is no compelling association between astrological signs and personality traits. (Adapted from Balch, W. R. "Testing the validity of astrology in class." *Teaching of Psychology*, 1980 7(4), 247-250.)

■ ONE-MINUTE MOTIVATORS

1. **Ask one student to describe** all the things that s(he) did, thought, and felt during the last five minutes. Point out that human behavior is exceedingly complex.

2. **Quickly collect demographic data** from the class by a raising of hands. What kind of generalizations can be made about the "kind of people" in that specific class?

3. **Add examples of the way humans talk** to public telephones, vending machines, automatic bank tellers, automobiles, and computers when the machines are "moody." Is there anything wrong with this kind of anthropomorphizing?

4. **To demonstrate "diffusion of responsibility,"** as it relates to prosocial behavior, drop something and count the number of students who rush to help. Do the same thing on the way to class when only a few students are present and bring that data to class for discussion.

5. **If your classroom is fairly soundproof,** scream once to demonstrate a potent stimulus and discuss the responses made by members of the class.

6. **After describing the academic preparation of psychology professionals,** ask, "What education and experience should a psychology professor have? Why?

7.   **To quickly illustrate the fallacies of astrology,** buy a bag of fortune cookies. Have each student read his or her fortune and then explain how it is "true" or "accurate" in some way. Remind students that they received fortunes on a random basis and that the fallacy of positive instances is a likely explanation of any "accurate" fortunes.

■ CLASSROOM EXERCISES

TO THE INSTRUCTOR:

The two exercises which follow should help to get the students involved in the subject matter of the chapter. The first is a take-home exercise intended to help the student to understand what the subject matter of psychology is. The second is an in-class activity that should impress the students with the difficulty of gathering objective data, especially by the method of introspection. Although students may deny relying on introspection, they do, in fact, treat their own sensory experiences as infallible.

Exercise #1: What is Psychology?

The purpose of this exercise is to help students to learn what psychology is about and to impress on them that what psychologists are doing is different from the popular notions held by persons who are not familiar with what psychologists study. This exercise is set up on the following pages in such a way that it can be duplicated and distributed. Students may record responses and write their analysis directly on the form provided.

Exercise #2: Introspection

This exercise is a classroom activity that should generate discussion on methodology and particularly on the validity of self-reporting personal experiences as a method of understanding behavior. With a few simple materials you can have students involved in this project. You can follow the directions, using three pairs, with the rest of the class as observers, or you can divide the whole class in pairs of "experimenters" and "introspectionists."

WHAT IS PSYCHOLOGY?

TO THE STUDENT:

The purpose of this exercise is to help you to understand what psychology is about and how it differs from the popular ideas about it that most people have. You probably had some of the same misconceptions before beginning this course. Begin by reading Chapter 1 of the text. Look for the definition of psychology given on page 1 and write it down so that you can complete this assignment. Then follow the directions, record responses, and discuss what you find.

1.   Ask five people what they think psychology is. Ask each to give a brief statement about what it is or what psychologists study. Select a variety of people. They should be persons of different ages, sexes, and educational levels.

2.   Record pertinent data about each subject (sex, approximate age, educational level) and the verbatim response to your question. Do not add to the response or try to clarify it.

3.   After you have collected all your responses, do an analysis, comparing what you were told by the respondents with the definition in the text. The questions which follow this data sheet should help you in your analysis.

WHAT IS PSYCHOLOGY?   DATA SHEET:

Subject #1   Sex_____   Age (approx.)_____   Education_____

Subject #2   Sex_____   Age (approx.)_____   Education_____

Subject #3   Sex_____   Age (approx.)_____   Education_____

Subject #4   Sex_____   Age (approx.)_____   Education_____

Subject #5   Sex_____   Age (approx.)_____   Education_____

Name_____

WHAT IS PSYCHOLOGY?   ANALYSIS OF RESPONSES:

A.   The definition of psychology given in your text is:

B.   What are some of the common elements in the statements made by your subjects?

C.   How do the popular notions about psychology given by your subjects differ from the definition given in the text?

D.   What are some of the major misconceptions that your subjects had about psychology?

Exercise #2

INSTROSPECTION

TO THE INSTRUCTOR:

The concept of structuralism as a philosophical underpinning to early psychological inquiry is sometimes difficult for students to comprehend. This is attributable somewhat to the difficulty students have with introspection, the methodology of structuralism. Many students perceive introspection to be a valid source of information and find it difficult to question findings from this methodology. (How many people doubt the truthfulness of their own sensory experiences?) The purpose of the following demonstration is to assist students in understanding the methodology of introspection, the inherent difficulties of relying on data generated with introspection, and what structuralists were trying to accomplish through the use of this method.

Equipment: A.   Data Sheets
            B.   Several simple objects (e. g. apple, pencil, cup, an aromatic liquid)

Demonstration: Begin by exploring with the class what structuralists attempted to discover about the "mind." Be sure it is understood that structuralists were attempting to discover the "building blocks" of conscious experience. Next, discuss the methodology of introspection and its attendant language (reporting on a "pure" immediate sensory experience). Once this discussion is complete, you can begin the demonstration.

Have six students from the class volunteer to participate in the demonstration. Randomly assign three persons to be experimenters and three to be introspectionists. Divide them into three pairs, each with an experimenter and an introspectionist. Conduct the demonstration in the following manner:

1.   Give one of the objects to each of the experimenters. The experimenter should present the object to the introspectionist briefly (about two seconds), then remove it from sight.

2.   During the time the object is being presented, the introspectionist should say whatever comes to mind about the qualities of the object being considered. Allow students to determine for themselves what constitutes a basic quality or irreducible conscious element. Be sure the students do not report on emotional experiences, but on their sensory experiences as objectively as possible. The experimenter should record the responses on the data sheet.

3.   Have the experimenters repeat this procedure 3 to 5 times for the same object.

4.   Rotate the objects among the pairs so that each pair introspects with each object.

5.   After all of the objects have been "introspected", collect the data sheets and note the similarities and differences among the reports given to the experimenters. These should be listed on the chalkboard in the form of a table.

6.   The instructor should, at the conclusion of the above demonstration, have the students respond to one or more of the questions on the data sheet. These may be used in small group discussions in class or as a take-home exercise.

(adapted from a demonstration by Dr. William C. Titus, Arkansas Tech University)

INTROSPECTION--DATA SHEET:

OBJECT	TRIALS				
	1	2	3	4	5
1.					
2.					
3.					
4.					

DISCUSSION QUESTIONS:

A.   Should we rely on this methodology as a way of obtaining consistent and unbiased data? Why or why not?

B.   What problems exist with interpreting data based on this methodology?

C.   What problems exist with regard to studying certain types of psychological phenomena using the method of introspection (e.g. altruism, aggression, psychopathology)?

D.   To what degree (or how) does this methodology violate the basic tenets of empiricism?

■ BROADENING OUR CULTURAL HORIZONS

1. **Ask students to read a short section** from an encyclopedia on the culture of Russia. Which school of psychology would a Russian most easily accept? Ask students to read about the Japanese culture. Which school of psychology would you guess would be most interesting to a person from Japan? Is it possible to have one valid psychology for all cultures?

2. **Psychology is a system for explaining behavior.** In western cultures psychology is approached as if it were a natural science, with great emphasis placed on empiricism and the scientific method. Is this a cultural preference? Or is it the most defensible approach to psychology, regardless of cultural values?

■ SUPPLEMENTAL LECTURE

It may be helpful for the students' understanding of where psychology is going to look at where it has been. The history of the study of man* goes back thousands of years. There has been lively discussion about man: his/her place in the universe, destiny, nature, and many other questions that have led to endless debate and theorizing. Philosophers have looked for answers to questions about man through reasoning, and theologians have added faith to the discussion.

If we go back to the medieval period in the history of western thought, we can trace a process that seems to go full circle--or perhaps it is more of a spiral than a circle. Looking at the history of this process can make our exploration more meaningful because it puts modern psychology in a broader context.

In this lecture the instructor should discuss with the students the major changes in the way man has been viewed during the past seven hundred years, since we have had extensive written records. This can be done by dividing the time into historical periods. If desired, the students could be divided into groups with each group researching one period. Probably, to save time, the instructor could develop the highlights of each period through lecture/discussion in class.

*In this context, the term "man" refers to human nature.

EVOLUTION OF THE STUDY OF MAN

I.   Medieval Period
- A.   Philosophical notion of man
  1.   Consists of   - body - animal nature
                       - soul - spiritual nature
  2.   Soul has two powers - reason - to think
                              - will - to choose
  3.   Philosophers discussed man's capacity to think and freedom to choose. Theories varied regarding the relationship between body and soul and the rational and volitional capabilities of man.
- B.   Theological notion of man
  1.   Theologians built their concept of man on the philosophical base.
  2.   Man's ability to choose made him praise-worthy or culpable, depending on whether his actions were in keeping with God's law as revealed in the scriptures.

II. Renaissance Period
- A.   Rebirth was cultural, social, economic, and philosophical.
- B.   Questioning of previously accepted ideas and ways of doing things was characteristic of this time.
- C.   Skepticism left people open to look at and for new ideas.
- D.   With the beginning of industry, people began to live in towns, become better educated, and have leisure to discuss ideas and share opinions. The result was new questions and a rejection of old ideas--scientific enquiry was called for.
- E.   The scientific method became accepted as the only valid way to attain knowledge.
- F.   Renaissance thinkers about man focused more on the body and less on the soul or spirit because the body could be observed and studied scientifically while the soul could not.
- G.   By 1700 A.D. the break from philosophy had occurred. The philosophers and theologians pursued their study of man through reason and faith. Those interested in scientific answers to questions about man began to move in a different direction with the body and its behavior as their focus. Psychology emerged as this new area of study.
- H.   The term "psychology" was in common use by the middle of the eighteenth century as the name of this new study of man.

III.   Modern Period
- A.   Psychology became established as a science. The focus was on the body as a behaving organism. The method was observation and measurement.
- B.   The new science was opposed by theologians and people of all religious faiths because it appeared to deny the existence of the soul which, of course, cannot be observed or measured.

C.   Psychology progressed through several schools or theories: Structuralism to Functionalism to Behaviorism, as the search for an explanation of behavior continued.

D.   As the twentieth century approached, psychologists expanded their subject matter to include all behavior, animal as well as human. This was due, to a large extent, to the acceptance of evolution as an explanation for the origins of man.

E.   Finally, by the middle of the twentieth century, Humanistic Psychology appeared with the focus on the self. Self-direction and self-determination were again in vogue. The Medieval ideas of man were rediscovered in a new way in Humanistic Psychology.

IV.   Discussion Questions
A.   Have the ideas of "man" come full circle or spiraled?
B.   How did psychological theories change as they moved from Structuralism to Functionalism to Behaviorism? Trace the progression.
C.   Where does Gestalt Psychology fit into this context? Did it serve as a precursor to Humanism?
D.   Where will psychological theories go from here?

■ SUGGESTIONS FOR FURTHER READING

History:

Atkinson, R. C. "Reflections of Psychology's Past and Concerns About Its Future." *American Psychologist*. 1977, 32, 205-210.

Hothersall, D. *History of Psychology*, 2nd ed.. McGraw-Hill, 1990.

Mueller, C. G. "Some Origins of Psychology as a Science." *Annual Review of Psychology*, 1979, 30, 9-29.

Definition:

Hebb, D. O. "What Psychology Is About." *American Psychologist*, 1974, 29, 71-79.

Jerome, L. E. "Astrology--Magic or Science?" in *Objections to Astrology*. Prometheus Books, 1975.

Koch, S. "The Nature and Limits of Psychological Knowledge: Lessons of a Century qua Science." *American Psychologist*, 1981, 36, 257-269.

Applications:

Career Associates. *Career Choices for Students of Psychology*. Walker and Company, 1985.

Grasha, A. *Practical Applications of Psychology*, 3rd ed. Harper & Row, 1987.

Holland, M and G. Tarlow. *Using Psychology: Principles of Behavior in Your Life*, 2nd ed. Little, Brown & Co., 1980.

Super, Charles, Ph.D. and Donald Super, Ph.D. *Opportunities in Psychology Careers*. Lincolnwood IL.: VGM Career Horizons, 1988.

■ FILM SUGGESTIONS

BEHAVIORISM AND BEYOND (1974, CRM Productions, 20 min.)
>   This film presents a discussion of the beginnings of modern behaviorism by B. F. Skinner. Skinner then goes on to present his interpretation of behaviorism's basic principles.

HISTORY OF PSYCHOLOGY (Educulture) Filmstrip, Module 1.
>   A survey of structuralist, functionalist, behaviorist, Gestalt, psychoanalytic, and contemporary theories.

ISSUES IN PSYCHOLOGY (1990, Coast Community College District Telecourses, 30 min.)
>   Part of the *Psychology - The Study of Human Behavior Series*, this video presents a discussion with leading psychologists and teachers of important topics in psychology.

RESEARCH METHODS (1990, Coast Community College District Telecourses, 30 min.)
>   Part of the *Psychology - The Study of Human Behavior Series*, this video shows footage of lobotomy, autism, and police investigators employing cognitive interview techniques.

WHAT IS PSYCHOLOGY (1990, Coast Community College District Telecourses, 30 min.)
>   Part of the *Psychology - The Study of Human Behavior Series*, this video describes the nature of psychology and what its practitioners do.

CHAPTER 2

Research Methods and Critical Thinking

■ BEHAVIORAL OBJECTIVES

The student should be able to:

1. Explain the problem in using common sense as a source of information.
2. List the five steps of the scientific method.
3. Define the term "hypothesis" and be able to identify one. Explain what an operational definition is.
4. Explain the purpose of theory formulation.
5. Describe the technique of naturalistic observation including both the advantages and limitations of this method. Define the terms observer effect and observer bias.
6. Describe what a correlational study is and list three advantages and disadvantages of such a method. Explain what a correlation coefficient is, how it is expressed, what it means, and how it is related to causation.
7. List and describe the three variables in the experimental method.
8. Explain the nature and the purpose of the control group and the experimental group in an experiment.
9. Explain the purpose of randomly assigning subjects to either the control or the experimental group.
10. Identify three advantages and two disadvantages of the experimental method.
11. Explain the purpose of the field experiment.
12. Explain what statistically significant results are.
13. Explain why replicability is so important in science.
14. Explain what a placebo is, how effective it is, how it probably works, and what its purpose in an experiment is.
15. Explain what single-blind and double-blind experimental arrangements are.
16. Explain the experimenter effect and how it is related to the self-fulfilling prophecy.
17. Briefly describe the clinical method of research including two advantages and three disadvantages. Give an example of a case in which the clinical method would be used.
18. Briefly describe the survey method of investigation including an advantage and a disadvantage. Define the terms gender bias, courtesy bias, and my-side bias and explain how they make evidence less useful.
19. List seven suggestions that the author gives to help the student become a more critical reader of psychological information in the popular press.
20. List and describe the three areas of ethical concern in psychological experiments, and explain the position of the APA in terms of ethical guidelines.
21. Briefly describe the polarity that exists in the debate concerning animal research. Describe the middle ground of the debate.

■ DEMONSTRATIONS, DRAMATIZATIONS, AND DISCUSSION

1.   **The theme of Chapter 2 can be summarized by a statement made by Bertrand Russell,** "...it is not <u>what</u> the man of science believes that distinguishes him, but <u>how</u> and <u>why</u> he believes it. His beliefs are tentative, not dogmatic; they are based on evidence, not on authority." (In the interest of using non-sexist language, it might be best to paraphrase this quotation, substituting "scientists" for "man of science" and using the plural pronoun "they.") This can be the start of a good discussion on what science is and how it differs from philosophy, mathematics, values, religion, magic, art, etc.

2.   **For some excellent examples of foolishness masquerading as science see Martin Gardner's** <u>Fads and Fallacies in the Name of Science</u>, New York, N.Y.: Dover Publications, 1957.

3.   **A problem for many students is an inability to recognize the dependent and independent variable(s)** in situations other than those provided in the text. To generalize these concepts, present the following descriptions and ask students to identify the independent and dependent variables in each.

   a.   A physiological psychologist injects several monkeys with male hormones and notes that by comparison to control animals they display more aggressive acts in a testing situation.

   b.   After being deprived of food for varying amounts of time, subjects show a progressive decline in hand dexterity and steadiness.

   c.   An educational psychologist finds no differences in the math achievement scores of elementary school students who have, or have not, been assigned to a special math-education program.

   d.   A social psychologist observes that subjects tested in crowded rooms have slower reaction times than those tested individually.

   e.   A psychologist decides to test the idea that you "can't teach an old dog new tricks." What would the dependent and independent variables be?

4.   **To clarify the various elements of a carefully controlled experiment,** and to review problems such as the placebo effect and experimenter expectancies, describe the following experiment to students and have them identify the mistakes that have been made:

   Let's say that I am interested in the effects of caffeine on memory. In order to test the effects of caffeine, I divide the class in half. All the students on the right are given five cups of coffee to drink, and one hour later they are given a test of memory. The students on the left are dismissed. After the first group has been tested, the second group returns and is given the same memory test as the first group. The average scores are compared, and they show that the first group remembered more than the second group.

Major errors that students should note are: The experimental and control groups were not formed by random assignment; subjects were not tested at the same time of day; no placebo was used; subjects were probably aware of the experimenter's hypothesis; the experimenter was not blind with respect to subject assignment. Extraneous variables were not identified or controlled. Pre-tests and post-tests were not given. (For a better model for this experiment, see Supplemental Lecture section which follows.)

5. **One way to illustrate the difference between casual observation and the empirical method** is to ask students to describe things in their environment that they "see" on a regular basis. The following questions regarding items that people observe all the time can serve as a starting point. Answers are indicated in parentheses. You may be surprised at how poor most students are at identifying things they have seen many times.

   1) Everyone knows that it's red with white letters, but what is the shape of a stop sign? (Octagon)
   2) Which way does Abe Lincoln face on a penny? (To his left, which means the viewer's right.)
   3) In which hand does the Statue of Liberty hold her torch? (The right)
   4) How many tines are on a standard dinner fork? (Four)
   5) Which two letters are missing on a standard telephone? (Q and Z)
   6) If a common pencil isn't cylindrical, how many sides does it usually have? (Six)
   7) On which side of their uniforms do police officers wear their badges? (On their left side)
   8) On the back of a $5.00 bill is the Lincoln Memorial, and on the back of a $10.00 bill is the U.S. Treasury Building. What is on the reverse side of a $1.00 bill? (The word ONE in large letters)

■ ONE-MINUTE MOTIVATORS

1. **Bring a camera to class the first day to take photos of students in order to better remember their names.** After a posed shot, take a series of "natural" shots or use a video camera while the class is doing a small group activity. Develop the photos and show that people act differently when they know they are being observed.

2. **To demonstrate the experimenter effect and the self-fulfilling prophecy, ask for a female volunteer.** Explain that you want to show that the reaction time of females is faster than that of males. You will drop a piece of paper. Her job is to catch it as quickly as possible. Ask another student to serve as timer. Before you start say things like, "Are you relaxed?" "Do you understand what I want you to do?" "Are you ready?" Of course, she will catch the

paper. Then ask for a male volunteer. Quickly say, "Ready, go!" He invariably misses the paper. Conclude, "Thus you can see that female reaction time is faster than male reaction time." Ideally, as you start to move on, someone will say, "But that wasn't fair. . ."

3.   **To demonstrate a representative sample, bring in two boxes of candy,** one filled only with nut chocolates and the other with a blend. (Plain M&Ms and peanut M&Ms would work.) Ask students to sample one piece from each box and then draw a conclusion about the whole box. While we need more than a piece or two to gain confidence in our conclusions, we really don't have to eat the entire box to be fairly accurate.

4.   **When talking about the limitations of surveys and the Gutek (1981) data on harassment,** ask the class to write down on a scrap of paper their gender and whether they believe they have experienced any form of sexual harassment in the prior year. While many males will have been harassed, you will probably find that a larger percentage of women have experienced such pressures.

■ CLASSROOM EXERCISES

TO THE INSTRUCTOR:

The following two exercises provide the student with opportunities to become involved with the concepts being studied. The first is an in-class activity which will make the concept of correlation more relevant to the student. The second is an exercise that requires students to look for reports of scientific "marvels" found in the supermarket tabloids. These often purport to be the astounding results of new research.

Exercise #1: Positive and Negative Correlation

In this exercise students are asked to respond to a questionnaire which will provide the class with raw data to be plotted on a scattergram. The students are more likely to give correct responses to the questions if they do not have to identify themselves, so keep the responses anonymous. Collect the questionnaires. They will provide you with plenty of data. You can read the data and have the students plot a scattergram. After plotting several pairs of variables, they will soon see that relationships are not all the same. You will find that some of the relationships will be positive and some negative. Other variables will show little or no relationship. (You and the class may wish to add other variables.)

Once the students see the relationships on the graph it is important to discuss cause and effect. Does it exist? How can you tell? Copy and distribute the prepared data sheets and the diagrams provided for this exercise.

Exercise #2:   "Scientific Marvels" in the News

Students should be able to evaluate reports of research using the principles of the scientific method discussed in this chapter. Students may find it fun to review some of the sensational reports found in the periodicals which are displayed in the grocery store check-out lines. This exercise should provide a clear demonstration of the absurdity of these reports when examined using scientific criteria.

POSITIVE AND NEGATIVE CORRELATION

TO THE STUDENT:

Complete this questionnaire giving information about yourself. You do not need to put your name on this sheet, so your information will be confidential. If you are not sure, estimate what you think the response should be.

Your responses will be collected, and the class will use the information to study correlation.

Age_____

Height_____

Weight_____

Shoe size_____

Grade-point average_____

Number of members in your family_____

Number of hours of study per week_____

Number of hours of part-time or full-time work per week_____

Number of credit hours being taken by you this term_____

Number of courses from which you withdrew last term_____

Number of courses which you completed last term_____

Number of movies attended per month_____

Number of parties attended per month_____

Number of sports in which you regularly participate_____

Number of books which you read for pleasure per month_____

POSITIVE AND NEGATIVE CORRELATION   SCATTERGRAMS:

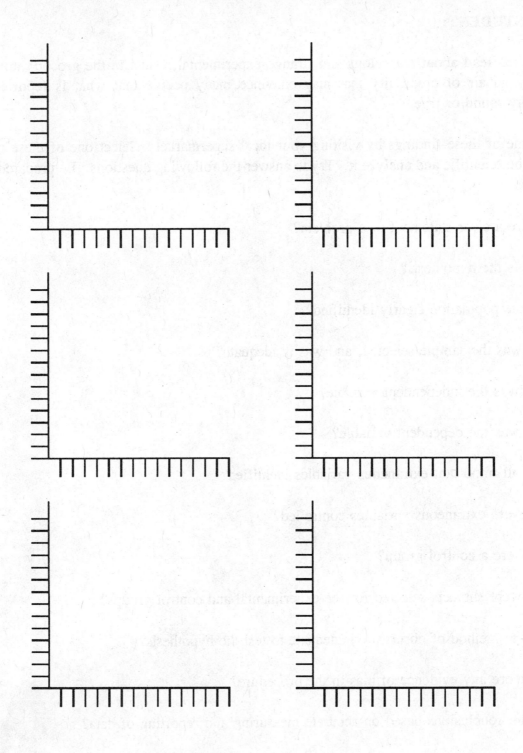

"SCIENTIFIC MARVELS" IN THE NEWS

TO THE STUDENT:

One can often read about marvelous and strange experimental results in the grocery store tabloids. They carry an air of credibility that may convince many people that what is reported is really scientifically sound or true.

Collect some of these findings by visiting your local supermarket. Select one of these reports that appears to be scientific and analyze it. Try to answer the following questions. Be prepared to discuss this in class.

1. Is there a clear statement of a problem?

2. What is the hypothesis?

3. Was the population clearly identified?

4. How was the sample selected, and was it adequate?

5. What was the independent variable?

6. What was the dependent variable?

7. Were all important extraneous variables identified?

8. How were extraneous variables controlled?

9. Was there a control group?

10. How were subjects selected for the experimental and control groups?

11. Was the method of observation adequate to test the hypothesis?

12. Was there any evidence of bias in the procedure?

13. Are the conclusions based on accurate measuring and reporting of data?

14. Are the conclusions warranted?

■ BROADENING OUR CULTURAL HORIZONS

Many people within the American culture value highly dogs and cats as pets. There are other cultures where such pets are not treated as part of the family. Think of how research in psychology would be different in those cultures as opposed to ours.

■ SUPPLEMENTAL LECTURE

The section in Chapter 2 entitled, "The Psychology Experiment--Where Cause Meets Effect," discusses the experiment. Terms are defined and some examples show how an experiment could be done.

It is important for students to know how experiments are carried out so that they will see the value of and problems in doing experiments with living organisms (humans or animals). In this lecture you will take the students through the process, step-by-step, so that they will see how the experiment is done. Prior to this lecture you should have the students read the section in the text referred to above. Your lecture can then be concerned with how an experiment works out in practice.

THE EXPERIMENT--NOT OUT OF CONTROL

I.   Cause and Effect

    A. The goal of the experiment is to show cause and effect.

        1.   Discuss the importance of control of all factors, i.e. the experimenter needs to know exactly what is causing the behavior that is being observed.

        2.   Begin by illustrating the following model on the chalkboard (or an overhead projector), noting that the stimulus affects the subject, and we observe a response:

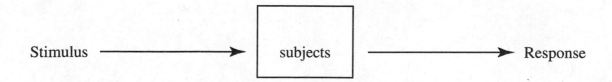

3.   This is the basic model: we do something to the subjects, then we observe/measure the response of each.

B.   An example: we want to know if caffeine improves retention.

     1.   Discuss this with the students. Could we give a group of students ten cups of caffeinated coffee and then test their memory? What if we did and found that they all did well on the test?

     2.   This discussion should reveal two things (or you should be sure it does):

           a.   You need a pre-test and a post-test to see if any <u>change</u> has occurred as a result of the caffeine consumption.

           b.   Changes in the response that did occur could have been caused by other factors, such as re-taking the same test, a change in time of day between tests, students being aware that they are subjects, etc.

C.   Some terms are needed at this point and should be introduced:

     1.   Variable - any condition that changes or is changeable. Elicit examples from the students: things such as air temperature, one's mood, time of day, etc.

     2.   Independent variable - this is the "stimulus" in the model above. It is the condition we will be applying to the subjects in order to get them to respond. In our example it is the caffeine.

     3.   Dependent variable - this is the "response" in the illustration above. In the example it will be the performance of the subjects on the pre- and post-tests for memory.

     4.   Extraneous variables - these are any conditions that could affect the behavior of the subjects and so influence the results. Some of the conditions mentioned by the students in the earlier discussion would fall into this category.

D.   So, back to the model:

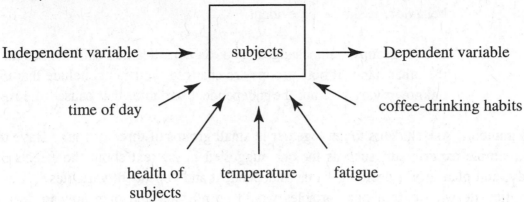

EXTRANEOUS VARIABLES

E.   Control of extraneous variables:

1.   Note that all significant variables need to be identified and controlled.

2.   The experimenter must identify all relevant variables—those that might influence the behavior of the subjects in this experiment.

3.   Control of these variables means either eliminating them where possible or holding them constant at a level where you know what their effect would be.

4.   Can we now attribute the change in behavior from pre- to post-test to caffeine? Most students will say yes, but elicit from them the problems of the unknown or unidentified extraneous variable. The dreaded unknown or unidentified extraneous variable! How do you know all variables are controlled? You don't! Not for sure. How can you find out?

F.   Experimental and Control Groups

1.   Discuss what these groups are and how subjects are randomly assigned to each.

2.   Discuss single- and double-blind techniques.

3.   Explain that the experimental group is exposed to the independent variable and the control group is not.

4.   Both groups are otherwise treated the same. Extraneous variables are dealt with equally in both.

5.   Both groups get the pre- and post-tests.

6.   Now you can compare the results. If caffeine is the cause of changed test behavior, it should be evident.

7.   If both groups are unchanged, you can conclude that caffeine has no effect. On the other hand, if both groups are changed, you can conclude that there was an unknown variable, not the independent variable, that caused the result.

II.   Assignment: Ask students to get together in small groups of three or four. Have them decide on a simple experiment, such as the one suggested in the text about the effects of music on study, and plan it out, deciding on the independent and dependent variables. They should try to anticipate what extraneous variables would be relevant and plan how to deal with them. Experimental and control groups should be set up once subjects are selected. Students could be asked to work it out on paper or actually design and carry out such an experiment.

■ SUGGESTIONS FOR FURTHER READING

Anderson, B. D. *The Psychological Experiment,* 3rd ed. Brooks/Cole, 1977.

Barber, T. *Pitfalls in Human Research: Ten Pivotal Points.* Pergamon Press, 1976.

Edwards, A. L. *Experimental Design in Psychological Research,* 5th ed. Harper & Row, 1985.

Elmes, D., B. Dantowitz, and H. L. Roediger. *Research Methods in Psychology,* 5th ed. West, 1995.

Goldstein, M. and I. Goldstein. *How We Know: An Exploration of the Scientific Process.* Plenum, 1978.

Kantowitz, B., H. L. Roediger, and D. Elmes. *Experimental Psychology: Understanding Psychological Research,* 5th ed. West, 1995.

Keith-Spiegel, P. and G. P. Goocher. *Ethics in Psychology: Professional Standards and Cases.* Random House, 1985.

Miller, A. G. (1986). *The Obedience Experiments: A Case Study of Controversy in Social Science.* New York: Praeger.

Monte, C. F. *Psychology's Scientific Endeavor.* Praeger, 1975.

Stanovich, K. E. *How To Think Straight About Psychology,* 3rd ed. Harper Collins, 1992.

■ FILM SUGGESTIONS

METHODOLOGY; THE PSYCHOLOGIST AND THE EXPERIMENT (1975, McGraw Hill/CRM, 31 min.)
This film provides an informative visual account of the standard methods which all research experiments employ. Independent and dependent variables, control groups, random assignment to groups, and other basic statistical concepts are explored. Schachter's experiment in "fear and affiliation" is documented as well as Riesen's physiological psychology experiment on the development of visual-motor coordination.

THE NATURE OF SCIENCE (1972, Coronet Films, 11 min.)
A look at some of the shortcomings of sensory experience as a primary source of information about the environment. Illusions are used to demonstrate situations where sensory experience is inadequate and to give examples of the ways in which scientific methods produce more reliable explanations.

■ COMPUTER PROGRAMS: *MIND SCOPE*

Exercise 2, Reaction Time

Gives students a feel for how early measurements of human behavior were made. Ask students to monitor their own reaction times carefully and to notice differences when different variables are operating. It is useful for explaining how variables affect human behavior and for explaining the difficulties early psychologists encountered in measuring human behavior. Students are asked to design an experiment after developing a hypothesis about variables that might affect reaction time.

Exercise 13, Randomness

Students are asked to generate a random sequence of pluses and minuses on the computer, while at the same time the computer is generating a truly random sequence. They compete with the computer to approximate real probability statistics. With experience, students generally become better randomizers. The exercise is useful for explaining random selection and the purposes behind it, i.e., fairness and getting nonbiased results in experiments.

CHAPTER 3

The Brain, Biology, and Behavior

■ BEHAVIORAL OBJECTIVES

The student should be able to:

1. Define biopsychology.
2. Name the basic unit of the nervous system, state what it is specifically designed to do, and list and describe its four parts.
3. Explain how a nerve impulse (action potential) occurs and how it is an all-or-nothing event.
4. Describe the effect of myelin on the speed of the nerve impulse.
5. Describe the difference between the nature of a nerve impulse and the nature of the communication between neurons. Name the four structures which possess receptor sites to which neurotransmitters attach.
6. Explain how nerve impulses are carried from one neuron to another.
7. Explain what determines whether a neuron will have an action potential triggered.
8. Explain the functions of neuropeptides, enkephalins and volume transmission.
9. Differentiate a nerve from a neuron.
10. Explain what determines whether or not a neuron or a nerve will regenerate. Explain how in some cases brain damage can be partially alleviated. Describe the ethical concern related to this intervention and how the dilemma may be resolved.
11. Chart the various subparts of the human nervous system and explain their function.
12. Differentiate between the two branches of the autonomic nervous system.
13. Explain the mechanism of the reflex arc.
14. Describe the main difference between the brains of lower and higher animals. Name what appears to be the foundation of human intelligence. Describe the main two differences between the brains of people who score high on mental tests and those who score low.
15. Identify the two hemispheres of the brain.
16. Describe the function of the corpus callosum.
17. Explain how and why a brain is "split" and describe what the resulting effects are.
18. Differentiate the abilities of the two hemispheres of the cerebral cortex.
19. Describe the functions of each of the following:
    a. occipital lobes
    b. parietal lobes (including the somatosensory areas)
    c. temporal lobes
    d. frontal lobes
    e. associative areas
20. Explain the relationship between the size of the various parts of the somatosensory and motor areas of the cortex and the degree of sensitivity of the corresponding body parts.
21. Explain how brain injuries are related to behavioral outcomes. Describe the problem

known as neglect.

22.   Describe the cause and effect of the three disorders aphasia, agnosia, and facial agnosia.

23.   List and be able to recognize the three areas of the subcortex.

24.   Explain the function of each of the following parts of the three areas of the subcortex:

        a.   Hindbrain (brainstem)   b.   Forebrain

           1)   medulla   1)   thalamus

           2)   cerebellum   2)   hypothalamus

           3)   reticular formation

25.   Name the structures that comprise the limbic system and explain its function.

26.   Describe the process of ESB --- how it is done, what it can be used for, and what its limitations are.

27.   List five basic functions of the brain.

28.   Explain the concepts of redundancy and plasticity. Describe the mechanism of plasticity.

29.   Briefly explain the purpose of the endocrine system and name and describe the mechanism by which this system carries out its function.

30.   Describe the effect that the following glands have on the body and behavior:

        a.   pituitary (include a description of giantism, dwarfism, and acromegaly)

        b.   pineal

        c.   thyroid

        d.   adrenal medulla

        e.   adrenal cortex

31.   Describe the relationship among handedness, brain dominance, and speech. State what is inherited in terms of handedness.

32.   Explain how a person can determine which hemisphere is dominant.

33.   State the incidence of left-handedness and discuss the relative advantages and/or disadvantages of being right-handed versus left-handed.

34.   Describe the following techniques for studying the brain: dissection, staining, ablation, deep lesioning, micro-electrode recording, CT scan, MRI, functional MRI, EEG, MANSCAN, PET scan, and MEG scan.

■ DEMONSTRATIONS, DRAMATIZATIONS, AND DISCUSSION

Unless you have access to sophisticated lab equipment, only rudimentary demonstrations can be done to illustrate concepts from Chapter 3. In many cases the most effective and expedient recourse will be to obtain one of the films listed at the end of this section. Visual aids can also be very helpful in clarifying these difficult concepts. A model brain which can be disassembled to show its components is particularly effective. These can often be obtained from biology or physiology departments of colleges and universities. *If you would like to try some simple classroom demonstrations, the following can be interesting:*

1.   **This demonstration is a sure-fire illustration of cortical localization and interference.**
Begin by asking the entire class to simultaneously move the right hand and right foot in a clockwise direction for a few seconds. This should be quite easy for everyone. Next ask

that the <u>right</u> hand and <u>left</u> foot be moved in a clockwise direction. This is also easy. Next have students make circular movements in <u>opposite</u> directions with the right hand and the left foot. This is more difficult, but most students will master it. Finally, have students attempt to move the <u>right</u> hand and <u>right</u> foot in opposite directions. This is extremely difficult for most people. After making these observations, students should be challenged to explain them. If they need a hint, ask them to think in terms of probable activity in the motor areas of the cortex.

2.   **A national news service recently reported the case of a child born without a brain.** According to the doctors interviewed at the time, such cases occur about once a year. In the most recent instance the defect was not discovered until the child was several months old. The baby, who appeared outwardly normal and healthy, began to cry excessively, and tests were performed to determine the cause. These tests revealed that the child had no brain. Doctors speculate that a cyst formed during prenatal development at the stem where the brain should have been and prevented further growth. The child survived because that portion of the brainstem which controls vital functions had already developed before the cyst formed. After students have read Chapter 3, they should be able to predict the kinds of abilities one might expect from such a child. You could ask them to describe the likelihood of this child having a personality, motivation, awareness, intelligence, etc.

3.   **Students are usually very interested in addressing the subject of the relationship between the brain and the mind.** You might begin a discussion of this topic by pointing out that many philosophical speculations regarding this issue have lost their relevance in light of new and innovative techniques (e.g., PET scans) for studying the human brain. The subject is, nevertheless, still very complex, and a lively class discussion can be generated by describing the following hypothetical experiment:

> You are looking at a PET scan of your brain while the radiologist taking the scan is sitting with you. You are discussing the activity depicted on the screen. Assume that the PET scanner is slightly advanced over what is presently available and depicts glucose utilization immediately. (State-of-the-art scans require a 30- to 45-minute lead time.) As you are staring at the PET scan, the radiologist points out that the most active areas seen on the screen are in the left hemisphere, particularly the language area and the visual areas toward the back of the brain. At this moment you hear some music, and almost immediately the activity pattern of the scan changes. Now there is activity in the right hemisphere as well, and you call the radiologist's attention to that change. "That's somewhere in the region of the music appreciation center," she responds. Then a few minutes later she asks, "Do you have any comments on the PET scan?" "What do you mean?" you reply, and, at this point, you notice another change. The auditory areas, as well as the frontal lobes, light up. You look toward the radiologist and see that she is smiling, and you finally realize that the PET scan is depicting your own brain activity! It is showing a shift as you change from one thinking activity to another.

Now ask the students to consider the following questions: Is this an example of their minds studying their brains, or can they adequately explain it as the brain studying itself? For more speculation on this topic see R. Restak's <u>The Brain</u>, Bantam Books, 1984.

■ ONE-MINUTE MOTIVATORS

1. **In order to conceptualize the firing of the neuron,** students often need analogies to concrete objects. Possible analogies include: a radio, a telephone, a fax machine, a stereo system, the process of sending mail, etc. The analogy must be developed carefully: it must clarify, not mystify or confuse. A cap pistol can be used to demonstrate the all-or-none quality of the action potential. Since the text refers to a "domino" effect of sorts, set up a domino chain on a table.

2. **The power of neurotransmitters can be demonstrated using a squirt gun** filled with laundry bleach. Squirt a colorful fabric; then squirt a glass or porcelain plate. The point to be made is that neurotransmitters must adhere to appropriate receptor sites before an action potential can be triggered.

3. **Without warning, suggest that it would be helpful to know more about the interests of students.** Explain, "In five minutes I will pick a student from the class and ask her/him to stand up and give a brief speech." After one student talks briefly, discuss the actions of the sympathetic nervous system in their own bodies during the past few minutes. Then guide students through a few minutes of deep breathing and relaxation to demonstrate the parasympathetic system. The transition from one to the other may be identified by asking students to indicate when they have sufficient saliva to actually swallow a cracker.

4. **To illustrate the enhanced surface areas of the cortex,** wad up a piece of foil or aluminum-backed cloth to create a convoluted brain surface. If you don't have these materials, crumpling a sheet of paper int a small ball will do.

5. **Ask left-handers to meet outside of class and make a list of all the inconveniences of living in a right-handed world.** Ask them to share any horror stories from their childhoods, such as having their left hands tied to their backs, etc.

■ CLASSROOM EXERCISE

TO THE INSTRUCTOR:

An in-class activity that will demonstrate the functioning of the left and right hemispheres of the brain and which many show dominance of one hemisphere over the other involves observing lateral eye movement. A study by Schwartz, Davidson, and Maer serves as a model for this exercise. They were able to show that spontaneous lateral eye movement reflects activity in one or other of the hemispheres of the brain. Eye movement to the left seemed to indicate involvement of the right hemisphere, and movement to the right appeared to involve the left side.

It has been observed that some people shift their eyes to the left more often than to the right. These are called left-movers. Others typically shift to the right and are called right-movers.

A conclusion drawn by researchers in this area is that left-movers have a right hemisphere dominance and tend to be more artistic, creative, and intuitive thinkers. Right movers have left hemisphere dominance and tend to be more logical, analytical, verbal, and numerical. These conclusions are considered to be general tendencies and therefore should be viewed with a skeptical eye. More study and research is needed to support these conclusions.

Lateral Eye Movement (or, Look Left and You'll Be Right)

1.   Select five students to be the subjects of the demonstration. Ask them to leave the room while preparations are made.

2.   Explain to the rest of the class that you will ask the subjects a list of questions. The students are to observe and record the eye movements of each subject when the questions are asked. Caution them that the eye movements may be slight and will be to the left or right. They will have to observe with care (and they will not have the benefit of slow motion or instant replays).

3.   Provide each student with a copy of the record sheet which contains the questions and a space to record the subject's responses.

4.   Admit the subjects, one at a time, and have each one stand in front of the class in full view of the students.

5.   You should ask each question and give the subject time to respond. The students will record their observation for each question. You should accept whatever answer is given and move on.

6.   After all subjects have been questioned, tally the number of observed left and right eye movements for each question and each subject.

7.   An analysis of the results should attempt to see:

    a.   which items tended to elicit a left eye shift, indicating right hemisphere activity and which elicited a shift to the right, pointing to a left hemisphere involvement.

    b.   if any subject had a tendency to shift more in one direction than the other, indicating a left or right hemisphere dominance.

8.   The record sheet provided has a series of questions which follow a pattern. All odd-numbered items should elicit left hemisphere activity (eye shift to the right), and even-numbered items should elicit right hemisphere activity (eye shift to the left).

9.   Discuss the results with the whole class, including the subjects who were observed. The class should try to see the left and right hemisphere patterns. Then they should ask the subjects about their preferences for left or right hemisphere activities to see if the eye movements do relate to hemisphere dominance.

10.   Finally, ask the students to critique the exercise as a scientific endeavor. Was it scientific? Are the results valid? reliable? or useful?

LATERAL EYE MOVEMENT   RECORD SHEET:

TO THE STUDENT:

Record your observations on this sheet. Mark an L for left and an R for right. Remember that you are recording the subject's eye movements to HIS or HER right, not to yours. Do not do anything to distract the subject, or yourself, since the eye movement may be slight.

SUBJECT				
1	2	3	4	5

1. How many weeks are there in a year?

2. On what coin is John F. Kennedy pictured?

3. What is the last line of the "The Star-Spangled Banner"?

4. Without looking at me, what is the color of my shirt (tie, skirt)?

5. Define the term "psychology."

6. In England, on which side is the steering wheel of a car?

7. Why do people pay taxes?

8. Who is pictured on the front of a five-dollar bill?

9. What do the letters in "NASA" stand for?

10. About how far is it to the moon?

■ BROADENING OUR CULTURAL HORIZONS

1. **Different religions have diverse attitudes concerning the rights of humans** to intervene medically to save a life and also concerning the disposition of a person's body after death. Compare and contrast the following views:

    a.   Blood transfusions should not take place.
    b.   The body should not be violated after death.
    c.   Parts of the dead should be immediately used for transplants.
    d.   A person's body should be cremated at death.

2. **Prepare two forms outlining hypothetical situations.** Put the students into small groups and give each group one of the forms to discuss and research how people of different cultural and/or religious backgrounds would respond to these situations.

    FORM #1: A 25-year-old woman is dying of cancer. She has asked that "no extreme procedures be used to prolong life." She is now comatose and can be kept alive only with machines. How would you decide whether her will should be respected?

    FORM #2: A 25-year-old man is dying of cancer. He has asked that "no extreme procedures be used to prolong life." He is now comatose and can be kept alive only with machines. How would you decide whether his will should be respected.

3. **In what ways might different cultures** make greater or lesser use of the various strengths of the right and left cerebral hemispheres?

■ SUPPLEMENTAL LECTURE

Students always have a difficult time learning the parts of the brain and their chief functions. Diagrams in most texts tend to appear complex and confusing because so many parts are identified and labeled. An instructor should take the time to simplify the structure, focusing on the major parts or areas of the brain. Once the students learn these, they can then add other structures and eventually see the whole thing--but first, they should see the stripped-down version, the basic model.

In this lecture the students will learn:
1.   that the brain is specialized with each area having a different function;
2.   that the brain is not really one organ but several "brains", all in the same location, in the skull;
3.   what each of the three parts or "brains" is called, where each is located, and what special tasks each performs;
4.   that all of these separate parts are really interconnected and work together in a kind of network to direct behavior.

This lecture would work out best if a model of the brain were used. The model should be able to be disassembled and put together again. Otherwise a large diagram would be good, or, if that is not available, drawing on the chalkboard, showing one part at a time, can be effective.

THE BRAIN

I. Introduction
    A.   Discuss the composition of the brain:
        1.   type of cells,
        2.   number of cells (estimated),
        3.   location of the brain,
        4.   size of brain in relation to the rest of the body.
    B.   Identify the three main parts or "brains" which make up what we call the brain:
        1.   medulla,
        2.   cerebellum,
        3.   cerebrum.
    C.   Discuss each of the parts, giving location and major functions:
        1.   Medulla
            a.   It is located at the top of the spinal cord.
            b.   It is a slightly rounded structure.
            c.   It controls involuntary functions--these are the vital functions necessary for survival of the physical organism.
            d.   Its functions include regulation of: circulation, respiration, digestion, and reproduction.

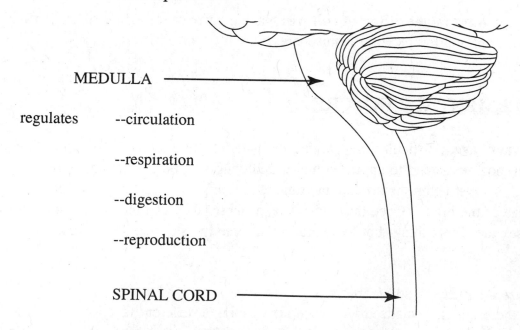

MEDULLA

regulates   --circulation

                --respiration

                --digestion

                --reproduction

SPINAL CORD

            e.   This is the most primitive part of the brain and is found in all living organisms. It is what keeps a human or animal alive.
            f.   Damage to this area could cause death.

2.   Cerebellum
   a.   It is located at the rear and base of the skull.
   b.   It is ball-shaped and consists of a left and right lobe
   c.   It controls the muscles and skeleton. It is responsible for motor coordination, balance, and fine motor movement.
   d.   Humans and all higher orders of animals have a well developed cerebellum.
   e.   Damage to this area results in impairment or loss of motor functions.

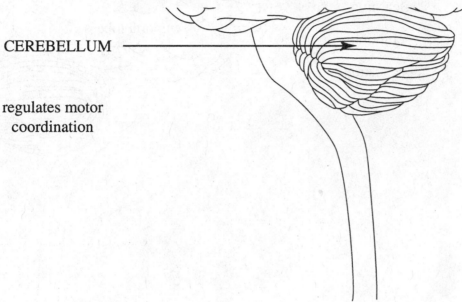

CEREBELLUM ⎯⎯⎯⎯⎯⎯

regulates motor
   coordination

3.   Cerebrum
   a.   It is located at the top and front of the skull and takes up most of the space in it.
   b.   It is walnut-shaped and has a left and a right section or hemisphere.
   c.   Each hemisphere is divided into 4 parts or lobes, each of which has special functions. One function of each lobe is coordination of sensations:
      1.   occipital lobe - vision
      2.   temporal lobe - hearing
      3.   parietal lobe - skin senses
      4.   frontal lobe - olfaction; and emotional control
   d.   The function of this complex part or "brain" is to coordinate sensations, regulate emotions, and direct thinking, learning, problem-solving, and other complex activities.

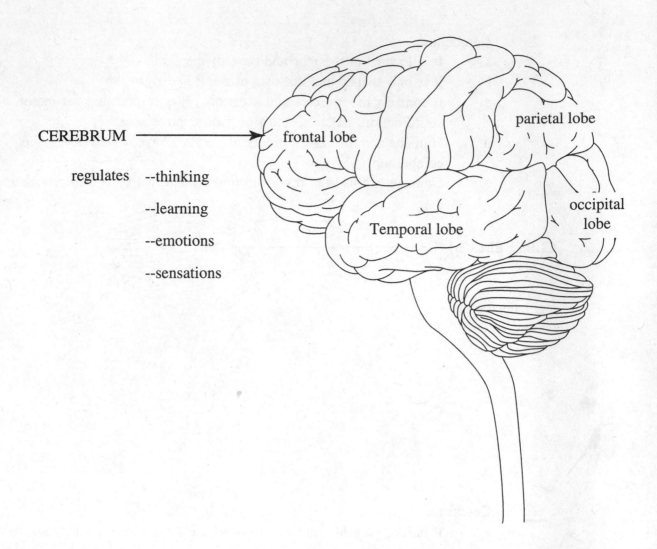

CEREBRUM ⟶ frontal lobe

regulates   --thinking

--learning

--emotions

--sensations

parietal lobe

occipital lobe

Temporal lobe

e.   This area is very large in humans and is smaller in other animals. Lower animals have very small cerebrums. Anthropologists have been tracing the evolution of humans from lower forms by finding skulls of various sizes leading up to the massive skull of the human. The size of the cerebrum is thought to correspond to the ability of the organism to solve problems and adapt to its environment.

f.   Damage to this area could lead to a variety of problems from minor dysfunctions to major disabilities and/or death.

D.   Having dissected the brain or brains, now you need to say that there is a constant flow of information to all parts so that our behavior is integrated. If time permits you could discuss structures on the underside of the brain that do some of the interconnecting. Mention should be made of the corpus callosum, thalamus, hypothalamus, and the reticular formation.

E.   As an activity students should be asked to identify all of the parts and structures discussed either by using a model or an outline drawing such as those in this lecture. Simply reproduce the drawings without the labels and have students identify what they see.

■ SUGGESTIONS FOR FURTHER READING

Corballis, M. C. "Laterality and Myth." *American Psychologist*,   March 1980: 284-295.

Gazzaniga, M. S. and S. E. LeDoux. *The Integrated Mind*. Plenum, 1978.

Gazzaniga, M. S. *The Social Brain: Discovering the Networks of the Mind*. Basic Books, 1985.

Herron, J. *Neuropsychology of Left-handedness*. Academic Press, 1979.

Kinsbourne, M. "Why Is the Brain Biased?" *Psychology Today*, May, 1979.

Levy, Jerre. "Right Brain, Left Brain: Fact or Fiction." *Psychology Today*. May 1985.

Robinson, D. N. *The Enlightened Machine*. Columbia University Press, 1980.

Rodgers, J. E. "Brain Triggers: Biochemistry and Behavior." *Science Digest*, January 1983.

Rosenzweig, M. R. and A. L. Leiman. *Physiological Psychology*, 2nd ed. McGraw-Hill, 1989.

Sacks, O. *Awakenings*. HarperCollins Publishers, Inc., 1990.

Sacks, O. *The Man Who Mistook His Wife for a Hat and Other Clinical Tales*. HarperCollins Publishers, 1985.

Scientific American, September, 1979. (This entire issue is devoted to the brain).

Snyder, S. H. *Drugs and the Brain*. W. H. Freeman, 1986.

Springer, S. P. and G. Deutsch. *Left Brain, Right Brain*. W. H. Freeman, 1981.

■ FILM SUGGESTIONS

THE BIOLOGY OF BEHAVIOR (1990, from *Psychology- The Study of Human Behavior Series*, Coast Community College District, 30 min.)
    Focuses on the human nervous systems and neurotransmission.

BIRTH OF A BRAIN (1983, McGraw-Hill/CRM, 33 min.)
    This film illustrates the genetic origins of the brain, the importance of the environment in its development, and the corresponding behavioral manifestations. Dramatic visuals include microphotography, computer graphics, and a live birth sequence.

DIVIDED BRAIN AND CONSCIOUSNESS (1977, Harcourt Brace Jovanovich,   22 min.)
    Discusses hemispheric specialization, the effects of brain damage, and split brain experiments. A sequence involving hypnosis demonstrates "divided consciousness."

THE HIDDEN UNIVERSE: THE BRAIN (CRM, Part I, 23 min., Part II, 25 min.)

With David Janssen as host, this film provides an overview of the functions of the brain, including motor control, memory, and sensory perceptions. Featured is a live scene in an operating room where doctors perform a craniotomy, probing different parts of the patient's brain as he indicates the sensation this causes. Following this, a discussion of the separate function of the right and left hemispheres is highlighted with scenes of a young man who has a "split brain." The film also features a woman who has an electric stimulator implanted in her back, and a doctor who is using computers in an effort to cure blindness.

LEFT BRAIN, RIGHT BRAIN (1980, Filmmakers Library, 56 min.)

Dr. Norman Geschwind introduces this film on recent break-throughs in brain research. As the film indicates, in most people the left hemisphere processes information with an analytic time-dependent sequential strategy, while the right hemisphere processes information with a holistic strategy that is independent of time and order. Researchers demonstrate a variety of tests which pinpoint the exact geography of brain functions.

THE NERVOUS SYSTEM: NERVES AT WORK (1985, Films for the Humanities and Sciences Inc., 26 min.)

This program on the nervous system focuses on the nerve signals and how they are transmitted. It looks at the part played by nerve messages in reflex activities and examines the chemical and electrical activities of networks of nerve cells.

THE NERVOUS SYSTEM: DECISION (1985, Films for the Humanities and Sciences Inc., 26 min.)

The focus in this film is on how the brain organizes input and output to make a simple but life-saving decision. It examines the cortex and how it assesses incoming information and sends outgoing messages to the muscles and stores maps of the world. It also includes a look at how circuits of nerve cells operate in the brain and how individual neurons function.

THE NERVOUS SYSTEM: OUR TALENTED BRAIN (1985, Films for the Humanities and Sciences Inc., 26 min.)

This film explores human culture--human's physiological brain capacity, use of memory, and use of symbols--and its relationship to the neural structure of the brain.

PATTERNS OF PAIN (1980, Filmmakers Library, 28 min.)

In this film a professor of psychology, a zoologist, and a doctor speak about the perception of pain in the nervous system. Illustrated and discussed are phenomena such as the absence of pain perception by the wounded during battle; pain control through hypnosis, acupuncture, and yoga; thresholds of pain; the body's ability to release its own analgesic; and finally, new surgical techniques for implanting electrodes in the brain to block pain.

PERIPHERAL NERVOUS SYSTEM (EMC, 19 min.)

Explanation and illustration of the transmission of nerve impulses and the relationship of reflex action to spinal cord and brain activity.

THE SPLIT-BRAIN AND CONSCIOUS EXPERIENCE (Harper and Row, 22 min.)

> Examines the implications of rare footage showing split-brain patients after surgery. Actual surgery is shown. Patients laugh when a nude is flashed to right hemisphere but cannot explain their reactions.

TRIUNE BRAIN (1985, National Film Board of Canada, 30 min.)

> Presents a detailed portrait of the human brain using models from antiquity through the more recently developed triune model, narrated by Paul McLean.

■ COMPUTER PROGRAMS: *MIND SCOPE*

Exercise 13, Chimeric Faces

Aspects of the specialization of the two brain hemispheres in people who have normal, intact connections between the hemispheres. This exercise is adapted from an experiment by Levy and Heller. Many people show a bias effect when performing the task, making affective judgments based on the information presented in the left visual field more than on the information presented in the right visual field.

Exercise 16, Neural Conduction Speed

Using Herman van Helmholz's logic, reaction time is measured in order to estimate the speed of neural conduction. By measuring the distance between two stimulation points and then measuring the difference in how long it takes to respond to a light tap, the speed of neural conduction can be estimated.

CHAPTER 4

Sensation and Reality

■ BEHAVIORAL OBJECTIVES

The student should be able to:

1. Explain how our senses act as a data reduction system by selecting, analyzing, and coding incoming information.
2. Explain how sensory receptors act as biological transducers.
3. Explain the concept of localization of function.
4. Explain the idea behind the statement, "Seeing does not take place in the eyes."
5. Define sensation.
6. Define the term "absolute threshold."
7. Explain the process of perceptual defense.
8. Define limen and describe subliminal perception including its effectiveness.
9. Explain Weber's law and the concept of the difference threshold (JND).
10. Describe hue, saturation, and brightness in terms of their representation in the visual spectrum of electromagnetic radiation.
11. Explain how the eye focuses and the process of accommodation.
12. Describe the following four conditions: hyperopia, myopia, astigmatism, and presbyopia.
13. Explain how the eye controls light.
14. Describe the functions of the rods and cones.
15. Explain how the visual area of the brain detects features.
16. Explain the relationship between the fovea and visual acuity.
17. Discuss peripheral vision. Include the structures responsible for it and how it affects night vision.
18. Discuss the trichromatic and opponent-process theories of color vision, including a description of afterimages.
19. Describe color blindness and color weakness.
20. Briefly describe the process of dark adaptation including the function of rhodopsin in night vision and night blindness.
21. Explain the stimulus for hearing.
22. Describe the location and explain the function(s) of the following parts of the ear:

    a. pinna
    b. eardrum (tympanic membrane)
    c. auditory ossicles
    d. oval window
    e. cochlea
    f. hair cells
    g. stereocilia
    h. Organ of Corti

23. Describe the frequency theory and the place theory of hearing.
24. List and describe the three general types of deafness.

25.   Describe the factors that determine whether hearing loss will occur from stimulation deafness. Discuss the relationship of stimulation deafness to temporary threshold shift and tinnitus.

26.   Describe the sense of smell including:
      a.   its nature and how it works.
      b.   a description of the lock and key theory
      c.   a description of the condition anosmia
      d.   how pheromones work and what they do

27.   Describe the sense of taste including:
      a.   its nature and how it works
      b.   the four basic taste sensations
      c.   the tastes to which humans are most and least sensitive
      d.   how the vast number of flavors is explained
      e.   how taste is affected by smell, genetics, and age

28.   List the three somesthetic senses and be able to describe the function of each.

29.   List and be able to recognize the five different sensations produced by the skin receptors.

30.   Explain why certain areas of the body are more sensitive to touch than other areas.

31.   Describe the concepts visceral pain and referred pain. Name and describe the two different pain systems in the body.

32.   List and discuss the three reasons many sensory events never reach conscious awareness.

33.   Discuss how endorphins explain some of the feelings associated with running, acupuncture, ESB, masochism, and childbirth.

34.   Discuss four techniques that can be used to reduce the amount of pain perceived.

35.   Describe the space adaptation syndrome, and explain how the otolith organs and the semicircular canals of the vestibular system are related to it.

36.   Describe how the sensory conflict theory explains motion sickness.

■ DEMONSTRATIONS, DRAMATIZATIONS, AND DISCUSSION

1.   **The senses do not simply mirror external "reality"--they** shape **our experiences in a multitude of ways.** The Archimedes spiral can produce a powerful distortion of sensory experience, and thus bring home the fact that what we take for "reality" is greatly affected by the functioning of sensory systems.

To construct an Archimedes spiral, obtain a phonograph turntable. (The author's is a child's phonograph with the tone arm missing. It was purchased from a thrift store for less than a dollar.) Cut a large circle of white posterboard (roughly 12-15 inches in diameter). Make a hole in the middle of the posterboard disk so that it can be placed on the turntable like a phonograph record. Leave the hole small so that the disk will remain attached to the turntable when the phonograph is laid on its side for the class to see. Use a black felt-tip marker to draw a wide, bold spiral from the edge to the center of the disk. When the disk is turning, the spiral may appear to be collapsing in toward the center, or expanding outward, depending on how it is drawn. Either type of spiral will work, but the inward-moving spiral tends to produce a stronger effect. It would be interesting to make one of each to see how each works.

Set the turntable on its side on the edge of a desk or table so that the cardboard disk can rotate freely and be seen by the class. Set the turntable at its lowest speed. Have students fixate on the center of the spiral for at least one minute. Then ask them to look immediately at some other object (a clock on the wall or your face, for example). If the collapsing spiral has been used, a figural after-effect occurs in which the object viewed after fixation appears to be expanding.

After the "oohs" and "ahs" die down, point out that a traditional test of the reality of an event is its consensual validation. If several people have the same experience simultaneously, it is thought to be "real." If only one has the experience, it may be considered a hallucination. The question becomes, then, did the clock (or your face) actually change size, or did it not? In terms of subjective experience, an entire classroom full of people could swear in court that it did. Yet in reality it did not.

2.   **As the text points out, "flavor," as we experience it subjectively, is actually a combination of olfaction and gustation.** This can be demonstrated relatively easily. Bring to class some apple, potato, and onion cut into tiny bits. Have a student volunteer taste bits of each while blindfolded. Discriminating between different foods should be simple in this condition. Next, test the blindfolded volunteer while he or she pinches the nostrils closed. With more olfactory cues reduced, correctly identifying the food bits should be more difficult (although not impossible). Even if they correctly identify the foods in the second test, subjects will usually report greater difficulty. Typically, they must rely more on texture than on "taste" when olfactory cues are reduced.

3.   **To demonstrate genetic differences in taste sensitivity,** obtain strips of litmus paper treated with the chemical phenylthiocarbamide (PTC). Most chemical supply houses carry this item, or the college biology department may have some in stock. It is inexpensive. Pass out one strip to each class member. Have everyone taste the strip and ask for a description of subjective experiences. As noted in the text, about seventy percent will have taste sensations, and about thirty percent will be genetic non-tasters.

4.   **Although the reproduction of the Ishihara plates in the text is not adequate for formal testing,** it is sufficiently accurate to allow detection of color-blind or color-weak students in the class. Usually such students can provide amusing anecdotes about their discovery of, or life with, impaired color vision.

5.   **In almost every classroom there are weak background stimuli that can be used to demonstrate selective attention.** The buzzing of neon lights, the hum of an air conditioner, the drone of street noise--any of these can be used to show that a stimulus may be present but not consciously perceived until attention is shifted to it. Simply stop in mid-sentence and call attention to one of these stimuli.

6.   **A type of stabilized vision can be demonstrated without the elaborate equipment used in formal research.** Tell students to close one eye and to place one finger on the outside corner of the upper eyelid of the open eye. From this position the finger can be used to gently push the eyeball against the nasal side of its socket. If it is gently held immobile in this way, the entire visual image will fade into darkness in about 20-30 seconds. This fading indicates that vision does undergo sensory adaptation, but that constant movement (physiological nystagmus) normally prevents it.

7.   **There is an age-old demonstration that students can do easily to demonstrate** that there are separate receptors for hot and cold and that temperature sensations are relative. Prepare three containers of water: one cold, one warm, and the third lukewarm. None should be extreme, not too cold or too hot. Have students put one hand into the cold water and the other into the warm. They should observe that one hand will feel cold and the other warm and also notice that the cold or warm feeling occurs mostly at the water line, where air and water meet. This is the only place on the skin where a comparison of air and water temperature can be experienced. The relative difference is what is reported as cold or warm. After being held in the containers for a few minutes, both hands should be put in the container of lukewarm water. Students will notice that the hand that was in cold water will feel warm, and the hand in warm water will now feel cold. Once again, a comparison of the sensations before and after is what is noted by the brain.

8.   **Before beginning this chapter, put a series of objects (fruit, pieces of cloth, something made of steel, etc.) in front of the class.** As students to describe these objects in writing. At the next class meeting pass the objects around. Ask students to explore them in more depth. After they have touched and smelled each object, ask them to again describe the objects. This time their descriptions should be richer and more detailed.

9.   **If you know a camera buff or a dynamic photography instructor,** ask to have a camera taken apart for the class. Point out the parts that function in a way similar to parts of the eye.

10.   **Ask students in pairs to observe each other's pupils.** Flip a coin to select the "subject." Darken the room for a few minutes. Turn on the lights and have students estimate how many seconds it takes their partner's pupils to return to their original degree of constriction.

■ ONE-MINUTE MOTIVATORS

1.   **Discuss how much sensory information there is** in a single flower, leaf, or other common object.

2.   **A child's battery-operated toy musical instrument can serve as an example of a transducer.** Pressing a key converts mechanical energy into an electrical current that activates a mechanical device that makes a musical sound.

3.   **To demonstrate the idea that information is continuously flowing into our sensory system,** but that it is not always attended to, play a tape of a waterfall or surf during your lecture. Ask students whether they feel they need to pay attention to information for it to trigger some kind of sensory response.

4.   **Demonstrate the difficulty of finding sensory thresholds in this way:** Tell the students you are going to drip five drops of perfume on a saucer. Ask students to tell you when they smell the perfume. Stop a few seconds between drops. Note after each drop how many say they can smell it and record the number. Use water until the final drop. Discuss the placebo effect, suggestion, and false positives.

5.   **Bring a dog whistle and a dog to class.** First have the class observe the behavioral response of a fellow student to "a very soft whistle." You may have false positives, so also fake blowing the whistle. Then bring in the dog and show the canine response.

6.   **Have students develop a series of analogies for each of the senses:** Which sense is most like a video? A CD? A TV? A computer? A battery-operated child's toy? A balloon? A musical instrument? A tea pot? In what important ways are the senses different in each case?

7.   **You can add the volley theory of hearing to your lecture by** giving three students cap pistols that must be reloaded after 5 shots. Have one student fire as quickly as possible and then reload and fire again. Then have all three students fire as quickly as they can, reloading when necessary. Stagger their starting times, and you will get a continuous flow of sound.

8.   **Drop a pebble in a dish of water.** Watch the compression and rarefaction of the waves. If you use a clear glass pie plate, this can be shown to larger classes with an overhead projector.

9.   **The smell of ammonia, rotten eggs, or kitty litter could (if you are somewhat sadistic) be brought to class.** Students rate the smell at the start of class and every 10 minutes after, and should quickly experience olfactory adaptation.

10. **Ask students to explain why individuals are often so insensitive to their own body and breath odor.** How does sensory adaptation contribute to this insensitivity? How have advertisers tried to capitalize on the situation?

■ CLASSROOM EXERCISES

TO THE INSTRUCTOR:

Two classroom exercises are developed in this section to help students understand some of the concepts in this chapter. The author of the text discusses the notions of cutaneous threshold and auditory localization. These are two types of sensory experience that can be demonstrated in the classroom in the following ways.

Exercise #1: Cutaneous Two-Point Threshold

This is an exercise to demonstrate the threshold for pressure on the surface of the skin. To carry out this exercise you need a subject and an experimenter and a device with two points. The two-point instrument could be a divider from a geometry set or some similar item that has two points which can be set at varying distances apart with some way to measure that distance.

This exercise can be done as a demonstration with several students selected to be subjects or by dividing up the whole class into pairs with each one alternating as subject and experimenter. The latter would require a large number of two-point instruments.

The procedure for this activity is as follows:

1.   Identify the subject and experimenter. If the class is paired, each couple can determine this. If it is a class demonstration, identify several subjects and an experimenter. You should direct the demonstration and not be either the subject or the experimenter.

2.   Blindfold the subject to be tested.

3.   Provide the experimenter, or the whole class, with the data sheet which indicates the area of the skin surface to be tested and the type of test to make. The experimenter will touch the surface of the skin with one point or two, varying the distance between the points with each trial. The subject will respond with "one" or "two" when each contact is made.

4.   Record all responses until the subject can no longer distinguish between one and two points on successive trials.

5.   If this is a class demonstration, have students record the responses for each subject. If the students are working in pairs, the experimenter will record each trial. After completing the trials, the two will change places and repeat the procedure. Provide students with enough data sheets for all subjects to be tested.

6.   After all testing is completed, collect the data and work out the thresholds for each part of the skin surface tested.

7.   Students should note and discuss differences found among students and differences from one part of the body to the other.

8.   Ask students to explain why there is a threshold and why it differs depending on the area of the body involved.

CUTANEOUS TWO-POINT THRESHOLD: DATA SHEET

TO THE EXPERIMENTER:

Some guidelines for doing this exercise--

1.   Be sure the subject is securely blindfolded.

2.   Apply even, firm, but not excessive pressure, with one point or two, as directed. You should avoid causing pain to (or breaking the skin of) the subject.

3.   Make exact measurements when setting the two points for each trial.

4.   Do not repeat any trials.

5.   Ask the subject for a response after each application of pressure.

6.   Do not give hints or clues to help the subject. Encourage the subject to make an immediate response.

7.   For each response made by the subject, put a 1 or 2 in the appropriate box.

DATA SHEET (cont.)

On the chart below, the distance (Dst) between points and the number of points (Pts) to be applied are indicated. Record the responses (Res.) of the subjects in the space provided.

lower back			palm			fingertip		
Dst.	Pts.	Res.	Dst.	Pts.	Res.	Dst.	Pts.	Res.
2"	1 2 2		1 1/2"	2 1 2		3/4"	2 1 2	
1 3/4"	2 1 2		1 1/4"	1 2 2		5/8"	1 2 2	
1 1/2"	1 1 2		1"	1 2 1		1/2"	1 2 1	
1 1/4"	1 2 1		3/4"	2 2 1		3/8"	1 1 2	
1"	2 1 2		1/2"	1 2 1		1/4"	2 1 2	
3/4"	2 2 1		1/4"	1 1 2		1/8"	2 2 1	
1/2"	1 2 1		1/8"	2 1 2		1/16"	1 2 1	
1/4"	1 2 1		1/16"	2 1 2				

Exercise #2: Auditory Localization

TO THE INSTRUCTOR:

Locating the direction of sound involves the binaural cue of time difference. Auditory stimulation reaches each ear at a different time because sound travels relatively slowly through the air. This is called the interaural time difference. This exercise will demonstrate this phenomenon. The subject will attempt to locate a sound with only auditory cues. Students will see that sound location will be most accurate when the interaural time difference is the greatest and least accurate when the difference is smallest.

In preparation for this demonstration, students should read the section on hearing in this chapter with particular attention to the discussion of auditory information processing.

The only materials needed are a blindfold, twelve noisemakers (such as a cricket clicker) that will give a clear, crisp sound, and thirteen chairs.

Procedure:

1.   Set up twelve chairs in a circle to resemble the numbers on a clock. Put the thirteenth chair in the center, facing six o'clock and away from the chalkboard.

2.   Select as many subjects as you want to use and send them out of the room during the preparation time. You will need one, and might consider two, if time permits.

3.   Select twelve persons to occupy the twelve chairs in the circle, all facing the chalkboard, and provide each with a noisemaker. Each student will be assigned a number corresponding to the numbers on a clock dial, with the student farthest from the chalkboard number six, and the student nearest the chalkboard number twelve.

4.   Ask the remaining students to be recorders. Each should be provided with a data sheet.

5.   Use a random procedure to determine the order of clicks. A good way would be to prepare 48 slips of paper with the numbers 1 to 12 (each number repeated four times). Draw these slips out of a hat. The order should then be put on the record sheets and on the chalkboard.

6.   Admit the student subject, seat him/her in the center chair facing away from the chalkboard, and put on the blindfold. Instruct the subject to face straight ahead, listen for the sound, and indicate the location by naming a position on the clock, with 6 o'clock being directly in front and 12 o'clock behind.

7.   The instructor or a student should act as experimenter and point to each location on the chalkboard, one at a time. The person seated at that location should make one clicking sound. Give time for the subject to respond and the recorders to note the location given.

8.   After all forty-eight trials are completed, students should check for the subject's accuracy at each of the twelve locations, noting the size of the error for each.

9.   If a second subject is to be used, the positions for the trials should be re-randomized.

10.   On completion of the trials for all subjects, the class should determine the average size of the error at each of the twelve positions.

11.   Some questions for discussion:

      a.   Is there a pattern to the error size? Where is it greatest and where is it smallest?

      b.   What is the explanation for the differences found?

      c.   Would there be any value in moving one's head when the location of a sound is ambiguous?

      d.   What would be the effect of deafness in one ear? Could the person locate a sound? Discuss reasons for a yes or no answer to this question.

(based on a demonstration by Dr. William C. Titus, Arkansas Tech University)

AUDITORY LOCALIZATION   DATA SHEET:

TRIAL	LOCATION	RESPONSE	TRIAL	LOCATION	RESPONSE
1	____	____	25	____	____
2	____	____	26	____	____
3	____	____	27	____	____
4	____	____	28	____	____
5	____	____	29	____	____
6	____	____	30	____	____
7	____	____	31	____	____
8	____	____	32	____	____
9	____	____	33	____	____
10	____	____	34	____	____
11	____	____	35	____	____
12	____	____	36	____	____
13	____	____	37	____	____
14	____	____	38	____	____
15	____	____	39	____	____
16	____	____	40	____	____
17	____	____	41	____	____
18	____	____	42	____	____
19	____	____	43	____	____
20	____	____	44	____	____
21	____	____	45	____	____
22	____	____	46	____	____
23	____	____	47	____	____
24	____	____	48	____	____

■ BROADENING OUR CULTURAL HORIZONS

1. **Various cultures have different approaches to pain management.** Some groups suggest that pain should be ignored; others acknowledge pain but suggest specific ways to deal with it. What did the "mini-culture" of your family suggest? If you suddenly feel pain in your chest, what has your culture taught you to do? Are these behaviors adaptive or maladaptive?

2. **Do various cultures emphasize different sensory channels to a greater or lesser degree?** For example, do some cultures place more emphasis on touch, taste, or smell than North Americans do? What does the American preoccupation with television tell us about our culture? The French reputation for cooking? The Italian tendency to touch a person when talking to her or him?

3. **Invite a hearing-impaired and/or vision-impaired person to class.** Discuss the person's sensory world with her or him, with an emphasis on the subculture that exists among hearing-impaired and/or vision-impaired persons.

4. **Using a world map, try to characterize the traditional cuisine of various regions as hot and/or spicy versus bland.** Do any patterns emerge? What hypotheses can be advanced to explain cultural preferences for spicy or bland tastes?

■ SUPPLEMENTAL LECTURE

Have the students read the section in the text on the skin senses, noting that pain is one of these. This lecture should interest students because it deals with a topic of interest to everyone, i.e. control of pain. You should establish what pain is and then discuss how to cope with it. You should be able to generate some lively discussion.

CONTROL OF PAIN

I.   The Skin Senses

    A.   Is there a sense of touch? Discuss the popular notion. Ask students to identify what makes up the so-called sense of touch.

    B.   Discussion should yield the information that there are really at least three distinct sensations (pressure, temperature, and pain) involved in what has been lumped together as the touch sense.

II. The Pain Sense

    A.   Is it one sense or many? Discuss the types of pain found in the skin, in the head, teeth, ankle, knee, etc., and in the internal organs.

    B.   Distinguish between sudden sharp pain, as in a pin prick, and chronic pain, such as a backache or headache.

III.   Treatment of Pain

A.   Sudden and sharp pain can often be diagnosed and treated because the source can be identified.

B.   Chronic pain may be harder to diagnose and treat. Some techniques may be useful to minimize the pain, even when the source of pain is unclear and/or untreatable as is found in arthritis, cancer, and lower back problems.

IV.   Techniques for Minimizing Pain

A.   Some techniques have been gaining recognition by professionals. The following are some examples. Others could be explored.

1.   Preparation

a.   Knowing what will happen is a good way to ease pain.

b.   Anxiety causes pain to be more intense. Preparation relieves anxiety. A good example is prenatal classes preparing for natural childbirth.

c.   Control over painful stimuli lessens anxiety and distress, resulting in less suffering.

2.   Reinterpretation

Pain tolerance can be increased by interpreting the circumstances or stimuli in a positive way. The pain of training for an athlete may be reinterpreted as good because it is evidence of progress: "no pain, no gain." Also the pain suffered for religious reasons by a martyr may be seen as sanctifying and a pleasurable "cross to bear."

3.   Selective Attention

a.   Paying attention to only part of the sensory input and shutting out (tuning out) the rest, including pain, may give relief. A headache may disappear when some emergency situation arises. Injured persons may not feel pain until after the traumatic experience is over.

b.   Distractions will help turn attention from pain. A dentist may give a patient headphones and soothing music while he is drilling. Fantasizing or daydreaming may relieve the pain of a teacher's lecture.

c.   Hypnosis is a way to direct attention and give relief from pain. For those who can be hypnotized, there could be considerable, or total, pain relief. It has been used in major surgery, dentistry, and childbirth.

4.   Sensory Gating

    a.   One type of pain may cancel another. Discuss this concept with the class.

    b.   Acupuncture is thought to work this way and has been used for centuries in the Far East to kill pain.

    c.   Electrical stimulation is an interesting modern technique to interfere with pain messages. Gating is said to explain how it works.

    d.   We often use counter-irritation to relieve pain. Pain in another area may relieve uncontrollable pain. As a result, someone who has a severe localized pain in one area may cause a controlled pain in another area to get relief. The "white knuckle" phenomenon in the dentist's chair may be an example of this.

5.   Drugs

    a.   Analgesics are pain-killing drugs. Aspirin is one of these. For severe pain major pain-killing drugs may be needed. Morphine has been used. Discuss the various types and the problems with side-effects including addiction.

    b.   Placebos are not real drugs but may give relief from pain. These may stimulate production of endorphins, or they may simply have some other psychological effects. Discussion of these may be interesting.

B.   A discussion of endorphins as nature's way of giving relief should be productive. How some of the above techniques might stimulate production of these chemicals should be examined.

C.   A class assignment which could be given prior to this lecture, or after, is to have students do some research on these techniques. Give each type to a group of students to study and report to the rest of the class.

■ SUGGESTIONS FOR FURTHER READING

Autrum H. et al. *Foundations of Sensory Science*. Springer-Verlag, 1984.

Barlow, H. H. and J. D. Mollon. *The Senses*. Cambridge University Press, 1982.

Fineman, M. *The Inquisitive Eye*. Oxford University Press, 1981.

Goldstein, E. B. *Sensation and Perception*, 3rd ed. Wadsworth, 1989.

Hurvich, L. M. *Color Vision*. Sineaur Associates, 1981.

Marr, D. *Vision*. W. H. Freeman, 1983.

■ FILM SUGGESTIONS

HEARING CONSERVATION (International Film Bureau, 22 min.)
> This film discusses the prevention of environmentally-caused hearing loss.

THE SENSES: SKIN DEEP (1985, Films for the Humanities and Sciences, Inc., 26 min.)
> This film looks at those sense receptors that depend on contact with the immediate world: taste buds, touch sensors, and olfactory cells. These senses lie in the skin--the largest organ of the body--which also senses heat, pain, and pressure. The complex world beneath the skin is seen from the viewpoint of the root.

SENSATION AND PERCEPTION (1990, from *Psychology- The Study of Human Behavior Series*, Coast Community College District, 30 min.)
> Demonstrates construction of reality from senses, interpretation and organization into meaningful patterns by the brain.

THE SENSES: EYES AND EARS (1985, Films for the Humanities and Sciences, Inc., 26 min.)
> This film looks at the "distance senses"--eyes and ears. Viewers are shown a young reckless driver careening down a road--and are then taken into his eye where the image of the potential crash site is shown. Also seen are scenes inside an ear, showing how the linked bones vibrate to a sound, and a computer graphic shows how the eye focuses on an image.

■ COMPUTER PROGRAMS: *MIND SCOPE*

Exercise 1, Blindspot Mapping

In the first part of the exercise, students map the size and shape of their blindspots. In the second part, the "filling-in" process that makes it seem that the visual field is continuous is explored.

Exercise 10, Sensory Homunculus

The sensitivity of the human skin surface to tactile stimulation is mapped in this exercise.

CHAPTER 5

Perceiving the World

■ BEHAVIORAL OBJECTIVES

The student should be able to:

1. Define perception.
2. Describe the following constancies:
    a. size
    b. shape
    c. brightness
3. Give examples of the following as they relate to the organization of perception:
    a. figure-ground
    b. nearness
    c. similarity
    d. continuity
    e. closure
    f. contiguity
    g. common region
4. Explain what a perceptual hypothesis is.
5. Define and give an example of an ambiguous stimulus.
6. Define depth perception and discuss the nativistic and empirical view of it.
7. Describe the following cues for depth perception and indicate in each case whether the cue is monocular or binocular:
    a. accommodation
    b. convergence
    c. retinal disparity
8. Describe the visual adaptations found among birds.
9. Describe the following two-dimensional, monocular, pictorial depth cues:
    a. linear perspective
    b. relative size
    c. light and shadow
    d. overlap
    e. texture gradients
    f. aerial perspective
    g. relative motion (motion parallax)
10. Describe the phenomenon of the moon illusion. Include in your explanation the apparent distance hypothesis.
11. Define "perceptual habit" and explain how it allows learning to affect perception.
12. Explain and give an example of context.

13.   Describe and give an example of the concept of adaptation level.

14.   Differentiate between an illusion and a hallucination.

15.   Describe at least one practical use of the stroboscopic movement illusion.

16.   Describe the Muller-Lyer illusion and explain how perceptual habits may account for this illusion.

17.   Define attention and list the factors which affect it. Distinguish between selective attention and divided attention.

18.   Differentiate habituation from sensory adaptation. Include the concept of the orientation response.

19.   Explain the "boiled frog syndrome" and how it may affect the ultimate survival of humans.

20.   Explain and give experimental evidence of how motives may alter attention and perception.

21.   Explain how perceptual expectancies may influence perception.

22.   Explain why most eyewitness testimony is inaccurate, including the concept of weapon focus.

23.   Explain what the term "reality testing" means.

24.   Explain Maslow's theory of perceptual awareness.

25.   Discuss how attention affects perception.

26.   Define extrasensory perception.

27.   Define the term parapsychology.

28.   Describe the following psychic abilities:
      a.   clairvoyance
      b.   telepathy
      c.   precognition
      d.   psychokinesis

29.   Explain why most psychologists remain skeptical about psi abilities.

■ DEMONSTRATIONS, DRAMATIZATIONS, AND DISCUSSION

1.   **This demonstration requires a bit of construction.** Obtain a cardboard carton (a half-gallon ice cream carton is about right). Paint the carton flat black. Punch two small holes in the bottom of the carton, one in the center and one near the rim. Place a flashlight inside, facing the bottom, and stuff crushed newspaper around it for support. Leave a space between the lens of the flashlight and the bottom of the carton so that both holes can be lighted.

Cover the center hole with opaque tape. Turn off the room lights and turn on the flashlight. Face the bottom of the carton toward the class and roll it from left to right across a tabletop. The rim light will describe a series of inverted half-circles. Next, uncover the center hole, cover the rim hole, and roll the carton again. The center light will make a straight line from left to right. You would expect, if the carton is rolled again, with both holes uncovered, the two patterns (half-circles and a straight line) would simply be superimposed on one another. Not so! Instead, the class will see a more unified and sophisticated pattern: The rim light will appear to move in complete circles around the center light. Students should be asked to account for this perceptual organization in terms of principles described in the text.

2. **For a simple illustration of convergence,** have students fixate on a distant point and then bring a finger up into the line of sight. The finger will appear "transparent" because the line of sight is nearly parallel. If students then look directly at the finger, it will once again become "solid" (convergence). A variation on this (which also illustrates retinal disparity and fusion) involves again fixating on a distant point. This time the tips of the index fingers of both hands should be brought together in the line of sight, about twelve inches from the eyes. Students should see a small "sausage" forming and disappearing between their fingertips as the two retinal images overlap.

3. **Students often underestimate the effect of the Muller-Lyer illusion because they are so familiar with it.** To demonstrate it in class, on a sheet of paper draw a horizontal line several inches long and place an "arrowhead" on one end and a "V" on the other. Be sure not to center the line within the borders of the page. Duplicate this figure and distribute it to the class. Ask the students to mark the spot that they think is the center of the horizontal line (without trying to correct for the illusion). Now fold the page so the tips of the horizontal line are matched up (to do this they will have to hold the paper up to the light), and crease the paper at the fold. Now ask them to unfold the page and compare the crease with the mark they made. The majority of the students will have erred in their bisection due to the illusion. This is a good launching point for a discussion of illusions.

4. **The role of contrast in selective attention can be demonstrated by** having two students read aloud simultaneously from different books. First this should be done by two students of the same sex who have similar voices. Then it should be done by a male and female pair. The class's ability to selectively attend to one message or the other will be greatly enhanced in the second condition.

5. **For a dramatic and time-honored demonstration of the inaccuracies of eyewitness testimony,** arrange for a confederate to "make a scene" in class. Ideally, the confederate should wear unusual or distinctive clothing (different colored socks, an outlandish hat, etc.). The confederate should charge into class, ask loudly if you are "Professor (your name), "douse" you with a bucket full of paper clippings, and then run out. Immediately after, ask the class to write a description of your "attacker." Then compare details of the descriptions. For an interesting twist, tell students to be sure to include the color of the visitor's socks in their descriptions. In this variation, of course, the confederate wears no socks!

6. **Provide students with apparent examples of "mental telepathy."** In groups have them decide how the following occurrences could be mere coincidences:

    "I suddenly woke up and knew that something tragic had happened to my mother. That morning I received a call that she had died at that precise hour."

    "My sister and I live 3,000 miles apart. We have never visited each other's homes. I didn't know what to buy her for a holiday gift but somehow knew she would like a specific set of towels. I was not surprised to learn that she had already bought a shower curtain of that brand

and color for her bathroom and needed the towels I sent to complete the décor."

■ ONE-MINUTE MOTIVATORS

1. **Show students a five-minute series of rapidly flashed abstract slides or an excerpt from an unusual Fellini-like film.** Ask them to describe what they think they saw. Discuss the diverse ways people can perceive the world.

2. **Develop a five-minute video of close-ups of common objects.** Show each close-up and have students guess what the object is. Then show the entire object. Discuss how perceptual hypotheses and figure/ground processes explain the way objects are normally perceived.

3. **Divide students into pairs.** Ask one student to sit with eyes closed. The other student claps to the left, to the right, and above that student. The "above" clap should be very difficult to localize.

4. **Pictorial depth cues can be demonstrated with a series of slides or transparencies.** Ask students to name each cue and explain how it contributes to perceived depth.

5. **Ask students to use a mirror to write their names, copy a geometric design, etc.** Ask an observing student to note the nature of the errors made as his/her partner adapts to this new perceptual world.

6. **Send three students outside to serve as subjects.** Put three others in front of the class. Invite one subject in and ask the person to estimate the height of the middle student. Ask the middle student to remain; ask two other students to come up to the front. Invite another subject inside. The guesses should change, depending on the height of the other two students as well as the height of the subject.

7. **Throughout your lecture, make a small but novel gesture every few minutes.** The gesture should be something that would draw little attention if done once. Do students become aware of the gesture as it is repeated? Or do they habituate to it? Discuss their perceptions near the end of the session.

■ CLASSROOM EXERCISES

TO THE INSTRUCTOR:

The two exercises outlined in this section should help students understand some aspects of perception that may lead to further discussion and investigation.

Exercise #1: Perception/Attention: The Stroop Effect

In 1935 J. R. Stroop developed an experiment, which now bears his name, on how we process conflicting sensory data. It is called the Stroop Effect. He found that conflicting sensory data slows down the process of perception and increases the chance of error. With a small amount of preparation you can do the experiment in class.

This exercise may be done as a classroom demonstration or as an all-class project. If you choose the former, select several subjects (about five would be sufficient) and ask them to leave the room. You will then bring them back, one at a time, and test them in front of the class, who will be observers and recorders. The latter method, involving the whole class, would require a bit more work to prepare but should pay off in greater student interest. You would pair up the students, having one be the subject and the other the experimenter. The roles could be reversed to test the bi-directional effect.

<u>Procedure</u>: This exercise should be carried out as follows:

1.   Prepare three word-color sheets. The words should be spaced equally on both the horizontal and vertical dimensions. The list and arrangement are found at the end of this exercise. Each of the sheets will be a list of four colors: yellow, blue, green, and red. They will be presented in identical order but in different ways.

      a.   List #1: This list will be done in black or blue ink. All will be the same color.

      b.   List #2: This list will not be words but color patches. Each patch will be the color of the word on the list. These patches can be done with crayons or markers, and should be small rectangles of color with no words.

      c.   List #3. The words on this sheet should be the same as on List #1, except that the words should be printed in color. The color used should always be different from the color named in the word.

2.   If this is to be a classroom demonstration, prepare your subjects, experimenters, and recorders. Otherwise, pair up the students in the class and identify the subjects and experimenters, who will also act as recorders. Each experimenter will need a watch which will measure seconds for timing the subject. The three sheets should be placed face down in front of the subject in order of presentation. Reading each list will constitute a trial. In each case, the subject will

be instructed to read the list from left to right from the top line down, as quickly as possible. When finished, the subject should say, "done." The experimenter will time the reading of each list and note it on the data sheet.

3.   Present List #1 and ask the subject to read the words in order. When presenting List #2, ask the subject to name the color on the patches in the same order as before. For List #3 ask the subject to name the color of the ink in which each word is printed.

4.   Collect the data for all subjects and work out a class average for each of the three lists. If the Stroop Effect has occurred, you should find that the subjects took about the same amount of time to read lists 1 and 2 and longer for 3.

5.   If you have time, reverse the roles of experimenter and subject and repeat the experiment. The only difference would be in reading List #3. The new subject would be asked to read the words on the third list instead of identifying the color of the word. This may provide a different average time when compared with the average time for the first subjects.

Some questions for discussion:

1.   Was the Stroop Effect evident? Explain how it manifested itself.

2.   How can you account for the differences in average time?

3.   Did the change in the reading of List #3 produce a different average time? How great was the difference? How could it be explained?

(based on a demonstration by William C. Titus, Arkansas Tech University)

THE STROOP EFFECT: COLOR-WORD LIST

YELLOW	YELLOW	BLUE	YELLOW
GREEN	RED	YELLOW	GREEN
GREEN	BLUE	RED	YELLOW
RED	GREEN	BLUE	RED
GREEN	BLUE	GREEN	BLUE
BLUE	RED	RED	YELLOW

THE STROOP EFFECT: DATA SHEET:

SUBJECT	TIME (in seconds)		
	LIST #1	LIST #2	LIST #3
1			
2			
3			
4			
5			
6			
7			
8			
9			
10			

Exercise #2: Mental Telepathy, or It's in the Cards

TO THE INSTRUCTOR:

You can easily demonstrate an ESP experiment looking for evidence of telepathy by using the Zener cards. The cards can be made if no real deck is available. The Zener cards are made up of five symbols, one of which is on each card. You should have 25 cards in the deck, five of each symbol. If you make your own, use heavy cardboard so the symbol cannot be seen through the back. Select five symbols that are easily distinguishable from each other. For example, you should not use a square and rectangle as two of the symbols because of possible confusion. The cards and symbols need to be small enough to be easily shuffled and large enough to be easily seen by the whole class when shown.

Duplicate the data sheet which follows so that each student in the class can participate as a subject. The sheet has a place for students to respond to each of five trial runs through the deck. The student can also tally the responses and work out the percentage of correct answers.

Procedure:

1.   Distribute a response sheet to each member of the class and explain how it is to be used.

2.   Shuffle the deck of cards thoroughly in full view of the class and place the deck face down on the table.

3.   Pick up one card at a time, look at it carefully for about two seconds, and place it face down on a new pile. Do not let students see the face of the card. While concentrating on the card, try to shut out any distracting thoughts.   If you are preoccupied with running the demonstration, have a student, prepared beforehand, do the telecommunicating.

4.   Give the students time to write down on their data sheets the symbol which they think you saw on the card. Note on your own record sheet what the symbol was. Proceed through the deck in the same way.

5.   After completing a trial (one run through the deck), shuffle the cards thoroughly and go through the stack again. Repeat this until you have completed five trials, being sure to shuffle the cards before each one. Also, be sure you have kept an accurate record of each card for each trial run.

6.   After the fifth run through the deck, give the students the correct listing of cards so they can score their sheets.

7.   Ask the students to total the number of correct responses for each of the five trials. They can work out the percentage for each run by dividing the number right by 25 and multiplying by 100.

8.   Then ask them to total the number right for all five trials. Divide this total by 125 and multiply by 100 to get a percentage for the whole experiment.

Discussion:

Ask the students to discuss their findings. They should first determine what they could expect to score by chance alone, i.e. by guessing. Then they can compare their scores with the chance score to see if they did as well, poorer, or better.

1. Do those who did better have ESP?

2. In this case, do they have the power of telepathy?

3. What would happen if you did it many more times?

4. Of what value is it to do better than chance?

TELEPATHY: DATA SHEET

	TRIALS				
	1	2	3	4	5
1					
2					
3					
4					
5					
6					
7					
8					
9					
10					
11					
12					
13					

	TRIALS				
	1	2	3	4	5
1					
2					
3					
4					
5					
6					
7					
8					
9					
10					
11					
12					
13					

■ BROADENING OUR CULTURAL HORIZONS

1. **Ask students skilled in languages other than English to share with the class** the alphabet of the language and few key words. Using Russian, Japanese, or Chinese characters is especially effective. Discuss how meaningless the characters or words may seem at first. Rewrite the letters each day on the chalkboard. After a few sessions, the words should become meaningful. Remind students that English appears just as meaningless at first to the non-English speaker as the characters or words appear to the English speaker.

2. **While some cultures may associate tallness with high status, other cultures value other attributes.** Describe a hypothetical culture where shortness and age are highly valued. How would these differing values affect the social structure of these two cultures? How would they affect the way people are perceived in job interviews?

3. **Find a science fiction story that includes a fourth and fifth dimension** (or have students write such a story. Discuss how our earthly existence constrains the way we perceive the world.

4. **Ask students to watch a half-hour of Saturday morning cartoons, including the commercials.** Ask groups of the class to watch the shows as if they were a child raised:

    a.   On a poor ranch 100 miles from the nearest town
    b.   In a middle class suburb of a large city
    c.   In the poorest section of a large city
    d.   In rural Guatemala

    Discuss assumptions we make about rural, suburban, and urban, and North American living and different perceptions of aggression, friendship, and materialism.

■ SUPPLEMENTAL LECTURE

Closure is one principle of perception that is often treated somewhat superficially. Many seldom go beyond seeing it as joining dots to form a line or a figure. It is interesting to think about ways in which closure may be a factor in our everyday experiences. This lecture should be a discussion with the class about their experiences with this phenomenon. They will be surprised to find that it is an important factor in their perception of the world.

CLOSURE

I.   Definition

A.   The common definition refers to closure as the tendency to complete a figure. Where gaps are found in a line, people tend to see it as continuous. This is a rather simplistic definition. The phenomenon presents itself in a number of other ways that are significant to the individual.

B.   A fuller definition of closure says that we have a natural tendency to perceive stimuli as wholes. This concept is basic to Gestalt psychology. It is the inclination to complete incomplete stimuli, the tendency to fill in the gaps when sensory data are incomplete.

C.   Another way to look at it is that we have a natural tendency to give meaning to our experiences. It is possible to extend the concept to explain how people interpret events in their lives, ideas about the world, news reports, etc. It helps us to see why people who have the same experiences interpret them differently.

II.   Applications of the Principle

A.   As gossip is spread, it grows and changes. Most of the time, gossip comes in fragments of information. The natural tendency to bring closure, to complete the picture, results in some embellishment or addition. When we pass it on, it is tidied up a bit, and some "gaps" are filled in. Each participant in spreading the gossip does the same. The story grows and becomes more interesting with each transmission.

B.   Projective tests use closure. They present ambiguous stimuli, and the subject is asked to fill in the gaps. The subject is required to tell what s/he sees in response to incomplete, vague, or inconclusive stimuli.

C.   Television makes use of closure. The picture on the screen is made up of a series of dots, and the viewer is required to fill in the spaces to produce the images which flow out of "the tube." Marshall McLuhan coined the expression, "The medium is the message." He believed that television shapes the viewer's perception of the world because the viewer must become involved with producing the images. He pointed out that the stories and pictures about the Viet Nam War which the American citizens saw on the evening news made them participants. He saw television as a "hot medium" because it got the viewer involved. This was, and is, the principle of closure at work in our perception of the world through television.

D.   Eyewitness accounts of an accident or crime almost always differ. Most viewers see only a part of the whole event, and what they see may pass by quickly. The natural tendency to want to make experiences complete results in a story by the witness which is only partially factual. Usually several witnesses are needed to piece together what really happened.

III.   With What Does a Person Fill in the Gaps?

    A.   This is a good discussion question because students should begin to see that it has to come from within the perceiver. It is from one's own experience. That is what makes a projective test work. The subject reveals something of himself/herself in the responses. People who hear a siren in the distance may think it is an ambulance or a police car or a fire truck, depending on their past, and often their most recent, experiences.

    B.   Discuss why people disagree about the meaning of world events reported in the news media.

    C.   Ask the students to think about the effects of television violence on viewers, especially on children. What would McLuhan say about this important question?

IV.   An Exercise

    A.   Ask the students to stand in straight lines of about ten persons each. Prepare ahead of time an ambiguous message about a test or assignment. Write the message on a piece of paper and give it to the first person in each line. Ask that person to read the message silently and return it to you. Then ask this person to whisper the message to the next person. Ask each one to pass the message on. Ask the last person to write the message on a pad.

    B.   Compare the message given at the beginning and the message received at the end. Discuss how closure is a factor in this process.

■ SUGGESTIONS FOR FURTHER READING

Bloomer, C. M. *Principles of Visual Perception*. Van Nostrand Reinhold, 1976.

Boff, K., K. Kaufman, and J. Thomas. *Handbook of Perception and Performance*. Wiley, 1986.

Carraher, R. G., and J. B. Thurston. *Optical Illusions and the Visual Arts*. Van Nostrand Reinhold, 1968.

Dember, W. N. and J. S Warm. *Psychology of Perception*. Holt, Rinehart and Winston, 1979.

Hansel, C.E. M. *ESP: A Scientific Evaluation*. Prometheus Books, 1980.

Locher, J. L., ed. *The World of M. C. Escher*. Abrahms, 1971.

Marks, D. and R. Kamman. *The Psychology of the Psychic*. 1980.

Randi, J. *Flim Flam!* Lippincott and Crowell, 1980.

Sekuler, R. and R. Blake, R. *Perception*, 3rd ed.   McGraw-Hill, 1994.

Wolman B. B. et al., eds. *Handbook of Parapsychology*. Van Nostrand Reinhold, 1985.

■ FILM SUGGESTIONS

ESP-THE HUMAN "X" FACTOR (Indiana University, 30 min.)
>   Illustrates extrasensory perception and interviews J. B. Rhine.

EXPERIMENTAL PARAPSYCHOLOGY (1977, CTV Television Network Ltd., 145 min.)
>   Looks at the problems and patterns of alleged cases of paranormal events. Program contains a series
>   of five cassettes 29 minutes each.

AN INTRODUCTION TO VISUAL ILLUSIONS (1970, Pennsylvania University, 12 min.)
>   Demonstrates illusions involving depth, direction, after-images, apparent movement, and others.

THE MIND AND PERCEPTION - PART TWO (1984, from *Using Your Creative Brain Series*, Educational
Dimensions Group, approximately 42 min.)
>   Discusses the psychology, biology, and sociology related to the perceptiveness of the brain.

PERCEPTION (1979, CRM/McGraw-Hill, 28 min.)
>   This film shows how perception is an individual and subjective means of viewing reality influenced by
>   upbringing, culture, and media. Several vignettes in business as well as social settings depict the
>   consequences of individuals perceiving the same situation differently. Although people strive for
>   objectivity, the film points out that diverse opinions can be normal and enriching as well as a means
>   to evaluate one's own judgments and decisions.

PERCEPTION (1970, Prentice-Hall, 15 min.)
>   This film provides many principles of perception not normally available for classroom demonstration.
>   It begins with an overview of the field and goes on to present illustrations of figure-ground
>   relationships. Bruner's experiment, phi phenomena, Benham's top, perceptual set, color satiation, color
>   mixture, and the trapezoidal window are included.

THE SENSES AND PERCEPTION: LINKS TO THE OUTSIDE WORLD (1975, Indiana University, 18
min.)
>   A look at the way in which sense receptors send information to the brain which then interprets it based
>   on the information itself as well as on past experience.

■ COMPUTER PROGRAMS: *MIND SCOPE*

Exercise 14, Contrast Effects

Students are asked to judge which of two panels, shown successively, contains more asterisks. The backgrounds against which the panels are displayed will be varied, so the effect of context on judgment can be determined. The purpose is to demonstrate that judgments are made against some kind of background. Whether it's a food item on display in a store or one's first introduction to another person, the context or circumstances can influence one's perception.

CHAPTER 6

States of Consciousness

■ BEHAVIORAL OBJECTIVES

The student should be able to:

1. Define consciousness according to William James.
2. Define "altered state of consciousness."
3. Explain how sleep is defined by Webb.
4. Define the term microsleep.
5. Describe the effects of 48 hours of sleep deprivation.
6. Name and describe the condition that occurs when a person is deprived of sleep for a longer period of time.
7. Discuss the concept of circadian rhythms. Describe the characteristics of long and short sleepers.
8. Explain the relationship between age and sleep needs.
9. Discuss the neurological control of sleep.
10. Explain the four stages of sleep.
11. Differentiate between the two basic states of sleep: REM and NREM.
12. Explain the relationship between REM sleep and dreaming.
13. State how many times per night most people dream and how long the dreams usually last.
14. Describe and differentiate between the sleep disturbances sleepwalking, sleeptalking, and nightmares vs. night terrors. List three steps that can be used to eliminate nightmares.
15. Describe narcolepsy and cataplexy.
16. Define insomnia. List and describe the characteristics and treatments of the three types of insomia.
17. Describe the effects of nonprescription and prescription drugs on insomnia.
18. List and describe six behavioral interventions for insomnia.
19. Describe the sleep disorder known as sleep apnea including its nature, cause, treatments, and relationship to SIDS. Describe the sleep position which seems to minimize SIDS in infants.
20. Describe the functions of REM sleep and the consequences of deprivation of REM sleep.
21. Explain how Freud viewed dreams, and present the evidence against his view.
22. Describe the activation-synthesis hypothesis concerning dreaming.
23. Define hypnosis. Describe the history of hypnosis from Mesmer through its use today.
24. Explain how a person's hypnotic susceptibility can be determined.
25. List the four common factors in all hypnotic techniques.
26. Explain what the basic suggestion effect is.
27. Describe the dissociation in awareness caused by hypnosis.
28. Explain how hypnosis may affect a person's acting in a way that he or she would not

normally act.

29. Explain what can and cannot be achieved with hypnosis.

30. Explain what sensory deprivation is and describe its positive and negative effects.

31. Define the term psychoactive drug.

32. Differentiate physical dependence from psychological dependence.

33. List and describe five different types of drug-taking behaviors.

34. Describe the following frequently abused drugs in terms of their effects, possible medical uses, side effects or long-term symptoms, organic damage potential, and potential for physical and/or psychological dependence:

    a.   amphetamines

    b.   cocaine (including the three signs of abuse)

    c.   caffeine

    d.   nicotine

    e.   barbiturates

    f.   alcohol

    g.   hallucinogens (including marijuana)

35. List and explain the three phases in the development of a drinking problem.

36. Generally describe the treatment process for alcoholism. Name the form of therapy that has probably been the most successful.

37. List and describe the four dream processes identified by Freud which disguise the hidden meaning of dreams.

38. Describe the dream theories of Freud, Hall, and Cartwright.

39. Outline procedures for using dreams to improve creativity.

40. Define lucid dreams and describe methods for increasing their frequency.

41. List the predictors of adolescent drug abuse.

42. Discuss the social and psychological factors involved in drug abuse.

43. Describe both traditional and contemporary approaches to the prevention of drug abuse.

■ DEMONSTRATIONS, DRAMATIZATIONS, AND DISCUSSION

1. **The Charcot Pendulum makes a good demonstration of the core elements of hypnosis.** Prepare three pendulums by tying a small weight to one end of three foot-long strings. A nut, pendant, washer, fishing sinker, or ring works well. In class ask for volunteers. Have them stand in front of the class. Each should hold a string (with attached weight). Proceed by giving suggestions similar to these:

The Charcot Pendulum has long been used as a prelude to hypnosis. Today I will not be hypnotizing you, so just relax. For the pendulum to work, you must be able to concentrate and focus your attention as I instruct you. Begin by holding the pendulum at arm's length and at eye level. Focus your attention on the pendulum. Notice its texture and the way the light reflects from its surface. Relax and take a deep breath. Watch the pendulum and focus on it intensely. Let everything else fade away until the pendulum is at the very center of your attention. Now I'd like you to begin to use your concentration to move the pendulum. Do not move your hand or body. Just apply the energy of your concentration to the pendulum. Try to push it away from you. Each time it moves away push again, with your eyes, with your attention. Push and release, push and release. Follow it with your eyes as it begins to move. Each time it swings out, push and release. It's as if a magnet were pushing and releasing, pushing and releasing. Relax and follow it with your eyes. Let it swing wider and wider. Push, release (and so forth).

With continued suggestions such as these, most subjects will respond by swinging the pendulum in a broad arc. When questioned they will deny that they consciously moved the hand. The major point here is that the pendulum seems to move of its own accord, aided only by the "concentration" of the subjects. In this respect the experience is similar to hypnosis. Suggestion brings about a temporary suspension of reality-testing and conscious intention--a change essential to hypnosis.

2.   **For a simple but dramatic demonstration of the fakery involved in much stage hypnosis, try the following.** Tell the class that one of the most reliable phenomena available with hypnosis is anesthesia or pain analgesia. Tell them that earlier you used self-hypnosis to make your hand totally insensitive to pain, and that now you need only use a post-hypnotic cue to produce numbness. Stroke your hand as if you were putting on a glove, and explain that this is the cue. Pinch your hand a few times as if testing to see if it has become numb. Ask the class to watch carefully as you strike a match (a paper match, <u>not</u> a wooden match) and hold the flame to the palm of your outstretched hand. The trick, of course, is to <u>keep the match moving at all times</u>. (You may want to practice this at home first!) It is quite possible to leave very impressive "scorch" marks (actually soot) on your hand without experiencing any pain. Explain to the students what you have done and point out that many examples of stage hypnosis rely on similar deception and a lack of questioning by the audience.

3.   **The spectacular stage trick of suspending someone between two chairs** (pictured in this chapter) is worth repeating in class. Have a volunteer recline as shown. Be sure the head and feet touch the backs of the end chairs. Ask the subject to lift, and remove the middle chair. The subject should have no difficulty maintaining this position. Now place a book on the subject's upper abdomen (diaphragm area). With the volunteer's permission, lean on the book with both hands to show that the subject can support extra weight <u>without</u> hypnosis. Then note that the upper abdomen is the only place a hypnotist could actually stand or sit on the suspended subject. For obvious reasons the entertainer is not going to position himself/herself on the subject's knees, pelvis, or chest. The only workable position is just a few inches from the front edge of the chair--which is why subjects can so readily support the weight.

4.   **A very interesting class discussion can usually be generated from comparisons** of individual differences in sleep patterns and unusual experiences associated with sleep. Look for people who:

     a.   sleep very little or much more than average;

     b.   have been deprived or sleep for long periods;

     c.   have done shift work or have maintained unusual sleep/working cycles;

     d.   have a relative or acquaintance who has had sleep disturbances such as somnambulism, night terrors, narcolepsy, sleep apnea, or insomnia;

     e.   have done problem-solving in dreams.

5.   **While many students express great interest in the topic of sleep and dreams,** it is a subject about which they have many misconceptions. Recently, J. Palladino and B. Carducci developed *A Sleep and Dream Information Questionnaire* designed to assess student awareness of current findings in sleep and dream research. This questionnaire can provide an interesting and informative way to introduce students to this material. Student responses can also be used to tailor lectures to meet the needs of the class. Finally, after students take the questionnaire, the instructor can discuss the items in class, thus giving students immediate feedback. Copies of the questionnaire, an appendix entitled "Explanation of Items Comprising the Sleep and Dream Information Questionnaire", and reprints are available from Joseph Palladino, Department of Psychology, Indiana State University at Evansville. For more information see J. J. Palladino and B. J. Carducci, "Students' Knowledge of Sleep and Dreams," *Teaching of Psychology*, Vol. II (3), October 1984.

■ ONE-MINUTE MOTIVATORS

1.   **Spend five minutes overloading the class with a videotape, a musical tape, three students reading different news stories aloud, and a thinking task or puzzle.** Contrast this with five minutes of the most dreary and monotonous lecture you have ever given. Have students discuss their reactions to these brief samples of too much and too little stimulation. Suggest that each of us attempts to find an "optimal level of arousal" that is appropriate to the task we are trying to do.

2.   **Ask students to close their eyes while you say, "Your body is becoming heavy. . ."** etc. Ask students if they felt at all hypnotized. If not, was their consciousness changed in other ways?

3.   **Ask students to predict their hypnotic susceptibility before they read this chapter.** Then bring several students to the front of the class and make some of the suggestions from the Stanford Hypnotic Susceptibility Scale. Identify students who responded to most of the suggestions as good hypnotic subjects.

4.   **Take students on the following meditative walk and discuss any alterations in consciousness they experience.**

Try to get comfortable in your seat. Close your eyes and begin deep breathing. Inhale through your nose and then exhale through your mouth, sitting deeper and deeper in the chair with each breath. Continue deep breathing as I talk. If you mind wanders away from what I am saying, let your thoughts go for a moment, then pull them back. Imagine that you are in a beautiful green meadow. You can feel the warm but shaded sun on your arms and your legs. Your feet are bare, and you are walking down a dirt path. Your right foot is on the warm, soft dirt; your left foot is on the cool grass. Watch yourself walk. Look at the rhythm of your movements as you focus on your left foot, then your right, then your left, then your right. Continue walking until you get to the end of the meadow and begin hearing and smelling the ocean. Watch yourself come out in a very warm clearing where suddenly the beach is in front of you. You walk down four warm, wooden steps, first putting your left foot, then your right then your left, then your right. Once on the beach you pause and listen very carefully to the surf. Hear the waves build up, break, roll into shore, and pull back out. Begin walking into the surf. Watch yourself get closer and closer to the water. Now you are on crusty sand that was wet a few hours ago. Hear it crunch as you walk. Now you are at mid-calf, then at your knees. and finally at your mid-thigh. Pause to listen to the surf, to hear the birds, to smell the sea. Take from a pocket in your shorts a list of ten worries that you have. Read that list very slowly: 1,2,3,4,5,6,7,8,9,10. You realize that you haven't even thought about those worries since you began your walk in the meadow. You realize that there is nothing you can do now to deal with these issues. You take your list and you tear up the biodegradable paper and toss the shreds on the sea beside you. You watch your worries scatter, the ink fading, and you let go of all worries for the moment. Then you look up at the sun and feel the glorious warmth on your face and your arms. You turn and begin walking back to the shore, feeling the water at your thighs, then at your knees, then at your mid-calf, and then at your ankles. When you get to the shore, you see a very special person about a hundred feet from you at the end of the beach. This is the person in your life who is most able to comfort and inspire you. You watch yourself approach this person; watch yourselves embrace; you hear yourself describe one problem that you did not think you could handle yourself but you hear yourself resolve the issue. You turn and leave your friend, stronger, more assertive, more competent than before.

5.   **Ask a student to role-play the feelings of the cocaine addict.** Others in class could verbalize the feelings of the addict's spouse, children, parents, and employer.

■ CLASSROOM EXERCISES

TO THE INSTRUCTOR:

This chapter in the text has a varied collection of topics. It is good to engage the students in looking at some experiences they have had that fall into one or another of these categories. Two types of altered states have been singled out for these exercises. You could select any others that appeal to you. The main objective is for students to become aware of their own experiences and begin to examine them more objectively. Understanding the dynamics of these experiences makes them more meaningful.

Exercise #1: Dreaming

Everyone dreams but few people remember their dreams, and those who do find that the memory of the dream seems to fade away soon after awakening. To analyze the dream, the student must record it as soon as possible after waking. Suggest that students purchase a book or use the forms provided for this exercise. Students should write down the substance of a dream each day for about a week. The following items should be recorded each time that dreaming has occurred:

A.   the main actions and events in the dream, including persons, known or unknown, who appear;

B.   events of the day (or days) prior to the dream that were significant to the student, even if they seem unrelated to the dream. Ask them to pay particular attention to major events and also to those thoughts or activities which preceded going to bed. After doing this for a couple of days, students should become adept at it.

After these items have been collected for a few days, ask students in class to form groups of three to discuss the dreams. Group discussion is best because individuals often do not see connections between their own dreams and past events, but others do because they are not personally involved. Some of the more interesting findings should be shared with the whole class.

Compare the findings in class with the discussion about dreams in the text. Do they support the author's ideas about dreams and their origins?

Exercise #2: Relaxation

Altered states such as hypnosis and meditation require the subject to relax. Relaxation is not always easy to achieve, and most people need to work at it to do it successfully. Biofeedback techniques can help people learn to relax and gain control of their bodies. Students can discover how easy it is to relax, even in the classroom, by a simple exercise. Having experienced the benefits of relaxation of the whole body, the students will want to do it again. They will find it easier to cope with stress and anxiety if they can gain control of their bodies through relaxation.

A.   This exercise requires students to:

1.   clear their minds of all thoughts,
2.   consciously relax their muscles,
3.   breathe deeply and regularly,
4.   concentrate on relaxing and breathing.

B.   Procedure:

1.   Ask students to sit comfortably in their chairs and close their eyes.

2.   Ask them to clear their minds of all thoughts, try not to think about anything, and listen to your voice.

3.   Tell them to breathe deeply and slowly in and out, in and out. You should set the pace very carefully so they hold each breath and exhale slowly.

4.   Tell the students to continue to do this as they begin to relax their muscles. First relax the toes, feel the toes relaxing. Then move to the feet, thighs, back, fingers, arms, chest, etc., progressing to the top of the head.

5.   Remind them periodically to keep breathing deeply in and out.

6.   As the exercise proceeds, you can interject relaxing scenes such as a tree swaying in the breeze, blue water on a lake, waves lapping at a shore, etc.

7.   This exercise should take only about five minutes. To terminate it, stop talking and let the students sit quietly for a minute or two. Gradually each one will return from the activity relaxed and refreshed.

C. Discussion:

1.   Ask students to comment on:

a.   how they felt after the exercise,
b.   what they felt during the exercise,
c.   their confidence (or lack of it) in the exercise before it started,
d.   their feeling about the effectiveness of the exercise after it is over.

2.   Discuss the use of relaxation as a way to deal with stress in daily life.

DREAMING: **DATA SHEET**

TO THE STUDENT: Record on this sheet the answers to the following questions about your dreams. Write your responses as soon as you awake in the morning.

1.   What dream(s) did you have last night? What happened? What people or animals were present?

2.   What were you doing or thinking about immediately before going to bed?

3.   What significant experiences did you have yesterday or in the last few days?

4.   Are you anticipating any important events today or in the next few days? What are they?

■ BROADENING OUR CULTURAL HORIZONS

1.   **What meaning or importance does American culture give to dreams?** Do you think that this applies to other cultures? Do you think that it is appropriate?

2.   **The members of many cultures seek altered states of consciousness as pathways to enlightenment and personal power.** What are the predominant means of altering consciousness in our culture? Are any of them potential pathways for personal growth?

3.   **In what ways is the "passive, alert" state sought in meditation** at odds with mainstream values in North American culture?

4.   **What role do drugs play in American culture?** In your life? To what extent is your use of drugs (including non-prescription drugs) an expression of cultural patterns and values?

5.   **What cultural values do you think would increase the likelihood of drug use or abuse?** What similarities would you guess would exist among drug abusers in various cultures, regardless of their race, gender, or ethnic background?

■ SUPPLEMENTAL LECTURE

The topic of drugs and alcohol abuse continues to be important for students to study and understand. Students in a class will come with varying backgrounds because of educational programs, television, and personal experience. The textbook gives detailed information on most of the popular, well-known drugs in use today. Class time would not be used efficiently, simply going over the list of drugs. Not only can the students read these in the text, but the names and types tend to change rapidly, so the list and teacher may appear to be obsolete.   Classroom time would be best used giving the students an overview of drugs. They should become aware of why drugs are harmful and what the effects are on the body and behavior of the user. The student can then fit in any specific drug in a more meaningful way.

DRUGS AND ALCOHOL

I.   Introduction

    A.   Begin the class with a discussion of chemicals in the body. Students should have an understanding of the body as a very complex chemical system. A delicate balance is needed to maintain the body and keep it operating at its best.

    B.   Remind students of what happens in the laboratory when chemicals are combined. Most will have seen demonstrations of clear liquids turning colored, colors changing, flashing explosions, fires starting, etc. These are standard "spectacular" demonstrations done to catch the interest of students. The point here is to be sure they understand the implications of mixing chemicals.

C.   Discuss with the class some of the known effects on the body of ingesting commonly obtained chemicals. Some common examples can be alcohol, aspirin, sleeping pills, cyanide. Students will think of others.

II.   Effects of Drugs

A.   Discuss the consequences of prolonged use of drugs. Chemicals that are added to the system in the body will affect it in many ways. One of these ways is that the body may begin to accept the chemical. It can be said to make room for it. When this begins to happen, the body expects to have it and may express a need to have it. ADDICTION is the result of this kind of adjustment. WITHDRAWAL is the behavior of the body when its need is not being satisfied. Explore the difference between physical and psychological dependence.

B.   The body may adjust to the effects of the drug and begin to function as if the drug were not there. The desired effect of the drug will diminish. More will be needed to produce the same effect. At some point even very large doses may not create the effect the body has come to expect and craves. The concept of TOLERANCE is important and should be explored.

C.   Mixing two or more drugs may have serious adverse effects on the body. Often these effects are not known. Some are. Alcohol and depressants in combination can cause loss of consciousness, brain damage, and death.

D.   Students need to be aware of the damage to organs in the body due to prolonged use of drugs. These "side effects" are often not mentioned and may not be thought to be important. It could be a useful project for students to investigate further.

III.   Types of Drugs

A.   The four types of drugs are:

1.   Stimulant - any chemical substance that excites or arouses the central nervous system,
2.   Depressant - any chemical substance that slows down the functioning of the central nervous system,
3.   Analgesic - any chemical substance that functions as a pain-killer,
4.   Hallucinogen - any chemical substance that produces hallucinations by distorting reality and disturbing sensory input into the central nervous system.

B.   Rather than trying to identify and categorize all known drugs you should discuss the four types and how they affect the user. The student can then look at individual drugs.

C.   For each type of drug:

1.   discuss the effects on the individual: addiction, tolerance, physical damage, etc.;

2.   examine the psychological effects as well as the physical;

3.   indicate some prominent and common examples of this type of drug, including legal as well as illegal drugs;

4.   distinguish between use and abuse of these drugs.

IV.   Class Discussion (as a whole or in discussion groups)

A.   What would be the consequences of legalizing all illegal drugs--for the individual and for society?

B.   What are the abuses of legal drugs? Identify some of the drugs and the abuses that exist.

C.   What is the difference between use and abuse of drugs?

D.   Discuss the relationship that exists today between the use of drugs and the punishment meted out for illegal acts.

E.   Find out what the penalties are. Either bring in a resource person (policeman, lawyer) or assign students to get information.

F.   Treatment for drug and alcohol abuse should be explored. Students could interview people involved. Clinics for alcohol and drug abuse, mental health centers, police officers, etc. are good sources.

G.   Side-effects of drugs are often overlooked. Discuss these. Moreover, it would be beneficial for students to select a drug and investigate this aspect. Some will have personal experiences or experiences with elderly relatives to share with the class since this is a serious problem with the aged.

■ SUGGESTIONS FOR FURTHER READING

Blane, H. T. and K. E. Leonard. *Psychological Theories of Drinking and Alcoholism.* Guilford Press, 1987.

Evans, C. *Landscapes of the Night: How and Why We Dream*. Viking, 1983.

Gibson, H. B. *Hypnosis: Its Nature and Therapeutic Uses*. Taplinger, 1977.

Huxley, A. *The Doors of Perception*.   Harper and Row, 1970.

Julien, R. M. *A Primer of Drug Action*, 6th ed.   W. H. Freeman, 1992.

Loftus, E. F. "Alcohol, Marijuana, and Memory." *Psychology Today*, March 1980: 42-56, 92.

Ray, O. S. *Drugs, Society, and Human Behavior*, 6th ed. C. V. Mosby, 1993.

Van de Castle, R. L. *Our Dreaming Mind*. Ballantine Books, 1994.

Vogler, R. E. and W. R. Bartz. *The Better Way to Drink*. Simon and Schuster, 1983.

Wallace, B. and L. E. Fisher. *Consciousness and Behavior*. Allyn and Bacon, 1987.

■ FILM SUGGESTIONS

AA AND THE ALCOHOLIC (1981, Motivational Media, 44 min.)
  This film presents answers to the most prevalent myths and most frequently asked questions about Alcoholics Anonymous. Made with the help of recovering alcoholics, the film combines documentary and dramatic forms.

ALCOHOL AND HUMAN PSYCHOLOGY (1985, Aims Media, 23 min.)
  Describes psychological aspects of alcohol consumption.

AN EASY PILL TO SWALLOW (1980, CRM/McGraw-Hill, 28 min.)
  As this film points out, anxiety has become a major medical problem and a very big business as indicated by the fact that well over one-quarter of the prescriptions filled in North America are for mood-altering drugs. This film explores this phenomenon in an examination of drug abuse issues illustrated by discussions with doctors and patients. It asks whether we have turned our common social and emotional problems into "diseases" and abandoned self-reliance or self-help in favor of drugs.

BIOCHEMICAL REVOLUTION: MOODS OF THE FUTURE (Document Associates, 17 min.)
  Examines future implications of the development of mood-altering drugs in a society populated by pill-taking adults.

CAPTIVE MINDS: HYPNOSIS AND BEYOND (1985, Filmakers Library, 55 min.)
  How do the Moonies hold on to their disciples? How can the Marine Corps generate fierce loyalty? Why do Jesuit priests submit to a lifetime of strict authority? The film shows how the indoctrination methods of these disparate institutions are quite similar. Recruits are isolated in unfamiliar environments, kept busy to the point of exhaustion, and often they become vulnerable to suggestion. The film goes on to show how other types of suggestion (e.g., hypnosis,

psychotherapy) also influence behavior.

I'M DEPENDENT, YOU'RE ADDICTED (1974, Time-Life, 47 min.)
Based on medical evidence from England and America, this film discusses amphetamines, barbiturates, LSD, and marijuana and analyzes their effects from the level of the individual brain core to the whole human psyche.

INTERVENTION AND RECOVERY (1982, Federal Mogul Service, 28 min.)
This film uses puppets to show how intervention teams of family, friends, and employees can help an alcoholic or drug addict to accept treatment. Also shown are ways to form intervention teams.

HARD DRUGS (Document Associates, 16 min.)
Offers insights into the development of an addiction. Addicts and former addicts participating in two therapy programs are interviewed.

PORTRAIT OF A TEENAGE DRUG ABUSER (1987, Barr Films, 23 min.)
Presents the individual and collective experiences of six young adults who are all recovering drug abusers. Presents insights into the causes and tragic fates of teenage drug abusers.

SECRETS OF SLEEP (1976, Time-Life, 52 min.)
This film covers all of the major sleep phenomena, including the effects of sleeping pills, jet lag, dreams and their interpretation. Also included are some fascinating interviews with individuals whose sleep needs are considerably less than most people's (e.g., one gentleman who has slept no more than 15 minutes a night for his entire life).

SLEEP AND DREAM RESEARCH (1977, CTV Television Network Ltd., 145 min.)
Gives and account of the history of sleep and dream research, problems of dream recall, factors effecting sleep and dreams and the effects of sleep deprivation. Program contains a series of five cassettes of 29 minutes each.

SLEEP AND DREAMING (1990, from *Psychology- The Study of Human Behavior Series*, Coast District Telecourses, 30 min.)
Demonstrates construction of reality from senses, interpretation and organization into meaningful patterns by the brain.

SLEEP: DREAM VOYAGE (1985, Films for the Humanities and Sciences, 26 min.)
What happens to the body during sleep? This film explores the mystery of REM sleep, observes a computer display of the waves that sweep across the brain during sleep, and presents an interesting piece of footage of a cat "acting out" its dreams. The analogy of sleep to a ship on automatic pilot illustrates how some functions must and do continue while the conscious brain is asleep.

SMOKING: GAMES SMOKERS PLAY (Document Associates, 26 min.)
Combines facts and humor to encourage viewers to seriously consider the real reasons for smoking.

CHAPTER 7

Conditioning and Learning

■ BEHAVIORAL OBJECTIVES

The student should be able to:

1. Define learning.
2. Define reinforcement and explain its role in conditioning.
3. Differentiate between antecedents and consequences and explain how they are related to classical and operant conditioning.
4. Give a brief history of classical conditioning.
5. Describe the following terms as they apply to classical conditioning:
   a. neutral stimulus (NS)
   b. unconditioned stimulus (US)
   c. unconditioned response (UR)
   d. conditioned stimulus (CS)
   e. conditioned response (CR)
6. Describe and give an example of classical conditioning using the abbreviations US, UR, CS, and CR.
7. Explain how reinforcement occurs during the acquisition of a classically conditioned response. Explain higher order conditioning.
8. Describe and give examples of the following concepts as they relate to classical conditioning:
   a. extinction
   b. spontaneous recovery
   c. stimulus generalization
   d. stimulus discrimination
9. Describe the relationship between classical conditioning and reflex responses.
10. Explain what a conditioned emotional response (CER) is and how it is acquired.
11. Explain the concept and the importance of vicarious classical conditioning.
12. State the basic principle of operant conditioning.
13. Contrast operant conditioning with classical conditioning. Briefly compare the differences between what is meant by the terms "reward" and "reinforcement."
14. Explain what response contingent reinforcement is.
15. Describe how Skinner's vision of behavioral engineering has been put into practice.
16. Explain how shaping occurs.
17. Explain how extinction and spontaneous recovery occur in operant conditioning.
18. Describe how negative attention seeking demonstrates reinforcement and extinction in operant conditioning.
19. compare and contrast positive reinforcement, negative reinforcement, and punishment and give an example of each.

20. Differentiate primary reinforcers from secondary reinforcers and list several examples of each kind.

21. Discuss three ways in which a secondary reinforcer becomes reinforcing.

22. Discuss the major advantages and disadvantages of primary reinforcers and secondary reinforcers (tokens, for example), and describe how tokens have been used to help "special" groups of people.

23. Explain how a secondary reinforcer can become a generalized reinforcer.

24. Explain how the Premack principle (involving prepotent responses) can be used as reinforcement.

25. Describe how the delay of reinforcement can influence the effectiveness of the reinforcement.

26. Describe response chaining and explain how it can counteract the effects of delaying reinforcement.

27. Explain why superstitious behavior develops and why it persists.

28. Compare and contrast the effects of continuous and partial reinforcement.

29. Describe, give an example of, and explain the effects of the following schedules of partial reinforcement:
    a. Fixed Ratio (FR)
    b. Variable Ratio (VR)
    c. Fixed Interval (FI)
    d. Variable Interval (VI)

30. Explain the concept of stimulus control.

31. Describe the processes of generalization and discrimination as they relate to operant conditioning.

32. Explain how punishers can be defined by their effects on behavior. Explain the concept of response cost.

33. List and discuss three factors which influence the effectiveness of punishment.

34. Differentiate the effects of severe punishment from mild punishment.

35. List the three basic tools available to control simple learning.

36. Discuss how and why reinforcement should be used with punishment in order to change an undesirable behavior.

37. List and discuss three problems associated with punishment.

38. List six guidelines which should be followed when using punishment.

39. Explain how using punishment can be habit forming and describe the behavior of children who are frequently punished.

40. Name two key elements that underlie learning and explain how they function together in learning situations.

41. Explain what two-factor learning is.

42. Explain classical and operant conditioning in terms of the informational view.

43. Define feedback, indicate three factors which increase its effectiveness, and explain its importance in learning.

44. Describe programmed instruction and computer-assisted instruction and discuss their application in learning and teaching.

45. Define cognitive learning.

46. Describe the concepts of cognitive map and latent learning.

47. Explain the difference between discovery learning and rote learning, and describe the students who use each.

48. Discuss the factors which determine whether or not modeling or observational learning will occur.

49. Describe the experiment with children and the Bo-Bo doll that demonstrates the powerful effect of modeling on behavior.

50. Explain why what a parent does is more important than what a parent says.

51. Briefly describe the general conclusion that can be drawn form studies on the effects of TV violence on children. Explain whether this means that TV violence causes aggression or not and why.

52. Describe the procedures and results of Williams' natural experiment with TV.

53. List and briefly describe the seven steps in a behavioral self-management program.

54. Describe how self-recording and behavioral contracting can aid a self-management program.

55. Describe and give an example of a fixed action pattern.

56. Define instinct and explain why most psychologists reject the idea that humans have any.

57. Discuss the concept of biological constraints.

58. Explain why some fears are easier to acquire than others and name the explanatory theory.

59. Discuss the concept of instinctive drift.

■ DEMONSTRATIONS, DRAMATIZATIONS, AND DISCUSSION

1. **The best demonstration of operant conditioning is to bring a Skinner box and a rat or pigeon to class.** In lieu of that, an entertaining (if somewhat artificial) illustration of shaping can be done with a human subject--you! Students provide reinforcement in this case by tapping their pens or pencils on their desks. Leave class for a few moments to allow the class to choose a response or a series of responses for you to perform. When you return, begin moving around the room. Students should tap each time you perform a response which approximates the final desired pattern. Your task, of course, is to keep the tapping as loud as possible (it's a little like playing "hot, warm, and cold"). The result can provide a hilarious interlude and a surprisingly instructive experience.

2. **B. F. Skinner published *Walden Two* in 1948.** It was the story of a model community based on behavioral engineering. That is, he applied the "technology of behavior", which he developed, to a community situation to show how an ideal community could exist if operant conditioning principles were applied. Organize the class into small groups and ask them to visualize and plan such a community. They should specify how the behavioral principles would be used and what kind of behaviors could be expected from the participants. They should try to think in terms of the details of daily life in the community as well as the overall welfare and spirit of the group. The groups should then come together and share their ideas as a class.

3. **The text discusses the way in which conditioned emotional responses can become phobias.** Generally those who have a phobia cannot identify its origins. However, some can do so, and

often family members will relate the phobias to some experience the person had in early childhood. Ask the students to generate a list of fears that they or their friends or relatives have. Try to restrict the list to only those fears that are intense and irrational (phobias) rather than other more common fears shared to some degree by most people. Ask those who contribute these items to try to recall or find out how they were acquired. Did the fear come from some legitimate unpleasant or painful experience, or did it come about vicariously? Some fears are learned from experience with the feared object. Sometimes children take on fears of their parents or some other person by imitation. Many of the fears will have no evident explanation. Be sure to discuss classical and operant conditioning principles in connection with these learned fears.

4. **Feedback is essential for effective human learning to take place.** To illustrate this and to introduce the concept of biofeedback, locate three class members who do not know how to wiggle their ears but think they might be able to learn. Have all three come to the front and face the class so that their ears are visible. Have them try for about a minute to master this skill. If anyone succeeds too easily, replace him/her with a new subject. When you have three subjects who clearly cannot wiggle their ears with more than minimal success, give each a hand mirror. Ask them to hold the mirror so that they can see their ears. Most will succeed with the addition of the feedback provided by the mirror.

5. **The role of modeling in learning often seems so self-evident to students that they may not fully appreciate its importance in learning theory.** To bring home the idea that modeling has a powerful and pervasive impact on human learning, invite a student to the front of the class and ask him/her to tell you verbally how to tie your shoe. Untie one of your shoes (make sure you're wearing shoes with laces), and follow the subject's instructions explicitly. Be sure not to lead, interpret, or show any signs of previous shoe-tying skill. If you are very literal in your interpretation of the student's instructions, the point will be made: In many cases learning would be virtually impossible or incredibly inefficient were it not for observational learning.

6. **One very good way to illustrate the existence of cognitive maps involves asking students to draw a map of the campus, or the layout in general of the community in which they live.** Selected maps can then be projected on a screen and compared to one another and/or to formal maps.

7. **The general approach of the "Behavioral Self-Management Application" in this chapter provides a good way to review learning principles.** Have students submit anonymous examples of troublesome habits (their own or those of family and friends). Select from these the most interesting and, at the next class meeting, ask students to apply chapter concepts by suggesting ways to alter the troublesome behaviors.

8. **Ask students to apply reinforcement principles to a "real world " problem such as waste recycling.** How would they engineer better paper recycling on a university campus? In a college dorm? In a selected neighborhood?

In actual experiments of this sort several techniques have proven effective. These include "recycling contests" (in which groups compete for a small cash award financed by selling the recycled paper), and raffles in which each bag of paper submitted for recycling earns a raffle ticket and a chance to win a small weekly prize. (E. S. Geller, J. L Chaffee, and R. E. Ingram, "Promoting Paper Recycling on a University Campus," *Journal of Environmental Systems*, 1975, 5, 39-57.)

■ ONE-MINUTE MOTIVATORS

1. **Begin the unit by asking students about their favorite foods.** Discuss briefly why they like these foods and whether they also eat these foods often. Use this as a preface to classically conditioned feelings and to the effect that reinforcers have on behavior.

2. **Demonstrate reflex pupil dilation** with a flashlight, the patellar reflex with a small rubber mallet, and the blink reflex by using a turkey baster to direct a puff of air to the eye.

3. **In pairs, have students answer these questions.** Why does your:
    a. dog drool when you open the can of food before the food is given to him?
    b. friend flinch when you tickle him or her?
    c. little sister tremble at the sound of a dentist's drill?
    d. fellow student begin blushing before s(he) is called on to give a speech?

4. **Ask students to describe superstitious behaviors** they have observed in televised sports events. Is it possible that these behaviors actually are reinforcers? What makes them superstitious?

5. **To demonstrate negative reinforcement and operant escape,** give half of the class this assignment: "As soon as you have written the alphabet backward three times, raise your hand and then write it a fourth time. Give this assignment to the other half: "As soon as you have written the alphabet backward three times, go outside and wait for further instructions." You will find those escaping from boredom writing much more quickly than those with no escape option.

6. **Give students a five-minute quiz on the preceding chapter.** Collect all the quizzes and place them in the trash. When students protest, discuss how frustrating it is not to receive knowledge of results, whether in terms of class exams, feedback at work, praise from friends, or even a thank you note when you send someone a gift.

7. **Have students stand and face the back of the room.** Have one student come to the front of the class and mime the motions needed to fry an egg (place pan on stove, turn on burner, add oil, pick up egg, crack egg open, add salt and pepper, turn with a spatula). As the student does this s(he) should try to tell the rest of the class what motions to make to do what she is doing--without making any reference to cooking or to any objects. Ask students to guess what

they are learning to do. When one does, discuss the model's frustration with verbal instruction and have her repeat the demonstration for those students who didn't guess what they were learning to do. Can they guess now?

8. **Show a short sequence of commercials** recorded from commercial television and discuss the kinds of role models that are being presented.

■ CLASSROOM EXERCISES

TO THE INSTRUCTOR:

The three exercises which follow give the students an opportunity to have some first-hand experience with the concepts being studied. In the first, students will observe or participate in the classical conditioning of the eyeblink response. In the second, the students will try to identify instances from their own experience in which they were conditioned to respond in a new way. The third illustrates how a simple skill is acquired.

Exercise #1: Classical Conditioning of the Eyeblink Response

I.   Introduction:

Students should have read the section in the text on classical conditioning and received classroom instruction to clarify the concepts involved. They should be clear on what is to happen in this demonstration. The purpose is to condition the eyeblink response to the sound of a clicker. Some other noisemaker may be substituted such as a buzzer or bell.

II.   Apparatus:

The apparatus for this exercise is easy to get together. A clicker or noisemaker is needed. One that makes a clear, sharp sound is best. The apparatus to deliver a puff of air to the eyes is a little more difficult. You need a piece of rigid plastic tubing attached to a stand. The stand can be made or clamp stands can be borrowed from the chemistry lab. Flexible plastic tubing (about 3 feet long) should be attached to the rigid tube at one end and to a squeeze bulb at the other. A kitchen baster will deliver a generous puff of air for this purpose.

III. Procedure:

A.   Organize the class into teams of three. One will be the subject, one the experimenter, and the third will be the recorder. If time permits, the students can rotate these roles so each one has an opportunity to be the subject.

B.   Seat the subject and set up the apparatus so that the tip of the rigid tube will be about two inches from his/her eyes. The experimenter should be behind the subject, holding the clicker and the squeeze bulb. The recorder should sit directly in front of the subject. Throughout the experiment the recorder will note whether or not the subject blinked at each trial.

C.   Begin the experiment by presenting the subject with a puff of air and observe the eyeblink response. This should be done at least twice to be sure that the puff of air (unconditioned stimulus) is producing the eyeblink (unconditioned response). Space the trials at fifteen-second intervals. A watch with a large second hand should suffice as a timer.

D.   The conditioning trials should be done as follows. Click the noisemaker and immediately after (not at the same time) present the puff of air. Wait about fifteen seconds and repeat. Do this fifteen times. This should be sufficient to establish the eyeblink (now a conditioned response) to the sound of the noisemaker (the conditioned stimulus). The recorder will note the eyeblink for each trial on the data sheet.

E.   After the fifteen conditioning trials, continue with fifteen more, presenting only the noisemaker with no puff of air. The recorder will note the presence or absence of the eyeblink at each trial. It should be possible to see when extinction has occurred.

F.   At this point the experiment could be concluded, or some variations could be tried. Here are some possibilities:

    1.   Give the subject a rest period and then resume trials with only the clicker and see if spontaneous recovery will occur.

    2.   Present the puff of air only occasionally while continuing clicking trials, then stopping the US to see how long it takes for extinction to occur.

    3.   See if more than fifteen conditioning trials will result in slower extinction.

G.   Discussion questions:

    1.   What is the change in behavior in this exercise?

    2.   Why did it occur?

    3.   Why did extinction take place?

    4.   Does this kind of "learning" have a real value in our lives?

CLASSICAL CONDITIONING--HUMAN EYEBLINK: DATA SHEET

TO THE STUDENT:

Record accurately what you observe. In this exercise it will be the presence or absence of an eyeblink when the stimuli are presented to the subject. You should be sure not to communicate your expectations to the subject. Simply record what you see.

Acquisition Phase			Extinction Phase	
TRIAL	BLINK (Y or N)		TRIAL	BLINK (Y or N)
1	___		1	___
2	___		2	___
3	___		3	___
4	___		4	___
5	___		5	___
6	___		6	___
7	___		7	___
8	___		8	___
9	___		9	___
10	___		10	___
11	___		11	___
12	___		12	___
13	___		13	___
14	___		14	___
15	___		15	___

Exercise #2: Conditioning as a Personal Experience

TO THE INSTRUCTOR:

Students should be asked to identify personal experiences in which they were conditioned. It might require some speculation on their part as to how it came about. However, it is important for them to realize the extent to which this type of learning occurs in their lives. If students use the classical conditioning model, Figure 7-2, they can see how the change in behavior occurred. For the operant conditioning experiences, they need to pay attention to the concept of reinforcement, or consequence of a response, when producing examples.

The students should be instructed to identify the source of motivation for the behavioral change and what is being associated in each example.

The data sheet which follows can be duplicated and given to students to write their examples. Many of the examples will be wrong the first time. You can help them to understand these concepts by going over the examples, showing them what is wrong, and suggesting how they could be done better. Then ask the students who were unclear to write some new examples.

CONDITIONING AS A PERSONAL EXPERIENCE: DATA SHEET

Instances of classical and operant conditioning occur in everyday life. Your assignment is to think of two personal examples of each type of conditioning that you have experienced and briefly describe each one. Do not use examples found in the text or presented by your instructor in class. In each example, identify where the association bond is and what the motivation is for the change in behavior.

<u>CLASSICAL CONDITIONING</u>
1.

2.

<u>OPERANT CONDITIONING</u>

1.

2.

Exercise #3: The Learning Curve

I.   Introduction

The purpose of this exercise is to give students an opportunity to see how learning follows a typical learning curve. This can be done by charting the progress of a student learning to follow a maze, provided the maze is not too easy or too complex.

II.   Procedure

A.   Divide the class into groups of three for this exercise. Designate one to be the subject, another the timer, and the third to be the recorder. Rotate the students so that all three will have an opportunity to be the subject.

B.   Provide each group with 45 copies of the maze, three data sheets, and three of each of the two graphs. Be sure that each group has a watch with a second hand to time the trials.

C.   Discuss with the students the way to do the timing, how to score the maze (time and errors), and how to plot points on the graphs.

D.   Sit back and enjoy a brief respite while the students go to work. Be sure they complete their trials and complete the data sheets while doing the exercise. It would be best to have them plot the graphs while in the classroom so they can help each other and seek your assistance, if needed. Once all three students have completed the exercise, each student should plot the data for all three subjects on the same graph. Different colors could be used to identify each.

III.   Discussion

A.   Did a learning curve occur? What was its shape?

B.   Did an error curve emerge? What was its shape?

C.   What conclusions can you draw about maze learning in general?

D.   Would similar curves appear in the learning of other types of material?

E.   Is what you have learned from this exercise of any value to you in your learning?

Bring the class together to go over the results. Try to find out what problems were encountered and what results appeared. Then ask students to discuss the questions above. You may have some of your own to add or substitute.

THE LEARNING CURVE: MAZES   DATA SHEET

Record the time for each trial and the number of errors made on each. Try to be as accurate as possible in timing the subject and recording errors. Before starting, number the maze sheets from 1 to 15 and have the subject use them in order. An error is made each time the subject raises the pencil, enters a blind alley, or crosses a line. Crossing a line and returning into the path constitutes one error (not two) since the line has to be recrossed to enter the path.

	SUBJECTS					
	1		2		3	
TRIALS	SECS.	ERRORS	SECS.	ERRORS	SECS.	ERRORS
1						
2						
3						
4						
5						
6						
7						
8						
9						
10						
11						
12						
13						
14						
15						

THE LEARNING CURVE: GRAPH I--LEARNING

To the Student: Plot the times for each trial on the graph.   Join the points to produce a learning curve. The horizontal axis represents the number of trials, and the vertical, the number of seconds per trial.

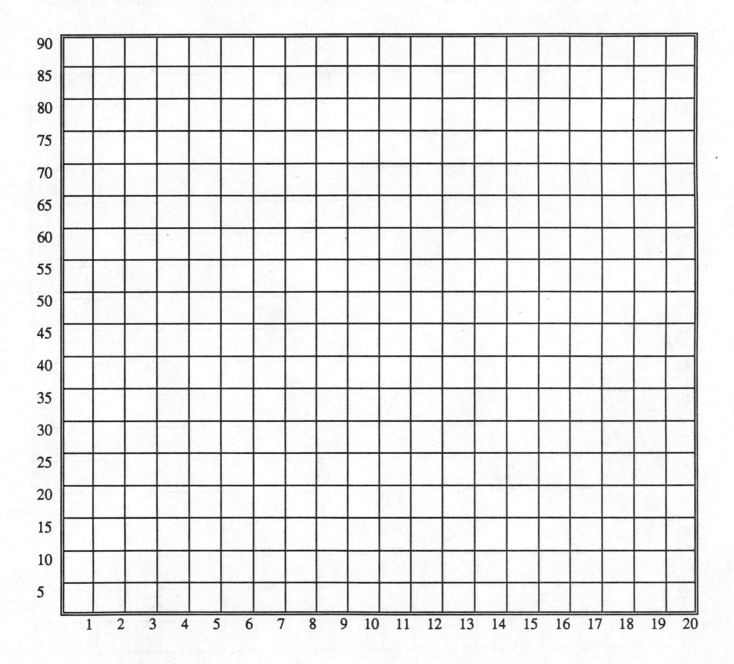

THE LEARNING CURVE: GRAPH II—ERRORS

To the Student: An error is made each time the subject raises the pencil, enters a blind alley, or crosses a line. Crossing a line and returning into the path constitutes one error (not two) since the line has to be recrossed to enter the path. Plot the number of errors made on each trial. Join the points to produce an error curve. The horizontal axis represents the number of trials, and the vertical axis, the number of errors.

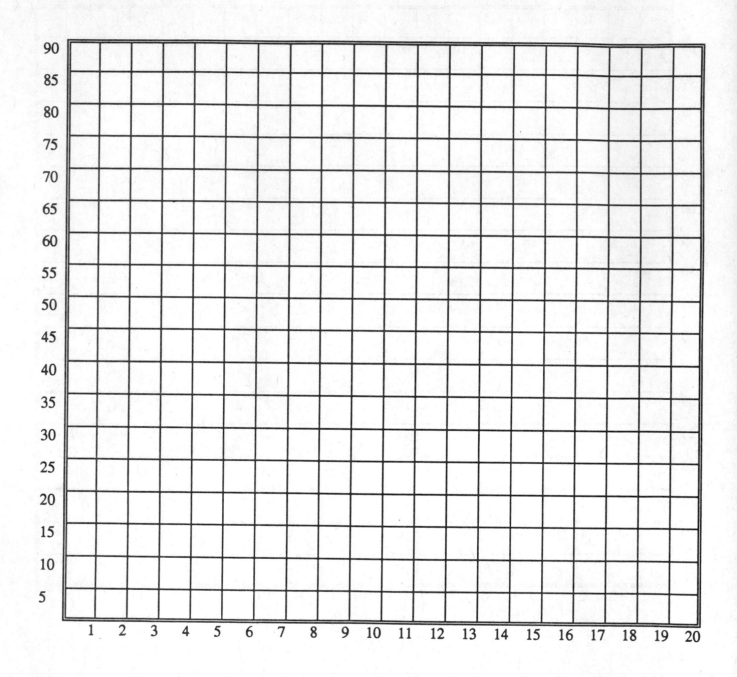

THE LEARNING CURVE: MAZE LEARNING

To the Student: Follow the maze from the center to the exit. Do not raise your pencil from the paper once you begin. If you cross a line or go into a blind alley, return to the point where the error was made without lifting your pencil from the paper. Work as quickly as you can.

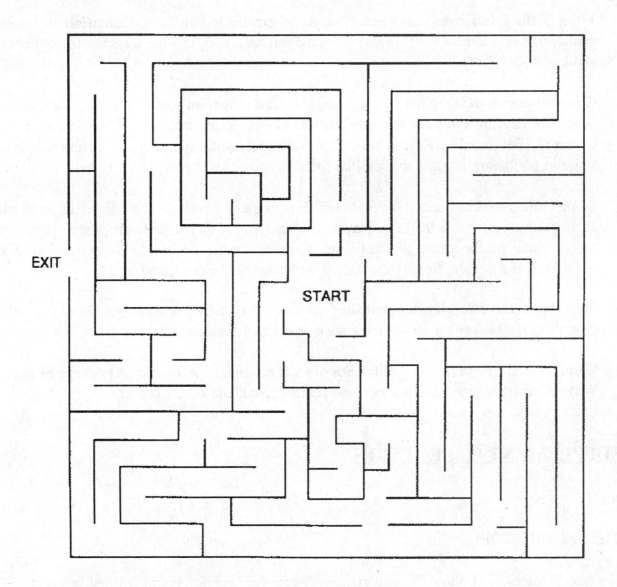

■ BROADENING OUR CULTURAL HORIZONS

1. **Have students make a list of symbols that have emotional meaning for a specific group of people.** For example, religious, political, or sexual symbols (words, objects, gestures) can provoke emotional responses. Explain these associations in terms of classical conditioning.

2. **What is the relationship between stimulus generalization and discrimination** and gender, ethnic, or racial stereotyping, prejudice, and discrimination? In what ways are these processes similar or different?

3. **Cultural norms develop because a specific behavior is reinforced.** Can you identify some behaviors that are typically reinforced in the United States that are not reinforced in other cultures? (For example, Korean businesspersons rarely smile at customers because people who smile in public are thought to look like fools.)

4. **Some cultures focus on and invest much time in game-playing.** Interview friends of yours about their attitudes toward game-playing. What types of games did their parents play? Was the outcome of the game primarily the result of chance or skill? What reinforced this behavior? If a person "lost" the game, what would be the consequences?

5. **Stereotypes have developed about the "work ethic" of different cultures.** Does your ethnic group or culture focus more on immediate or delayed reinforcers?

6. **What view did your family and friends of your parents take toward physical punishment?** What cultural factors explain why some parents spank and others don't?

■ SUPPLEMENTAL LECTURES

Lecture I

TO THE INSTRUCTOR:

This lecture is intended to show the importance of secondary reinforcers in learned behavior. The discussion will include both positive and negative reinforcers. It is the secondary reinforcers that can maintain behavioral change in the absence of the primary reinforcer. This can be good or bad depending on the situation. Students should be aware of the dynamics involved so they can use reinforcement more effectively to bring about behavioral change.

SECONDARY REINFORCERS

I.   Introduction

    A.   Discuss the meaning of the terms involved:

        1.   reinforcement
        2.   positive reinforcement
        3.   negative reinforcement
        4.   primary reinforcer
        5.   secondary reinforcer

    B.   It should be made clear that all reinforcers, whether positive or negative, change behavior. You may need to distinguish between negative reinforcement and punishment to be sure the concept of negative reinforcement is understood.

    C.   It is important to make it clear that a secondary reinforcer receives its reinforcement properties by being associated with a primary reinforcer. This would be a good time to draw from the students (if you can) that this association results from classical conditioning.

II.   Positive Reinforcers

    A.   A positive primary reinforcer can be used to establish a change in behavior. B. F. Skinner used food pellets to establish bar-pressing behavior in a rat.

    B.   When Skinner connected a light to the apparatus, it would go on when the bar was pressed and as the pellet of food was released. After several such instances, when the food machine was turned off and only the light flashed when the bar was pressed, the rat continued the conditioned response much longer than when no light was presented with the food. The classically conditioned association between the light and the food maintained the learned behavior for a much longer period of time. The presence of the secondary reinforcer, the light, resulted in slower extinction.

    C.   Now for an example of human behavior:

        1.   Let us say that I want to get my daughter to clean her room on Saturday mornings. The reinforcement will be $20 each time she cleans up on Saturday. The operant conditioning model looks like this:

STIMULUS ————————————————————→ RESPONSE

$20   .   room-cleaning behavior

This should establish the behavior after a few repetitions as the S and R become associated.

2.   As I go broke, I stop giving the money, and the behavior extinguishes very rapidly--no more room cleaning. One way to keep it going longer, perhaps forever, is to plan for some secondary reinforcers--stimuli that become associated with the primary reinforcer, in this case, the $20.

3.   What might I try to associate with the primary reinforcer? Ask the class to suggest ideas. Some that come to mind are the following:

a.   a compliment when inspecting the room and handing over the cash;
b.   a privilege, like a movie, granted when the job is done;
c.   allowing her to have a girlfriend over to visit in her room;
d.   her ability to find things more easily;
e.   her sense of satisfaction in having a neat room.

The model would, at this point, look like this:

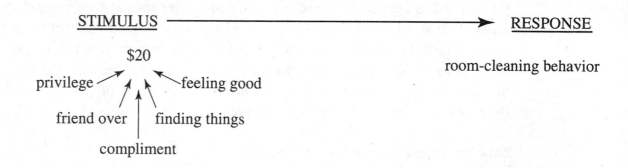

STIMULUS ————————————————————→ RESPONSE

$20   room-cleaning behavior

privilege   feeling good

friend over   finding things

compliment

4.   Now, if the money (primary reinforcer) is absent, the secondary reinforcers should keep the room cleaning behavior going indefinitely, I hope. The model now looks like this:

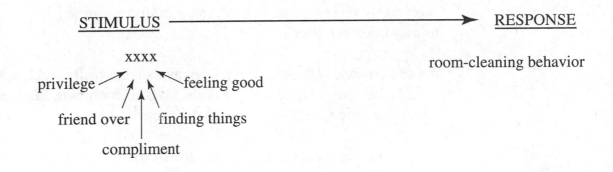

STIMULUS ⟶ RESPONSE

xxxx

privilege   feeling good   room-cleaning behavior

friend over   finding things

compliment

She now has many stimuli which, initially, might not have stimulated the change in behavior, but now they do because they were associated with the primary reinforcement.

III.   Negative Reinforcement

A.   A negative reinforcer is a stimulus which brings about a change in behavior to escape from or avoid an aversive stimulus. Skinner used a mild electric shock in the Skinner Box to produce bar pressing behavior. This would shut off the current and remove the shock. The rat learned quickly to escape the shock by pressing the bar (escape behavior). After very few trials the rat would anticipate the shock and press the bar before receiving the stimulus. It is now avoidance behavior. Any stimulus associated with the shock would also produce avoidance behavior. The approach of the experimenter or white colors, which resembled the smock worn by the experimenter, would cause the same response as the primary reinforcer. They are secondary reinforcers because they are associated with the shock.

B.   Now back to my daughter! Could I get the room cleaning behavior using negative reinforcement. I think so.

1.   The negative reinforcement will be a good solid swat that will send her scurrying to her room to clean up. The model would look like this:

STIMULUS ⟶ RESPONSE

swat

room-cleaning behavior

Most likely this response will become established quickly and go from escape to avoidance behavior.

2.   As was the case with Skinner's rat, so my daughter will quickly associate other stimuli with the primary one. Ask the class to contribute some ideas on this. Some that they should be sure to include are:

   a.   Dad (or whoever administers the swat),
   b.   home (where the negative stimulus is received),
   c.   her room (the cause of her misery),
   d.   Saturday morning (The dreaded day is anticipated.).

The model, at this point, looks like this:

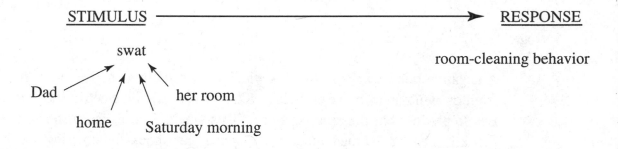

STIMULUS ⟶ RESPONSE

swat

room-cleaning behavior

Dad

home   Saturday morning

her room

3.   It is important to make students aware that once avoidance behavior is established there are no more "swats" being administered. However, the behavior persists, and extinction may be slow because she does not wait for the negative stimulus so doesn't know that it will no longer be administered.

4.   The most significant factor to impress on students is that the avoidance behavior (to the swat) is now extended to the stimuli which are associated with the primary reinforcer. These are secondary reinforcers. She will want to avoid Dad, home, her room, Saturday mornings, etc.--not a pretty picture. Yet my intention was good, to teach her to clean her room. In this case, the secondary reinforcers, unknown to me, are creating problems between me and my daughter. She maintains a clean room, but at a heavy price!

IV.   This lecture should provide lots of food for thought and material for discussion. Some questions that should be addressed:

   A.   Which form of reinforcement is most efficient in establishing and maintaining new behavior?

   B.   What about the use of negative reinforcement as a way to teach children how to behave?

   C.   Should children be punished?

   D.   Why do young teenagers often run away from home? Can this be explained in terms of secondary reinforcers?

   E.   How can a parent who uses negative reinforcement minimize the problems of having the child react negatively to the parents, home, Saturday, etc.?

Lecture II

This lecture concerns observational learning. Students should be aware of learning that is not the direct result of reinforcement. Many new, complex behaviors appear without the benefit of operant conditioning as we are studying it. Once the role of models and imitation is understood, the students will see more clearly how a variety of complex behaviors may be acquired.

OBSERVATIONAL LEARNING

I.   Introduction

   A.   Discuss with the students incidents of learning where new behaviors do not seem to be reinforced. In particular, cite instances in which someone imitates the behavior of another. Examples of such behavior occasionally hit the news. A philanthropist makes a generous donation to a worthy cause, receives a good deal of publicity and praise as a reinforcement, and many people follow suit, giving donations with no apparent fanfare or reward. Often a serious crime is committed, such as a murder, which gets a great deal of attention. In recent years the cyanide in Tylenol capsules was such a case. Soon after, similar instances of cyanide in foods of various kinds were reported.

   B.   Ask the students to think of examples of this and speculate on why it occurs.

   C.   Refer to the work of Albert Bandura and others, studying the dynamics of modeling and imitation. The classic experiment with children and the Bo-Bo doll should be discussed in this context.

II.   The Dynamics of Observational Learning

A study of this type of learning indicates that some specific factors are involved and are necessary for the change in behavior to occur.

A.   The model:

1.   the model must be observed performing the behavior;
2.   the model must be observed receiving the reinforcement;
3.   the model must be a significant person to the observer--this is where the motivation comes from--this is what gets the attention of the observer.

B.   The observer:

1.   must pay attention to the model and his/her behavior;
2.   must observe the reinforcement being received by the model;
3.   must be capable of remembering (encoding) the behavior;
4.   must be capable of reproducing the behavior.

C.   The behavior:

1.   is performed by the model and reinforced;
2.   is performed by the observer without reinforcement or the expectation of it.

D.   The reinforcement:

1.   the model's reinforcement is not received by the observer, nor is it expected;
2.   the observer repeats the behavior without reinforcement and continues to do so;
3.   some say that reinforcement is received by the observer, but perhaps in a different way. Let us look at the possibilities!

E.   Reinforcement, "Let us count the ways":

1.   direct - the observer does, in fact, receive the same or similar reinforcement as the model;
2.   vicarious - the observer receives no reinforcement but experiences pleasure or pain in sympathy with the model, or is simply pleased that the model was reinforced.
3.   indirect - the observer receives a different kind of reinforcement, usually internally in the form of self-reinforcement. It's like giving oneself a pat on the back or a kick in the pants.

III.   Discussion

This topic is loaded with potential for discussion. There are so many interesting ways to look at this phenomenon. Discuss the role of television and the models that are set before us daily.

A.   Advertising displays significant models: sports figures and actresses show and use the product, hoping that the viewer will buy the product and imitate the behavior. Usually there is no expectation that (s)he will receive the same reward as the model.

B.   Violence on television is an area of concern. Is it being modeled for children and adults?

C.   Parents are significant models. Is it true that abusive parents were themselves abused? Do alcoholic parents raise children who become alcoholic?

D.   The potential for using models in education should be explored.

E.   Discuss how modeling could be used to promote pro-social behaviors in children.

F.   Discuss the types of models that are found in our society.

■ SUGGESTIONS FOR FURTHER READING

Bower, G. H. and E. R. Hilgard. *Theories of Learning*, 5th ed. Prentice-Hall, 1981.

Comstock, G. S., S. Chaffe, N. Katzman, M. McCombs, and D. Roberts. *Television and Human Behavior*. Columbia University Press, 1978.

Drowatzky, J. N. *Motor Learning: Principles and Practices*. Burgess, 1975.

Flaherty, C. F. *Animal Learning and Cognition*. Knopf, 1985.

Hill. W. F. *Principles of Learning: A Handbook of Applications*. Chandler, 1982.

Holland, M. K. and G. Tarlow. *Using Psychology*. Little, Brown, 1980.

Kalish, H. I. *From Behavioral Science to Behavior Modification*. McGraw-Hill, 1981.

Kazkin, A. E. *Behavior Modification in Applied Settings*. Dorsey Press, 1975.

Leahey, T. H. and R. J. Harris. *Human Learning*. Prentice-Hall, 1985.

Pavlov, I. *Conditioned Reflexes*. Clarendon Press, 1927.

Pew, T. W. Jr. "Biofeedback Seeks New Medical Uses of Yoga." *Smithsonian*, December, 1979.

Powers, R. B. and J. G. Osborne. *Fundamentals of Behavior*. West, 1976.

Rubinstein, E. A. "Television and the Young Viewer." *American Scientist*, November-December, 1978.

Schwartz, B. *Psychology of Learning and Behavior*, 3rd ed. W. W. Norton, 1989.

Skinner, B. F. *Behavior of Organisms*. Wiley, 1938.

---. *Beyond Freedom and Dignity*. Knopf, 1971.

---. *The Shaping of a Behaviorist*. Knopf, 1979.

---. *Walden Two*. Macmillan, 1960.

Walters, G. and J. Grusek. *Punishment*. W. H. Freeman, 1977.

■ FILM SUGGESTIONS

BIOFEEDBACK: LISTENING TO YOUR HEAD. (1979, Document Associates, 19 min.)
   This film explains how biofeedback is used to control involuntary functions.

BEHAVIOR THEORY IN PRACTICE (PARTS I-IV) (1966, Prentice-Hall, each part is 20 min.)
   Basic and informative, these films present behavioral principles in considerable detail. Included in Part I is respondent versus operant behavior, selection of a response for basic research, the cumulative record, and operant conditioning and extinction. Part II covers schedules of reinforcement, shaping various operants, and programmed instruction. Part III features generalization, discrimination, motivation, reinforcement, punishment, avoidance, and intracranial reinforcement. Part IV describes sequences of behavior, homogeneous and heterogeneous chains, alternative responses, and multiple stimulus control.

B. F. SKINNER AND BEHAVIORAL CHANGE. (1979, Research Press, 45 min.)
   Distinguished professionals from various disciplines join B. F. Skinner in facing the issues and controversies generated by behavioral psychology. The viewer observes on-site interventions with patients, clients, and students as the film visits (1) a home where parents work with their mentally retarded child, (2) a hospital for treatment of an epileptic child, (3) a youth center where children with social problems learn more effective skills, (4) a marital counseling session, and (5) a school of dental medicine where a child is taught to control fear of dental procedures.

BUSINESS, BEHAVIORISM AND THE BOTTOM LINE (CRM, 22 min.)
   A discussion of the application of operant procedures in business and industry. B. F. Skinner is interviewed.

CLASSICAL AND INSTRUMENTAL CONDITIONING. (1978, Harper & Row, 20 min.)
   Laboratory footage and graphics are used to present the principles of conditioning and to show how they are applied to humans. Includes a sequence which involves the viewer in a classical conditioning experiment.

A DEMONSTRATION OF BEHAVIORAL PROCESSES BY B. F. SKINNER. (1971, Prentice-Hall, 28 min.)
> In this documentary, B. F. Skinner offers an introduction to operant conditioning. In a classroom setting, Skinner reviews the history of operant conditioning and explains the experimental apparatus. He demonstrates differential reinforcement and "shaping" techniques used on a pigeon while showing how pigeons shape their own behavior. Finally, Skinner applies principles of operant conditioning to human behavior.

LEARNING (1990, from *Psychology- The Study of Human Behavior Series*, Coast District Telecourses, 30 min.)
> Focuses on classical conditioning, operant conditioning and real-world applications to behavioral psychology.

MIND OVER BODY (1974, Time-Life, 49 min.)
> This documentary looks at a wide spectrum of cases to show a whole new area of research that straddles psychology, physiology, and medicine. The links are demonstrated by the re- search explained in the film. In the future, many persons may be able to use self-therapy to alleviate psychosomatic illnesses.

OBSERVATIONAL LEARNING (1978, Harper & Row, 23 min.)
> This film shows the famous Bo-Bo doll experiment, vicarious emotional conditioning, modeling therapy, and children imitating what they have seen on television.

PAVLOV HIMSELF. (Film for the Humanities, 25 min.)
> Presents an historical view of Pavlov and incorporates rare documentary footage of Pavlov at work in his laboratory. Produced by USSR Central Television with English narration.

THE POWER OF POSITIVE REINFORCEMENT (1978, McGraw-Hill Films, 27 min.)
> Documents the systematic on-site application of behavior management and its emphasis on positive reinforcement. Examines its use in the Valley Fair Amusement Park in Minnesota, on the defensive line of the Minnesota Vikings and in the streets of Detroit, Michigan, with the Sanitation Department. Portrays behavior modification as a powerful tool for managing human performance.

REWARD AND PUNISHMENT (CRM, 30 min.)
> Dr. James Gardner narrates this film which focuses on operant techniques used in the management of children's behavior. The appropriate uses of reward and punishment are also discussed.

THE SKINNER REVOLUTION. (1979, Research Press Films, 45 min.)
> This film presents interviews and conversations with B. F. Skinner, attempting to show him as an individual against the background of his contributions to science and philosophy.

■ COMPUTER PROGRAMS: *MIND SCOPE*

Exercise 15, Schedules of Reinforcement

Students are exposed to five different schedules of reinforcement. They are asked to describe the rule for each schedule after they have been exposed to it for three minutes.

CHAPTER 8

Memory

■ BEHAVIORAL OBJECTIVES

The student should be able to:

1. Explain the three functions of memory.
2. List the three interrelated memory systems.
3. Explain sensory memory. (Include an explanation of how icons and echoes function in this memory system.)
4. Explain how information is transferred from sensory memory to short-term memory.
5. Describe short-term memory in terms of capacity, how information is encoded, permanence, and susceptibility to interference.
6. Describe long-term memory in terms of permanence, capacity, and the basis of how information is stored. (Include a brief description of dual memory.)
7. Describe chunking and the two types of rehearsal and explain how they help memory.
8. Discuss the permanence of memory including the work of Penfield and the Loftuses.
9. Explain how memories are constructed. (Include the concepts of constructive processing and pseudo-memories.)
10. Discuss the effects of hypnosis on memory.
11. Briefly describe how long-term memories are organized including the network model and redintegration.
12. Differentiate procedural (skill) memory from declarative (fact) memory.
13. Differentiate the two kinds of fact memory--semantic memory and episodic memory.
14. Explain the tip-of-the-tongue phenomenon (including the feeling of knowing).
15. Describe and give an example of each of the following ways of measuring memory:
    a. recall
    b. recognition (compare to recall and include the concept of distractors)
    c. relearning (include the concept of savings)
16. Distinguish between explicit and implicit memories.
17. Describe eidetic imagery and its effects on long-term memory.
18. Describe the concept of internal imagery and explain how it differs from eidetic imagery and exceptional memory.
19. Explain Ebbinghaus's curve of forgetting.
20. Discuss the effects of cramming versus spaced review on memory.
21. Discuss the following explanations of forgetting:
    a. encoding failure
    b. decay of memory traces
    c. disuse (also giving three reasons to question this explanation)
    d. cue-dependent forgetting

114

e.   state-dependent learning

f.   interference (also list and explain the two types of interference as well as how they are investigated in the laboratory)

g.   repression (and differentiate it from suppression)

h.   retrograde and anterograde amnesia

22.   Define and give an example of positive and negative transfer.

23.   Describe the role of consolidation in memory.

24.   Describe the effects of stimulants and alcohol on memory.

25.   Name the structure in the brain that is responsible for switching information from STM to LTM. (Include a discussion of the relationship between learning and transmitter chemicals, brain circuits and receptor sites.)

26.   Describe each of the following in terms of how it can improve memory:

a.	knowledge of results	h.	cues
b.	recitation	i.	overlearning
c.	rehearsal	j.	spaced practice
d.	selection	k.	sleep
e.	organization	l.	review
f.	whole versus part learning	m.	strategy
g.	serial position effect		

27.   Define and explain the role of mnemonic systems in storing and retrieving information.

28.   Discuss the validity of recovered memories, presenting evidence for each side of the debate.

■ DEMONSTRATIONS, DRAMATIZATIONS, AND DISCUSSION

1.   **You can do a quick test of short-term memory in the classroom.** Use a set of random digits like the sample given in this demonstration. Do not give the students any hints about how to memorize effectively. Simple tell them that you are giving them some sets of digits to write down.

To illustrate the limited capacity of short-term memory, read a series of random digits to the class. Instruct the students to listen to the numbers and, after you stop, to write down as many as they can remember. Begin by reading a series five-digits long: 5 1 9 2 3

Then try six: 9 1 9 2 5 8
       seven: 9 8 2 2 9 3 1
       eight: 3 8 5 4 9 6 5 7
        nine: 3 8 0 4 7 1 3 6 9
         ten: 5 3 2 1 9 6 1 2 1 6

Reread the digits so the students can check their accuracy. The seven- (plus or minus two) bit capacity of short-term memory should become quite apparent to the students.

2. **Chunking can greatly extend the capacity of short-term memory.** This can be shown by instructing half the class in a chunking strategy while allowing the other half to memorize more haphazardly. Hand out to half the class an instruction sheet which reads:

> A long list of words will be read to you. Try to memorize the entire list using "raw" memory ability. You should listen to the list and try to remember as much as you can, but do not attempt to apply any system or special technique in memorizing the list.

The second half of the class should receive a sheet which reads:

> A long list of words will be read to you. Try to memorize the entire list. Your task will be easier if you memorize the words in groups of three. Try to form a mental image that includes the first three items as read and then try to form a new image for each following set of three. For example, if the first three words were, "skate, bone, and piano," you might picture a roller-skate with a bone in it on top of a piano.

After students have read their respective instructions, read the list below. Read loudly and clearly, allowing a relatively long pause between words:

CAR TREE TOOTH PENCIL WATCH CHAIR VIOLIN FLOWER HOUSE
BICYCLE RECORD PIZZA BOOK DISH NAIL TOWEL APPLE MATCH
FISH SKY SHOE

After completing the list, ask students to write as many items as they can remember.

Notice that there are twenty-one items on the list. Students who use the chunking strategy will have only seven chunks to contend with, which should be a manageable number for most. To determine if chunking improved retention, compute the mean number of items recalled by each group.

3. **One of the simplest and most obvious indications of organizational structure in memory is clustering** (the tendency for related words to appear together in a free-recall situation). To demonstrate clustering, ask students to memorize the following list:

APPLE	HAMMER	SUMMER	RED	PEACH	SAW
SPRING	YELLOW	BANANA	WINTER	BROWN	LEMON
PLIERS	AUTUMN	GREEN	PLUM	WRENCH	FALL
BLUE	SCREWDRIVER				

A satisfactory means of presentation is to read the list slowly. Afterward ask them to write as many items from the list as they can recall, in any order. Then ask them to circle adjacent items representing clusters from the categories: fruit, tools, seasons, and colors. Students with particularly good examples of the clustering effect should be encouraged to share them with the class.

4. **To demonstrate the serial position effect,** the following word list should be read aloud fairly quickly (to avoid the use of mnemonic devices by the students). After one reading, ask the students to write down as many of the items as they can remember. Then present the list to the students using an overhead projector and check by a show of hands how many remembered each item. More students will recall the first and last portions of the list than the middle, showing the serial position effect.

    Use the following list of words:

house	cheese	star	pen	dish
book	highway	melon	horse	uncle
class	ocean	doorway	model	moustache
creature	cloud	prairie	train	plastic

5. **A discussion of mnemonic strategies and examples can provide skills of lasting value to students.** It may be useful to begin by asking for examples of terms or information students have had difficulty learning in other classes. With the help of the class you can then devise a mnemonic strategy for each. Names also make good examples. For interest, use names from the class roster, making transformations such as these: *Aaron = hair on, Carifiol = care if I oil, Chomentowski = show men to ski, Sellentin = sellin' tin,* and so forth.

    The mnemonic device of loci, or places, was developed by Simonides. In this approach, each item to be remembered is pictured in association with familiar locations--around the home, along a street, on campus, or on parts of the body.

    To show how powerful mnemonic strategies can be, have the class call out a list of twenty objects. As each object is added, encourage students to imagine it placed on, or associated with, a part of the body. For example, if the first item is "pencil," students might imagine a pencil stuck between their toes; if the second is "bird," a bird might be imagined in place of the foot, and so forth. Identify a body part to be used with each new item as it is added. The following loci work well: toes, foot, heel, ankle, calf, knee, thigh, hip, waist, navel, ribs, chest, fingers, palm, wrist, forearm, ear, forehead, hair. This provides 19 loci, so the last item must be remembered by rote.

    After the list has been practiced once through, ask the class to recall it by trying to picture the object associated with each body part. Nearly all the items will be remembered by most class members--a unique experience for many of them.

6. *Psychology Today* **has surveyed its readers regarding their earliest memories.** Ninety-six percent of the respondents reported having memories prior to the age of six, with sixty-eight percent reporting recall for events occurring when they were two or three. Further, a surprising seven percent said they had memories prior to age one, and a few even claimed to have prenatal recollections as well as memories of their own birth! While some of the early memories were of traumatic experiences (such as the birth of a sibling, being injured, or the

death of relatives or pets), the majority of recollections were of more mundane things (like being given a bath, having a picture taken, or being pushed in a swing). Interestingly, most of the memories involved images rather than events. People remembered things like curtains blowing in the breeze, a light shining on someone's face, and a mobile hanging in the air. This is probably because small children generally lack the language skills necessary to encode a complicated series of events. Many psychologists, in fact, believe that it is rare for people to remember things that occurred before they were able to talk.

Since students are usually fascinated by their own early lives, you can generate a high amount of interest in this topic by asking them to write the answer to the same question *Psychology Today* asked its readers: "What is your earliest memory and how old were you?" Before starting, your students need to be cautioned to try to make sure that it is a real memory and not something they've been told about or seen in photograph albums, etc. After they've finished, you should have them read some of the responses for the class. For more details see E. Stark, "Thanks for the Memories," *Psychology Today*, November, 1984.

7. **Give students two comparable lists of terms.** Ask students to recall one list and give them a recognition test for terms from the other list. Embed the terms in a longer list and have students circle those that they learned. Compare their memory scores.

■ ONE-MINUTE MOTIVATORS

1. **During the last five minutes of class before beginning this chapter,** weave into your lecture/discussion an announcement of a quiz for the next class session (or write the announcement in some obscure corner of the chalkboard). Only one or two people should notice. Begin class asking students to take out a piece of paper for the quiz. When students protest, begin a discussion of why we often fail to remember, including inattention and failure to record the information in the first place.

2. **Use a T-scope to flash images quickly to demonstrate sensory memory.** Read a series of words to the class to be remembered. Ask them to introspect about their initial processing of the words. Are they aware of an echo? Do they silently rehearse the words? Do they attempt to chunk them in some way? Do they try to link them to knowledge in long-term storage?

3. **Ask each student to state his or her favorite musical group and favorite food.** Have students try to remember each classmate's favorites. Discuss to what extent students used visual cues, the order of the information, and chunking to remember the information. What mnemonic strategies would make this task easier?

4. **In the first week of class take a picture of the class members.** In a class session at least three weeks later, to demonstrate redintegration, ask students to try to remember the activities, demonstrations, and discussions that took place on the day the picture was taken. Then show them the photograph you took in class and remind them of major national and local news

events that took place that day. As one memory leads to another, discuss how important memory cues are.

5.   **Ask a student to tell what her or his hobby is (or favorite movie, sport, food, color, etc.).** The next student repeats what the first student said and adds his or her own information. Continue in this way until 10 students have spoken. Students will find that they remember what the first few students said, and the person just before their turn. Discuss the serial position effect.

6.   **Add a few posters to the classroom.** Do not draw attention to them. Take them down and ask the class about them. Discuss how difficult it is to remember if we never encoded the information in the first place. Share strategies for selective listening and note-taking.

7.   **Ask students to report a "flashbulb" memory that is especially vivid for them.** What role did emotion play in the formation of the memory? Have they rehearsed and retold the memory unusually frequently? How can flashbulb memories be explained?

■ CLASSROOM EXERCISES

TO THE INSTRUCTOR:

The two exercises included in this section deal with the importance of making information meaningful to maximize storage and recall. Efficiency in learning, good retention, and significant recall hinge on a number of factors, one of which is meaning. The first exercise is a simple demonstration to show that organization of information increases meaning and recall.

The second exercise shows how varying degrees of meaning result in corresponding amounts of recall. This is a take-home exercise. Students should follow the directions given, gather the data, answer the discussion questions, and then meet in class for a review of the concepts involved.

Exercise #1: Organize for Meaning

I.   Introduction

This exercise is intended to show that when information is organized in a meaningful way it is learned, retained, and recalled more easily. You should be sure to relate this exercise, and the discussion before and after it, to the study habits of the students. They may not see the value of what they learn here unless it is pointed out. It is even better if they can be led to conclude this for themselves.

Two handouts are provided for this exercise. They should be distributed in such a way that half of the class gets Handout #1, and the other half gets Handout #2. A good way to do this would be to stack the handouts ahead of time alternating #1 and #2 in the pile.

List #1 contains a set of terms that are organized in a logical meaningful way. List #2 has no particular logic, meaning, or order to the presentation. Only the form and raw content are the same as #1.

II.   Procedure

A.   Explain to the class that they will be given a brief learning task. Ask them to do their best on it, so they can see a learning principle at work.

B.   Distribute the handout sheets, alternately stacked, to the students, face down. Give each student a data sheet for responding, also face down.

C.   Ask the students to turn the list over and study it for forty-five seconds.

D.   At the end of the time period, instruct the students to turn the list face down and write as many words as they can remember on the data sheet. Give them about two minutes to do this.

E.   Ask the students to check their work to see how many they got right.

F.   Total the number right for those who had lists #1 and #2 separately, and find the mean for each group. Those who studied list #1, which was organized in a meaningful way, should receive a higher mean score than those who did list #2.

III.   Discussion

A.   What is the difference between the two lists? You should project the two lists together on an overhead projector so the students can compare them.

B.   Why is there a difference in performance on the two lists?

C.   Some students who had the second list, the one lacking organization, will still do as well as or better than those in the other group. Identify those persons and try to find out what they did to recall so much. This could lead to some interesting discussion of memory techniques.

D.   Can what has been found in this exercise apply to the study habits of the students? Discuss ways to make it work for them.

ORGANIZE FOR MEANING: **LIST #1**

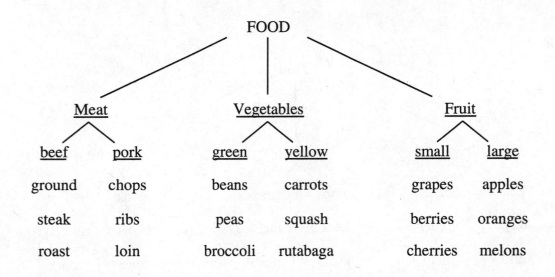

FOOD					
Meat		Vegetables		Fruit	
beef	pork	green	yellow	small	large
ground	chops	beans	carrots	grapes	apples
steak	ribs	peas	squash	berries	oranges
roast	loin	broccoli	rutabaga	cherries	melons

ORGANIZE FOR MEANING: **LIST #2**

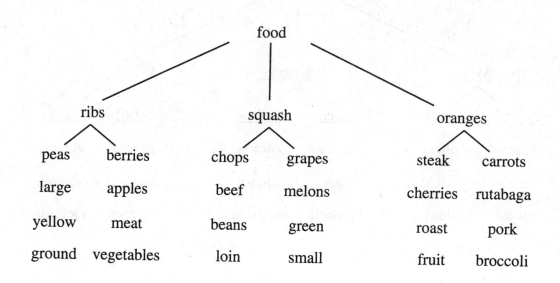

ORGANIZE FOR MEANING:　　　　　**DATA SHEET**

TO THE STUDENT:

Write as many words from the list you have studied as you can, in any order. If you are not sure, you can guess.

1._____	15._____
2._____	16._____
3._____	17._____
4._____	18._____
5._____	19._____
6._____	20._____
7._____	21._____
8._____	22._____
9._____	23._____
10._____	24._____
11._____	25._____
12._____	26._____
13._____	27._____
14._____	28._____

Exercise #2: MEANING AND MEMORY

TO THE STUDENT:

A.   Background and Purpose

Psychologists have found that meaningful information is easier to remember than that which is not. This is because it is associated with information that is already in memory. The purpose of this project is to show that material which is higher in association value is easier to store in memory and recall.

B.   You will be testing subjects with three word lists. One list has high association value, the second has medium value, and the third has low association value. Each subject will be given all three lists; however, they should be given one at a time, at separate times, with some time interval between the administration of each list. The subjects will be asked to write down as many words as they can remember after hearing the list once.

C.   Directions

1.   Select three subjects for this study. They should be over ten years of age.

2.   You need to meet with each subject three times to administer each of the three word lists.

3.   Provide the subject with a pencil and sheet of paper.

4.   Give each subject the high association word list first, then the medium list, and finally the low. Each should be given separately with a time interval in between.

5.   Read the wordlist to the subject. Read the words in order, slowly, about one word per second. Practice this by yourself ahead of time to get the timing right.

6.   The subject should listen carefully. After you complete reading the list, have the subject write down as many as he/she can remember. Do the same for each list.

7.   Record the results for each subject on each word list. Find the average number of words recalled correctly for each type of list.

8.   Answer the questions about your results, discussing what you found, and relating it to the material on memory in the text.

Exercise #2 (cont.)

Word Lists

High	Medium	Low
the	bee	yad
dog	nor	cif
ate	can	mul
two	but	bix
and	fee	pog
did	lob	zel
not	sit	riv
eat	old	mib
for	doe	daf
you	run	hib

Results

Subject	Scores (number of correct words)		
	High	Medium	Low
1.			
2.			
3.			
Average Score			

Exercise #2 (cont.)

D.   Discussion

    1.   Based on the data you gathered, to what extent does association play a part in memory? Give reasons for your answer based on what you have learned about remembering and forgetting.

    2.   What are the implications of an associationistic theory of memory for student learning?

    3.   Give some examples of how a student might organize his/her study to take advantage of the association value inherent in the material.

Exercise #3: POSITIVE TRANSFER

TO THE INSTRUCTOR:

This is a simple exercise that should demonstrate positive transfer of a learned perceptual-motor skill. In this instance students will learn a skill using their dominant hand and then see how much transfers to the non-dominant hand. The equipment needed is a small bucket or wastebasket, a small rubber ball that bounces with some enthusiasm, and tape to mark a line.

I.   Procedure

  A.   Divide the class into small even-numbered groups. Four persons in each group would be ideal if you have enough buckets and balls to go around.

  B.   Set up a can or bucket as a target for each group. About ten feet from the bucket, mark a line with the tape. If the success rate is too high, you should move the line back. This could be determined beforehand to save time.

  C.   The groups of four should be divided into two persons who are the experimental subjects and two who are control subjects.

  D.   Provide all subjects with the data sheets to keep a record of hits and misses.

  E.   Provide each group with a rubber ball. Explain to them that the object is to toss the ball, bounce it once, and get it into the bucket. Twenty tosses constitutes a turn. Record each hit or miss on the data sheet.

  F.   The two experimental subjects will go first and toss the ball twenty times each with their <u>dominant</u> hands. The control subjects will then toss the ball twenty times with <u>non-dominant</u> hands. Finally, the experimental subjects will toss the ball twenty times with their <u>non-dominant</u> hands.

  G.   Once all turns are completed and recorded, calculate the mean for the number of hits for each group. They should end up with a mean for the experimental group's dominant hand and one for their non-dominant hand. They should also have a mean for the control group's non-dominant hand.

  H.   If transfer has occurred, it will be evident when comparing the performance of the non-dominant hand for the experimental and control groups.

  I.   It may be interesting to combine all scores in all groups and make the same comparison.

II.   Some Questions for Discussion

  A.   Did transfer occur?

  B.   What is transfer of learning in a skill such as this?

  C.   Can we move from this demonstration to any conclusions about transfer of learning in other areas?

  D.   Can we assume that learning transfers from one situation to another?

  E.   How can we insure that maximum transfer will occur?

POSITIVE TRANSFER: DATA SHEET

To the Student: Record each of the trials for each subject. A hit is recorded when the subject, standing behind the line, bounces the ball once and gets it into the bucket.

TRIALS	EXPERIMENTAL GROUP DOMINANT HAND				CONTROL GROUP NON-DOMINANT HAND				EXPERIMENTAL GROUP NON-DOMINANT HAND			
	#1	#2	#3	#4	#5	#6	#7	#8	#9	#10	#11	#12
1												
2												
3												
4												
5												
6												
7												
8												
9												
10												
11												
12												
13												
14												
15												
16												
17												
18												
19												
20												
TOTAL HITS												
AVG HITS												

■ BROADENING OUR CULTURAL HORIZONS

1. **Members of cultures that trade beads can remember** color patterns of long strands of beads; those who herd cattle can remember and recognize dozens of individual animals. Can you name some type of information that is easily remembered in our culture, but that might be difficult for a member of another culture to encode? (For example, the year and make of a number of automobiles, baseball or football statistics) In what ways does cultural experience prepare us to remember some things easily and others with difficulty.

2. **Why might a person who speaks English and Spanish equally well** prefer to study physics in English and to learn poetry in Spanish.

3. **You are visiting a foreign country.** You speak the language but are unfamiliar with the culture. You stop a passerby on the street and ask for directions. Why might you find it difficult to remember the directions and why might your helper have trouble giving them.

4. **Talk to people in your class or on campus who were born in another country.** Ask them how they remember the number of days in each month, for example, or any other information you remember with a mnemonic device. What poem do they use? Is it very different from the device you were taught?

5. **Why is it often difficult for new immigrants to learn a country's monetary system?** (Consider perceptual effects, such as a dime being smaller than a nickel, as well as memory.)

■ SUPPLEMENTAL LECTURE

The study of memory can be the most practical and useful topic for students. Some time should be spent in class on how the student can benefit from a study of memory. This lecture is intended to do that. You may have some knowledge or insights that could be added to what is outlined here. Whatever you present should be made meaningful by relating it to established psychological principles. This lecture is specifically concerned with helping students to see how they can improve their capability to store information and retrieve it when needed.

STUDY FOR RETRIEVAL

I.   Introduction

A.   There are several important concepts to be reviewed or learned before this lecture can proceed.

1.   Be sure students know about the role of the brain in long-term memory and the process of storage. Of particular interest is the role of the hippocampus, its location and function.
2.   Students should be familiar with sensory, short-term, and long-term memory.
3.   Also, it is useful to have discussed the various explanations for forgetting.
4.   The concept of consolidation should have been introduced.
5.   The role of sleep in storage, consolidation, and recall should be part of the students' background.

B.   Effective storage and retrieval do not occur by themselves. Students often believe that if they are "in the presence" of learning, by sitting through a lecture or being in front of a book for several hours, that learning will occur. Some even try playing tapes of material to be learned while sleeping, expecting to awaken with some new learning. The idea that learning is "absorbed" or "not absorbed" is time-honored but invalid.

Introduce this lecture by discussing the misconceptions about learning. Be sure to emphasize that learning, in this case effective storage with the hope of efficient retrieval, takes time, effort, and energy. There are no magic formulas or shortcuts.

C.   The purpose of this lecture is to make students aware of some ways to make the "time, effort, and energy" pay dividends in the form of new learning.

II.   Studying for Retrieval

A.   What follows is an outline of suggestions. These need to be fleshed out with discussion and readings.

B.   Students need to be conscious of what they are doing until habits are formed. Old habits often inhibit new ones. A struggle to change may be part of the process of becoming a better learner.

C.   The following six factors are outlined with brief comments. Students should explore them more fully.

1.   Motivation:
      a.   This is the key to success--without it little or no learning occurs.
      b.   Students need to find it if it isn't already present.
      c.   Discuss intrinsic and extrinsic motivation.

       d.   It can be enhanced by: looking for novel ideas, relating material to what the learner already knows, telling others about it.

2.   Meaning:

       a.   Look for ways to make material to be learned more meaningful. A geography lesson about a distant country can come to life if the student is asked to plan a trip to visit the place.

       b.   Meaning often comes when material is organized so relationships are evident.

       c.   Associations among the concepts and with already known ideas helps to hold new material longer.

3.   Repetition:

       a.   Once over the material to be studied won't do the job. Except for special instances of startling stimuli or high motivation, frequent repetition is needed for long-term retention. Repetition and frequent review (rehearsal) are needed.

       b.   Overlearning is suggested. Review until the material is learned, and then review again. Wouldn't you want your brain surgeon to have overlearned his surgical skills?

4.   Techniques:

       a.   Recitation is the key to success. Students should try to express the learned material in their own words. Be able to tell someone, explain the concept.

       b.   Memory aids help recall. They not only make it easier to recall, but the time and effort put into doing this, establishing a mnemonic scheme, for example, involves many of the study and learning concepts already discussed, especially establishing relationships and repetition.

5.   Use all of the senses:

       a.   As many of the senses as possible should be used to take in and review information. It makes it more certain that the material will be stored and will be more easily retained.

       b.   The major senses, vision and hearing, should be involved as much as possible. Visual stimulation has been found to be the most productive.

6. Consolidation:

       a.   This refers to the setting or establishing of learning in long-term memory.

       b.   This is not an instantaneous process. Time is needed as well as the effort put forth using the methods discussed above.

       c.   The time between the learning and the establishment of long-term memory is critical.

       d.   Rest and relaxation, including a good night's sleep, are considered important for consolidation to occur. Be sure students understand that these come after the study, not instead of.

III.   Discussion

    A.   This topic should generate a good deal of discussion with students offering their experiences and opinions. Their ideas about what will work and what won't should provide for an interesting session.

    B.   The age-old adage, "You can't teach an old dog new tricks" should be discussed. Can students with twelve or more years of study habits, no matter how bad or good, change?

    C.   Discuss the role of sleep as an aid "after study," not during study.

    D.   Can drugs enhance memory, storage, and retrieval?

    E.   Does hypnosis improve recall?

■ SUGGESTIONS FOR FURTHER READING

Best, J. B. *Cognitive Psychology*, 4th ed. West Publishing, 1995.

Bower, G. H. "Mood and Memory." *American Psychologist*, 1981, 36: 129-148.

Cermak, L. S. *Improving Your Memory*. McGraw-Hill, 1976.

Cohen, G., M. W. Eysenak, and M. E. LaVoi. *Memory: A Cognitive Approach*. Open University Press, 1986.

Donahoe, J. W. and D. C. Palmer. *Learning and Complex Behavior*. Allyn and Bacon, 1994.

Donahoe, J. W. and M. G. Wessells. *Learning, Language, and Memory*. Harper and Row, 1980.

Ellis, H. C. and R. R. Hunt. *Fundamentals of Cognitive Psychology*, 5th ed. Brown, 1993.

Harris, J. E. and P. E. Morris. *Everyday Memory: Actions and Absent-Mindedness*. Academic Press, 1984.

Klatzky, R. L. *Memory and Awareness: An Information-Processing Perspective*. W. H. Freeman, 1984.

Linton, M. "I Remember It Well." *Psychology Today*, July 1979: 81-86.

Loftus, E. F. *Memory*. Addison-Wesley, 1980.

Luria, A. R. *The Mind of a Mnemonist*. Basic Books, 1968.

Lynch, G. "A Magical Memory Tour." *Psychology Today*, April 1984: 29-39.

McGaugh, J. L. "Preserving the Presence of the Past: Hormonal Influences on Memory Storage." *American Psychologist*, 1983, 38: 161-174.

Neisser, U. *Memory Observed: Remembering in Natural Contexts*. W. H. Freeman, 1982.

Spear, N. E. and D. Riccio. *Memory: Phenomena and Principles*. Allyn and Bacon, 1994.

Tulving, E. *Elements of Episodic Memory*. Oxford University Press, 1983.

Wingfield, A. and D. Byrnes. *The Psychology of Human Memory*. Academic Press, 1981.

■ FILM SUGGESTIONS

HUMAN MEMORY (1978, Harcourt, Brace, Jovanovich, 28 min.)
> This film describes the various processes of memory, memory aids, and the cognitive distortions created while reconstructing memories. It begins with a segment about what it is like to have no memory at all and then goes on to establish the difference between short-term and long-term memory, with some brief experiments illustrating the limited capacity of short-term memory. Gordon Bower then shows how learning involves the transfer of information from short-term to long-term memory and reviews several learning methods, including rote repetition and the invention of meaningful associations.

INFORMATION PROCESSING (1971, CRM/McGraw-Hill, 28 min.)
> Actor David Steinberg introduces this film which utilizes isolated, stimulus-rich sequences from a complex social environment--a Hollywood cocktail party--to illustrate some of the aspects of human information processing. Donald Norman acts as "anchorman," observing behavior from a booth situated above the party. Norman and Steinberg explain what each scene reveals about the ways in which people receive information, store it in memory, and then retrieve it when necessary.

MEMORY (1980, CRM/McGraw-Hill, 30 min.)
> This film opens with descriptions of three basic types of recall: sensory memory, short-term memory, and long-term memory. The film concentrates on improvement of long-term memories, illustrating a variety of very effective methods of categorizing and referencing memories in order to facilitate recall.

MEMORY (1990, Coast Community College District Telecourses, 30 min.)
> Explains research in the nature and workings of memory; defines amnesia and Alzheimer's disease.

SHORT-TERM VISUAL MEMORY (Bell Telephone, 18 min.)
> This film presents a discussion of research methods involving the temporary storage of information.

■ COMPUTER PROGRAMS: *Mind Scope*

Exercise 3, Scanning Short-Term Memory

This exercise examines how people use information in short-term memory and is based on an experiment by Saul Sternberg. The exercise helps determine whether people use information in short-term memory by using parallel comparison or serial comparison techniques.

Exercise 5, Serial Position Effects

Students participate in an experiment which examines free recall of serially-presented lists under two conditions. With some lists, students are asked to recall items as soon as the list is presented; with others they are asked to recall after a short delay.

Exercise 8, Semantic Memory

A theory developed by Collins and Quillian that suggests that semantic information is organized in the brain in a method analogous to the way it is typically organized in a dictionary is studied in this exercise. An important implication of this dictionary-search model of the operation of semantic memory is that search time will take longer for some kinds of information than for others.

Exercise 12, Iconic Memory

This exercise is based on a technique called "partial report," developed by George Sperling. It is based on the idea that people who have to report all the items in a large display simply forget some of the items before they can report them all--that is, people see more than they are able to report. Sperling developed his technique to demonstrate the existence of iconic memory.

CHAPTER 9

Cognition and Creativity

■ BEHAVIORAL OBJECTIVES

The student should be able to:

1. Define the term "thinking."
2. List the three basic units of thought.
3. Describe mental imagery and synesthesia. Explain how both stored and created images may be used to solve problems (including how the size of a mental image may be important).
4. Explain how kinesthetic imagery aids thinking.
5. Define the terms "concept" and "concept formation," explain how they aid thought processes, and describe how they are learned.
6. Define the terms conjunctive concept, disjunctive concept, and relational concept.
7. Explain the difference between the denotative and connotative meaning of a word or concept, and describe how the connotative meaning of a word is measured.
8. Explain how language aids thought.
9. Define semantics.
10. Briefly describe the following three requirements of a language and their related concepts:
    a. symbols
        1) phonemes
        2) morphemes
    b. grammar
        1) syntax
        2) transformation rules
    c. productivity
11. Explain why forms of language other than speech are believed possible.
12. Explain the extent to which primates have been taught to use language.
13. Describe both the criticisms and the practical value of attempts to teach language to primates.
14. Differentiate between mechanical problem-solving and problem-solving through understanding.
15. Define heuristics and explain how they aid problem-solving.
16. Tell how each of the following contribute to insight:
    a. selective encoding
    b. selective combination
    c. selective comparison
17. Explain how fixation and functional fixedness block problem-solving, and give an example of each.
18. List and explain four common barriers to creative thinking.
19. Define the term artificial intelligence (include a description of what it is based upon).
20. Describe both the potential uses and drawbacks of artificial intelligence.

21. Describe the following four kinds of thought:
    a. inductive
    b. deductive
    c. logical
    d. illogical
22. Describe the following characteristics of creative thinking:
    a. fluency
    b. flexibility
    c. originality
23. List the two most common daydream themes and discuss how fantasy (daydreams) relates to creativity.
24. Explain the relationship of creativity to divergent and convergent thinking.
25. Describe how the ability to think divergently can be measured.
26. List and describe the five stages of creative thinking.
27. Discuss the five qualities which characterize creative persons.
28. Explain the following three common intuitive thinking errors:
    a. representativeness (include representativeness heuristic)
    b. base rate
    c. framing
29. List and explain three common problems which cause difficulties in thinking and problem-solving.
30. Describe six practical steps to encourage creativity.
31. Describe the process of brainstorming, and explain how it can be used to solve problems.
32. Describe thinking in animals as exemplified by delayed response problems and insight.
33. Give two examples of apparently intelligent thought by an animal.

■ DEMONSTRATIONS, DRAMATIZATIONS, AND DISCUSSION

1. **The research team of Sue Savage-Rumbaugh, Duane Rumbaugh, and Sarah Boysen has advanced a cogent argument** against the notion that true language usage has been achieved by apes trained in ASL or computer language systems. For a critical and thought-provoking appraisal of primate language programs, see their article, "Do Apes Use Language?" in *American Scientist*, Jan.-Feb. 1980: 49.

2. **The semantic differential provides an interesting look at the subtleties and similarities of the connotative meanings of words.** To illustrate, duplicate the semantic differential scales shown in the text and give copies to the class. Then have them rate words such as: MOTHER, FATHER, MONEY, SEX, LOVE, STUDENT, PROFESSOR, COLLEGE, POLITICS, LIBERAL, etc. To what degree are connotations shared? Do individual differences in connotative meanings match students' perceptions of themselves, their interests, and values?

3. **Mednick's Remote Associates Test (RAT) is a good example of a creativity test that**

combines divergent and convergent thinking. The RAT consists of groupings of three words. The words in each group have a single word in common associated with them. The object is to find that word. For example, if the words were, "shake, cow, and carton," the common element is "milk" (milkshake, milk cow, and milk carton). The items below are similar to the RAT. They may be used in class to raise the question of what distinguishes creative thought from other types of problem-solving. The class may also want to discuss whether or not the RAT actually tests creativity.

1) ball home naval
2) stream goose town
3) dance ladder door
4) dog pepper rod
5) sand mouse door

6) ball shake lotion
7) puff whipped ice
8) bowling cushion hair
9) sun bulb sky
10) wrench stove line

Answers for the preceding items are: 1) base 2) down 3) step 4) hot 5) trap 6) hand 7) cream 8) pin 9) light 10) pipe.

4. **Is "brainstorming" really superior to individual problem-solving for producing creative solutions?** A small in-class experiment may shed some light on this issue for students. Begin by dividing the class in half. Form four-person groups out of one-half of the class. If possible, separate the groups from the remaining individuals. Beforehand, prepare a brief summary of brainstorming from the discussion in the text and give it to the four-person groups to read. Tell the students their task is to imagine as many possible uses for a brick as they can. Groups are to work according to the rules for brainstorming. Individuals are to work by themselves. At the end of a five-minute period, collect the lists of uses, and arbitrarily group the solutions of individuals by fours. Then compare the number of uses generated by the brainstorming groups to the number produced by groups of four individuals working independently. In addition to determining if the cross-stimulation produced more ideas, the originality of group and individual solutions can be compared.

You may wish to use this exercise to illustrate the value of breaking sets. Write the following attributes on the board: weight, color, rectangularity (sharp edges, flat surfaces), porosity, strength, roughness, storage and conduction of heat, electrical insulation, hardness. Then ask students to try adding to their lists of uses by considering each of the listed attributes. Does this increase the number, flexibility, and originality of their answers? (Adams, J. L. *Conceptual Blockbusting*. San Francisco: W. H. Freeman, 1974.)

5. **There are many ways in which fixation in problem-solving can be illustrated.** A typical problem you may wish to pose to students is this: How could you put your left hand completely in your right hand pants pocket and your right hand completely in your left hand pants pocket at the same time while you are wearing the pants? The answer is to put the pants on backward, whereupon the task becomes quite easy. Students often miss this solution due to conventions about the "right" way to wear a pair of pants.

A large number of problems similar to the preceding are offered by Eugene Raudsepp in a *Psychology Today* article. They cannot be reprinted here, but the article will provide you with an excellent collection of creativity problems for class use. The article appears in the July 1980 issue of *Psychology Today*: 71-75, 88-90.

6. **Ask each student to think of 5 different groups of people.** The groupings can be based on physical qualities, age, gender, ethnic or racial background, etc. Create columns describing each group's socioeconomic status, happiness, creativity, intelligence, emphasis on family, value of independence, honesty, and industriousness. Ask the students to rate the likelihood (1 = not likely; 7 = very likely) that these qualities would exist in an individual member of each group. Have students share their ratings in pairs. Then discuss the ways in which informal concepts of what various groups are like can color our attitudes toward individuals. Discuss stereotypes as a type of over-simplified concept.

7. **Charles Croll has interviewed children of different ages, asking them, "Is Santa Claus real? Why, Why not?"** Students can ask children the same question regarding Santa, the Tooth Fairy, the Easter Bunny, magic, cartoon characters, animals, germs, and so forth. The percentage of children who respond correctly shows a nice progression through ages 4-7. This is an easy way for students to get a glimpse into the cognitive world of younger children.

8. **Richards and Siegler found that movement was the attribute most frequently cited by children as a criterion for life.** Younger children rely heavily on qualities of life that are true of animals but not of plants. Older children cite attributes that are true of both plants and animals.

    A simple replication of part of the study would be to have students ask children of various ages (4-11) "Can you tell me how things that are alive are different from things that are not alive?" List the attributes cited at each age and the percentage of children who mentioned them. This provides a nice picture of children's increasingly complex knowledge structures. Discussion can focus on how the development of knowledge and cognition can be best explained. (Richards, D. D. & Siegler, R.S. [1986]. "Children's understanding of the attributes of life." *Journal of Experimental Child Psychology*, 42, 1-22.)

■ONE-MINUTE MOTIVATORS

1. **Ask students to spend a few moments summarizing the contents of their thoughts just before class began.** What elements of thinking were present?

2. **Ask students to process these numbers:** 15 x 2 x 7 divided by 3 - 20 (the answer is 50); to think of all the words they can make from the letters T-H-I-N-K; to say without looking how many circles there are on the back of a one-dollar bill; to say what dogs, cats, parakeets, and goldfish have in common. Do students use different elements of thought to answer these questions?

3. **Bring an unusual object to class.** Keep the object covered. Allow students to ask questions about the object until they can identify it. How much did they rely on language? Concepts? Imagery?

4. **Ask a student to describe how to get to** the bookstore, the nearest theater, how to run a special football formation, or to describe what he/she did yesterday, and to describe feelings about a recent holiday. Ask a few students to watch the degree to which hand movements took place.

5. **Categorize these concepts as** conjunctive, disjunctive, or relative: yellow fruit, American state capitals, female vocalists, all-star athletes, under, spouse, student, west.

6. **Ask students to make a list** of entertainers, politicians, athletes, or other prominent people. Rate each person according to the semantic differential categories.

7. **Flash a series of slides** that show atypical chairs, vases, trees, animals. Discuss prototypes.

8. **Ask students to develop a list of oxymorons** ("government intelligence," "jumbo shrimp"). Discuss semantic problems.

9. **Ask students to describe the specific problem-solving strategies** they used to select this course, and would use to select a job, a book, or a movie.

■ CLASSROOM EXERCISES

TO THE INSTRUCTOR:

The exercises which follow show the effects of mental set on behavior. Solving problems may become difficult or impossible because of a predisposition, or set, to see the problem in a particular way or to try to solve it by a predetermined method. Students should readily see that they have fallen into this trap when they do these exercises.

The first exercise involves a story problem that is sure to baffle the listeners because of the obvious (but faulty) solution. The second exercise establishes a mental set in the first five problems. Because of the set which is now established, the students will have a harder time doing the next three.

Exercise #1 It Pays to Tip

This is a classroom exercise which demonstrates the effect of set on thinking and problem-solving. Students should be asked to read the section on mental set in the text prior to this exercise. You should have a stopwatch or some other timing mechanism to inform students of the time it takes them to solve the problem. The value of this exercise lies in the discussion that should follow concerning the students' attempts at problem-solving and the evident mental set which made the problem difficult or impossible to solve.

A.   Procedure

   1.   Ask students to have a sheet of paper and pencil or pen handy for problem-solving purposes. Advise them that you are going to read a story and ask a question. They are to solve the problem and note the time, in seconds, that it took them to find the solution.

   2.   After reading the story, watch the time and note the elapsed time in ten-second intervals on the chalkboard, as the students work on the solution.

   3.   Stop the exercise after five minutes regardless of how many are finished.

   4.   The following story should be read slowly and clearly while the students listen:

   Three friends went to a restaurant to have a leisurely drink and lunch. They finished their meal and paid their bill while lingering over coffee and conversation. The bill came to $30.00, so each paid $10.00 to the waiter, who went off to pay the bill. The bartender, who handled the cash register, noticed that the waiter had charged full price for the drinks, which were on a two-for-one special. The actual bill should have been $25.00, so he gave the waiter $5.00 and told him to return the money to the customers. On the way back to the table the waiter decided that since the diners did not know they had been overcharged, he would return one dollar to each and keep $2.00 for himself. That is exactly what he did. Now each of the diners had paid $9.00 for the food and drinks, and the waiter kept $2.00. Three times nine equals 27 plus 2 equals 29. Where is the other dollar?

   (There is no "other dollar." Twenty-five dollars went to the restaurant, three to the diners, and two to the waiter.)

B.   Discussion

   1.   Find out how many solved the problem.

   2.   Ask students to discuss how they tried to find a solution. See how many ways were tried.

   3.   Discuss what factors made it difficult to solve this problem.

   4.   See if students can see how mental set can be a factor in their day-to-day experiences.

Exercise #2: Measure for Measure

Beginning with an apology to Shakespeare for that title, we can also give thanks to Luchins for his classic experiment with the water jars. The subject is given a set of three jars of varying sizes and a goal to achieve. The person is to fill and empty the three jars until the goal of a specified number of pints of water is attained. Since the goal is never identical to the capacity of any of the three jars, some strategy needs to be developed to end up with the exact amount. Suppose, for example, the subject were given a 20-pint jar, a 4-pint jar, and a 3-pint jar and had to end up with exactly 10 pints of water. The solution requires the subject to fill the 20-pint jar and then pour out 3 pints twice and four once, leaving 10 pints. It could be written as $20 - 3 - 3 - 4 = 10$.

I.   Procedure

      A.   Explain the exercise to the class, indicating the type of problem being presented. Students should be given the demonstration item above and shown how to record their answer on the data sheet.

      B.   Distribute a data sheet to each student.

      C.   Write the problems given below on the chalkboard, one at a time, asking the students to record their solution after each one.

      D.   After all eight are completed, discuss items 1-5. Two elements are needed for a correct solution to each of these items. The correct amount of water remaining is essential. Also, the way it was arrived at is important because it will demonstrate mental set. In each case manipulation of the jars of water was needed to arrive at the exact amount.

      E.   Go on to items 6-8. These can be solved directly without manipulation of the amounts of water. However, after solving 1-6, students will probably try manipulation first and may never see the direct method. (Note that for item 6, $7 + 8 = 15$.)

Exercise #2: Measure for Measure

| PROBLEM | WATER JAR SIZE | | | |
	A	B	C	GOAL
1	20	31	2	7
2	20	57	3	31
3	5	48	8	27
4	20	100	11	58
5	3	84	7	67
6	7	38	8	15
7	4	17	3	7
8	9	29	6	15

(From: Luchins, A. S. "Mechanization in Problem-Solving: The Effect of 'Einstellung.'" Psychological Monographs, 54 (Whole Number 248), 1942.)

II.   Discussion

   A.   Discuss the trial-and-error method needed to learn the best way to solve the problem when starting out.
   B.   Have students identify the mental set that was established by the first five items.
   C.   How many made the shift to the easy way to solve items 6 - 8? How many stuck to the "old-fashioned" way while doing items 1 - 5?
   D.   Discuss the extent to which mental set plays a part in our everyday lives?

Exercise #2: **MEASURE FOR MEASURE   DATA SHEET**

TO THE STUDENT:

In the space provided, show any calculating that you need to do to arrive at a solution. You will have two minutes to do each problem. Your instructor will demonstrate how the problems are to be done and how your answer should be written.

ITEM	SOLUTION	CALCULATIONS
1		
2		
3		
4		
5		
6		
7		
8		

■ BROADENING OUR CULTURAL HORIZONS

1.   **To what extent does cultural or ethnic background affect** the kinds of prototypes we use to categorize objects and events? Would these prototypes affect the way we think?

2.   **Discuss the ways in which connotations can be culture-specific.** Ask students for examples of misunderstandings they have encountered that can be traced to differences in connotative meaning.

3.   **Ask students who speak English as a second language** to discuss their feelings about learning and using a new language and about what effect this has had on their thinking.

4.   **Invite a person to class who is fluent in American Sign Language.** Would a non-hearing person perceive the world differently than a hearing person because of using a different language structure? Teach students to sign the words to a current popular song.

5.   **What cultural "rules" or values could contribute to functional fixedness?** Why are some cultures regarded as more inventive than others?

■ SUPPLEMENTAL LECTURE

This lecture on creativity is intended to bring together several significant aspects of the topic. All are alluded to in the text in different places. Students should be made aware not only of what creativity is, but also what mental functions make it possible for us to exhibit this capability.

CREATIVITY

I.   Introduction

A.   Discuss with the students Guilford's model of intelligence. He sees human intellectual functioning as being comprised of three aspects:
1.   operations - kinds of functions that can be done;
2.   content - the kinds of information that can be operated on;
3.   products - the results of applying an operation to content.

B.   Of the several types of operations, two are of most interest for our discussion of creativity:
1.   Convergent thinking:
   a.   This involves solving problems by arriving at a single correct or best solution.
   b.   It includes using logic, following rules, producing a solution.
   c.   It is an activity of the left hemisphere of the brain.
   d.   It is not conducive to creative thinking.

        2.   Divergent thinking

            a.   It involves using one's knowledge to develop many solutions to a problem.

            b.   Several hypotheses can be proposed and a variety of answers considered when confronted with a question or problem.

            c.   It is an activity of the right hemisphere of the brain.

            d.   Creative thinking is more likely to occur in this approach to problem-solving.

C.   It is a good idea to tie into this discussion a review of the left and right hemispheres of the brain, examining the special functions attributed to each.

D.   The question of "nature versus nurture" might be explored at this point. Do we inherit a tendency to one operation or the other? Can we learn or develop either or both? These are valuable questions to consider since the relationship between intelligence and creativity always comes up. What is the relationship?

        1.   Intelligence and school success are highly correlated. Schooling focuses on left hemisphere types of functions more than those of the right hemisphere. At least, this is true in our society.

        2.   Creativity is more closely allied to right hemisphere activities and functions, which are emphasized less in school.

        3.   Intelligence tests, therefore, do not measure creativity.

        4.   Creativity and intelligence, as defined by what tests measure, are separate and different. A person can be high on intelligence and low on creativity, or vice versa. On the other hand, he/she can be high on both or low on both.

        5.   Divergent thinkers often have problems in school because they don't think in a logical, disciplined way. Often creative people do poorly in school.

II.   Creativity--What is it?

     A.   Refer to the studies done by Jackson and Messick (P. W. Jackson and D. Messick, *Foundations of Abnormal Psychology*, eds. P. London and D. Rosenbau. New York: Holt, 1968). From their studies they have developed four criteria for creativity. They say that for something to be creative it must be all of the following:

        1.   Novel - something new, not thought of before;

        2.   Appropriate - makes sense and is useful for whatever it is intended;

        3.   Transcending constraints - goes beyond the boundaries of the traditional or what is expected;

        4.   Coalescing over time - The value may not be apparent at first but becomes obvious over time. Its value increases and is appreciated more as time goes on.

B.   Some examples could be discussed.   Be careful to make a clear distinction between the notion of creativity as defined here and the popular conception.   When a painter paints a pretty picture or a dancer performs well, we tend to refer to them as creative. However, neither of those fit the criteria indicated above.   A distinction should be clearly drawn:

1.   Artistic - refers to a job well done.   A dancer performs beautifully, a singer sings well, a painter paints a beautiful sunset, etc.   The important point here is that no new form has been produced.   It does not transcend beyond traditional boundaries.   Rather, the artist or performer is simply doing well in the art form that was already created and developed.

2.   Creativity should be restricted to those activities that produce new art forms and new ways of thinking, acting, painting, singing, etc.

3.   Now the class should try to identify who the creative persons were who pioneered an art form or an idea.   Frank Lloyd Wright was the creative person who produced a novel design for a house which gave rise to a variety of modern housing styles.   The Beatles were creators of a new form of music. Who are some others?

III.   Assignment

Divide the class into groups of about six persons.   Give them each a problem that is either insoluble or has no simple solution, such as achieving peace in the Middle East.   Ask them to brainstorm--come up with as many solutions as possible.   They need to be uncritical, with no holds barred; no solution should be considered unacceptable.   Instruct them to keep a list of all suggested solutions.   They will soon find that their natural tendency is to look for one solution and to argue about why other people's solutions are not as good as their own.   This should be resisted.

After the brainstorming session, ask a person from each group to read its list.   See the variety of responses that are presented.   An alternative would be to reproduce the lists and give all students a copy of all the suggested solutions.   Ask each student to find from the lists one good, workable, novel solution--not his/her own--and try to defend it.

■ SUGGESTIONS FOR FURTHER READING

Anderson, J. *Cognitive Psychology and its Implications*, 4th ed. W. H. Freeman, 1995.

Best, J. B. *Cognitive Psychology*, 4th ed. West Publishing, 1995.

Bramsford, J. D. *The Ideal Problem Solver: A Guide to Improving Thinking*. W. H. Freeman, 1984.

Chomsky, N. *Rules and Regulations*. Columbia University Press, 1980.

DeBono, E. *Lateral Thinking: Creativity Step-by-Step*. Harper and Row, 1970.

DeLuce, J. and H. T. Wilder (Eds.). *Language in Primates: Perspectives and Implications*. Springer-Verlag, 1983.

Ellis, A. and G. Beattie. *The Psychology of Language and Communication*. Guilford Press, 1986.

Gardner, H. *Art, Mind, and Brain: A Cognitive Approach to Creativity*. Basic Books, 1982.

Guilford, J. P. "Transformation Abilities or Functions." *Journal of Creative Behavior* (17) 1983: 75-83.

Koberg, D. and J. Bagnall. *The Universal Traveler*. Crisp, 1991.

Koestler, A. *The Act of Creation*. Macmillan, 1964.

Mayer, R. *Thinking, Problem Solving, and Cognition*, 2nd ed. W. H. Freeman, 1992.

Miller, G. A. *Language and Speech*. W. H. Freeman, 1981.

Patterson, F. and E. Linden. *The Education of Koko*. Holt, Rinehart and Winston, 1979.

Premack, D. "Animal Cognition." *Annual Review of Psychology* (34) 1983: 351-362.

Wesells, M. G. *Cognitive Psychology*. Harper & Row, 1982.

■ FILM SUGGESTIONS

APE LANGUAGE - FROM CONDITIONED RESPONSE TO SYMBOL (1986, Aims Media, Inc., 23 min.)
>   This video illustrates and documents research into the nature of language acquisition through the study of symbolic and syntactical skills in chimpanzees.

CREATIVE PROBLEM SOLVING: HOW TO GET BETTER IDEAS (1979, CRM/
McGraw-Hill, 28 min.)
>   The film shows how creative problem-solving can be developed in each individual but is often inhibited by criticism or lack of self-confidence. Animated sequences explore the sources of creativity according to Freud and also according to the "split-brain" theory.

DECISION MAKING AND PROBLEM SOLVING (1990, Coast Community College District Telecourses, 30 min.)
>   Part of the *Psychology - The Study of Human Behavior Series*, this video explains rational and irrational influence on human thought.

LANGUAGE (1990, Coast Community College District Telecourses, 30 min.)
>   Part of the *Psychology - The Study of Human Behavior Series*, this video describes how language is the product of learning, environmental influences, and human genetic endowments.

MATURITY AND CREATIVITY (1982, Karol Media, 30 min.)

In this film Rollo May discusses his views on maturity and his own work on the process of creativity. In this interview, he also evaluates his contributions to psychology, reacts to his critics, and discusses his future plans.

THE MIND MACHINES (1979, Time/Life, 57 min.)

This film discusses artificial intelligence, including chess-playing machines, computerized medical diagnosis, and computer controlled robots that can "see" and "learn."

PROBLEM-SOLVING STRATEGIES: THE SYNTHETICS APPROACH (1980, CRM/ McGraw-Hill, 27 min.)

This film depicts an actual Problem-Solving Laboratory conducted at Synectics, a unique consulting firm in Cambridge, MA, which specializes in teaching the process of creative problem-solving. Viewers are given a simple set of innovative strategies that can be used to stimulate organizational creativity and streamline problem solving.

A PSYCHOLOGY OF CREATIVITY (Macmillan, 31 min.)

Creative behavior and achievement are portrayed, and techniques for encouraging creativity are explored.

SIGNS OF THE APES, SONGS OF THE WHALES (1984, Time/Life, 57 min.)

This film is a NOVA production that updates progress in the attempts to teach language to animals. It features segments on dolphins, whales, sea lions, chimps, and gorillas.

■ COMPUTER PROGRAMS: *Mind Scope*

Exercise 4, Mental Paper Folding

When people are asked to "imagine" something visually, a surprising amount of information can be revealed. This exercise is based on an experiment by Shephard and Feng. It seeks to determine if an imaginal process mimics a physical one in its time requirements.

Exercise 6, Sentence-Picture Comparison

This exercise is adapted from an experiment by Clark and Chase on the process of comparing sentences and pictures. It seeks to answer the question of whether the structure of a sentence influences the way it is understood and used by the person who reads it.

Exercise 11, Tower of Hanoi

The children's game that is the basis of this exercise is an example of an artificial problem that has proven to be extremely useful in the study of problem solving. There are various ways to approach the problem, some more successful than others. Students are asked to develop their own strategy to solve the problem and, after they have completed it, are exposed to other strategies that are helpful in solving it.

CHAPTER 10

Motivation and Emotion

■ BEHAVIORAL OBJECTIVES

The student should be able to:

1. Define motivation.
2. Describe or analyze a motivational sequence using the "need reduction" model.
3. Explain how the incentive value of a goal can affect motivation, and describe how incentive value is related to internal need.
4. List and describe the three major types of motives and give an example of each.
5. Define homeostasis.
6. Discuss why hunger cannot be fully explained by the contractions of an empty stomach.
7. Describe the relationship of each of the following to hunger:
   a. blood sugar
   b. liver
   c. hypothalamus
      1) feeding system (lateral hypothalamus)
      2) satiety system (ventromedial hypothalamus)
      3) blood sugar regulator (paraventricular nucleus)
   d. cultural factors
   e. taste
8. Explain how a person's set point is related to obesity in childhood and adulthood.
9. Explain the paradox of yo-yo dieting.
10. Explain the relationship between how much a person overeats and the person's obesity.
11. Describe the relationship between emotionality and overeating.
12. Explain how a taste aversion is acquired, give a practical example of the process, and briefly explain why psychologists believe these aversions exist.
13. Describe the essential features of the eating disorders anorexia nervosa and bulimia nervosa. Explain what causes them and what treatment is available for them.
14. Name the brain structure that appears to control thirst (as well as hunger). Differentiate extracellular and intracellular thirst.
15. Explain how the drive to avoid pain and the sex drive differ from other primary drives.
16. Describe the evidence for the existence of drives for exploration, manipulation, curiosity, and stimulation.
17. Explain the arousal theory of motivation including the inverted U function. Relate arousal to the Yerkes-Dodson law and give an example of it.
18. Describe the two major components of test anxiety and describe four ways to reduce it.
19. Explain how circadian rhythms affect energy levels, motivation, and performance. (Include an explanation of how and why shift work and jet lag may adversely affect a person and how to minimize the effects of shifting one's rhythms.)

20. Use the ideas of Solomon's opponent-process theory to explain how a person might learn to like hazardous, painful, or frightening pursuits.
21. Define need for achievement (nAch) and differentiate it from the need for power.
22. Describe people who are achievers, and relate nAch to risk-taking.
23. List three reasons why people might avoid success.
24. Explain why women may have extra reasons to fear success. (Include an explanation of the sex differences or similarities in the fear of success as well as parental influences which encourage success.)
25. Explain the influences of drive and determination in the development of success for high achievers.
26. List (in order) the needs found in Maslow's hierarchy of motives.
27. Explain why Maslow's lower (physiological) needs are considered prepotent.
28. Define meta-need and give an example of one.
29. Distinguish between intrinsic and extrinsic motivation, and explain how each type of motivation may affect the person's interest in work and leisure activities.
30. Explain what is meant by the phrase "emotions aid survival."
31. List and describe the three major elements of emotions.
32. List the eight primary emotions proposed by Plutchik and explain his concept of mixing them.
33. Describe, in general, the effects of the sympathetic and parasympathetic branches of the ANS during and after emotion.
34. Describe the relationship between pupil dilation and emotion.
35. Define "parasympathetic rebound" and discuss its possible involvement in cases of sudden death.
36. Explain how the polygraph detects "lies."
37. Discuss the limitations and/or accuracy of lie detector devices.
38. Discuss Darwin's view of human emotion.
39. Describe the evidence that supports the conclusion that most emotional expressions are universal.
40. Define kinesics. List and describe the emotional messages conveyed by facial expressions and body language. Explain how overall posture can indicate one's emotional state.
41. Discuss the behavioral cues to lying, including a differentiation of illustrators from emblems. Explain how they and the ANS reveal lying.
42. Describe the commonsense theory of emotion.
43. Briefly describe the James-Lange theory of emotion.
44. Briefly describe the Cannon-Bard theory of emotion.
45. Briefly describe Schachter's cognitive theory of emotion and give experimental evidence to support his theory.
46. Describe and give an example of the effects of attribution on emotion.
47. Briefly describe the facial feedback hypothesis.
48. Discuss the role of appraisal in the contemporary model of emotion.
49. Explain what is meant by behavioral dieting, and describe the techniques which can enable you to control your weight.
50. Explain Sternberg's triangular theory of love (including the three "ingredients").
51. Describe the emotional states resulting from the various combinations of Sternberg's factors.

■ DEMONSTRATIONS, DRAMATIZATIONS, AND DISCUSSION

1. **An exercise can be developed around the results of a projective approach to assessing nAch.** Find a somewhat ambiguous photo in a magazine and ask students to write a short story telling what led up to the situation portrayed, what is happening now (including the feelings of the characters), and what will happen next. Stories can be scored (rather loosely) for the number of references to achievement themes and imagery (references to striving, trying, goals, excellence, success, planning, achievement, and so forth). Interview students with unusually high nAch as a basis for discussion and illustration. Other themes that can be interesting to look for are power, affiliation, and fear of success.

2. **Have the class rate the importance of each of the following clusters of needs on a 10-point scale** (1 = of little importance to me; 10 = extremely important to me). Which cluster gets the highest rating? Where does this place the individual on Maslow's hierarchy of motives? Does this placement correspond to his or her self-perception? In what way does one's culture affect the area of emphasis on the hierarchy? Do students agree with Maslow's ordering of needs?

    1)   A safe and secure house, dependable income, good health, predictable future, general sense of security.
    2)   Respect from colleagues or co-workers, valued by others in the community, self-respect, and self-esteem.
    3)   Perfection, justice, beauty, truth, autonomy, meaningfulness, simplicity.
    4)   Close circle of family or friends, loved and cared for by others, loved by a special person, accepted in the community.
    5)   Good food, drink, sex, physical comfort, rest and vigorous activity, good night's sleep, life's physical pleasures.

    It is fairly obvious that the items tap (in this order): 1) safety and security; 2) esteem and self-esteem; 3) self-actualization (meta-needs); 4) love and belonging; and 5) physiological needs. The items are likely to be transparent even for a naive subject. Therefore, to get the most out of this exercise, it should probably be given before students have studied the material in Chapter 10 but discussed when the chapter has been read.

3. **Since most college students hold jobs,** you might begin a discussion of motivation by asking them to list all of the major reasons that they have for working. You could then compare their motivations with what Sylvia Porter in *New Money Book for the Eighties* (Avon Books, 1980), cites as being the 12 most-often mentioned reasons people give for working. In order of importance they are 1) security, 2) interesting work, 3) opportunity for advancement, 4) recognition, 5) good working environment, 6) wages, 7) autonomy, 8) social contacts, 9) opportunity to learn new things, 10) good working hours, 11) ease of job, and 12) fringe benefits. Your students probably placed wages a good deal higher than sixth. Do they feel that their motives for working will change after they finish school, and if so, how and why?

4.　**Discuss the notion of willpower with students.** This is a problem for many people. Most of us have "too little" of it, whatever it is. Have the students examine this concept in the light of the theories they have been studying. Behaviorists would say there is no such thing; our actions are simply the result of association and reinforcement. The notion of motivation as a force to generate behavior would be unacceptable to a Behaviorist. Willpower, from a cognitive point of view, is an internal force that moves a person in some direction. Behavior is powered by strong needs, or guilt, or anxiety. How would Humanistic psychologists view this concept? Using this kind of discussion, you should be able to get students to see how these theories explain behavior more clearly. Instead of willpower, you could use conscience as the concept to be discussed.

5.　**Try to show how Maslow's theory helps us understand everyday problems.** How could an owner of a business use the hierarchy of needs to understand the situation of his employees, and how could he change conditions to improve morale and increase productivity? How could the theory apply to your own classroom, to problems between parent and child, boyfriend and girlfriend, etc.

6.　**A good way to clarify the cognitive view of emotion is to seek examples from the class** in which they were "fooled" by an emotional situation, so that an initial reaction of fear or apprehension gave way to relief or laughter. Point out that the foundation of physiological arousal remained--only the perception or interpretation changed.

7.　**If you can obtain a galvanic skin response instrument,** you can show the sympathetic nervous system in action. Attach the sensors to the fingers of a volunteer and have the class ask some provocative questions. (You may need to screen them ahead of time to avoid being provoked or embarrassed yourself.) Even without a verbal response from the subject, the GSR will show an increase in the level of moisture on the skin (perspiration) due to the arousal of the SNS.

8.　**Chapter 10 addresses the topic of the elusive emotion of love.** As a way of allowing students to explore their own ideas about this subject, they can be put into small groups and asked to write a definition of love on a 3" x 5" card or slip of paper. Then all of the groups should shuffle their cards and place them face down in the center. Each person in turn should select a card, read it aloud, and comment on the definition. After they all have been discussed, the groups should be instructed to arrive at one definition acceptable to all of the members. The group definitions should be presented to the class as a whole for discussion and debate.

9.　**Ask students to identify a fear they once had but have conquered.** How did they extinguish the fear? Did they learn anything from the way they handled that fear which can be used to conquer fears that remain?

10.   **You have discussed the polygraph and how it works.** Students are aware of its usefulness and its limitations. Raise some questions with the class about its use and abuse. Ask them to respond to the following questions:

   a.   How would you react if your employer were to demand regular polygraph tests of all employees?

   b.   Should the polygraph be used to check up on government officials?

   c.   What do you think about "lie detecting" in the future? How will it be different?

■ ONE-MINUTE MOTIVATORS

1.   **Depending on the season and your classroom,** you can demonstrate homeostasis by turning the thermostat in your room up or down and waiting until a student complains and asks you to alter the temperature.

2.   **Provide students with many baskets of chips and salty peanuts.** Be sure that no one has any liquid in class to drink. Wait until one student asks to run outside for a drink of water. Discuss intracellular thirst.

3.   **Give students the first five minutes of class to complete a large wooden or jigsaw puzzle.** Stop students before the puzzle is complete and return to lecture/discussion. Be sure the puzzles are within touching distance of many students. Before class ask a student to count the number of times students reach out to complete the puzzles. Discuss human curiosity and manipulation needs. You may also want to discuss the motivational properties of frustration that results from interrupted goal-seeking.

4.   **Arrange students in pairs.** Ask half of the pairs to engage in five minutes of aerobic exercise. Ask the other half to meditate. Then give each pair some pick-up sticks. Each pair decides who is the observer and who is the subject. Count the number of sticks that can be carefully picked up. Discuss optimal arousal.

5.   **Play a quick series of games with points.** Ask trivia questions, guess numbers, or the like. Keep track of each student's points. Ask students to share feelings about winning and losing with a person sitting near them. What does this say about each person's need to achieve?

6.   **Ask students working in pairs** to conduct an entire conversation using only facial expressions and gestures. How much was understood? Why?

7.   **Ask students to spend one day intentionally smiling.** Ask them to jot down their feelings and the reactions of others to them. Share feelings the next day of class.

8.   **Ask students to put a pencil crosswise between their teeth** during a ten-minute lecturette. Did the smiling affect their feelings?

9.   **Call on people for impromptu speeches.** Break a balloon or turn on a buzzer just prior to pulling out a name. Discuss the role of anxiety and arousal as they relate to the fight/flight reaction. Remind students that these are normal reactions and that the challenge is to channel such responses into adaptive behaviors.

■ CLASSROOM EXERCISES

TO THE INSTRUCTOR:

The exercises which follow are designed to give students an opportunity to evaluate motivation and emotion in an objective manner. They should be able to see how a psychologist tries to assess motivation. At the same time, they should become aware of the difficulty of doing it scientifically and getting hard data to work with. Emotions are interesting to study and discuss in class because they touch everyone. The classroom climate needs to be accepting before students will share feelings with each other.

Exercise #1 deals with the need for achievement. This is near and dear to the hearts of students since they spend a great deal of time and energy in pursuit of goals that will satisfy this need. Students should be able to arrive at a need level for themselves and also see what characteristics are found in people who have high and low need levels.

Exercise #2 is intended to help students see the way in which Maslow's hierarchy of needs functions in their lives. Students should begin to see that they are "on the road" and not yet "at the destination" as far as personality development is concerned.

Exercise #3 should be nonthreatening and will open up discussion of some personal experiences. In this exercise students are asked to identify some fears that they have, and they are then asked to think about ways to reduce them.

Exercise #4 illustrates the way that some words take on emotional overtones. People show this by their behavior when they are confronted with these words or ideas.

Exercise #1: nAch(oo!)

Pardon the pun! But just as the sneeze is a precursor of a cold, so some behaviors indicate the existence of a need and the intensity of the drive to satisfy it.

I.   Introduction

The items in this exercise describe some behaviors which are related to achievement motivation. People do not experience them all to the same degree, but put together they can be an indicator of the strength of the need for achievement. Have the students respond to the scale, total the points on all items, and report their scores. The highest possible score is 50 points;

the lowest would be 10. On the scale, achievement motivation could be evaluated as follows:

High: 40 - 50   Medium: 20 - 40   Low: 10 - 20

This could leave some people on the borderline with scores of 20 or 40. Other factors may need to be taken into account to determine in which group the student belongs.

Students should be put at ease about this exercise. Be sure they understand that the results will not affect their standing in the class nor will it be a basis for personal judgments.

II.   Procedure

A.   Distribute the scale to the students. Ask them to read the directions and follow them. They should be given as much time as needed--about 10 minutes.

B.   Ask students to total their ratings to arrive at a score for the scale. They should note their own scores for future reference.

C.   Collect the scales for further analysis.

D.   Prior to the next class develop the following data:
1.   Find a mean score for the class.
2.   Identify the high and low achievers.
3.   Pick out the items on which all or most low achievers scored lowest, and high achievers scored highest.

III.   Discussion

A.   Make copies for the students of the items identified as common to high and low achievers. Discuss achievement motivation using these items as a starting point. Begin by asking students why they responded as they did.

B.   Ask students if they felt this scale adequately sampled their achievement motivation. Could it be improved? How? (For this discussion you could put a copy of the scale on an overhead projector.)

Exercise #1: MOTIVATION--NEED FOR ACHIEVEMENT (nAch)

TO THE STUDENT:

This is a five-point rating scale. Your responses should be based on how you feel about each item at the present time. This is not an evaluation of your work in this course, and your responses will be anonymous. Try to respond as accurately as you can. Rate each item as follows:

not characteristic of me	1
seldom characteristic of me	2
sometimes characteristic of me	3
usually characteristic of me	4
very characteristic of me	5

1. I tend to be competitive and strive to excel in most activities I undertake.   _____

2. I often go out of my way to take on outside responsibilities in the college and community.   _____

3   When thinking about the future, I emphasize long-term goals more than short-term goals.   _____

4. I get bored easily by routine.   _____

5. I tend to get upset if I cannot immediately learn whether I have done well or poorly in any situation.   _____

6. I am generally not a gambler; I prefer calculated risks.   _____

7. In choosing a career, I would be more interested in the challenge of the job than in the pay.   _____

8. When I cannot reach a goal I have set for myself, I strive even harder to reach it.   _____

9. If given the choice, I would prefer a highly successful stranger as a co-worker to a friend as a co-worker.   _____

10. I believe people should take personal responsibility for their actions.   _____

TOTAL FOR THIS SCALE   _____

Exercise #2: NEEDS: A HIERARCHY

TO THE INSTRUCTOR:

I.   Introduction--This is an exercise that should help students understand Maslow's hierarchy of needs. The goal is to have students examine their own experiences and find ways in which they satisfy needs at each of the five levels. They should use everyday examples such as the following:

    A.   Physiological needs:

        1.   the need to get a sweater when the classroom is cold

        2.   the need to get a cup of coffee after a "long, hard class"

    B.   Safety needs

        1.   stocking up on canned tuna so it will be there when needed

        2.   putting a double lock on the front door

    C.   Love and belonging needs:

        1.   joining the French Club at college

        2.   checking on your best friend when he/she is sick

    D.   Esteem needs:

        1.   working hard to get good grades

        2.   helping mother with dishes after supper

    E.   Need for self-actualization:

        1.   taking dancing lessons to be better at it

        2.   volunteering to work with handicapped children at the park district pool

II.   Procedure

    A.   Pass out the worksheets to students to use for this exercise.

    B.   Group the students in threes so they can discuss their experiences and select those that fit each level more easily.

    C.   Ask students to produce their own list after sharing and discussing their ideas. Each student should produce his/her own list.

    D.   Allow about ten minutes for this part of the exercise, then ask them to return to their own places.

    E.   Now ask the students to evaluate these levels and try to see where they are at the present time. Each student should try to determine the level at which he/she has the most difficulty and why. They should be asked to explain this in the space provided at the end of the worksheet.

    F.   Have students turn in the worksheet for your review. You should not grade the sheet, but read it and make supportive comments on what is said. You will learn a good deal about your students from this exercise.

HIERARCHY OF NEEDS: A WORKSHEET   STUDENT'S NAME_____

TO THE STUDENT:

In the space provided, try to identify and record some things that you do which are intended to satisfy needs at each level. Provide several examples of each. You can discuss this with your group members, but put down your own behavior, not theirs.

1.   Physiological needs

2.   Safety needs

3.   Love and belonging needs

4.   Esteem needs

5.   Need for self-actualization

Indicate the level of needs that you feel takes up most of your time and energy at the present time. At what level do you find yourself functioning most of the time? Explain what you do at that level and why it is keeping you occupied at present. (Use back of page.)

Exercise #3: Personal Fears

TO THE INSTRUCTOR:

I.   Introduction

This exercise is intended to get students to think about their own fears. Fears can be a serious problem if they affect the quality of life of an individual. Often people don't face up to their fears but instead develop a lifestyle that avoids confronting situations that might cause feelings of fear to occur.

In doing this exercise students can, in a non-threatening way, assess their fears and try to evaluate the effect they have on their lives. If they are willing to share some of these with the class, they will have an opportunity to think them over and perhaps do something to change.

II.   Procedure

A.   Hand out to students a copy of the fear intensity scale which follows this exercise.

B.   Ask students to record on the scale those fearsome things, events, or situations that they can think of. They should place these items on the scale where they think they should fall. Each item should be clearly stated.

C.   Students should then be asked to think about ways to reduce the fears. Begin with the top item and work down.

III.   Discussion

A.   Start off some discussion in class by asking students to volunteer to give their top-rated fear. If a cooperative environment exists, students will try to help each other with suggestions.

B.   Be sure to bring in some psychological principles. You could have them explore the possibility of using techniques for extinction of unwanted behavior and reinforcement and shaping of new behaviors.

C.   Either individually or in groups, students should think of ways to change this behavior. Ask them to write down ideas for changing their fear behaviors.

PERSONAL FEARS: INTENSITY SCALE

TO THE STUDENT: Indicate on the
scale the intensity of some of your
fears. Below write some of the reasons
for the more intense fears and some
ideas you have for changing them.

INTENSE   100-

          95-

          90-

          85-

          80-

          75-

          70-
STRONG
          65-

          60-

          55-

          50-

          45-

          40-
MILD
          35-

          30-

          25-

          20-

          15-

          10-
WEAK
          5-

Exercise #4: Words and Emotion

TO THE INSTRUCTOR:

I. Introduction

Words and numbers, as symbols, have no special significance in themselves besides their designated meaning. However, they take on added meaning and/or value as they are used in a culture. A number sequence such as 38-22-36 may have no special significance in itself, but when the number sequence is attributed to anatomical measurements, it takes on additional meaning. Word association techniques are used for diagnostic purposes because words are both motivational and emotional. Freud used word association in his psychoanalytic approach to behavior problems. Free association is initiated by words that have emotional content for the patient.

Some psychologists have found significance in not only the word or words used, but also to the length of time taken to respond and the behavior of the subject while responding. This exercise is designed to determine whether words which are emotional in content produce a different behavior from neutral words. For this study, the variable under observation will be the length of time between the stimulus word and the response.

II. Procedure

A. Make copies of the word list and data sheet for the students in the class.
B. Divide the class into groups of three. Ask each group to identify a subject who is immediately sent out of the room. The other two in each group should divide up the work to be done; one will be the experimenter and the other the timer.
C. Distribute a copy of the word list to each experimenter. Ask the experimenters to read over the directions while you read them aloud. Be sure both experimenters and timers know what they are to do. Review the role of each as follows:
    1. Experimenter - present one word at a time, waiting after each for a response from the subject.
    2. Timer - use a watch with a large second hand or a stopwatch. Note the period of time between the stimulus word and the reaction time. Do not stop timing until the subject has given a complete word. Utterances such as, "uh," laughter, remarks such as, "That's a tough one," are not responses.
D. Instruct the students to work out the average response time for the neutral words and the emotionally-laden words.

III.   Discussion

Some questions that can be raised with students should include the following:

A.   Was there any difference in response time between the neutral and emotional words? If a difference occurred, how do you account for it?

B.   Were there any differences between response times for the neutral words? Were reaction times to neutral words given after an emotional word any different than to those after a neutral word? If so, can you explain why?

C.   Does the level of association value make a difference in response time?

D.   If no significant differences occurred between the two means, does that mean that emotional connotations do not affect reaction time?

WORDS AND EMOTION: **WORD LIST**

TO THE EXPERIMENTER:

Read the following list of words to the subject, one at a time. Pause after each word to give the person time to respond. Give the recorder time to write the response and time. Emotion-laden words are designated by an asterisk (*).

Say to the subject:

   I am going to give you a list of words, one at a time. After each word say the first word that comes into your mind. My partner will write down what you say. Here is the first word.

        1.   cloud

        2.   rape*

        3.   leaves

        4.   chair

        5.   brother

        6.   failure*

        7.   flower

        8.   communism*

        9.   dog

        10.   abortion*

        11.   holiday

        12.   paper

        13.   table

        14.   chocolate*

        15.   groceries

WORDS AND EMOTION: **WORD LIST**

TO THE RECORDER:

Be sure to note the exact time (number of seconds) between the stimulus word given by the experimenter and the response of the subject. Also, make a note of the response in the appropriate place. Emotion-laden words are designated by an asterisk (*).

STIMULUS WORD	RESPONSE	RESPONSE TIME
1 cloud		
2 rape*		
3 leaves		
4 chair		
5 brother		
6 failure*		
7 flower		
8 communism*		
9 dog		
10 abortion*		
11 holiday		
12 paper		
13 table		
14 chocolate*		
15 groceries		

MEAN response time for: NEUTRAL WORDS   _____

                                 EMOTIONAL WORDS   _____

■ BROADENING OUR CULTURAL HORIZONS

1. **Some cultures encourage people to eat a sweet, fat, high-variety diet.** Other cultures encourage more savory, low fat, and less-varied foods. Ask students to study the eating habits of different cultures. Is the Far Eastern diet becoming Westernized? Or is the Western diet becoming Easternized?

2. **Ask students to bring to class the most unusual ethnic foods they can find.** Ask students to taste the foods; then have the provider describe the food and its cultural background.

3. **What cultures do you guess would have the least frequency of anorexia?** Why are most people with eating disorders female? As women play a more prominent role in business, will this gender difference change? How? Why or why not?

4. **What cultural biases may exist in the Zuckerman Sensation-Seeking Scale?** What assumptions does this scale make about human behavior?

5. **Make a list of all the ways a culture could reinforce social behaviors.** What social behaviors do you perform? How are these reinforced? Do different ethnic groups and subcultures encourage different social behaviors?

6. **Look at your own family culture.** What forms of success are you encouraged to work toward? Do you think that other cultures share the same goals or define "success" in the same way?

7. **Are Maslow's motives universal?** Imagine a culture where social needs were more important than self-actualization needs. How would you test the universality of self-actualization? Are there many different ways self-actualization can be expressed?

8. **Most colleges have an increasingly diverse student population.** Imagine that you are one of five student government leaders wanting to put together a recycling campaign. One student is a 40-year-old Indian man; another is a 25-year-old single woman; another is a 32-year-old white single father; another an 18-year-old man; and finally a 22-year-old married Japanese woman. How would you go about motivating this diverse group of people?

9. **Identify some ethnic churches in your area.** Arrange for some students to attend a wedding ceremony. Observe how the people in that culture celebrate a happy event. If several different ethnic churches have been visited, the students could then share their experiences and compare them with traditional American celebrations.

10. **Invite someone from a non-Western cultural background to come to the class to discuss love and marriage in his/her culture.** It is always interesting to discuss arranged marriages as are found in India or Korea.

11.   **Assign students the task of interviewing people from various cultures on how anger is typically expressed.** Find out what is socially accepted and what is not. Try to interview persons from places such as Central America, South America, Asia, the Middle East, Africa, Great Britain, etc. Compare the findings with the way anger is treated in North America.

■ SUPPLEMENTAL LECTURES

Lecture #1:

The concept of motivation, as that which initiates, sustains, and directs the behavior of an organism, can be presented to the students using the motivational cycle as a model. The following lecture is a development of the concept in a way that appeals to the eyes as well as the ears of the students.

MOTIVATIONAL CYCLE

I.   Introduction

    A.   Begin the lecture by discussing the notion of homeostasis as a way to understand motivation. This mechanistic idea of behavior as an attempt to find equilibrium sets up the idea that all behavior has a purpose.

    B.   Develop this idea that all behavior has a purpose. It is goal-directed. Its purpose is to satisfy the needs of the individual. It is easy to move on to discuss needs of the organism as motivators of behavior.

II.   Needs as Motivation

    A.   If behavior is motivated by needs of the organism, then the starting point is the need.

    B.   You can illustrate your explanation on the chalkboard by using a circle (cycle) as the basis. You will put the term "need" at one spot on the circle and at the same time define and explain the term. The definition should also be written on the board. At this point your chalkboard will look like this:

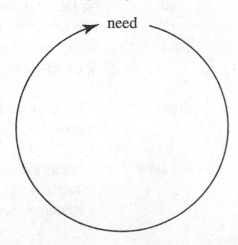

need-- a lack of something the organism has to have or wants for its well-being

C.   The need is a lack of something. You can use an example of eating behavior. The need is for nourishment. The organism lacks nourishment.

D.   A need usually gives rise to a drive, which is the urge to satisfy the need. In our example it would be hunger. When the body needs nourishment, we feel hunger, the urge to satisfy it. It would appear on the cycle as follows:

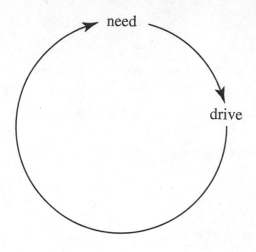

need-- a lack of something the organism has to have or wants for its well-being

drive-- the urge to satisfy the need

E.   Need and drive are distinct. We can need nourishment and not feel hungry. We can feel hungry and have the urge to eat when we don't need nourishment. Think about Thanksgiving dinner and the pumpkin pie (with lots of whipped cream) for dessert! However, need and drive do occur together most of the time, and the terms are often used interchangeably.

F.   The drive is what generates behavior. The urge to satisfy the need moves (motivates) the organism to do something (behave). Two kinds of behavior are generated. The first is to identify a suitable goal to satisfy the need. The second is to do what is necessary to achieve the goal. Here's what the cycle looks like at this point:

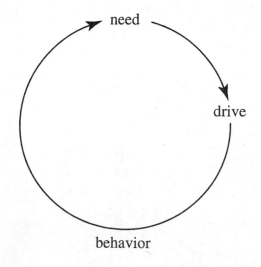

need   -a lack of something the organism has to have or wants for its well-being

drive   - the urge to satisfy the need

behavior   - identification of a suitable goal
            - attaining the goal

G.   The goal is whatever will satisfy the need. Let us say that the hungry student decides a cup of coffee and a donut in the cafeteria is a suitable goal. That is the first type of behavior. Then follows the second, actually going to the cafeteria, buying the goodies, and consuming them. The goal either eliminates or reduces the need, and the cycle is complete. It would look like this on the chalkboard:

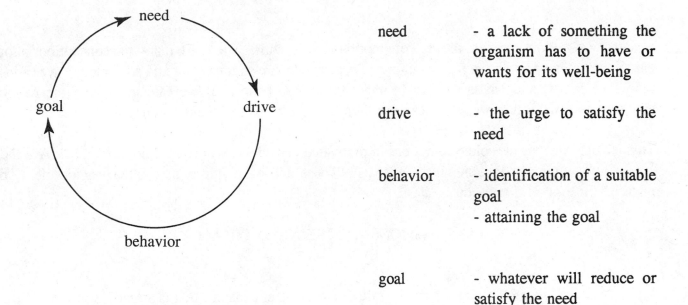

need   - a lack of something the organism has to have or wants for its well-being

drive   - the urge to satisfy the need

behavior   - identification of a suitable goal
              - attaining the goal

goal   - whatever will reduce or satisfy the need

III.   Discussion

A.   Students should be clear on the dynamics of needs as motivators. This approach helps them to see it. Try another example or two. If the students began to notice black smoke coming into the classroom through the ceiling vents, their behavior might seem automatic, but would, in fact, be motivated by a need and would be goal-directed. See if they can fill in the cycle.

NEED   -   This would be a need for survival--to save one's skin.

DRIVE   -   The urge would be to be somewhere else.

BEHAVIOR -   First, a split-second decision is made to head outside; that is the suitable goal.
              -    Then, you head for the nearest exit at top speed.

GOAL   -   The outside of the building, when attained, will satisfy the need for survival.

B.   Discuss what happens if unsuitable goals are selected. For example, what if the students decided to hide under their desks.

C.   Also, have the class consider what would happen if the need or drive were absent in those circumstances.

D.   The next session with the class should consider the types of needs: primary, stimulus, and secondary needs.

Lecture #2

Students are seldom clear on the role of emotions in behavior. There are many misconceptions about emotions that have appeared in our culture. Because they are so important and so personal, we cannot ignore emotions, and we should try to understand them better. If we can understand the role of emotions in behavior, perhaps we can use them more effectively to enrich our lives.

This lecture is about the role of emotions in motivated behavior. Where do emotions fit in? Are they a help or a hindrance to achieving our goals? These and other questions should provide plenty of material for a good discussion in class.

EMOTIONS--DO WE NEED THEM?

I.   Introduction

A.   This lecture deals with the role of emotions in behavior that is already motivated. That is, we are talking about goal-directed behavior, behavior seeking to satisfy a need. This idea is not clear to students.

A common misconception is that the emotion is the motivator. An example that students give is, "I was afraid of dying, so I ran out of the burning building." If you ask people why they ran, they will reply, "because I was afraid!" If you ask what motivated them to run, they will say it was fear.

As discussed in the needs theory of motivation discussed in this chapter, if it's true that all behavior is goal-directed to satisfy needs, then their reasoning does not seem to fit. Fear is not a need. Rather, fear seems to be aroused when a need already exists, in this case, the need to escape from a burning building in order to survive.

B.   Remind students of the definition of emotion as a state of arousal. The example above would sound more reasonable if we were to say that the fear aroused a person to act swiftly and expeditiously to exit the building. However, if fear is not the motivator, what is?

II.   Need reduction is the basis for behavior.

A.   Use the motivational cycle discussed in Chapter 10 as the model. A shorthand version of it could be drawn as follows:

NEED - DRIVE ⟶ GOAL

behavior

Notice that there is no place in this scheme for emotion.

Let us take our example again. If we insert into this model, "when I become aware of the fire and interpret it as dangerous to me," a need becomes apparent; a drive follows; goal-seeking and goal-attaining behavior is the result. What are these specific elements:

NEED - survival, to avoid pain and death.
DRIVE - the urge to leave the vicinity of the threat to my well-being.
GOAL - somewhere outside, preferably far away.
BEHAVIOR - two kinds of behavior usually occur at this point:
1.   looking for a suitable goal and means of getting there;
2.   doing whatever needs to be done to reach that goal.

B.   Let us look at the behavior portion of this model. It is important to my safety and well-being that I find a goal that will, in fact, save my life. Hiding under a table, or shutting my eyes won't do. Also, it is important that I move quickly to attain that goal. If I decide to rescue all my belongings before leaving, it may be too late. Therefore, I have to assess the urgency of the situation and act accordingly, even if my life savings are in jeopardy.

III.   Emotions to the Rescue

A.   What does the emotion of fear do for me? It makes it more certain that I will perform the necessary behavior to satisfy the need. No fear may mean that I identify and seek an unsuitable goal. The presence of fear strengthens and supports the behavior so that I will do what is needed to survive.

B.   The role of emotions could be diagrammed as follows:

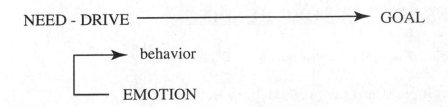

NEED - DRIVE ⟶ GOAL

behavior

EMOTION

C.   The role of emotions, then, is to strengthen and reinforce the already-motivated behavior to be sure the needs are adequately satisfied. An example, using the emotion of pleasure: We eat for nourishment, but the emotion of pleasure makes it more likely that we will pick a greater variety of foods, more nourishing food, and that we will spend the money to get it and go to the trouble to prepare it well. The hunger drive could be satisfied by something as simple as a few slices of bread, but we would not be well nourished. Pleasure at the taste of food gives us the necessary push to do better. We may know people who take no pleasure in food. They often eat irregularly and inadequately. Their bodies may not be adequately nourished.

IV.   Discussion

  A. It will be difficult for students to assimilate this concept because of long-standing erroneous ideas about emotions. You need to use several examples and help them to think them through.

  B. An objection students will raise is that emotions often are not helpful, as when one gets angry and breaks furniture, or punches or even shoots someone. Fear may cause someone to be petrified and he/she will not run from danger. Ask for some of these examples.

   This should open up a discussion of the effects of too little or too much emotion. Too little makes it less likely we will satisfy our needs adequately. Too much will also jeopardize our well-being. The discussion should center on use of emotions in moderation--only as much as needed to do the job. Too much pleasure can lead to overeating. Too much fear can lead to immobilization. Too much anger can lead to the destruction of a relationship.

  C. A good discussion can be held, and should be, on the way our society looks at emotions:

   1. Do we teach our children how to use emotions effectively?
   2. Do we tolerate emotional expression in our society? Under what conditions?
   3. How do cultures differ in how they encourage or discourage emotional expression? Talk about mourning for the dead in our society and in other cultures.

■ SUGGESTIONS FOR FURTHER READING

Bennett, W., and J. Gurin. *The Dieter's Dilemma*. Basic Books, 1982.

Berlyne, D. E. *Conflict, Arousal, and Curiosity*. McGraw-Hill, 1960.

Bolles, R. C. *Theory of Motivation*, 2nd ed. Harper and Row, 1975.

Brody, N. "Social Motivation." *Annual Review of Psychology*, (31) 1980: 143-168.

Darwin, C. *The Expression of Emotions in Man and Animals*. University of Chicago Press, 1965   (first published in 1872).

Ekman, P. and W. V. Friesen. *Unmasking the Face*. Prentice-Hall, 1975.

Geen, R., R. Arkin, and W. Beatty. *Human Motivation*. Benjamin Cummings, 1995.

Grossman, S. P. "The Biology of Motivation." *Annual Review of Psychology* (30) 1979: 209-242.

Kubler-Ross, E. *On Death and Dying*. Macmillan, 1969.

Lepper, M. R. and D. Greene. *The Hidden Costs of Reward*. Erlbaum, 1978.

Lykken, D. T. *A Tremor in the Blood: Uses and Abuses of the Lie Detector*. McGraw-Hill, 1981.

McGee, M. G. and M. Snyder. "Attribution and Behavior: Two Field Studies." *Journal of Personality and Social Psychology* (32) 1975: 185-190.

Orbach, S. *Fat Is a Feminist Issue*. Paddington Press, 1978.

Plutchik, R. *Psychology and Biology of Emotion*. Harper Collins, 1994.

Schultz, R. *The Psychology of Death, Dying, and Bereavement*. Addison-Wesley, 1978.

Seligman, M. "Fall into Helplessness." *Psychology Today*, June 1973: 43-48.

Spence, J. T. (Ed.). *Achievement and Achievement Motives*. W. H. Freeman, 1983.

Walster, E. and G. Walster. *A New Look at Love*. Addison-Wesley, 1978.

■ FILM SUGGESTIONS

CONSTRUCTIVE USE OF THE EMOTIONS (1970, University of California, 22 min.)
    This film reviews the different responses to anxiety and the apparent adaptability of most of them.

DEATH (1968, Filmakers Library, 42 min.)
    Documents the last days of a terminal cancer patient. Discusses psychological defenses used to face death and the reactions of family, nurses, and others.

EMOTION (1990, Coast Community College District Telecourses, 30 min.)
    Part of the *Psychology - The Study of Human Behavior Series*, this video illustrates the universality of certain human emotions.

EMOTIONS: FRIEND OR ENEMY (1954, Indiana University, 30 min.)
    This film discusses the importance of emotions for adaptation and contrasts this with their capacity to disrupt behavior.

EMOTIONAL STYLES IN HUMAN BEHAVIOR (1962, University of California, 24 min.)
    Relates emotional response to personality functioning.

GRIEF (1976, Carousel Films, 18 min.)
    This film discusses the nature of grief and grief therapy.

MARJOE (1972, Cinema 5, 88 min.)
    This is a documentary illustrating how an evangelist induces high states of arousal to motivate his
    audience.

MOTIVATION (1990, Coast Community College District Telecourses, 30 min.)
    Part of the *Psychology - The Study of Human Behavior Series*, this video describes what motivates
    people to think, behave, and make choices.

MOTIVATION AND SELF-ACTUALIZATION (1969, Psychological Films, 60 min.)
    This film discusses Maslow's hierarchy of needs and variables related to the attainment of self-
    actualization.

MOTIVATION: IT'S NOT JUST THE MONEY (1981, Document Associates, 26 min.)
    Through interviews with employees, managers, and behavioral scientists, the factors which contribute
    to satisfaction and productivity on the job are examined. As the film shows, it is becoming increasingly
    evident that while wages and benefits are important, a range of non-material needs must also be met
    by modern organizations. The film features a look at the Volvo plant in Sweden, where an innovative
    approach to manufacturing was established that better met the needs of employees.

NEED TO ACHIEVE (1963, Indiana University, 30 min.)
    Documents the research of David McClelland on various aspects of achievement motivation. It shows
    that people with a high need for achievement are moderate risk-takers.

A NEW LOOK AT MOTIVATION (1980, CRM/McGraw-Hill, 32 min.)
    Studies have shown that even when a job itself provides neither intrinsic nor extrinsic rewards, the
    social environment within an organization may provide an incentive to work. This film examines these
    needs as they are defined by David McClelland and illustrates the categories and personality types
    which are usually associated with each.

NONVERBAL COMMUNICATION (1976, Pennsylvania State University, 22 min.)
    This film features interviews with leading figures in the field. Stanley Milgram discusses the nonverbal
    cues involved in body language.

THE PSYCHOLOGY OF EATING (1978, Harcourt, Brace, Jovanovich, 29 min.)
    What motivates animals and humans to seek food? Why do we choose some foods and avoid others?
    Why do some people eat more than they need and become obese? These questions provide the
    framework for the consideration of the psychology of eating in this film. Illustrated research includes
    taste preferences in newborns, conditioned aversions, physiological responses to novel foods, and the
    capacity of animals to control their body weight by regulating the amount they eat.

THE SELF-MOTIVATED ACHIEVER (1967, University of Illinois, 25 min.)
>   In addition to covering some of the research on achievement motivation, this film shows how to enhance self-motivation.

WHAT HAPPENS IN EMOTION (1957, Indiana University, 30 min.)
>   This is a brief overview of physiological and behavioral changes in emotion.

WITHOUT WORDS: AN INTRODUCTION TO NONVERBAL COMMUNICATION (1977, Prentice-Hall, 23 min.)
>   Illustrates the role of nonverbal communication in daily life.

■ COMPUTER PROGRAMS: *Mind Scope*

Exercise 19, Signal Detection

Students participate in a signal detection experiment by making a decision about whether a particular stimulus, or "signal," is present in a complicated task. Students perform the task under two separate motivational conditions.

Exercise 9, The Stroop Effect

This exercise examines the phenomenon of automatization. It gives students the opportunity to examine their ability to turn off the attention that they normally pay to the orthographic features of words that are relevant to the skill of reading.

CHAPTER 11

Health, Stress, and Coping

■ BEHAVIORAL OBJECTIVES

The student should be able to:

1. Define the terms health psychology and behavioral medicine.
2. Light eight behavioral risk factors that can adversely affect one's health. Briefly describe the relationship between health-promoting behaviors and longevity.
3. Explain how health psychologists work to lessen behavioral risks to health. Describe the impact of refusal-skills training and community health programs on illness prevention.
4. Define the term wellness by listing five characteristics of wellness.
5. Explain the similarity between your body's stress reaction and emotion.
6. List five aspects of stress that make it more intense and damaging.
7. Describe burnout. List and describe the three aspects of the problem. Describe three things that can be done to help reduce it.
8. Give an example of how primary and secondary appraisal are used in coping with a threatening situation.
9. Explain how the perception of control of a stressor influences the amount of threat felt.
10. Differentiate problem-focused coping from emotion-focused coping and explain how they may help or hinder each other.
11. List and describe the two different kinds of frustration.
12. List four factors which increase frustration.
13. List and describe five common reactions to frustration (see Figure 11-6).
14. Explain how scapegoating is a special form of displaced aggression.
15. Describe and give an example of each of the following four types of conflict:
    a. approach-approach
    b. avoidance-avoidance
    c. approach-avoidance (include the terms ambivalence and partial approach in your response)
    d. double approach-avoidance (include the term vacillate in your response).
16. Define the term defense mechanism and discuss the positive and negative aspects of using them.
17. Describe the following defense mechanisms and give an example of each:
    a. denial   e. projection
    b. repression   f. rationalization
    c. reaction formation g. compensation
    d. regression   h. sublimation
18. Describe the development of learned helplessness and relate this concept to depression and attribution. Explain how helplessness may be unlearned.

19.   Describe the five problems which typically contribute to depression among college students.

20.   List the five conditions of depression and describe how it can be combatted.

21.   Discuss the relationship between life changes and long-term health. Describe the SRRS. Explain how hassles are related to immediate health and how acculturative stress can cause problems.

22.   Distinguish between psychosomatic disorders and hypochondria.

23.   List the causes of psychosomatic disorders and name several of the most common types of psychosomatic problems.

24.   Discuss biofeedback in terms of the process involved, its possible applications, and the contradictory evidence as to its value.

25.   Differentiate between Type A and Type B personalities.

26.   Be aware of the twelve strategies for reducing hostility and be able to apply them.

27.   Describe what a hardy personality is and list the three ways such people view the world.

28.   Explain the concept of the General Adaptation Syndrome. List and describe its three stages.

29.   Explain how stress affects the immune system and how control may be related.

30.   List the three categories of responses that are triggered by stress.

31.   Discuss the stress management techniques that can be used to diminish or break the cycle of stress responses. (Include a discussion of the effective ways to avoid frustration.)

32.   Define stereotyped response and give an example of it.

33.   Discuss three effective ways to avoid frustration and four strategies for coping with conflict.

34.   Distinguish between concentrative and receptive meditation.

35.   Discuss how concentrative meditation can be used as a self-control technique in reducing stress.

■ DEMONSTRATIONS, DRAMATIZATIONS, AND DISCUSSION

1.   **Although everyone has plenty of experience with frustration and can provide numerous examples,** creating a little frustration in class can dramatize the subject and encourage discussion. The music department on your campus may own a device called an Echoplex (or a similar device). Internally it has a continuous tape loop which allows auditory input to be delayed for short time intervals for replay. You will also need a microphone, a small amplifier, and a speaker. Connect and adjust the equipment so that a word spoken into the microphone is heard from the speaker with a delay of about one-half second. The resultant delayed auditory feedback makes it virtually impossible to speak into the microphone without tremendous interference and frustration. (This effect is similar to the interference caused by the echo of a poor public address system in a large auditorium.) Invite a student to the front of the class and ask him/her to tell the class some things about him/herself (college major, interests, what he or she has been doing for the last few days, etc.). The speaker should speak into the microphone, and the speaker volume should be as loud or slightly louder than his/her voice. Under these conditions, the speaker will stutter, stammer, and become thoroughly frustrated. Allow the tension to build, and then interview the student about the frustration experience.

2.   **Obtain a large, narrow-mouthed jar.** You will also need two metal rods about three-sixteenths of an inch in diameter and eighteen inches long. (These may be obtained at most hardware stores; welding rods also will work well.) Place a marble or ball-bearing in the bottom of the jar. In class, ask if someone would like to play a game. Tell the volunteer that he/she has one minute to use the metal rods to lift the ball out of the jar. The jar may not be picked up or touched; the lifting must be done directly with the rods. To make things more interesting you might offer to add five points to the student's last test score for succeeding within the time limit. Be sure to test the task first before using it in class to be sure it will work. If the dimensions are right, it hovers right on the edge of possibility--and is devilishly frustrating. Discussion can clarify conditions under which frustration is likely to occur.

3.   **To introduce the topic of conflict, it might again be valuable to create a little conflict in class.** Ask if someone would like to play a "game of chance" with you. Tell the volunteer that you are going to flip a coin. If it comes up heads, three extra points will be added to the student's last test score. If it is tails, five points will be subtracted from the last test score. Give the student a few moments to decide if he/she still wants to play. Then discuss the approach-avoidance conflict that has been created.

If the student declines or wins, ask if anyone else wants to play. Tell this volunteer that he/she must guess if heads or tails will appear when you flip the coin. If he/she guesses wrong, five points will be deducted from his or her last test score; if he/she guesses right, three points will be deducted. When the student says he/she does not want to play, tell him/her that choosing not to play will result in ten points being subtracted from his or her last test score. This should produce a good spontaneous display of emotion. Force the choice and discuss the conflict created (avoidance-avoidance). After demonstrations such as these, it is probably best to announce that three points will be added to each volunteer's grade for class participation and that the supposed effects of their decisions will be ignored.

4.   **Type A personality characteristics can be illustrated in this way:** Give each student three pages completely covered with random digits. (These can be duplicated from a table of random numbers.) Tell students that their task is to cross out as many single, odd digits as they can after you say, "begin." Start students and let them work for thirty seconds. Have students count the number of digits crossed out. Announce that students will get a second try at the task, and have each student write down his or her goal for the second trial. Give the class thirty seconds to work. Students should again record their scores and set a goal for the third test. This completes the demonstration, since it is not necessary to conduct the third test; the point of this exercise is the goal-setting.

On the board make a distribution of the number of digits students set as a goal for the third test. Research has shown that on similar tasks Type A's and Type B's do not differ on average performance. However, Type A's consistently set higher goals than Type B's. This pattern of goal-setting seems to reflect the Type A's preference for a rapid pace of activity. Students whose announced goals were at the top of the distribution are presumably Type A's; those at the bottom, Type B's. (Based on B. R. Snow. "Level of Aspiration in Coronary

Prone and Non-Coronary Prone Adults." *Personality and Social Psychology Bulletin* (4) 1978: 416-419.)

■ ONE-MINUTE MOTIVATORS

1. **Suddenly give students a pop quiz or lecture very rapidly.** They will quickly tell you that the quiz isn't fair or to speak more slowly. Use this to begin a discussion of stress.

2. **Ask students to interview each other,** making a list of activities found to be "boring," "relaxing," "fun," and "stressful." Most likely, many activities will be listed in different categories by different people. Discuss perceptual differences in primary appraisal.

3. **Put students in groups of six.** One person stands in the middle, and the other five put their arms around the waists of the people on either side. The person in the middle has five minutes to break out of the circle. Count backwards for the final 30 seconds. Usually you will see students increase the vigor of their attempts during the last few seconds. Caution students against expressing their frustration aggressively.

4. **Use a pillow to be the recipient of displaced aggression.** Ask students to think of someone they're angry at while briefly pounding the pillow. Do they feel better? Why or why not?

5. **Ask students to make an honest estimate of the amount they spend** on alcohol and tobacco for one week. Collect the amounts and total them; then multiply by 52.

■ CLASSROOM EXERCISE

The exercise which follows should provide students with a good deal of thought-provoking material. It is based on the idea that stress in a person's life can lead to a crisis, illness, and/or accidents. Changes in one's life, whether positive or negative, can be stressors. Because we live through these events one by one, we may not put them together or see how much stress we are under at any particular time. This questionnaire forces the student to look back over the past year to see what stressful events occurred. The Social Readjustment Rating Scale is reproduced in Chapter 11 of the text. It is Table 11-2. Students are asked to take from that list any events which they have experienced over the last twelve months. The total score can then be interpreted by the values given on the interpretation sheet.

Exercise #1: Stress in Your Life

TO THE INSTRUCTOR:

I.   Procedure

A.   Provide all students with a data sheet, an interpretation and reaction sheet, a Health Problems sheet, and a discussion sheet.

B.   Ask them to go over the list of life events in Table 11-2 of Chapter 11 in the text. It is the Social Readjustment Rating Scale (SRRS). They should pick out those events which apply to them and record them on the data sheet.

C.   Instruct students to get a total of the Life Change Units (LCUs) and proceed with the interpretation and reaction sheet.

D.   Finally, ask the students to check off the health problems from the list provided and arrive at a total.

E.   Ask students to complete the Discussion sheet and submit it with the figures for their total LCUs and their total health problems. This can be done anonymously.

F.   Select the 25% of the LCU scores that were the highest and the 25% that were the lowest. Find the average of LCUs from the high group and the low group. Find the average number of health problems for the high and low groups. See what differences there are, and let the class discuss these.

STRESS IN YOUR LIFE: **DATA SHEET**

TO THE STUDENT:

This data sheet consists of two parts. The first is an inventory of significant life events that you have experienced in the last twelve months. **Table 11-2 of Chapter 11** in your text lists forty-three life events which could add stress to your life. No doubt you could think of others. For this exercise, restrict yourself to those listed in the Table. You will see that each event has a value, stated in Life Change Units (LCUs). Go through the list in Table 11-2 and pick out those events which you have experienced over the past year (12 months). List them below with their corresponding units. Then total the LCU scores and compare yours with the standards given on the interpretation sheet.

SIGNIFICANT LIFE EVENT   LCU

_____   _____

_____   _____

_____   _____

_____   _____

_____   _____

_____   _____

_____   _____

_____   _____

_____   _____

_____   _____

                                                        Total   _____

STRESS IN YOUR LIFE: **INTERPRETATION**

Interpretation of the LCU score is based on samples of subjects who have been given the Social Readjustment Rating Scale. See if you fit the description of those who had scores similar to yours.

SCORE   DESCRIPTION

0 - 150   Persons scoring in this range should be suffering very little stress. Their chances of suffering illness or crisis are small.

150 - 199   Scores in this range indicate that you are experiencing MILD stress with a possibility of crisis or illness being fairly low—about 33%.

200 - 299   Scores in this range indicate a MODERATE stress situation. This could result in a greater possibility of accident, illness, or some other crisis—about 50%.

300 or more Those scoring in this range are experiencing high levels of stress and therefore run a much higher risk of crisis or illness. This is considered a major risk area—about 80% chance of experiencing some problems.

My LCU score _____

Reaction: Indicate how you feel about the significance of your score. Are you surprised? Did you expect it to be higher? or lower? Has this been a typical year for you?

STRESS IN YOUR LIFE: HEALTH PROBLEMS

Below is a list of health problems that are common in the population. You will recognize many as old friends. Try to think back over the past twelve months and see if you can recall having had some of these. Check off all of those that you can remember.

___ allergies	___ diarrhea	___ minor accident
___ appendicitis	___ earache	___ muscle strains
___ asthma	___ eye problems	___ nausea
___ athlete's foot	___ flu	___ nerves (anxiety)
___ backache	___ hay fever	___ sexual problems
___ blisters	___ headaches	___ shortness of breath
___ bloody nose	___ hearing loss	___ sinus problems
___ boils	___ hernia	___ skin disease
___ bruises	___ high blood pressure	___ skin rash
___ chest pains	___ hives	___ sleep problems
___ colds	___ indigestion	___ sore throat
___ constipation	___ injury to joints	___ stomach problems
___ cough	___ insomnia	___ tonsillitis
___ cuts	___ kidney problems	___ ulcers
___ dental problems	___ major accident	___ urinary problems
___ depression	___ menstrual problems	___ vomiting

TOTAL HEALTH PROBLEMS _____

STRESS IN YOUR LIFE: **DISCUSSION**

TO THE STUDENT:

Enter your LCU score and your total number of health problems in the space provided. Then write brief comments on the discussion questions.

LCU score   _____

Health Problems   _____

1.   In which of the four LCU categories did you find yourself? Does this seem to fit in with your idea about your stress level and possibility of crisis or illness?

2.   How does your level of health problems compare with your LCU score? Do you see any relationship between the two?

3.   Are you taking any significant steps to reduce the stress level in your life? Do you see any need to do so?

■ BROADENING OUR CULTURAL HORIZONS

1. **Poverty is the norm in many cultures,** and it is a continuing problem in the U.S. Discuss the helplessness that occurs with poverty. How do the poor feel? What can be done to help each of us feel less helpless in dealing with poverty?

2. **Rewrite the "Life Change Units" scale** in terms of the principal stressors of the poor. Would the stressors be the same as for others? Would the rankings be the same? Why or why not?

3. **What cultural values would encourage Type A behavior?** Type B behavior? More hardy personalities? Why?

4. **Some cultures, especially those marked by poverty and privation, place a high value** on stoicism and quiet tolerance of suffering. How does this compare with the hardy personality? How might it be adaptive? How is it unadaptive?

■ SUPPLEMENTAL LECTURE

This is a lecture on frustration and the reactions to it. The purpose is to show that:

1. We all experience frustration in daily life.
2. We look for ways to deal with the problems.
3. In the process of learning to cope with frustration and its consequence, anxiety, we develop rigid patterns of behavior; that is, we use the same means even when circumstances differ.
4. These coping mechanisms may be helpful but may eventually cause problems.

I. Introduction

    A. Begin this lecture by reminding students about needs as motivators. When a need is apparent and a drive is generated, one begins to search for a suitable goal and, on finding one, tries to attain it. Frustration occurs when an obstacle stands in the way of satisfying the need. Either no suitable goal is found or something interferes with its attainment. Draw the model on the chalkboard like this:

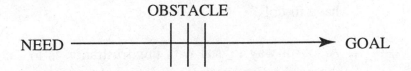

        OBSTACLE

        NEED ──────────────┤┤┤────────▶ GOAL

    Remind students that this is an everyday occurrence. Elicit some examples such as: your pen runs out of ink when you need to write; you can't find any gloves, and it's cold outside; you are late for work, and a freight train is slowly rumbling through the crossing.

B.   For our classroom example let us say that you have been studying in the library. It's 5:00 p.m., you are starving, and dinner will be on the table at home at 5:30 p.m. You head for the parking lot and find your car won't start. The model would now look like this:

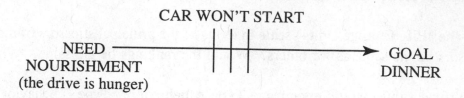

II.   Responses to Frustration

A.   Ask the class to think of the possible courses of action. The most difficult part of this example is to keep the students' attention focussed on the need for nourishment. They naturally begin to think of the need to fix the car. The question is, what about satisfying the need for nourishment, with the hunger drive as the motivator?

B.   Draw attention to the fact that there could be a number of ways to satisfy the need. See how many you can elicit from the class.

1.   Probably the most obvious way would be to remove the obstacle, that is, get the car started. Some trial and error behavior may take place, such as running down the battery trying the starter, looking at the engine and jiggling the wires, kicking the fender, crying, pounding the steering wheel; well, you get the idea!

2.   Another possibility would be to circumvent the obstacle. If you can get around it and reach the goal, your need will be satisfied. Call home and ask for a ride, hitchhike home, ride with a friend, walk home. In this way, the same goal is attained in another way.

3.   If the need is urgent and the goal seems unattainable, you might change the goal. A substitute goal can satisfy the need, perhaps as well as the original, or is at least better than nothing. In our example you might satisfy your hunger drive by heading for the college cafeteria and eating there. Or, you might get a candy bar from a machine. It may not be as good as home cooking but it will have to do!

4.   A fourth way to deal with this frustration is to abandon the attempt to satisfy the need. For example, if you need your car to get to work, it may be more urgent to get it fixed, so you don't eat at all, but attend to the car and go to work. Or, you may simply feel unable to deal with the problem and give up, neither eating nor fixing the car.

C.   Now the model looks like this:

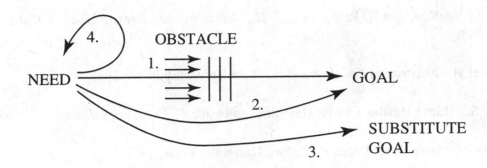

1.   Discuss this model. Ask students to think about which is the best way. They should, with your help, arrive at the conclusion that no one way is always best, that it depends on the circumstances.

2.   Help them to see that we need to be flexible so that when we are confronted with an obstacle, we can evaluate the situation and choose the best alternative for that circumstance. It will depend on what is possible.

3.   Students should be made aware that when important needs are frustrated, especially when it happens often, we tend to become anxious. Anxiety hampers judgment. We tend not to look carefully at all the alternatives. Often we fall back on what worked before, even though it may not be appropriate or adequate in this new situation.

4.   Inadequate and inappropriate responses to frequent frustration leads to more and new frustrations--and more anxiety. Over time, one can develop behavior patterns that are counterproductive.

D.   A Style of Coping--Flexibility may give way to rigidity, and rigidity results in maladaptive behaviors. Ask students to think about this. A good example is the mother who is annoyed with the children. She tells them to be quiet. They don't, so she shouts at them to be quiet. They keep misbehaving, so she yells some more. Eventually she has a screaming fit or hits them to get them to stop. Notice the rigidity in her behavior. She repeats a behavior that is not satisfying her need for peace and quiet, and finally resorts to a major maladaptive behavior to try to cope.

■ SUGGESTIONS FOR FURTHER READING

Cherey, L. "The Man Who First Names Stress." *Psychology Today*, March 1978: 64.

Davis, M., M. McKay, and E. R. Eshelman. *The Relaxation and Stress Reduction Workbook*, 3rd ed. New Harbiner, 1988.

Dollard, J., et al. *Frustration and Aggression*. Yale University Press, 1939.

Lazarus, R. S. "Little Hassles Can Be Hazardous to Health." *Psychology Today*, July 1981: 12-14.

Levi, L. *Society, Stress, and Disease*. Oxford University Press, 1971.

Mandler, G. *Mind and Body: Psychology of Emotion and Stress*. Norton, 1984.

Meichenbaum, D. "Stress-Inoculation Training." In *Cognitive Behavior Modification*. Plenum, 1977.

Schafer, W. *Stress, Distress, and Growth*. Responsible Action, 1978.

Selye, H. *The Stress of Life*. McGraw-Hill, 1976.

Woolfolk, R. and F. Richardson. *Stress, Sanity, and Survival*. Signet, 1978.

■ FILM SUGGESTIONS

HEALTH, STRESS, AND COPING (1990, Coast Community College District Telecourses, 30 min.)
> Part of the *Psychology - The Study of Human Behavior Series*, this video presents a discussion of Hans Selye's General Adaption Syndrome (GAS), stress and physical illness, and psychological stress.

LEARNING TO LIVE WITH STRESS: PROGRAMMING THE BODY FOR HEALTH (1979, Document Associates, 19 min.)
> This film contains interviews with two authorities in the study of stress and its effects on the human brain and body: Dr. Hans Selye, who introduced stress into the medical vocabulary, and cardiologist Dr. Herman Benson of Harvard. Both describe stress as a force causing heart problems, hypertension, and a multitude of other known and unknown threats to health.

MANAGING STRESS (1979, CRM/McGraw-Hill, 33 min.)
> This film takes a holistic approach to the study of stress, investigating both the physiological and psychological effects it may have. It is designed to help the viewer recognize common sources of stress, assess his or her own capacity to tolerate stress, and become more aware of alternative means of coping with stress.

STRESS: A DISEASE OF OUR TIME (Time-Life, 35 min.)
> Different types of stress are demonstrated in experiments, and their implications are discussed.

CHAPTER 12

Child Development

■ BEHAVIORAL OBJECTIVES

The student should be able to:

1. Define developmental psychology.
2. Name and describe four adaptive reflexes of a neonate.
3. Describe the intellectual capabilities and the sensory preferences of a neonate.
4. Discuss the concepts of maturation, readiness (principle of motor primacy), and practice (training).
5. Identify the three unlearned basic emotional reactions. Describe (in general) the course of emotional development according to Bridges. (Include an explanation of the interplay between the emotions of infants and adults.)
6. Explain what is meant by the nature-nurture controversy and give supporting evidence for each position. Discuss the outcome of this debate.
7. Explain the basic mechanisms of the transmission of heredity.
8. Define or describe each of the following terms:
   a. chromosome
   b. DNA
   c. gene
   d. polygenic
   e. dominant trait (gene)
   f. recessive trait (gene)
   g. sex-linked trait
9. Explain how sex is determined.
10. Characterize the three types of children according to temperament.
11. List the three factors which combine to determine a person's developmental level.
12. Distinguish between congenital and genetic problems.
13. Discuss the effects of environmental influences (including drugs and tobacco) on an unborn child. Include a description of the relationship between the blood supplies of the mother and her developing child.
14. Describe the fetal alcohol syndrome.
15. Explain how prepared childbirth differs from conventional deliveries and discuss the advantages and disadvantages of each. Include an evaluation of how important it is for the father to be present at the time of birth.
16. Briefly describe the Leboyer method of childbirth including the possible advantages and disadvantages.
17. Describe the range of effects of the maternal caregiving styles.
18. Discuss the importance of paternal influences in child development.

19. Explain the importance of self-awareness and social referencing in development.
20. Discuss the concepts of critical periods, imprinting and emotional attachment (including the concept of separation anxiety).
21. Differentiate between the three types of attachment identified by Mary Ainsworth.
22. Discuss the effects of daycare on children's sense of security and whether or not extended early contact is essential for mother/infant bonding.
23. Describe Harlow's "motherless monkey" research and its outcomes. Relate these findings to the importance of meeting a baby's affectional needs and to the incidence of child abuse.
24. List and briefly describe five stages of language acquisition.
25. Describe the "language dance" and explain why children probably do it.
26. Define the term psycholinguist. Describe the role of learning in the acquisition of language.
27. Explain how parents communicate with infants before the infants can talk. Include the ideas of signals, turn-taking, and parentese.
28. Explain how a child's intelligence and thinking differ from an adult's. Explain the concept of transformation.
29. With regards to Piaget's stages of cognitive development,
    a. explain the concepts of assimilation and accommodation.
    b. list (in order) and briefly describe each stage
    c. evaluate the usefulness of Piaget's theory including a review of current research on infant cognition.
30. Regarding moral development in humans,
    a. list (in order) and briefly describe each of Kohlberg's three levels (six stages) of moral development
    b. describe how Kohlberg's moral development levels are distributed among the population
    c. explain Gilligan's argument against Kohlberg's system, and describe the current status of the argument.
31. Compare, contrast, and give examples of the effects of enrichment and deprivation on development. Include a description of the two factors or elements in early deprivation.
32. Describe the effects of poverty on emotional and intellectual development.
33. Describe Harlow's experiment dealing with contact comfort, and state the results of the experiment. Relate his findings to the merits of breast and bottle feeding.
34. Discuss the effects of deliberate enrichment of the environment in infancy.
35. Describe the benefits of early childhood education programs (e.g., Headstart).
36. Describe White's practical advice on effective parenting for each of the following areas:
    a. attachment
    b. overindulgence
    c. the outside world
    d. respecting individual variation (include a differentiation between the statistical child and the particular child)
    e. enrichment
    f. responsiveness
    g. forced teaching

37. Describe the methods of encouraging intellectual development in children at each of Piaget's cognitive stages.

38. Define, describe and discuss the social implications of each of the following terms:
    a.   artificial insemination
    b.   in vitro fertilization
    c.   sex selection
    d.   genetic counseling
    e.   amniocentesis
    f.   eugenics
    g.   genetic engineering

■ DEMONSTRATIONS, DRAMATIZATIONS, AND DISCUSSION

1. **Given that Chapter 12 is concerned with development in childhood,** observing children at various ages makes a good outside assignment. Children may be observed at home, in a college preschool or day-care center, or at private nursery schools. Students should write a detailed description of a half-hour sample of a child's behavior, giving special attention to cognitive skills such as those described by Piaget. Such observations provide many examples of chapter concepts for class discussion. Prior to the observation, discuss with the class appropriate guidelines for behavior during objective observation.

2. **If you have willing parents in class,** arrange for an infant and a preoperational (four- or five-year-old) child to visit the class. With the infant you can demonstrate a lack of object permanence (or its presence, depending on the age of the child), by holding a toy in the child's view and then behind your back. Simple sensory-motor coordination and purposeful behavior will be apparent in the child's attempts to touch a desirable toy. Separation anxiety can be illustrated by having the parent briefly leave the room. Bring some props for the preoperational child so that you can demonstrate a lack of conservation of length, volume, or area. Conversations with preoperational children can be entertaining and instructive.

3. **Although few psychologists would deny the pervasive effects of heredity on development,** the general public often tends to over-emphasize hereditary effects. To illustrate, you may want to approximate a technique originated by David Rosenhan of Stanford University. Professor Rosenhan shows a slide of his two children and encourages students to note the ways in which the children resemble each other and him. Once students are thoroughly drawn in, he tells the class that his children are adopted! To make the same point you could show a slide of two unrelated persons and tell the class they are siblings; then, after discussion, reveal that they have no hereditary connection. Follow with a discussion of hereditary/environmental interactions.

4. **While deciding whether or not to become a parent is one of the most important decisions anyone will ever make,** it is surprising how little thought students have given to this subject. It is particularly surprising since the overwhelming majority of them will, in fact, one day

become parents. As a way to explore their motives for producing children, you could have students fold a sheet of paper down the center and on the left side list all the advantages of parenting and on the right side all the disadvantages. After they are finished, put some of their responses on the board and use them to generate a class discussion.

5. **Raise the question that is a burning issue today:** When is the developing organism a human being? The abortion issue and the Right-to-Life movement focus on this question. At what point between conception and birth is the organism human? Opinions will vary from the point of conception to the time when the fetus is viable. You should not try to convince students about your personal opinion. Rather, try to keep the discussion focused on the issue using as much scientific data as possible. One way to get students to step back from their positions, which may be somewhat hardened, is to ask them what scientific evidence they would require to change their opinions.

■ ONE-MINUTE MOTIVATORS

1. **Collect photographs of students taken during their childhood years.** Ask students to try to guess which classmate matches which childhood picture.

2. **Pass a lump of clay around the room.** Ask each student to note what it looks like when they first touch it and to mold it in some way. Continue lecturing during this process. At the end, point out that the lump's genetic material never changed, that its form often changed, and that each student made an imprint on the clay. Have the class explain how this demonstrates our own development.

3. **Conservation of volume can be easily demonstrated** with two glasses of unequal size. Ask students how to handle the following situation: Your four-year-old wants the same amount of milk as your eight-year-old receives. You only have two glasses of different sizes. How could you resolve this situation to the satisfaction of both children?

4. **Show the class four slides, 8 x 10 photos, or a short home video of a "family" composed of two unrelated parents and two unrelated children.** Ask the class to describe ways the children resemble each other and their parents. Students will try to be "helpful" and will find many similarities among the family members. Then explain that the children are not related to either each other or the adults. Discuss issues of heredity and environment. (This is a variation of the Rosenhan demonstration, described in the preceding section.)

■ CLASSROOM EXERCISES

There are two exercises which focus attention on some aspects of development. **The first** is a way to demonstrate conservation, or the lack of it. This exercise usually illustrates a difference in cognitive functioning between preoperational and concrete operational children. This one takes some preparation and planning. Children of appropriate ages need to be found and brought to class. It may be difficult to get a natural and normal response from young children when they are being observed by a large number of adults.

The second exercise demonstrates some hereditary characteristics. No props or preplanning is needed. This exercise will provide a natural opportunity to discuss dominant, recessive, and sex-linked traits and characteristics.

Exercise #1: Conservation

TO THE INSTRUCTOR:

These demonstrations of conservation are certain to impress the students with the idea that there is a qualitative difference in the cognitive functioning of a preoperational and a concrete operational child. They will see, furthermore, that this change does, in fact, occur at about seven years of age, as Piaget theorized it would.

This exercise can be done individually by each student if he/she can find enough subjects of the right ages. However, it would probably be easier to import a group of children for the class period. Students will probably have enough brothers, sisters, cousins, or neighbors of the right ages to do the project. Ask members of the class to volunteer to bring a child. This will take some planning since students will have to get the child's consent, the agreement of the parents, and permission from their schools to be absent on that day.

I.   Preparation

    A.   Get students to volunteer to bring the subjects. You will need ten altogether, a boy and a girl at each of the following ages: 5, 6, 7, 8, and 9. Set up a day and a time for the children to be at the school. The student or parent should bring them.

    B.   Prepare a set of materials ahead of time. You will need two short, fat beakers filled with colored liquid (use food coloring); and one tall, thin beaker; two large balls of modeling clay; and ten square cubes (these can be small toy blocks).

    C.   On the day of the exercise seat the students and the children in a way that will be non-threatening and make the children comfortable. Have the class and the children talk a bit, perhaps even mingle so they get used to each other. The students should have been prepared ahead of time to observe these children to see how they behave. Does their behavior square with the theories about what is appropriate for their ages?

D.   Select a student to be the experimenter ahead of time. Be sure he/she has run through the experiment a few times to be ready for whatever happens. You can play the child's role for the practice session.

II.   Demonstration

A.   Remove the children from the room and set up the three exercises. They will be presented to each child one at a time. The experimenter should be trained so that he/she knows what to expect. Provide each student with a Data Sheet.

B.   Bring the children in one at a time, starting with the youngest, and have them do each of the three exercises. The students in the class are observers and should record on the Data Sheet what they observe unobtrusively so that they do not disturb the subject.

C.   When all subjects have been tested, they should be assembled again, given a treat (the whole class should give themselves a treat), and sent on their way home. The students should look over their results and, on the next class day, discuss the observations.

III.   The Three Demonstrations

A.   Place the two short, fat beakers, filled almost full of liquid in front of the subject. Ask the subject, "Are they both the same, or does one have more than the other?" The child will reply that they are both the same. If he/she says one has more and one less, then pour a little from one to the other until the child says they are the same.

Now pour the liquid from one of the beakers into the tall, thin one. Ask the child, "Are they both the same, or does one have more than the other?"

If the child says the tall one has more, do not argue or question the child further, but, instead, simply pour the liquid back into the short, fat beaker. Again ask if they are now the same. After an affirmative answer, pour the liquid into the tall, thin glass and ask the question again. See if you get the same response.

B.   Place the two round balls of modeling clay in front of the subject. Ask the child, "Are the two balls of clay the same size, or is one bigger than the other?" When you have an affirmative answer, take one ball and, in full view of the subject, roll out one into a long, thin shape, like a sausage. Now ask the child, "Are they the same, or is one bigger than the other?" This one need not be repeated regardless of the answer.

C.   Place the ten blocks in two rows of five each in front of the child. Ask the child, "Do the two rows have the same number of blocks, or does one have more than the other?" After you get an affirmative answer, spread out the blocks in one row so the five blocks make a row about twice as long as the other five-block row. Now ask the child, "Do both rows have the same number of blocks, or does one have more than the other?" This one need not be repeated.

IV. Discussion

A.   All observations should have been recorded by the students on their data sheets. It should have been evident at what age the change took place on each of the three tasks. You can also see if there were any differences between the boys and the girls.

B.   What can you conclude about conservation in children?

C.   Would the results obtained here be the same for all children of the same ages?

CONSERVATION: **DATA SHEET**

TO THE STUDENT:

Record your observations on the chart. Indicate the responses for females (F) and males (M) separately for each age. Enter an S if the subject says the two are the same and a D if he/she says they are different.

AGE	LIQUID		CLAY		BLOCKS	
	M	F	M	F	M	F
5						
6						
7						
8						
9						

Exercise #2: It's In The Genes

TO THE INSTRUCTOR:

You can generate some interest in the genetic influences on behavior by a few simple exercises in the classroom. The purpose is to show the direct relationship between genes and behavior. Be sure to emphasize the point that practice does not improve one's ability to do any of the tasks. It's in the genes.

Try any or all of the following exercises:

1.   Tasting: This activity requires the use of paper soaked in phenylthiocarbromide (PTC). You can obtain this from the chemistry department.

Ask the students to place the treated paper on their tongues and report the taste. Although a variety of tastes may be reported, a significant number in the class will report a bitter taste. Those who do are called "tasters" because they have a dominant gene for this trait. Those who experience anything else are "non-tasters." They have a pair of recessive genes for this "taste" trait.

It has been estimated that about 70-75% of a typical class will be tasters. See how your class compares with this standard.

2.   Color blindness: Figure 4-15 in Chapter 4 of the text is a replica of the Ishihara test for color blindness. This is not a true test since the real color plates are of a different size and may differ in color quality. However, students can get some idea whether or not they are color blind. No doubt color blind persons will already know it, so this test will hold no surprises for them.

Ask the students to look at each of the sixteen plates and note what they see. When finished, have them check their responses with the information printed at the bottom of Figure 4-15.

If the class is big enough, you will almost certainly find one or more color blind persons. Students will likely know someone among family or friends who is color blind.

Ask students who are color blind to talk about their experiences. What were some amusing things that have happened to them? How do they handle traffic signals, clothing styles, color coding on forms and documents, etc.? They can recount many more such circumstances that could be problems.

Color blindness is recessive and sex-linked. This means that it appears more often in males than in females.

3.   Tongue curling: There are two ways a person can curl the tongue. The first is known as tongue rolling. The second is tongue folding.

In tongue rolling the person sticks the tongue straight out and turns the sides of the tongue up to form a U-shape.

In tongue folding the person folds the tip of the tongue back to touch the back of the tongue.

Some can roll and fold their tongues; others cannot. Those who can have a dominant gene, and those who cannot have the double recessive.

4.   Attached earlobes: A quick check of the students will verify the statement that not all earlobes are alike. They take on various shapes and sizes, some being very small and others large. However, a few people have what are called "attached" earlobes. This means the lobes are nonexistent, and the bottom of the ear slopes gently down to meet the neck.

Determine the proportion of persons in the class with attached earlobes. The number will be small. It is a recessive trait so it will appear in about 20-25% of the population.

Students could trace one of these traits in their family. As an additional exercise ask them to check among their relatives and try to draw up a family tree identifying those who had the trait. Tracing attached earlobes can be amusing and instructive.

(Based on a demonstration by Dr. William C. Titus, Arkansas Tech University)

■ BROADENING OUR CULTURAL HORIZONS

1.   **Ask students to collect information on the Israeli kibbutz system of child-rearing.** What are the advantages and disadvantages of this system?

2.   **Different cultures "see" children in different ways.** How do you view children? Circle the number that is closest to your views:

I see children (age 5 to 12) as:

big babies	1	2	3	4	5	*little adults*
helpless	1	2	3	4	5	*responsible*
dependent	1	2	3	4	5	*independent*
fragile	1	2	3	4	5	*sturdy*
not smart	1	2	3	4	5	*very smart*
self-centered	1	2	3	4	5	*other-directed*

Share your views with others in class. In what ways are your views similar and different?

3.   **Often step-families blend two very different "cultures" in terms of rules and expectations of behavior.** What would you suggest that step-families do to minimize the cultural shock as the families merge?

4.   **Research suggests that certain facial expressions are universally expressed.** What does this suggest about the possibility of effective international communication?

5.   **If any of your students are bilingual, ask them to discuss the advantages and disadvantages they have encountered.** If any of your students are visiting from other countries, or if they are recent immigrants, ask them to tell how child-rearing practices are different in their home culture.

■ SUPPLEMENTAL LECTURE

This lecture is on the principles that guide the developmental process. They may appear to be self-evident but need to be stated and discussed to be sure that students know and understand them. Once they have been stated and explained, students should be asked to see how they apply to each of the five areas of development.

Before this lecture students should already have been prepared, in a previous class session, with the following:

   1.   A definition of development--the process of change that occurs from conception to death;
   2.   The stages of development--prenatal stage, infancy, childhood, adolescence, adulthood, old age;
   3.   The five areas that developmental psychologists study:
         a.   physical
         b.   cognitive
         c.   personality
         d.   social
         e.   moral.

The above topics should have been discussed sufficiently to provide students with an orientation to the subject matter. The following discussion of principles of development will finish the introductory material and prepare students for a discussion of the major theories.

PRINCIPLES OF DEVELOPMENT

I.   Introduction

      A.   Explain that psychologists have found that development follows some rules, principles, guidelines, or whatever you want to call them. These principles guide or direct development in all five areas.

B.   Review the five areas of development to be sure everyone is clear on what you are talking about.

C.   The guiding principles are most evident in physical development because we can most easily observe and measure in that area. Arnold Gesell and his researchers developed the data to support these principles in the physical area.

D.   As theories emerged and were developed in the other four areas, it became evident that the principles applied to them as well. As you discuss the various theories, you should refer back to these principles.

II.   Guiding Principles

Explain and discuss each of these. Be sure to look at the implications so that students can relate them to their own experiences and observations.

A.   Nature-nurture: This means that both heredity and environment play a part. Discuss the relative contributions of each. Students should be aware that their relative influence will vary in each area and at different stages of development.

B.   Sequential development: Development occurs in a sequence that is predictable and is the same for all members of a species. This is clearest in the physical area where an infant develops the ability to stand before it walks, and walk before it runs, etc. It is less evident but holds true in other areas as well, e.g. Piaget's stages of cognitive development follow a sequence.

C.   Growth rates: The rate or speed with which each individual moves through the sequence varies from one individual to another. This means we should not expect any two children of the same chronological age to be at the same point in the developmental sequence in any of the five areas. An important point to be made here is that the rate is the result of many factors, genetic and environmental, which are outside the control of the child. Yet parents, teachers, and others often make comparisons among children and make judgments about their intelligence or learning capacity based on these comparisons, with possible disastrous consequences.

D.   Readiness: The child needs to have all of the essential structures in place and all previous steps established before a new step can begin. An example is that of a child standing. This cannot be done until the bones can support the weight, the muscles control the skeleton, and the nerve fibers transmit the appropriate messages.

E.   Optimum time: This refers to the best time for a new behavior to occur. Some authors call this the critical period or the sensitive period. For critical period, refer to Lorenz's story about the imprinting of the "following" behavior of ducks. It is the only time that the behavioral change can occur.

The sensitive period is the best or optimum time for the change to occur. Usually it is difficult or impossible to do it earlier and difficult or impossible later. The best time is when the child is "ready"--the readiness is all important.

A good example of optimum time is in language development. A child learns its native language with relative ease in the four years between ages one to five. However, when he/she reaches high school and tries to learn a second language in four years, it is a different story. Why wouldn't an older, wiser, more experienced person learn more easily and faster? The high schooler is well beyond the optimum time! Many adults who try to learn a second language never can pronounce it correctly or use proper grammar, yet a young child can learn two or more languages and speak them correctly and fluently. The optimum time for language development is the first five years of life!

III.   Discussion

A.   Students should be asked to look at the effects of "hurrying" children through the developmental sequence. Some parents want to move their children along faster to give them a head start or to make them appear to be gifted or talented. This should provide material for a good, lively discussion. For a more thorough look at this problem, suggest that students read *The Hurried Child* by David Elkind.

B.   See if students can see how starting all children off at the same age in school is contrary to developmental principles. Should all children begin reading at age six and arithmetic at age seven? Should they all play Little League Baseball at eight? Should they all start anything at the same chronological age?

C.   How should schooling be handled to take into account these developmental differences and to capitalize on readiness and optimum time?

D.   How can developmental level be determined in order to take advantage of readiness? This will give you an opportunity to discuss developmental tests, whether psychological or physical (such as x-rays of bone development).

■ SUGGESTIONS FOR FURTHER READING

Bartz, W. R. and R. A Rasor. *Surviving With Kids*. Ballantine, 1980.

Curtiss, S. *Genie: A Psycholinguistic Study of a Modern-Day Wild Child*. Academic Press, 1977.

Dworetzky, J. P. *Introduction to Child Development*, 5th ed. West Publishing Co., 1993.

Flavell, J. H. *Cognitive Development*, 3rd ed. Prentice-Hall, 1993.

Ginsberg, H., and S. Opper. *Piaget's Theory of Intellectual Development.* Prentice-Hall, 1969.

Hall, E., M. Perlmutter, and M. Lamb. *Child Psychology Today.* Random House, 1982.

Harlow, H. F. and M. K. Harlow. "The Effect of Rearing Conditions on Behavior." *Bulletin of the Menninger Clinic,* September 1962: 213-224.

Kagan, J. *The Growth of the Child: Reflections on Human Development.* W. W. Norton, 1978.

Miller, G. A. *Spontaneous Apprentices: Children and Language.* The Seabury Press, 1977.

Pines, M. "Superkids." *Psychology Today,* January, 1979: 53-63.

Restak, R. M. "Newborn Knowledge." *Science 82,* Jan./Feb., 1982.

■ FILM SUGGESTIONS

BABYMAKERS (1980, CRM/McGraw-Hill, 43 min.)
     This film explores the many controversies surrounding artificial insemination, egg-embryo manipulation (babies created outside the body--"test-tube babies"), and the use of surrogate mothers. It also offers unusual footage of the actual freezing of embryos.

CHILD'S PLAY (1976, Harcourt, Brace, Jovanovich, 20 min.)
     This film provides an introduction to the aims, methods, and perspectives of the developmental psychologist. Through a wide variety of scenes of children at play the film shows how children work out and practice their relations with others and with their world, and how they acquire increasingly complex perceptions of themselves.

COGNITIVE DEVELOPMENT (1990, Coast Community College District Telecourses, 30 min.)
     This film explores cognitive development and Piaget's theories.

A CROSS-CULTURAL APPROACH TO COGNITION (1976, Harper and Row, 27 min.)
     This film illustrates Piaget's cognitive stages using children from Japan, Guatemala, and Kenya.

DEVELOPMENT (1971, CRM/McGraw-Hill, 33 min.)
     This film presents a sampling of the current research methods in the study of human psychological development. Featured are a number of different areas of study and the psychologists who work in these areas. Included are Jerome Kagan demonstrating inborn motor reflexes and some of the more complex perceptual responses in experiments with infants. Also shown is Mary Ainsworth's "strange situations" experiment in which a mother and child are placed in a room alone with toys for the child.

EVERYBODY RIDES THE CAROUSEL (1980, Pyramid Film & Video, 72 min.)
     This video presents psychologist Erik Erikson's theory of personality development, using delightful animation. The eight stages of life are presented in three main parts: infancy to childhood, school-age to young adulthood, and maturity to old age.

PARENTS AND CHILDREN (1979, Research Press Films, 24 min.)

This film examines the parent-child relationship as a special learning experience in which the purposeful use of rewards plays a crucial role. Concepts presented in this film include:
1) how and when to use rewards effectively; 2) attention, activity, and material rewards;
3) strengthening or maintaining good behavior; 4) teaching new or complex behavior; and
5) eliminating undesirable behaviors.

PIAGET ON PIAGET (1977, Yale University, 42 min.)

Piaget's ideas and writings have been influential throughout the world in the study of child development and in education. In this film, he clarifies certain concepts and corrects some misunderstandings about his ideas. For example, Piaget sets forth his ideas on the nature and grounds of knowledge, as seen in some of the classic experiments in his research with children.

NEWBORN (1978, Filmakers Library, 28 min.)

This film documents the amazing capabilities of the newborn. It demonstrates the infant's readiness to face challenges, perceive its environment, and establish its individuality. Neonatal researchers Barry Brazelton, Lewis Lipsitt, and Louis Sanders demonstrate the components of normal infant development and how these are measured.

ROCK-A-BYE BABY (1972, Time-Life, 30 min.)

The film examines some of the techniques used by psychologists to measure mothering practices around the world. Children raised in orphanages, who have not been cuddled and carried, become listless and withdrawn. The film shows that even monkeys raised in isolation from their mothers develop human-like schizophrenia. The film suggests that from birth to about three years, the mother-child relationship is critical in human development.

WALK BEFORE YOU RUN (1989, Access Network, 29 min.)

This video demonstrates through a dramatization how students differ in their development and thinking skills at different ages.

CHAPTER 13

From Birth To Death: Life-Span Development

■ BEHAVIORAL OBJECTIVES

The student should be able to:

1. List the life stages experienced by all people.
2. Define developmental task.
3. Explain, according to Erikson, how the resolution of the psychosocial dilemmas affects a person's adjustment to life.
4. State the nature of the psychosocial crisis and the nature of an adequate or inadequate outcome for each of Erikson's eight life stages. Match each crisis with the corresponding age range.
5. Compare and contrast the following three parenting styles and their effects on children:
    a. authoritarian
    b. overly permissive
    c. effective (authoritative).
6. Discuss the positive and negative aspects of stress on a developing child.
7. List and describe (where applicable) nine "normal" childhood problems.
8. Give a brief description of the following childhood disorders and their possible causes:
    a. enuresis
    b. encopresis
    c. overeating
    d. anorexia nervosa
    e. pica
    f. delayed speech
    g. stuttering
9. Describe what the label "learning disability" includes.
10. Briefly describe the disorders *dyslexia* and *ADHD* in terms of symptoms, causes, and treatments.
11. Describe childhood autism in terms of symptoms, causes, and treatment.
12. Describe the characteristics of abusive parents and the conditions likely to foster abusive behavior.
13. Describe what can be done to prevent child abuse.
14. Define and differentiate between the terms adolescence and puberty.
15. Discuss the advantages and disadvantages of early and late puberty for males and females.
16. Explain what Elkind means by children being "hurried into adulthood." Explain how social markers are related to "hurried" adolescence.
17. With regards to the adolescent search for identity:
    a. explain what that means;
    b. discuss the importance of imaginary audiences;
    c. describe the interactions between an adolescent and his/her parents and peers as identity formation occurs; and,
    d. explain how being a member of a minority influences the identity search.

18. List and describe the four broad phases (and any stages therein) of career development.
19. State the single best predictor of the job category a person will enter. In addition, describe the two steps which aid a person in selecting a realistic and rewarding vocation. Include the influence of vocational counseling.
20. Generally describe the pattern of adult life stages proposed by Roger Gould.
21. Describe what a midlife crisis is and how it can be both a danger and an opportunity. Explain what a transition period is.
22. Distinguish between menopause and the male climacteric, and describe the typical reactions to each.
23. Contrast biological aging with our society's expectations of aging. Include a description of the differences between fluid and crystallized abilities.
24. Differentiate the concepts maximum life span and life expectancy. List six suggestions for increasing life expectancy.
25. Describe and distinguish between the disengagement and activity theories of aging.
26. Describe what is meant by the term ageism.
27. List the myths of aging refuted by Neugarten's research as will as Ryff's criteria of well-being in old age.
28. Regarding our emotional reactions concerning death,
    a. explain what people fear about death and how they cope with that fear;
    b. list and briefly characterize the five emotional reactions typically experienced by people facing death;
    c. explain how knowledge of the reactions to coping with death is important; and
    d. describe the general reaction of people who survive a near-death experience (N. D. E.).
29. Discuss the general characteristics of each stage of the bereavement process. Explain how suppressing the grieving process is related to later problems.
30. Name the two most important areas of parent-child relationships.
31. Explain the importance of consistency in disciplining children.
32. Give a brief description of each of the following child-rearing techniques and describe their effects on children:
    a. power assertion
    b. withdrawal of love
    c. child management (include the concept of self-esteem)
33. List seven guidelines that should be followed if physical punishment and/or withdrawal of love are used in disciplining a child.
34. Briefly describe each of the four basic ingredients of a positive parent-child relationship.
35. Describe the four methods which can be used to improve communication between parents and children.
36. Describe the philosophy and functions of hospices.
37. Explain the purpose of a "living will."
38. Define the terms active euthanasia, passive euthanasia, and cryonics.

■ DEMONSTRATIONS, DRAMATIZATIONS, AND DISCUSSION

1. **The topics of alternative birthing practices and maternal-infant bonding are approached by many students with vehemence and polarization.** Given that feelings are strong, a debate or panel discussion can be quite interesting. Try to involve students who have had experience with alternative birth procedures, who work in medical settings, or who have a strong interest in the topics (e.g., prospective parents). Ask each to do research and find evidence for his or her position before the discussion is held.

2. **If your community has an Adopt-a-Grandparent program, a Gray Panthers group, Council on Aging, or similar organization,** invite a speaker to discuss the problems of the aged and misconceptions about aging.

3. **For an interesting outside assignment or project on aging and changes over a lifetime,** ask students to interview one or more people from each of the following age brackets: 15-25, 35-55, 65 or up. Questions can deal with issues such as, "What is middle age?", "When does a person become old?", "Do you (or did you) look forward to retiring some day?, and "What has been the best period of your life so far?"

4. **To stir up a rousing discussion on parenthood, try reading this news excerpts to the class:**

    > BOULDER, COLO. (UPI)--Tom Hansen doesn't like the way his life has turned out and says it's because he was reared improperly. Hansen, 25, has filed suit against his mother and father, seeking $350,000 in damages because they reared him improperly and he will need psychiatric care the remainder of his life.

    What would the class consider evidence of "parental malpractice?" Should or could parents be held responsible for the way their children turn out? If placed in the position of the judge, would students hear the case? (It was thrown out of court.)

5. **Within a decade suicide has moved from fourth to second place** as the leading cause of death among American teenagers. Of the approximately 25,000 Americans who commit suicide every year, seven percent are between the ages of fifteen and nineteen. (It is estimated that there are twenty times that number of suicide attempts.) The class discussion could discuss these statistics and focus on the unique problems of adolescents. What are the problems? How do parents and schools contribute to them? How might the pressures on teens be reduced?

6. **For better or worse, psychology has had a sizable impact on widely held beliefs about child-rearing practices.** It is interesting to compare beliefs rooted in the experiences of various generations. A simple but highly informative project involves having students interview their own parents (or other parents of about their parents' ages) and their grandparents (or other adults who are roughly 60+ in age). The student should briefly record (in essay form) respondents' attitudes and beliefs regarding the following topics: breast

feeding, thumb-sucking, toilet training, proper discipline, a child's status in the home, and a child's capacity for early learning and the parents' role in early teaching. Students should also briefly summarize their own beliefs on each topic. Finally, students should discuss and compare the collected descriptions of child-rearing practices and relate them to the findings of contemporary psychology.

7. **A study by Handel examined two major components of personal theories** about the development of self over the life-span. Elements of the study can be replicated by asking students to write a brief autobiography and brief descriptions of themselves now, 5 years ago, 10 years ago, and 15 years ago. Students should then analyze their biographies for assumptions made about continuity and change. Comparisons should also be made between present self-perceptions and the three retrospective selves. Handel found that his subjects were impressed by the impact of chance events on their development. Also, progress toward actualizing a perceived "true self" stood out as a major criterion for evaluating the course of one's own development. (Handel, A. [1987]). "Personal theories about the life-span development of one's self in autobiographical self-presentations of adults". *Human Development*, 30(2), 83-98.)

■ ONE-MINUTE MOTIVATORS

1. **Bring a box of household items to class.** Put them on your desk. Divide the class quickly into groups. Give each group 3 minutes to devise ways that the items on the desk could be transformed into exciting toys for preschool children.

2. **Have a "T-shirt day"** on which everyone wears a shirt that has specific message printed on it. Ask students to state briefly why their message is important to them and how it helps to communicate their identity to others.

3. **Make a sign that says, "You are getting older and older minute by minute."** Place it near the classroom clock. A few times during the class ask students their age (to the minute). At the end of class remind students that "None of us will ever get these minutes back. I hope you feel we invested them well."

4. **On the day when aging is discussed,** ask students to bring a snack and a friend over 65. While discussing aging, solicit the ideas of your guests and end with a celebratory feast. Be sure to provide a name-tag for each guest, perhaps a flower, and perhaps even a banner saying, "In Celebration of Wisdom."

5. **To demonstrate a limitation of power assertion,** come to class with a number of objects of value to children and teens. Include a set of car keys. Ask one student to select those items that could be taken away from a 3-year-old, an 8-year-old, a 13-year-old, and finally an 18-year-old to encourage compliance to a parentally imposed rule. Plan the items so that the only item of value to an 18-year-old is the car keys. Remind students that it is primarily through

communication that one can encourage cooperation from many young adults. The ability to withdraw privileges can be limited.

■ CLASSROOM EXERCISES

TO THE INSTRUCTOR:

The purpose of these exercises is to get students thinking about the various stages of development. It is easy for people to lose sight of the fact that everyone is at some developmental level and that the level others are at may not be the same as the one they are at. It would help people to be more tolerant of others if they recognized this truth and accepted people at their own levels of development.

Exercise #1: Ages and Stages

The first exercise is based on Erikson's psychosocial stages.

Students are asked to evaluate people they know, using Erikson's descriptions of the stages of development. They need to be encouraged to look at the behaviors of the person first, then see what stage it fits into. The temptation may be to assume that the person is, in fact, at the stage which Erikson says is appropriate for his/her age. This may not be true. When the exercise is completed, it should be shared with class members. A good way to do this is to form groups of four. Ask the students to explain to each other what their subjects are like and why they chose to see them at the stages they did. See if the group members agree. If not, what changes would they make?

Exercise #2: Aging

The second exercise focuses attention on old age. There are many myths and stereotypes. People often see the elderly in those terms rather than as individuals who are all different, each living with and coping with a unique set of circumstances and problems. Most of all, students need to think of the elderly as persons and of old age as part of development.

The set of myths and stereotypes listed in the exercise are all false. Do a tally of the responses. See how many marked true for each item. Then ask students to explain their reasons. This should serve as a vehicle for a fruitful discussion on aging and old age.

■ BROADENING OUR CULTURAL HORIZONS

1. **Have students interview persons from various cultural backgrounds** to find out how they treat the elderly in their societies. The status of the elderly and who cares for the infirm should be part of the investigation. The findings should be shared with the class.

2. **Investigate the place that children occupy in a family setting in various cultures.** Compare the findings with the way children are raised in our culture.

3. **Talk with people from various cultural backgrounds about the relationships within the family.** Try to assess the extent to which family members are interdependent or independent.

4. **Find out from people of various cultural backgrounds** what is done in their culture about the care of very young children. Do mothers or fathers stay home? If both work, what provisions are made for children?

■ SUPPLEMENTAL LECTURE

IDENTITY STATUS

I. Introduction

A. Erik Erikson's stage theory of psychosocial development provides many opportunities for study and discussion. One of his stages that has been of great interest is the fifth, encountered in adolescence. He refers to this as identity vs. role confusion. This lecture is based on work done by James E. Marcia on identity status.

B. It is useful here to review the principles of development which were discussed in the last chapter and which were the subject matter of the Supplemental Lecture for Chapter 12 of this manual. Those principles apply at this stage of development as will be seen in this lecture.

C. Marcia proposes four identity statuses which he found in adolescents as they moved from childhood to adulthood. He suggested two criteria which determine the status of the adolescent:

1. Crisis: This refers to the extent to which an adolescent is actively involved in choosing alternatives. Any or all facets of one's life may be examined--occupation, beliefs, values, etc. may be under scrutiny.

2. Commitment: This refers to the degree of personal investment that the adolescent puts into the attitude, belief, or occupational choice (s)he is making.

II.   Identity vs. Role Confusion

   A.   Marcia studied adolescents and identified four identity statuses. Each have identifiable
          characteristics which he described. It is interesting to extend his idea and to see the
          four statuses as four stages of identity development which adolescents go through. In
          this way of looking at it we could think of Marcia having taken a "snapshot," catching
          his adolescent subjects at one or other of these stages.

   B.   Let us look at the statuses. By discussing them in the order which follows, we can see
          a sequence in terms of crisis and commitment.

          1.   Identity diffusion

                 a.   The adolescent is impulsive, disorganized, and shows very little self-
                        direction;

                 b.   may avoid getting involved in school work or personal relations;

                 c.   does not consider major issues--may appear to be avoiding them
                        altogether;

                 d.   has not thought much about a future occupation, sex role, or values.

          2.   Moratorium (identity crisis)

                 a.   The adolescent is aware of being in a crisis;

                 b.   has given thought to identity questions but has found no satisfactory
                        answers;

                 c.   is generally dissatisfied with high school or college, or whatever else
                        (s)he is doing;

                 d.   if in college, changes majors often;

                 e.   tends to daydream a lot;

                 f.   has intense, short-lived relationships with others;

                 g.   tends to reject parental values and ideals.

3.   Identity achievement

    a.   The adolescent has begun to make some commitments--may include a firm occupational choice, but probably not set on sex role behavior or religious values;

    b.   does not yet have everything in order in his/her life, but is working on it;

    c.   any trauma will bring back the identity crisis, but the hope of recovery and advancement is good.

4.   Identity foreclosure

    a.   The adolescent has no doubts about occupational choice, values, sex role, etc.;

    b.   often accepts and endorses the occupational choice, values, etc. of the parents;

    c.   may have made these decisions and choices at an early age and so has not been troubled with the identity crisis for any great length of time;

    d.   appears self-assured, knows where (s)he is going; is not troubled by doubts and fears.

C.   Role Confusion

1.   When the struggle for identity ends up in confusion, the adolescent may turn to defiant and destructive behavior. (S)he may develop a negative identity.

2.   Negative identity

    a.   This is characterized by a disdain for or a hostility toward roles and behaviors that are desired by the family and community. The adolescent may deliberately do what is forbidden.

    b.   (S)he may find it easier to identify with what should not be done than with what should be done. What is forbidden may be clearer and more evident than what is expected.

    c.   Punitive parents and society may then confirm the adolescent in these behaviors.

3.   Cults, gangs, etc.

     a.   One way to look at adolescents' participation in cults and gangs is as a way out of identity confusion.

     b.   Cults and gangs require a stable set of behaviors and relieve the member of choices and confusion which have caused intense anxiety.

     c.   Also, cults and gangs can be seen as a way of establishing a negative identity, doing the forbidden.

III.   Discussion

    A.   There should be plenty of opportunity to discuss Marcia's statuses since students can relate to these. Almost all students will see themselves in one or other of them. They will be able to identify where brothers or sisters are at, even parents.

    B.   Try to lead the discussion along the lines that there may be a developmental sequence here. Point out that all persons go through the four stages at their own rate. It is interesting to consider the moratorium phase. It is one that can be easily identified by students. Some will have passed through it, others will not. The question is, will they ever pass through it? In this context ask them to consider the "midlife crisis" as the moratorium stage. Does it fit the description by Marcia?

    C.   The concept of negative identity should be explored. Students will see it and understand it. Ask them to think about cults and gangs as examples of this. If this is true, then discuss what should be done about an adolescent who has joined a cult. Is deprogramming the way to go? What will happen once the adolescent cultist finds him/herself and his/her true identity?

■ SUGGESTIONS FOR FURTHER READING

Bettelheim, B. *The Empty Fortress: Infantile Autism and the Birth of the Self.* Free Press, 1967.

Comfort, A. *A Good Age.* Crown, 1976.

Elkind, D. *The Hurried Child.* Addison-Wesley, 1981.

Erikson, E. *Childhood and Society*, 2nd ed. Norton, 1963.

Erikson, E. (ed.) *Adulthood.* Norton, 1978.

Fischer, K. *Human Development: From Conception Through Adolescence.* W. H. Freeman, 1984.

Fontana, V. J. *The Maltreated Child*. Thomas, 1974.

Ginott, H. *Between Parent and Child*. Macmillan, 1965.

Gordon, T. *P.E.T.: Parent Effectiveness Training*. Wyden, 1970.

Kermis, M. *The Psychology of Human Aging: Theory, Research, and Practice*. Allyn and Bacon, 1984.

McKenzie, S. *Aging and Old Age*. Scott, Foresman, 1980.

Schaie, K. W. (ed.) *Longitudinal Studies of Adult Psychology*. The Guilford Press, 1983.

Williams, G. J. and J. Money. *Traumatic Abuse and Neglect of Children at Home*. Johns Hopkins University Press, 1980.

■ ADDITIONAL SOURCES OF INFORMATION

National Association of Anorexia Nervosa and Associated Disorders
Box 271
Highland Park, IL 60035

The National Association for Autistic Children
101 Richmond St.
Huntington, West Virginia 25701

Parents Anonymous
22330 Hawthorne Blvd.
Torrance, CA 90505

■ FILM SUGGESTIONS

ADOLESCENCE: THE WINDS OF CHANGE (1974, Harper and Row, 25 min.)
> This film considers the problems of growing up in the modern industrialized world, particularly the United States. The physical, sexual, and cognitive changes of adolescence are reviewed along with adolescents' responses to them. The film stresses the importance of democratic, authoritative child-rearing practices.

AGING (1985, Films for the Humanities and Sciences, 26 mins.)
> This film covers the physical processes of aging and examines the various body systems to see how and why they change as they age. It is shown that not all of the changes in older people are inevitable and that some, in fact, can be slowed down or reversed.

DEVELOPMENT OF THE ADULT (1977, Harper and Row, 25 mins.)

Examines adult crises and stages, social schedules, developmental differences between men and women, and the effects of culture on adult development.

GROWING OLD (1978, CRM/McGraw-Hill, 58 mins.)

This film discusses how adults see themselves and myths about old age. It emphasizes the importance of social support for the elderly.

SOCIALIZATION - MORAL DEVELOPMENT (1980, Harper Collins, 22 min.)

This video explores theories of morality and moral development through the demonstration of classic experimental work in social and developmental psychology.

THE ADULT YEARS - CONTINUITY AND CHANGE SERIES (1985, Pennsylvania State University Audio-Visual Services, 196 min.)

This is a seven-part series which explores the aging process as a complex mixture of continuity and change rather than a series of predictable steps or stages.

THE LAST OF LIFE (1979, Filmakers Library, 27 mins.)

"Our aim is to add life to years, not years to life," states Dr. Ronald Cape in this informative survey of the biology of aging and the emotional aspects of this stage of life. The film emphasizes that aging is not a disease but a normal part of development, and this is illustrated by a sequence of Rembrandt's self portraits in which he gradually grows older. Using micro-photography, the film also shows how the cells of the young differ from those of the old in their ability to multiply.

LIFE WITH BABY (1985, Filmakers Library, 27 mins.)

Every year children are neglected and abused by parents who are overwhelmed and feel that they can't do a good job. In this documentary, the viewer meets three families who are trying to adjust to the real life demands that a baby brings as well as the emotional impact.

TRANSITIONS (1979, CRM, 29 mins.)

This film examines the process of making major life changes and the personal, internal, and emotional adjustments required; focuses primarily on effects such changes have within work settings.

CHAPTER 14

Intelligence

■ BEHAVIORAL OBJECTIVES

The student should be able to:

1. Explain what the savant syndrome is.
2. Describe Binet's role in intelligence testing.
3. State Wechsler's definition of intelligence.
4. Explain what an operational definition of intelligence is.
5. Define the term aptitude. List and briefly describe the three levels of aptitude testing.
6. Define the terms validity, reliability, objective, and standardization as they relate to testing.
7. Generally describe the construction of the Stanford-Binet Intelligence Scale - 4th Edition.
8. Define the components of the Stanford-Binet intelligence quotient (IQ) and use an example to show how it was computed.
9. Differentiate between the Stanford-Binet IQ and deviation IQs.
10. Explain how age affects the stability of intelligence scores and how aging affects intelligence. Define the term terminal decline.
11. Regarding the types of intelligence tests:
    a. distinguish the Wechsler tests from the Stanford-Binet tests; and
    b. distinguish between group and individual intelligence tests.
12. Describe the pattern of distribution of IQ scores observed in the general population.
13. Describe the sex differences in intelligence.
14. Describe the relationship between occupation and intelligence.
15. Regarding Terman's study of gifted children,
    a. list five popular misconceptions concerning genius and their corrections; and
    b. explain how successful subjects differed from the less successful ones.
16. Explain why basing judgment of giftedness on IQ scores may be misguided.
17. Describe Gardner's broader view of intelligence and list the seven different kinds he discusses.
18. State the dividing line between normal intelligence and retardation (or developmental disability) and list the degrees of retardation.
19. Differentiate between organic and familial retardation.
20. List and describe the four types of organic causes of retardation.
21. Briefly describe the cause and effects of the following conditions:
    a. PKU
    b. microcephaly
    c. hydrocephaly
    d. cretinism
    e. Down syndrome

22. Briefly describe the maze-bright, maze-dull rat study as evidence for and against the hereditary view of intelligence.

23. Explain how the twin (identical and fraternal) studies can be used to support either side of the heredity/environment controversy.

24. Describe the evidence that most strongly supports the environmental view of intelligence.

25. Describe the studies which indicate how much the environment can alter intelligence.

26. Answer the question "Can training in thinking skills increase tested intelligence?" Explain your answer.

27. Explain Zajonc's confluence model relating the IQ of the children to the size of the family.

28. Discuss how the heredity/environment debate is resolved.

29. Define the term culture-fair test, and explain how IQ tests may be unfair to certain groups.

30. State four arguments against Jensen's claim that the IQ difference between blacks and whites can be attributed to genetic inheritance.

31. Discuss the general validity of IQ testing and the advantages and disadvantages of standardized testing in public schools.

32. Describe the overall controversy in the Larry P. case.

33. Explain what SOMPA is and how it helps solve many of the problems of using standardized IQ tests to assess the abilities of minority children.

■ DEMONSTRATIONS, DRAMATIZATIONS, AND DISCUSSIONS

1. **To impress upon students the arbitrary nature of operational definitions of intelligence,** have them write a list of skills or capacities they believe an intelligence test should measure (e.g., memory, computation, verbal ability, etc.). Ask a student to read his or her list, and no matter how long it is, ask, "Is that all that's meant by intelligence?" Then call on others to add to the list. When the class has exhausted all its additions, point out that the definition is still vague, limited, and arbitrary. Also ask students to imagine how all these abilities might be tested by one or several tests. It might also be interesting to note the degrees to which student definitions of intelligence have been shaped by their many years of exposure to schooling.

2. **The quotations and notes which follow are almost sure to stir up worthwhile class discussion:**

   a. "One thing I know. The IQ test does not truly measure intelligence. Our tests focus on such narrow things, the ability to acquire knowledge. What of human feelings? Are not these also important?" (Samuel C. Kohs, who helped develop the Stanford-Binet while a student of Lewis Terman.)

   b. Economist Thomas Sowell of Stanford University has found that during World War I, the IQs of European and Asian immigrants were nearly identical to black IQs today. Due to acculturation, education, and upward mobility, these immigrant groups now have IQs at or above the national average. Presumably, when socioeconomic and educational differences between blacks and whites are narrowed, the black-white gap will close as well.

c.   From a psychologist testifying for the defense in the Larry P. case (see discussion in Chapter 14 of the text): "...the surest and most effective action the Negro community could take by itself to achieve equality and education and jobs would be to limit dramatically the birthrate in those families providing the least effective environment for intellectual development." On the other hand, Professors Phillip Kunz and Evan Peterson of Brigham Young University have data suggesting that, "children in lower socioeconomic classes have lower grade point averages than those in the middle or upper class, regardless of family size."

d.   "I don't see any use for IQ tests during public school, except when a child has difficulty in learning. In that case, they are a valuable diagnostic tool. They can indicate a person lacks some ability to understand the world around them (sic)." Arthur Jensen speaking in 1980.

e.   "Absolutely wrong," and "biological nonsense" were but a few denouncements by Nobel Prize winners when they learned of the Repository for Germinal Choice set up by a U.S. businessman as a bank for sperm contributed by Nobel laureates. Three women have reputedly been fertilized with the sperm. One of the contributors was Dr. William B. Shockley.

f.   "The evidence about college entrance tests as predictors of academic success is no longer a subject of legitimate dispute...Most educators are quite familiar with the fact that the scores work in more cases than not, popular belief to the contrary notwithstanding." (William W. Turnbull, President of ETS in a 1974 speech.) According to figures ETS presented in 1977, the average accuracy of ETS aptitude tests in predicting first-year grades is seldom better than random predictions:

Percentage of Predictions in which Random Predictions with a Pair of Dice Is as Accurate as an ETS Test

SAT (college) 88%
LSAT (law school) 87%
GRE (graduate school) 89%
GMAT (business school) 92%

The compilation of ETS validity studies found that high school grades alone are about twice as good as the SAT in predicting college grades. (Quote and table from The Reign of the ETS by Allan Nairn and Associates, The Ralph Nader Report on the Educational Testing Service.)

g. Warner Slack and Douglas Porter of Harvard Medical School reported in the May 1980 Harvard Educational Review that coaching substantially improves scores on the SAT. ETS denies that coaching affects test results. Slack and Porter hold that the SAT tests measure "little-used vocabulary and tricky math," and that tutoring can raise scores enough to make the difference between acceptance and rejection to college.

3. To help students appreciate the difficulty in understanding what intelligence is, propose the following as measures of intelligence. Ask the students to decide which would be best:

   a.   a standardized IQ test;
   b.   a person's college GPA;
   c.   giving the person $100 to invest and seeing how much (s)he has after twelve months;
   d.   leaving the person out in the wilderness for three days with only an axe and a box of matches;
   e.   giving an extensive exam of general knowledge;
   f.   a person's grade in his/her course in psychology.

There will likely be a good deal of disagreement about which would be best. Most students will know someone whom they consider to be very bright but who has done poorly in college or high school. Ask them how they know the person is bright in the first place. What are their criteria? Challenge the class to propose a better way to measure intelligence.

■ ONE-MINUTE MOTIVATORS

1. **Ask students to write a short IQ test** that their instructor will flunk.

2. **Describe the smartest person you have ever known.** Do you think that person would score high on an IQ test? Or did s(he) possess other kinds of intelligence?

3. **All of us have talents** that others may not have. What is yours?

4. **Brainstorm unusual uses** for a brick, ways to conserve water, uses for discarded "pop-top" tabs. Analyze potential solutions in terms of fluency, flexibility, and originality.

■ CLASSROOM EXERCISE

Exercise: Analogies

TO THE INSTRUCTOR:

This exercise can serve at least two purposes. One is to arouse interest in the topic of intelligence. The second is to illustrate the use of analogies as a measure of this ability. Most tests of mental ability use some items of this kind, acknowledging that this is a measure of intelligence. The Miller Analogies Test, used as an entrance examination into some graduate programs, is a series of one hundred analogies. Charles Spearman's theory of intelligence, discussed in the Supplemental Lecture for this chapter, describes operations of general intelligence (g) which can be measured by analogies. Simply stated, an analogy requires the subject to see a relationship in the first half of a statement and to apply it in the second half. Spearman referred to these operations as eduction of relations and eduction of correlates. This test is timed. Spearman believed that speed of response is a factor in intelligence. On this test, students get four minutes with the understanding that most will not finish. This should make the test more discriminating at the top levels.

I.   Procedure

    A.   Giving the test

        1.   Make enough copies of the test so that each student will have one.

        2.   Without discussion distribute the tests, placing them face down on the students' desks. Ask them not to look at the test until told to do so.

        3.   When everyone is ready, ask them to turn over the test and read the directions as you read them aloud.

        4.   After the directions have been read, do the examples with the students. Point out the correct answer in the first. Ask a student to give the answer to the second. Clear up any questions before continuing.

        5.   Tell the students to begin. After four minutes ask them to stop and put their pencils down. DO NOT ALLOW STUDENTS TO CONTINUE IF NOT FINISHED.

        6.   Ask the students to put their names on the test papers, and collect them. Do not leave the test with the students if you plan to use it again.

B. Scoring the test

1. Check the items and find the number of correct responses for each student. The scoring key follows.

2. Work out the mean and standard deviation for the class. If you have given it to several classes, include all scores. The larger the number of scores, the more meaningful the results. You can develop a set of percentiles for the group which will tell each student how (s)he did in relation to all those who have taken the test.

3. You can convert the mean and standard deviation into T-scores with a mean of 100, and you will have a deviation IQ score.

4. Report the results to the students in a way that maintains the confidentiality of their scores, but do not return the tests.

II. Discussion

A. You can discuss the test items for validity.

B. You can discuss the results obtained and what they mean.

C. The simple statistics used can also be explained to show how data is assembled and interpreted by psychologists.

III. Analogies Scoring Key

1. kitten	7. fruit	13. finished	19. chairperson	25. L
2. herd	8. floor	14. 81	20. 48	26. Wednesday
3. shoe	9. trees	15. author	21. betray	27. laziness
4. light	10. dust	16. cuff	22. rim	28. create
5. door	11. deaf	17. seed	23. client	29. surface
6. quart	12. sap	18. sparrow	24. vice	30. run

(based on the Laycock Mental Abilities Test, S. R. Laycock, University of Saskatchewan, Canada)

ANALOGIES

TO THE STUDENT:

Read each item, then find and circle the word which best completes the statement. First, do the sample items. If you do not understand what to do, ask your instructor. You will have four minutes to complete the test. Work quickly but do not be concerned if you do not complete the test in the time allotted.

SAMPLES:

1.   Day is to night as yes is to--perhaps, no, maybe, if.

2.   Ship is to ocean as car is to--land, desert, forest, lake.

DO ALL OF THE FOLLOWING LIKE THE SAMPLES

1.   Dog is to puppy as cat is to--mouse, dog, rat, kitten.

2.   Sheep are to flock as cattle are to--herd, pack, bunch, group.

3.   Head is to hat as foot is to--toe, hair, shoe, knee.

4.   Dry is to wet as heavy is to--light, hard, soft, firm.

5.   Handle is to hammer as knob is to--lock, key, door, brass.

6.   Sugar is to pound as milk is to--cream, quart, sweet, barrel.

7.   Table is to furniture as apple is to--fruit, cherry, seed, leaf.

8.   Wash is to face as sweep is to--broom, nail, floor, straw.

9.   Book is to pages as forest is to--wood, trees, leaves, deer.

10.   Chat is to flat as must is to--how, cow, shop, dust.

11.   Eye is to blind as ear is to--hear, deaf, wax, hearing.

12.   Man is to blood as trees are to--leaves, branches, sap, water.

13.   Die is to dead as finish is to--finishing, finishes, will finish, finished.

14.   8 is to 64 as 9 is to--54, 81, 90, 45.

15. Picture is to painter as book is to--author, artist, school, library.

16. Neck is to collar as wrist is to--hand, cuff, coat, elbow.

17. Peach is to pit as apple is to--peel, red, tree, seed.

18. Fish is to trout as bird is to--sing, nest, sparrow, tree.

19. Trial is to judge as meeting is to--rules, speakers, chairperson, hall.

20. 3 is to 12 as 12 is to--24, 36, 48, 60.

21. Promise is to break as secret is to--betray, keep, guess, trust.

22. Lake is to shore as plate is to--horizon, beach, rim, ford.

23. Doctor is to patient as lawyer is to--judge, trial, prisoner, client.

24. Honesty is to virtue as stealing is to--vice, lying, criminal, trial.

25. H is to C as Q is to--P, M, L, N.

26. Monday is to Saturday as Friday is to--Tuesday, Sunday, Wednesday, Thursday.

27. Success is to ambition as failure is to--loss, defeat, energy, laziness.

28. Discover is to invent as exist is to--find, create, know, remove.

29. Point is to line as line is to--surface, curve, dot, solid.

30. Evolution is to revolution as crawl is to--baby, stand, run, creep.

■ BROADENING OUR CULTURAL HORIZONS

1. **Ask each student to think of 5 different groups of people.** The groupings can be based on physical qualities, age, gender, ethnic or racial background, etc. Create columns describing each group's socioeconomic status, happiness, creativity, intelligence, emphasis on family, value of independence, honesty, and industriousness. Ask students to rate the likelihood (1 = not likely; 7 = very likely) that these qualities would exist in an individual member of each group. Have students share their ratings in pairs. Then discuss the ways in which informal concepts of what various groups are like can color our attitudes toward individuals. Discuss stereotypes as a type of over-simplified concept.

2. **To what extent does cultural or ethnic background affect the kinds of prototypes we use to categorize objects and events?** Would these prototypes affect the way we think?

3. **Discuss the ways in which connotations can be culture-specific.** Ask students for examples of misunderstandings they have encountered that can be traced to differences in connotative meanings.

4. **Ask students who speak English as a second language** to discuss their feelings about learning and using a new language and about what effect this has had on their thinking.

5. **Invite a person to class who is fluent in American Sign Language.** Would a non-hearing person "perceive" the world differently than a hearing person because of using a different language structure? Teach students to sign the words to a current popular song.

6. **What cultural "rules" or values could contribute to functional fixedness?** Why are some cultures regarded as more inventive than others?

7. **Discuss with students if it is possible to develop a "culture-free" test.** If a test cannot be culture-free, can it be "culture fair"?

■ SUPPLEMENTAL LECTURE

Because intelligence is a concept that arouses a lot of curiosity and is considered vital to success in our society, there is a good deal of speculation and discussion about what it is. Also, because intelligence cannot be directly observed, there is a lot of disagreement about what it is. We can only infer someone's intelligence from observable behavior, whether it is their problem-solving, their test-taking, or their cutting in front of us on a busy highway. The inferences are judgments based on a limited sample of their behavior. What behavior should we look at? What behavior is "intelligent" and what is not? These are questions to which everyone has an answer but on which there is no agreement. As a result, many theories have been put forth to explain intelligence. At the risk of oversimplifying here, we will look at three theoretical orientations. Most of theories can fit, albeit uncomfortably, into one or other of these.

THEORIES OF INTELLIGENCE

I.   Introduction

    A.   Begin the session by asking students to give examples of behavior that they consider to be evidence of intelligence. It will soon become apparent that there is a wide diversity of opinion and possibly much disagreement.

    B.   A good discussion starter is to ask students to consider memory. Is memory a factor in intelligence? The question to ask is whether those who have a better memory are more intelligent than those who have a poorer memory. You need to avoid discussion of types of memory here. Keep it to factual memory to avoid complications. You should generate good discussion, pro and con.

    C.   Point out to students that they are facing the same dilemma as psychologists. What behavior is the best evidence of intelligence? How do you measure it?

II.   Theories of Intelligence

    A.   The theories can be grouped into three major types. There are, no doubt, others, but students at this level don't need to exhaust all the possibilities. They will get a better perspective if you keep it simple.

    B.   The three theoretical approaches give very different views of intelligence:

        1.   Connectionism

            a.   This is based on the idea that intelligence is a function of the brain. Thinking is setting up neural connections and pathways. Frequently used pathways are easier to access than those less frequently used. Repetition establishes connections and pathways.

            b.   One of the early proponents of this view was E. L. Thorndike, who, late in the nineteenth century, proposed this theoretical explanation of intelligence.

            c.   More recent explanations by behaviorists seem to build on this idea.

        2.   Multi-factor Theories of Intelligence

            a.   This approach is based on the concept that there is not one intelligence but many intelligences, each operating independently of the others. For example, one might have mathematical ability, musical ability, or mechanical ability. They are all separate and distinct abilities.

b.   An early proponent of this type of theory was L. L. Thurstone, who, in the early part of the twentieth century, proposed as many as thirty abilities. He, however, concluded that some were more important than others and eventually identified seven primary mental abilities which he believed were basic to all thought.

c.   Primary Mental Abilities (PMA) of Thurstone:

1)   verbal fluency
2)   numerical ability
3)   spatial ability
4)   memory
5)   perceptual speed
6)   inductive reasoning
7)   deductive reasoning

d.   A modern-day psychologist who holds a similar view is Howard Gardner, who, in 1985, stated that intelligence consists of seven intelligences, similar to Thurstone's PMA. See Highlight 14-1 in Chapter 14 for a discussion of these.

3.   Intelligence as a Single Power or Ability

a.   Theories that explain intelligence as a single power or ability that underlies all behavior have been very popular. People usually think of intelligence in this way. When we say, "He is an idiot," we are commenting on his intelligence and implying that he does stupid things. We don't distinguish one area of behavior from another, or one ability from another.

b.   The classical theory was enunciated by Charles Spearman, a British psychologist, in the early part of the twentieth century. It is commonly called the two-factor theory. The basic factor is what he called general intelligence (g), and it underlies all intelligent behavior. The second factor was many specific abilities (s) which give the person specific capabilities to behave in a variety of ways.

c.   Spearman said that general intelligence (g):

1)   underlies all intelligent activity,
2)   is inherited, not learned,
3)   exists in differing amounts in each person.

d.   The g factor consists of three operations:

1)   apprehension of experience--understanding what is going on around you--benefitting from experience;

2)   eduction of relations--being able to see relationships between or among objects or events;

3)   eduction of correlates--being able to apply relationships and principles to specific situations.

e.   Measuring intelligence could be done by measuring the person's ability to perform those three operations.

f.   See the Classroom Exercise for this chapter, which precedes this lecture, for a sample of a test that measures this type of intelligence.

III.   Discussion

A.   Students should look at some sample tests. Most tests try to sample a variety of behaviors but end up with one score which appears to fit the single power approach. Other tests give a number of separate scores as one would expect from a multi-factor approach.

B.   Ask students which of the three theoretical approaches seems best.

C.   Have students try the Analogies test in the Classroom Exercise section of this chapter. It should get them interested and help them to see what the g factor means.

■ SUGGESTIONS FOR FURTHER READING

Brody, E. B. and N. Brody. *Intelligence: Nature, Determinants, and Consequences.* Academic Press, 1976.

Cronbach, L. *Essentials of Psychological Testing,* 3rd ed. Harper and Row, 1970.

Eysenck, H. J. and L. Kamin. *The Intelligence Controversy.* Wiley, 1981.

Garcia, J. "IQ: The Conspiracy." *Psychology Today* April 1972: 40-43.

Goleman, D. "The 1,528 Little Geniuses and How They Grew." *Psychology Today* February 1980: 28+

Kamin, L. J. *The Science and Politics of IQ.* Erlbaum/Wiley, 1974.

Pines, M. "Superkids." *Psychology Today* January 1979: 53-63.

Rosenthal, R. and L. Jacobson. *Pygmalion in the Classroom.* Holt, 1968.

Sattler, J. M. *Assessment of Intelligence and Special Abilities.* Allyn and Bacon, 1981.

Scarr, S. *Race, Social Class, and Individual Differences in IQ.* Lawrence Erlbaum, 1981.

■ FILM SUGGESTIONS

THE EXCEPTIONAL CHILD (Time-Life, 51 mins.)
> Research on nonaverage intelligence and its causes is examined. Both the gifted and slow learners are discussed.

INTELLIGENCE (1990, Coast Community College District Telecourses, 30 min.)
> Part of the *Psychology - The Study of Human Behavior Series*, this video discusses the origin of IQ tests and whether they reveal aptitude or achievement.

INTELLIGENCE: A COMPLEX CONCEPT (1978, CRM/McGraw-Hill, 20 mins.)
> Beyond the notion that intelligence helps a person score well on tests, there are hundreds of different ideas about the nature of intelligence. When people on the street were asked, their filmed answers revealed much confusion between what intelligence tests measure and intelligence in daily life. The film explores some of the varied definitions of intelligence including those of Piaget and Guilford.

INTELLIGENCE TESTS ON TRIAL - LARRY P. AND P. A. S. E. (1982, San Diego State College, 46 min.)
> This video focuses on the major issues involved in two federal court cases dealing with the cultural bias of individually administered intelligence tests and the use of the tests in placement of black children in EMR/EMH classes.

IQ MYTH (1975, Carousel Films, 51 mins.)
> This is an extremely good documentary, narrated by Dan Rather, on the many ways in which IQ scores are misunderstood and misused. Topics include the origin of IQ testing in America, ways in which tests are standardized and administered, and interviews with leading psychologists, like Wechsler and Kamin, who take different positions on the utility of IQ testing.

MAY'S MIRACLE (1983, Filmakers Library, 28 mins.)
> This is a fascinating presentation of the abilities of a musical idiot savant. The film consists of an interview with his parents who describe the evolution of his remarkable ability, and he is shown through photographs as he slowly developed his talent.

MENTAL RETARDATION: THE LONG CHILDHOOD OF TIMMY (Contemporary/McGraw-Hill, 53 mins.)
> This is a compassionate portrayal of a child with Down Syndrome and his move from the family to a school for the retarded.

NO TWO ALIKE (1963, Indiana University, 30 mins.)
    The film explores measurement of abilities and the meaning of intelligence. It also shows methods of developing creative thinking in the classroom.

■ COMPUTER PROGRAMS: *Mind Scope*

Exercise 7, Digit Span

Some psychologists have suggested that differences between individuals in digit span can be used as a measure of intelligence. In this exercise students explore strategies that can be used to increase digit span.

CHAPTER 15

Personality

■ BEHAVIORAL OBJECTIVES

The student should be able to:

1. Define the term personality and explain how personality differs from character and temperament. Discuss the stability of personality (Highlight 15-1).
2. Define the term trait. Describe the trait approach and the type approach to personality, and explain the shortcoming of the type approach.
3. Explain what the self-concept is and how it affects behavior and personal adjustment.
4. Define the term personality theory. List and describe the four broad perspectives covered by this author.
5. Characterize the general approach to the study of personality taken by a trait theorist.
6. Distinguish common traits from individual traits.
7. Define, differentiate, and give examples of Allport's cardinal traits, central traits, and secondary traits.
8. Distinguish between surface traits and source traits, and state how Cattell measures source traits.
9. Explain how Cattell's approach to personality traits differed from Allport's approach.
10. Discuss the five-factor model of personality.
11. Explain what a trait-situation interaction is.
12. Explain how twin studies are used to assess the relative contribution of heredity and environment to a person's personality. Discuss how the similarities in the personalities of twins can be explained. Assess the relative contributions of heredity and environment to the makeup of personality.
13. Explain why Freud became interested in personality.
14. List and describe the three parts of the personality according to Freud.
15. Describe the dynamic conflict between the three parts of the personality and relate neurotic and moral anxiety to the conflict.
16. Describe the relationships among the three parts of the personality (according to Freud) and the three levels of awareness.
17. List and describe Freud's four psychosexual stages. In your answer include an explanation of fixation and the corresponding age range for each stage.
18. Discuss the positive and the negative aspects of Freud's developmental theory.
19. Define the term neo-Freudian and explain why many of Freud's followers eventually disagreed with him.
20. Describe Horney's view of neurosis and emotional health including the concept of basic anxiety.
21. Describe Jung's view of personality by defining or explaining the following terms:

    a.   persona

    b.   introversion/extroversion

    c.   personal unconscious

    d.   collective unconscious

    e.   archetype

        1.   anima

        2.   animus

    f.   self archetype

22. Explain how behaviorists view personality.

23. Explain how learning theorists view the structure of personality. Include in your discussion the terms habit, drive, cue, response, and reward.

24. Explain how learning theory and social learning theory differ. Include in your discussion a description of the terms psychological situation, expectancy, reinforcement value, and self-reinforcement. Explain how self-reinforcement is related to self-esteem and depression (see Highlight 15-4).

25. Using the behavioristic view of development, explain why feeding, toilet training, sex training, and learning to express anger or aggression may be particularly important to personality formation.

26. Describe the role of social reinforcement, imitation, and identification in personality development.

27. Briefly explain how the humanists set themselves apart from the Freudian and behaviorist viewpoints or personality.

28. Describe the development of Maslow's interest in self-actualization.

29. Using at least five of the characteristics of self-actualizers listed in your text, describe a self-actualizing person. From the original list of ten, evaluate yourself and explain what may be helping or hindering your self-actualization.

30. List and briefly explain or describe (where applicable) eight steps to promote self-actualization.

31. Differentiate Freud's and Rogers' views of the normal or fully functioning individual.

32. Describe Rogers' view of an incongruent person.

33. Explain how "possible selves" help translate out hopes, dreams, and fears and ultimately direct our future behavior.

34. Explain how "conditions of worth" and "organismic valuing" may affect personality formation.

35. Compare and contrast in general terms the strengths and weaknesses of the trait, psychoanalytic, behavioristic, and humanistic theories of personality.

36. Discuss the following assessment techniques in terms of purpose, method, advantages, and limitations:

    a.   structured and unstructured interviews

    b.   direct observation (combined with rating scales, behavioral assessment and situational testing)

    c.   personality questionnaires (MMPI)

    d.   honesty tests

    e.   projective tests (Rorschach, TAT).

37. Describe the personality characteristics of sudden murderers, and explain how their characteristics are related to the nature of their homicidal actions.

38.	List and describe the three elements of shyness. State what usually causes shyness.

39.	Compare the personality of the shy and nonshy. Include the concepts labeling and self-esteem.

40.	List and discuss the four major areas that can help reduce shyness.

41.	Define the term "self-monitoring" and differentiate high self-monitoring behavior from low self-monitoring behavior. Explain the advantages and disadvantages of each.

■ DEMONSTRATIONS, DRAMATIZATIONS, AND DISCUSSION

1.	**For an ambitious exercise,** administer a complete personality inventory to class members. Appropriate tests are the Guilford-Zimmerman Temperament Survey, the Allport-Vernon-Lindzey Scale of Values, the Edwards Personality Preference Schedule, and the Sixteen Personality Factor Questionnaire. The first three tests can be obtained from The Psychological Corporation, 757 Third Avenue, New York, NY 10017. The 16-PF is published by the Institute for Personality and Ability Testing, 1602-04 Coronade Drive, Champaign, IL.

	An excellent alternate source of psychological tests is a trade book by Rita Aero and Elliot Weiner, titled *The Mind Test* (New York: William Morrow, 1981). This book includes a variety of scales and questionnaires appropriate for class administration. Some of the areas covered are personality, stress, fear, anxiety, depression, marriage, vocation, and interpersonal relationships. Most of the scales presented were drawn from journal articles and are of good quality. The following listings are particularly suitable for classroom use: Locus of Control Scale, Self-Consciousness Scale, Death Concern Scale, Marital Adjustment Test, Beck Depression Inventory, Interest Check List, Social Interest Scale, and the Assertion Questionnaire.

	As an alternative to in-class testing, plot the personality profiles of one or two individuals (real or hypothetical) on the rating forms for one of the tests mentioned above. Duplicate the profiles for class distribution or present them with an overhead projector. Discuss the meaning of the various scales and the picture that emerges of the individual's personality.

2.	**A good way to introduce the topic of androgyny** is to select a number of terms from the Adjective Checklist that appears in Chapter 16. Write them on the board and ask students to indicate by a show of hands whether men (then women) tend to rank high or low in the quality named by the adjective. Plot two profiles to compare ratings of males and females. This should define some clearcut "masculine" traits, "feminine" traits, and "neutral" traits--at least as they exist in the minds of many.

3.	**Students can simulate a Rorschach test by making their own ink blots.** The instructor should bring a large bottle of a dark-colored liquid and an eyedropper. Ask students to fold a sheet of paper in half, then open it up. Put a few drops of the liquid into the fold and close it, pressing it flat. More than one application of drops may be needed to create a blot that is symmetrical and large. Students can then compare blots and discuss what they see.

An additional exercise might be to ask students to show their blots to several persons not in their class and record their responses. They should ask their subjects to respond to both the overall image and to particular parts of it.

Student discussion of the results should center on similarities and variations in responses with some speculation on reasons for this.

4.   **It might be wise in connection with this chapter to remind students of the problems** associated with easy acceptance of overly generalized and self-contradictory personality descriptions. These are frequently found in magazine articles and popular psychology books. A recent example is a book purporting to analyze personality on the basis of one's color preferences (*Analyze Your Personality Through Color*, by A. W. Munzfert, Hemisphere Publications, 1980). Here's a sample to share with your class:

> If your choice is red, your are an aggressive, extroverted person with strong desires and a craving for action. You are energetic, impulsive, and have a tremendous drive for success. You are quick to take sides and make judgments. However, you are not unreasonably stubborn, and in fact, may sometimes be too easily swayed in your feelings and attitudes. You dislike monotony in any form, and your search for activity may sometimes make you appear fickle. You tend to lack perseverance but may reach success through sheer energy and force of personality.

5.   **Fidgeting is described as engaging in actions that are peripheral to ongoing tasks or activities.** The cited article offers a 40-item fidgeting questionnaire and scoring instructions. High scores on the questionnaire are related to tendencies to engage in extraneous activities (consuming alcoholic drinks, cigarette smoking, eating, daydreaming, restlessness, insomnia). High scores are also correlated with binge eating, physical activity, anxiety, hostility. This is an interesting individual difference that students can easily relate to. Fidgeting can be viewed in state or trait terms and offers a chance to discuss correlations among related behaviors and the disposition-situation debate. (Mehrabian, Albert and Friedman, Shari [1986]). An analysis of fidgeting and associated individual differences. *Journal of Personality*, 54(2), 407-429.

6.   **Piliavin presented subjects with pairs of hypothetical mayoral candidates who differed in sex, race, or age.** Subjects' votes showed a strong preference for the candidates most similar to themselves in age. By leaving out differences in sex and race in descriptions of hypothetical candidates, this could be made into a good demonstration of ageism—one especially instructive for students who believe that they are free of age-based prejudice. (Piliavin, J. A. [1987]). Age, race, and sex similarity to candidates and voting preference. *Journal of Applied Psychology*, 17(4), 351-368.

7.   **To convey the flavor of the Freudian view of unconscious thought patterns, meanings, and associations,** try having students follow a <u>chain</u> of associations to see where it leads. Begin by asking the class to write the first word or thought that occurs to them when they hear one

of these words: *mother, father, death, birth, money, love, failure, breast, gun, rival.* (Choose words you consider most interesting or likely to produce interesting responses.) After the first association has been written, ask students to write their first association to <u>that</u> word or idea. Continue through a series of eight or ten associations, then select a few papers for discussion. The linkages and end-points can be fascinating.

8. **For a further investigation into Freudian dynamics,** have students complete the statements which follow. Can the resulting statements be categorized as id, ego, or superego responses?

> I want to...   One should never...
> If I could do anything, I would...   I won't ever...
> Why do I...?   Realistically, I...
> My plan is to...   I can't seem to...
> I think a responsible person...   Ideally I...

9. **To illustrate the importance of situational determinants of behavior,** you might find it interesting to share this bit of information with students: L. R. Kahle of the University of Michigan has reported that nearly half of the male students he tested cheated when they were deliberately given a chance to change test answers. Kahle used hidden pieces of pressure-sensitive paper to find out which students did or did not change answers on the test. You may want to discuss this finding in conjunction with the concepts of the psychological situation, expectancy, and reinforcement value.

10. **Another good way to illustrate situational determinants and the behavioral view is as follows:** Instruct students to keep a careful record for a day of each person they talked with. Students should include a brief description of the circumstances, setting, nature of the interaction, and apparent reinforcement (information, approval, needed goods, etc.) provided by interacting with others. When the records are brought to class, ask students to discuss the external variables influencing how "sociable" their personalities appeared on the day in question.

11. **You can give the students a chance to experience a projective test by preparing a TAT-like card.** Find a picture that is ambiguous and which can be copied. It should fit on an 8 1/2 x 11" sheet of paper. Make copies so that each student can have one. Ask the students to write a story about the card. What is going on in the scene? What led up to the action? What will happen next? When they are finished, ask the students to look over their responses. Look for themes and motives, such as aggression, achievement, love, anger. Students should be asked to share some of their stories with others. Ask other students to look for themes and motives in the reader's story.

■ ONE-MINUTE MOTIVATORS

1. **Interview a set of identical twins.** Talk to each twin separately (with one waiting outside class). In what ways do they feel they are similar and different? Then bring them together for a joint discussion.

2. **Have a conversation with a student who is directed to act unsocialized.** Discuss how difficult it is to put aside our socialization.

3. **Develop a file of 8½" x 11" pictures from magazines (or a series of slides).** Show students one picture or slide and ask each person to write a story. Ask students to share their stories with the class or with the person next to them. Were there any sexual or aggressive interpretations? Did people fabricate bizarre interpretations? How do psychologists know whether a person taking a personality test is telling the truth or lying?

4. **Group the students in pairs and tell them to engage in a five-minute conversation.** Have the pairs join to form groups of four and continue to converse for five more minutes. Ask students how they felt about the dialogue? Did they feel shy? What did they do effectively in the conversation? What could they have done more effectively?

5. **Sophie Tucker once said,** "From birth to 18, a girl needs good parents; from 18-25, good looks; from 33-55, a good personality; and from 55 on CASH." Type this four ways, using "girl," "boy," "woman," and "man." Distribute the forms randomly to the class and discuss whether the statement is true. Interestingly, many men in the class will find the term "boy" offensive, but "girl" appropriate. Discuss gender-based differences in personality and expectations.

6. **To demonstrate the preconscious,** ask students to dredge up their earliest memory of a family holiday celebration.

7. **Give each student a 3 x 5 card.** Ask students to write three statements of self-praise for some behavior done frequently during the week. Pass these around the class so everyone can read the statements. Collect the cards and read a few of them. Then ask students to take their own card home and place it in a visible location for a week. A week later discuss whether students noticed the card and whether they think it had any impact on their view of themselves.

8. **Sigmund Freud was born on May 6, 1856.** You can celebrate his birthday or the birthday of other key psychologists discussed in this chapter.

■ CLASSROOM EXERCISES

Three exercises follow which are related to personality and should be of interest to the students. The first requires the student to involve others in exploring his/her personality traits and needs to be done outside class. The second can be done in class or at home by the student. The third exercise deals with ways to look at one's own personality. Interest in the topic and classroom discussion should be easy to develop after one or all of these exercises. The instructions for the third exercise follow the instructions and data sheets for the first two exercises.

Exercise #1: Personality Traits

The purpose of this exercise is twofold. The first is to force the students to think about traits and to try to determine which are important. The second is to give each student a chance to see that his/her view of the self may not be the same as what others see or think is important.

This exercise is complete with instructions, a rating sheet, and a summary sheet to collect all the ratings. The student is given directions and some questions to stimulate thought. You may wish to add to these.

You will need to duplicate sufficient copies of the rating sheet so that each student will be able to rate him/herself and have three or four raters. Each student will need one copy of the directions and the summary sheet.

Exercise #2: Personality Types

This is an Introversion-Extroversion scale developed by the author of this text. It can be administered to students in class or as a take-home project. It should generate interest in personality types and illustrate a typical self-report instrument.

Once the scores are obtained, you should give students an opportunity to discuss the results. They will have some immediate reactions to the validity of the scale based on their scores and their perceptions of themselves.

Another interesting classroom activity would be to plot all the scores on a single scale to see what kind of distribution would be found in the whole class. A graph could be constructed that would give the students an idea of the variability that exists.

PERSONALITY TRAITS: **INSTRUCTIONS**

TO THE STUDENT:

Attached is a list of terms that describe personality traits which are commonly found in the population. You can probably think of many others, but stick with these for this exercise.

The purpose of this exercise is to compare your own ratings of yourself with the ratings of others. Do others see you in the same way that you see yourself? Follow the directions to find out.

1.   Make several copies of the list of terms. Ask three people to each separately rate you on the list of traits. You should also rate yourself. Select a variety of people to do the rating, such as a family member, a friend, a co-worker, a neighbor, a teacher, a spouse, etc.

2.   You and each of your raters should select and check off 20 traits which describe you best. It may be hard to stick to 20, but force yourself (and your raters) to do so.

3.   On the summary rating sheet, check off your choices and the choices of each of the raters.

4.   Now you can compare how you see yourself with the way others see you. You can also compare the responses of the different raters. They may not all agree with you or with each other!

PERSONALITY TRAITS: **RATING SHEET**

Rater's I.D._____(Rater may wish to be anonymous.)

Identification of personality traits of _____

<u>Instructions</u>: Check the twenty (20) traits from this list that <u>best</u> describe the person named above.
Your evaluation should be based on behavior that you have observed.

__boastful	__generous	__optimistic	__shy
__candid	__good-natured	__orderly	__sincere
__clumsy	__gracious	__outgoing	__skeptical
__compulsive	__grouchy	__patient	__sloppy
__considerate	__headstrong	__perceptive	__sly
__cooperative	__honest	__persistent	__smart
__cordial	__idealistic	__persuasive	__sociable
__courageous	__imaginative	__pessimistic	__studious
__courteous	__kind	__prejudiced	__suspicious
__crafty	__logical	__prideful	__tactful
__daring	__loyal	__punctual	__tense
__dependable	__mature	__reasonable	__truthful
__diligent	__methodical	__rebellious	__understanding
__efficient	__modest	__reliable	__unselfish
__energetic	__naive	__respectful	__vain
__ethical	__neat	__sarcastic	__versatile
__forgetful	__nervous	__sexy	__warm
__friendly	__open-minded	__short-tempered	__wholesome

PERSONALITY TRAITS: SUMMARY SHEET

In order to compare your own rating of yourself with the ratings of others, put your own twenty (20) checks on this chart first. Then put each rater's checks in the boxes provided.

	RATERS		
	ME	1	2	3
boastful				
candid				
clumsy				
compulsive				
considerate				
cooperative				
cordial				
courageous				
courteous				
crafty				
daring				
dependable				
diligent				
efficient				
energetic				
ethical				
forgetful				
friendly				
generous				

	RATERS		
	ME	1	2	3
good-natured				
gracious				
grouchy				
headstrong				
honest				
idealistic				
imaginative				
kind				
logical				
loyal				
mature				
methodical				
modest				
naive				
neat				
nervous				
open-minded				
optimistic				
orderly				

PERSONALITY TRAITS: SUMMARY SHEET (cont.)

	RATERS			
	ME	**1**	**2**	**3**
outgoing				
patient				
perceptive				
persistent				
persuasive				
pessimistic				
prejudiced				
prideful				
punctual				
reasonable				
rebellious				
reliable				
respectful				
sarcastic				
sexy				
short-tempered				
shy				

	RATERS			
	ME	**1**	**2**	**3**
sincere				
skeptical				
sloppy				
sly				
smart				
sociable				
studious				
suspicious				
tactful				
tense				
truthful				
understanding				
unselfish				
vain				
versatile				
warm				
wholesome				

PERSONALITY TRAITS: **EVALUATION**

Now you need to evaluate the results. The following questions should help you.

1.   Overall, does <u>your</u> selection of traits present a favorable or unfavorable picture of your personality?

2.   Do the traits identified by <u>your raters</u> present a favorable or unfavorable picture?

3.   How different are the traits selected by your raters from yours? In what ways do they differ?

4.   How do you explain the difference?

5.   Which of your traits appear to be most <u>positive</u> based on all ratings?

6.   Which of your traits appear to be most <u>negative</u> based on all ratings?

7.   What do you think about this type of evaluation of personality? Explain what you mean.

INTROVERTED? EXTROVERTED? WHICH ARE YOU?

To find out, mark true (T) or false (F) next to each of the statements below, and then follow the scoring instructions.

____ 1) I tend to keep in the background at social events.

____ 2) I prefer to work with others rather than alone.

____ 3) I get embarrassed easily.

____ 4) I generally tell others how I feel regardless of how they may take it.

____ 5) I really try to avoid situations in which I must speak to a group.

____ 6) I am strongly motivated by the approval or interest of others.

____ 7) I often daydream.

____ 8) I find it easy to start conversations with strangers.

____ 9) I find it difficult to make friends of the opposite sex.

____10) I particularly enjoy meeting people who know their way around the social scene.

____11) I would rather read a good book or watch television than go out to a movie.

____12) I would rather work as a salesperson than as a librarian.

____13) I spend a lot of time philosophizing and thinking about my ideas.

____14) I prefer action to thought and reflection.

____15) I am often uncomfortable in conversations with strangers.

____16) I am mainly interested in activities and ideas that are practical.

____17) I would prefer visiting an art gallery over attending a sporting event.

____18) I enjoy open competition in sports, games, and school.

____19) I make my decisions by reason more than by impulse or emotion.

____20) I have to admit that I enjoy talking about myself to others.

___21) I like to lose myself in my work.

___22) I sometimes get into arguments with people I do not know well.

___23) I am very selective about who my friends are.

___24) I make decisions quickly and stick to them.

SCORING:

1.   Go through the odd-numbered items and add the number of true and false responses. Put the numbers in the appropriate boxes.

2.   Go through the even-numbered items, adding the true and false responses. Enter the numbers in the proper boxes.

3.   Add only the ODD-false items to the EVEN-true items.

4.   The total thus obtained should be marked on the introversion-extroversion scale.

ODD ITEMS	True	False			
		True	False	EVEN ITEMS	
	TOTAL				

INTROVERT				EXTROVERT
0	6	12	18	24

Exercise #3: Who Am I?

I.   Introduction

This exercise on self-concept is built around Louis Zurcher's *Twenty-Statement Test (TST)*. The students are asked to complete the statement, "I am..." twenty times. Then they are asked to categorize the statements into the four categories as outlined on the Interpretation Sheet. Zurcher found that the TST statements of an individual often fall into one category more than the others. He labeled the four categories as follows:

Category 1: the physical self
Category 2: the social self
Category 3: the reflective self
Category 4: the oceanic self (selfhood independent of the preceding three categories)

II.   Procedure

A.   Pass out the **Response Sheets** to the students. Ask them to follow the directions and complete the forms.

B.   When they have finished, pass out the **Interpretation Sheet** and ask them to follow the directions. Circulate and help those who are uncertain about how to categorize a statement.

C.   Ask them to indicate in which category their answers predominate.

III. Discussion

A.   How do most students see themselves? Is there a majority in any one category?

B.   Speculate on why the results came out as they did.

C.   Zurcher says that a balance among all four components would be best for a person. Ask students if they agree and why.

IV.   Reference

For more information consult, L. A. Zurcher's *The Mutable Self,* Sage, 1977.

WHO AM I?: RESPONSE SHEET

TO THE STUDENT:

Complete each of the twenty "I am" statements below. Complete each sentence saying something about yourself. Do not be too concerned about exactness. Say whatever you think of as it occurs to you.

1.   I am _____

2.   I am _____

3.   I am _____

4.   I am _____

5.   I am _____

6.   I am _____

7.   I am _____

8.   I am _____

9.   I am _____

10.   I am _____

11.   I am _____

12.   I am _____

13.   I am _____

14.   I am _____

15.   I am _____

16.   I am _____

17.   I am _____

18.   I am _____

19.   I am _____

20.   I am _____
     _____

WHO AM I?: INTERPRETATION SHEET

TO THE STUDENT:

You now have a difficult job to do. You need to classify each of your statements into one or another of four categories below. Read over all four categories. Be sure you understand what they are. Ask your instructor if you need clarification. Put each of the item numbers under the heading that seems most appropriate based on the descriptions below:

Category 1: Physical or traditional identification--includes one's sex, age, address, religion, etc. For example, "I am a woman," "I am a Green Thing from Mars."

Category 2: Social relationships--family, occupation, membership, etc. For example, "I am a student," "I am a middle child."

Category 3: Situation-free behavior--likes, dislikes, attitudes, etc. For example, "I am a lover of music," "I am for nuclear disarmament."

Category 4: Identity--this is how you describe yourself. You say who you are. For example, "I am a citizen of the world," "I am a living individual," "I am a person."

Place the number for each of the twenty statements in the columns below as you make your decision about which category is best.

Category 1	Category 2	Category 3	Category 4
_____	_____	_____	_____
_____	_____	_____	_____
_____	_____	_____	_____
_____	_____	_____	_____
_____	_____	_____	_____
_____	_____	_____	_____
_____	_____	_____	_____
_____	_____	_____	_____

■ BROADENING OUR CULTURAL HORIZONS

1. **Imagine a society where people are rewarded when they give to the poor, live humbly, and stay physically fit.** What common traits would you expect to find in such a society? What do you think are the common traits of American society?

2. **Researchers traveling in China claim that they have never encountered a shy Chinese child.** What kinds of cultural differences do you think would account for this observation? How should you change our culture to reduce the incidence of shyness?

3. **Who are your heroes?** Who do you identify with? How has this affected your self-concept? How has your culture helped define your heroes and models? Would other cultures make heroes of the same people we do?

4. **How universal are Freud's concepts?** Would the strength and the role of each of Freud's structures of personality differ in various cultures? For instance, aren't some cultures more pleasure-oriented than others? Don't some acknowledge more libidinal energy than others? Could a boy develop a conscience if he never felt any rivalry with his father?

5. **Cultures vary widely in their views** of toilet-training and breast-feeding. What patterns are considered normal and desirable in mainstream American culture? What variations are you aware of in cultural and ethnic groups with which you are familiar?

■ SUPPLEMENTAL LECTURE

SELF-CONCEPT

I. Introduction

This lecture is about self-concept. The Humanistic psychologists focus attention on the self. As infants, and later as children, as they gather information about themselves from their environment, they sort it and organize it into a perception of the self as a person. The self emerges through experience and changes throughout one's lifetime. This lecture is a look at the self-concept which is the result of this interaction with the environment.

    A. The development of self-concept is a very complex psychological process which:

        1. has a developmental course that can be described and predicted;

        2. is influenced by learning (experience);

        3. is constantly changing, though the rate of change varies with age;

4. can be studied scientifically because it is reflected in the behavior of the individual.

B. The self-concept can be defined as the person's perception of himself/herself as distinct from other persons or things.

C. The function of the self-concept is to provide a frame-of-reference for the person. One evaluates new experiences and makes choices and decisions using what (s)he knows about him/herself as the reference point.

II. What Is the Self-Concept?

What is it that makes up the self-concept? How does it develop? Where does it come from? All of these are important questions. In the process of examining the idea of self-concept we can see the answers.

The self-concept is made up of three elements: self-identity, self-evaluation, self-ideal.

A. Self-identity

1. At birth the neonates make no distinction between their body and the environment.

2. The first consciousness of self comes from an awareness of the body as its senses probe the environment and collect data about the world. This is the beginning of the development of BODY IMAGE.

3. Body Image--how the person views his/her own body.

   a. This is the core of self-concept.

   b. It remains important to the self-concept throughout life.

4. Initially infants equate the self with their own feelings and actions (bodily functions). With time and experience they begin to relate to things outside themselves.

5. Interaction with others reinforces (positively or negatively) this image of the self. How adults react to the infant will be important. As the child gets older, peer reactions become more important. Abused and neglected children suffer because they have a poor quality of experience and interaction as do children whose parents are unrealistic in their expectations.

6.   As children develop, they learn several social roles, or, we could say, they have several "selves" which need to be integrated for a real sense of identity. If the roles are conflicting or unclear, problems are sure to follow.

B.   Self-evaluation

1.   As self-identity grows, so children begin to make value judgments about the self. Such values as superior-inferior, adequate-inadequate, good-bad, etc., become a part of the self-concept.

2.   In the early years the value placed on the self will be dependent on what others say and think. These will become internalized and form the person's value system. They should be reevaluated as the child gets older.

3.   Growth in the self-concept requires new values and reevaluation of old attitudes and feelings. This may be hard to do as one grows older.

4.   SELF-ESTEEM is the term used to identify the value a person places on her/himself. It is the feeling of personal worth that each of us has. It reflects the attitudes of others toward us but should eventually become a realistic appraisal of ourselves as we mature. This is not always easy to achieve.

5.   Family and peer standards form the basis for our self-evaluation.

C.   Self-ideal

1.   Ideals and aspirations develop as the child grows and matures. Hope is a key ingredient. Those who have it can look beyond today into the future. Those who can see far into the future make plans based on the self-ideal, the person's image of what (s)he should be or would like to be.

2.   Hopes and aspirations come from many sources:

    a.   A child sees what (s)he likes in others and wants to be like them-- parents, relatives, movie stars, etc.

    b.   Movies and television glamorize statuses and roles.

    c.   Parents and relatives may impose values and ideals.

    d.   Institutions such as church and school, the culture, and social organizations influence the child.

3.   Level of Aspiration

      a.   This encompasses the person's goals. "Where am I going?" "What will I do with my life?" The answers may or may not be thought about or stated.

      a.   This may be high or low depending on many factors.

      b.   It NEEDS TO BE realistic:

            1)   If it is too high, the person is doomed to failure.

            2)   If it is too low, the person will be unhappy and feel unfulfilled. His/her talents will be wasted.

      c.   A child may accept the values of others at an early age before having enough self-knowledge to make independent decisions.

      d.   A child needs to evaluate and reevaluate goals and ideals as (s)he matures. It's all right for a child, at the age of seven, to want to be a movie star or a fireman or a cowboy. Is it still all right to have the same aspirations at age seventeen or twenty-seven?

II.   Development of Self-Concept

    A.   This is subject matter for another lecture. However, a few comments to end this lecture are appropriate.

      1.   The child needs to have an opportunity to develop his/her own self-concept. It should not be imposed by others.

      2.   The child needs direction to develop significant, as opposed to trivial, ideals.

      3.   Models are probably most significant in this process.

      4.   Learning about oneself requires experience--interaction with the environment. Well-intentioned adults often deny the child the opportunity to try new things, especially if there is a chance of failure.

      5.   Success and failure are both valuable. A child needs to succeed, but failure is also a good teacher. Adults should help a child to evaluate failure and learn from it. It should lead to growth. Also it gives a child a chance to test his/her limits.

6.   Overly protective parents, overly permissive parents, overly authoritarian parents, and negligent parents make it difficult for a child to develop a realistic self-concept.

III.   Discussion

A.   This lecture is full of opportunities for students to contribute from their experiences. Examples of good and bad practices abound.

B.   Be sure to focus attention on three elements:

1.   Experience is needed--interaction with the environment. Being told what you can and cannot do is not as useful as trying things yourself.

2.   No one can predetermine what is best for a child. However, opportunities for growth are vital. Parents can provide these opportunities and so influence the development of the child's self-concept.

3.   Helping the child to translate experiences into growth is the best way for adults to promote positive self-concept.

■ SUGGESTIONS FOR FURTHER READING

Adler, A. *The Science of Living*. Doubleday, 1929.

Aero, R. and E. Weiner. *The Mind Test*. Morrow, 1981.

Allport, G. *Pattern and Growth in Personality*. Holt, 1961.

Bem. S. L. "The Measurement of Psychological Androgyny." *Journal of Consulting and Clinical Psychology* (42) 1974: 155-162.

----. "Sex-Role Adaptability: One Consequence of Psychological Androgyny." *Journal of Personality and Social Psychology* (31) 1975: 634-643.

Cattell, R. B. *The Scientific Analysis of Personality*. Penguin, 1965.

Cronbach, L. J. *Essentials of Psychological Testing*, 3rd. ed. Harper and Row, 1970.

Fadiman, J. and R. Frager. *Personality and Personal Growth*. Harper and Row, 1976.

Freud, S. *An Outline of Psychoanalysis*. Norton, 1949.

Girodo, M. *Shy? (You Don't Have to Be!)*. Pocket Books, 1978.

Hall, C. S. and G. Lindzey. *Theories of Personality*. Wiley, 1978.

Harris, I. D. *The Promised Seed: A Complete Study of First and Later Sons*. Free Press, 1964.

Jones, E. *The Life and Work of Sigmund Freud* (3 vols.). Basic Books, 1953-1957.

Jung, C. G. *Memories, Dreams, Reflections*. Random House, 1963.

____. *Man and His Symbols*. Doubleday, 1964.

Lanyon, R. I. "Personality Assessment." *Annual Review of Psychology* (35) 1984: 667-701.

Loevinger, J. and E. Knoll. "Personality: Stages, Traits, and the Self." *Annual Review of Psychology* (34) 1983: 195-240.

Maddi, S. R. *Personality Theories: A Comparative Analysis*. Dorsey, 1968.

Mahoney, J. J. "Reflections on the Cognitive Learning Trend in Psychotherapy." *American Psychologist* (32) 1977: 5-13.

Mischel, W. *Personality and Assessment*. Wiley, 1968.

-----. *Introduction to Personality* (3rd ed.). Holt, Rinehart, and Winston, 1981.

Olds, L. E. *Fully Human*. Prentice-Hall, 1981.

Pervin, L. A. *Personality Theory, Assessment, and Research* (3rd ed.). Wiley, 1980.

Pleck, J. H. *The Myth of Masculinity*. MIT Press, 1981.

Rogers, C. R. *On Becoming a Person*. Houghton-Mifflin, 1961.

Rorer, L. G. and T. A. Widiger. "Personality Structure and Assessment." *Annual Review of Psychology* (34) 1983: 431-465.

Rotter, J. B. *The Development and Application of Social Learning Theory: Selected Papers*. Praeger, 1982.

"Why You Do What You Do: Sociobiology--A New Theory of Behavior." *Time* 1 Aug 1977: 54-63.

■ FILM SUGGESTIONS

CONSCIENCE OF A CHILD (1963, Indiana University, 30 mins.)
   This film illustrates the development of personality, especially as it is affected by imitation and identification. A good portrayal of social learning theory.

DISCUSSION WITH DR. CARL JUNG (1968, Pennsylvania State University, 36 mins.)
>In this film Jung talks about his theories of personality and discusses his differences with Freud and Freudian psychoanalysis.

DR. HENRY MURRAY (Part I) (1966, Pennsylvania State University, 50 mins.)
>This is an introduction to the TAT in which Murray discusses Freud and Jung and their association techniques.

FREUD: THE HIDDEN NATURE OF MAN (1970, University of Illinois, 29 mins.)
>This film depicts the life of Sigmund Freud from his youth to his later years. It shows his early work with patients in Vienna and presents his theories of the Oedipus complex, the role of the unconscious, and infantile sexuality.

THE HUMANISTIC REVOLUTION: PIONEERS IN PERSPECTIVE (Psychological Films, 32 mins.)
>This film begins with an interview with Maslow on self-actualization followed by interviews with other pioneers in this field: Gardner Murphy, Carl Rogers, Rollo May, Paul Tillich, Fritz Perls, Victor Frankl, and Alan Watts.

MASLOW AND SELF-ACTUALIZATION (PARTS I AND II) (1969, Psychological Films, 30 mins. each)
>Maslow discusses themes of honesty and awareness in Part I and of freedom and trust in Part II.

OUTSTANDING CONTRIBUTORS TO THE PSYCHOLOGY OF PERSONALITY SERIES (Pennsylvania State University, 50 mins. each)
>Interviews with well-known personality theorists. Films appropriate for this chapter cover Gordon Allport and Raymond Cattell.

PERSONALITY (1971, CRM/McGraw-Hill, 30 mins.)
>An advertisement was run in a major newspaper asking for subjects for psychological testing. From many replies, one individual was selected to be the subject of this film: the personality was described and psychologically assessed. The description was obtained by processes including interviewing, outside descriptions, and self-description. The film also includes a discussion of standard psychological assessment tests--MMPI, Forer Sentence Completion, WAIS, TAT, and Holzman Inkblot Test.

REACTIONS TO PSYCHOANALYTIC CONCEPTS (1982, Karol Media, 30 mins.)
>In this film Rollo May discusses his reactions to the ideas of Sigmund Freud, Otto Rank, Harry Stack Sullivan, Alfred Adler, Alan Watts.

REFLECTIONS, CARL ROGERS (1976, American Association for Counseling and Development, 59 mins.)
>This video shows Warren Bennis, President of the University of Cincinnati, interviewing Carl Rogers. Rogers' theories and how they were formed are discussed.

YOUNG DR. FREUD (Films for the Humanities and Sciences, 99 mins.)
>This docudrama is an introduction to Freud's work and explores the influences that made Freud what he was: the effects of alienation, of medical studies which he neither enjoyed nor mastered, and of his discovery of a subject area in which he could make a unique contribution. Also discussed are the men who shaped his ideas: Breuer, Charcot, Janet, and Fliess as well as some of the famous cases, such as that of Anna O.

CHAPTER 16

Abnormal Behavior: Deviance and Disorder

■ BEHAVIORAL OBJECTIVES

The student should be able to:

1. Define psychopathology.
2. Present information to indicate the magnitude of mental health problems in this country.
3. Describe the following ways of viewing normality including the shortcoming(s) of each:
    a. subjective discomfort
    d. situational context
    b. statistical definitions
    e. cultural relativity.
    c. social nonconformity
4. State the conditions under which a person is usually judged to need help.
5. Explain the caution which is necessary to keep in mind when using psychiatric labels.
6. Explain why more women than men are treated for psychological problems.
7. Generally describe each of the following categories of mental disorders found in the DSM-IV.
    a. psychotic disorders
    f. somatoform disorders
    b. organic mental disorders
    g. dissociative disorders
    c. substance related disorders
    h. personality disorders
    d. mood disorders
    i. sexual and gender identity disorders
    e. anxiety disorders
8. List the four general categories of risk factors for mental disorders (Table 16-3).
9. Differentiate psychosis from insanity.
10. Describe the general relationship between violence and mental illness.
11. List and briefly describe the ten different types of personality disorders (see Table 16-4).
12. Describe the distinctive characteristics, causes, and treatment of the antisocial personality.
13. Explain the difference between public and private standards of sexual behavior, what sets true sexual deviations apart from other sexual activity, and what generally causes sexual deviations.
14. List and define eight behavior patterns (paraphilias) that fit the definition of sexual deviation.
15. Describe exhibitionism including who the offenders are, why they do it, and how one's reactions may encourage them.
16. Describe pedophilia (child molestation) including who does it, what the offenders are like, and the factors that affect the seriousness of the molestation. Explain how parents should react to an incident of molestation.
17. Explain how one can recognize signs of molestation from a child's behavior.
18. Explain why rape is not viewed by experts as primarily a sexual act.
19. Explain how sex role stereotyping may encourage the act of rape.
20. Differentiate anxiety from fear.
21. Outline the general features and characteristics of anxiety-related problems.
22. State what is usually meant when the term "nervous breakdown" is used. Differentiate this

category from an anxiety disorder.

23.   Define the key element of most anxiety disorders. Differentiate generalized anxiety disorders from panic disorders.

24.   Describe the following conditions:
   a.   specific phobia
         1.   *differentiate a social phobia from a simple phobia*
   b.   agoraphobia
   c.   obsessive-compulsive disorder
   d.   post-traumatic stress disorder
   e.   acute stress disorder
   f.   dissociative reactions:
         1.   *amnesia*
         2.   *fugue*
         3.   *multiple personality (dissociative identity disorder)*
   g.   somatoform disorders
         1.   *hypochondriasis*
         2.   *somatization pain disorder*
   h.   conversion reactions

25.   Discuss how each of the three major perspectives in psychology views neurosis. (Include the terms self-defeating, paradox, avoidance learning and anxiety reduction hypothesis.)
   a.   psychodynamic
   b.   humanistic-existential
   c.   behavioral

26.   Briefly describe Rosenhan's pseudo-patient study, and explain how his results relate to the idea of labeling.

27.   Explain how legal sanity or insanity is determined and present an argument for and against the existence of an insanity plea.

■ DEMONSTRATIONS, DRAMATIZATIONS, AND DISCUSSION

1.   **Although the emphasis in Chapter 16 is psychopathology and perspectives on abnormality,** it should be useful to devote some class time to the concept of mental health. Earlier discussion of Maslow's research on self-actualization advances one view of mental health. What does the class perceive as the basic attributes of a psychologically healthy individual? Can psychopathology be defined in the absence of some notion of health? As a starting point for discussion, you may want to present Jahoda's list of attributes:

   a)   accurate self-concept, self-awareness, self-acceptance;
   b)   self-actualization, full use of potential;
   c)   autonomy;
   d)   integration, a coherent outlook on life;
   e)   accurate perceptions of reality, social sensitivity;
   f)   competence and mastery of the environment.

(The preceding list is from M. Jahoda, *Current Concepts of Positive Mental Health*, Basic Books, 1958.)

2.   **A good way to illustrate the relativity of most definitions of abnormality** is to ask the class to describe examples of odd or unusual behavior they have observed in public. After getting several examples, return to each and ask if there is any set of circumstances under which the behavior observed might be considered normal. (For example, the person observed had lost a bet, was undergoing an initiation, was practicing a part for a play, was part of a psychology experiment, etc.) The point is that the behavior may have been truly eccentric, and perhaps pathological, but that few behaviors are universally normal or abnormal.

3.   **Here are some statistics you may want to discuss with your classes:** According to recent figures, an average of thirteen teen-age youths commit suicide each day in the United States, producing a yearly total of about five thousand. Since 1960 the number of suicides in the 15-24 age range has more than doubled. In the 10-14 age range there has been an increase of thirty-two percent since 1976. There has been an increase of roughly three hundred percent in youth suicides in the last eighteen years. At one time the incidence of suicide increased directly with age, reaching a peak in the 50-70 age range. Now there is a second peak--at about age twenty. There are now more suicides in the 15-24 age group than in the 50-70 group. Suicide is the number two cause of death among the young, with accidents number one.

4.   **A visit by a staff person from a local suicide prevention center** or crisis intervention team is always worthwhile.

5.   **The Audio-Visual Center at Indiana University** has recently produced a fascinating videotape that consists of interviews with four individuals suffering from a Bipolar Affective Disorder. In the first sequence a young woman is interviewed by a therapist while she is in the depressive phase of this disorder. This same young woman is then shown being interviewed during a manic episode. The change is so dramatic that students have great difficulty believing it is the same person. The tape then shows interviews with three different young men, each of whom is experiencing a hypomanic episode. Students find these interviews extremely interesting, and they produce a great deal of class discussion. The half-hour videotape can be obtained by writing to Indiana University Audio-Visual Center, Bloomington, IN 47401 and requesting BIPOLAR AFFECTIVE DISORDERS, tape No. EVH 2198.

6.   **Learning DSM-IV was daunting even for many mental health professionals.** In class, adding a game-like quality and a little competition to the learning process can work wonders. Assign each student the task of writing five Trivial Pursuit-type questions based on DSM-IV (to get even coverage it helps to assign major topic areas to different students). At the next class meeting combine the questions and divide the class into teams. Team members should be allowed to discuss their group answer before replying to a question. Keep score as you present questions, and reward the winning team with a special privilege or other form of recognition.

◼ ONE-MINUTE MOTIVATORS

1. **Prepare a list of unusual behaviors** and ask students if they are normal or abnormal for: a man? a woman? a person? a culture emphasizing passivity? a culture emphasizing aggression?

2. **During the late 1980's support groups developed to assist people who were victims** of abuse, neglect, alcoholism, rape, family violence, etc. What are the advantages and the disadvantages of a "victim mind-set"?

3. **Read definitions of major DSM-IV categories** and see if students can name the defined disorder.

4. **Have students estimate the number of parties they attended** during the preceding month. Make a frequency distribution on the chalkboard. Challenge the class to help you draw a line that defines "compulsive partying." As an alternative, collect data on the number of hours of television watched per week and define "TV addiction" by establishing a cut-off point.

5. **Ask students to help you name some humorous new phobias such as Muzakaphobia** (fear of being trapped in an elevator with piped-in music), cellulitophobia (fear that one's thighs are turning to cottage cheese, or Katophobia (this one is self-defining).

◼ CLASSROOM EXERCISES

TO THE INSTRUCTOR:

Abnormality has many different meanings. Certainly students come to this course with misconceptions and fixed ideas. To get students thinking along the same lines, you can use one or both of these exercises. By the time they finish the exercises and your class discussion of what they produced, they should be open to a more realistic appraisal of what is "normal" and what is not.

The first exercise focuses on the students' ideas about "normality". It should help them to see that there are many ways to be abnormal, depending on your definition and what you are looking for.

The second exercise is an attempt to observe what people generally do when confronted with behavior that is outside the expected.

Exercise #1: What Is Normal?

In this exercise students will be asked to distinguish between what is normal behavior and what is abnormal. There are a number of ways to do this:

1.   Statistically--this approach says that the mean is the norm, and any deviation from the mean is abnormal. The farther one's behavior is from the mean, the less normal the person is; or, conversely, the more abnormal. Those farthest from the mean are the most abnormal. Notice that from this viewpoint, both positive and negative deviations are equally abnormal.

2.   Clinically--people are judged as abnormal only if they display behaviors which deviate negatively from the norm. The greater the deviation, the greater the abnormality.

3.   Humanistically--well-adjusted people are somewhat rare, and they occupy the top of the distribution: they are self-actualizers. All others are maladjusted to some degree. Those who are farther down the scale are more maladjusted than those higher up. (See the Supplemental Lecture for a discussion of this approach.)

Procedure

A.   Discuss the three approaches to normality/abnormality outlined above.

B.   Distribute the student worksheets for their responses.

C.   Organize the class into small groups of three or four students so they can discuss the questions and record their conclusions on their worksheets.

D.   After the students have completed the discussion, you should ask them to report their conclusions. As each group reports, the whole class can comment. This should generate a good deal of interest in the topic of behavior disorders.

E.   Collect the students' work. Be sure that each student has written something. This is the best way to get students to think about the concepts being discussed.

WHAT IS NORMAL?   **WORKSHEET**

TO THE STUDENT:

In the space provided, report your group's decisions about each of the questions below. If you disagree with the rest of your group, indicate your disagreement and reasons. You will be asked to turn in this sheet after the discussion.

A.   List five types of behavior that would be considered abnormal according to all three approaches to the question of maladjustment explained by your instructor: statistical, clinical, or humanistic:

  1.

  2.

  3.

  4.

  5.

B.   List five types of behavior that would be considered statistically abnormal, but not from the other two points of view:

  1.

  2.

  3.

  4.

  5.

C.   List three types of behavior that would be considered mentally healthy from the humanistic point of view:

  1.

  2.

  3.

                                              Name_____

Exercise #2: The Deviant Among Us

This exercise, if carefully planned and executed, can be very beneficial to students. The main objective is to provide an opportunity for them to observe people's reactions to deviant behavior. They will, moreover, get to try out some observation techniques and will need to look more closely at behavior than they are accustomed to doing.

The students will observe people's responses to deviant behavior. It will be their own deviant behavior! Organize the students into groups of three for this exercise. One will be the deviant behaver, and the other two will be the observers. If time and opportunity permit, they could rotate and each take a turn at being deviant.

Students should form groups and plan a deviant behavior to perform and one or more locations in which to perform it. You should monitor this closely, so that the behavior is inoffensive, and the locations are appropriate. Any mistakes here could be embarrassing and/or costly!

Suggest that the "deviant" student might join a table of two or three who are eating lunch in the cafeteria. He/she could then be unresponsive to any gestures of friendship and/or mumble to him/herself while eating. The observers should be at a nearby table appearing to eat lunch but unobtrusively noting the behavior of those at the table. Other possibilities might be talking loudly (to no one) while walking down a crowded hall or sobbing uncontrollably in a busy lounge. Other ideas will come up. Be sure the students clear their plans with you before proceeding.

When the students return to class after completing the assignment, you should have a great discussion, including:

1.   reactions of the unsuspecting subjects to the "deviant;"

2.   the negative sanctions applied by the subjects;

3.   the feelings of your students before, during, and after the assignment was carried out;

4.   their thoughts about what it means to be normal or abnormal. Have their ideas on that changed with this exercise?

It would be good to ask the students to write up this project as an assignment for credit. They should describe the deviant behavior, the location, the reactions of the subjects, and his/her own reactions. This is a good way to give the students a chance to deal with their feelings about this assignment.

THE DEVIANT AMONG US: **WORKSHEET**

1.   "Deviant" student_____

2.   Observer students_____

3.   Location_____

4.   Description of deviant behavior:

5.   Description of subjects (number, sex, approx. age, etc.):

6.   Reactions of subjects:

Name_____

■ BROADENING OUR CULTURAL HORIZONS

1.   **What effect might living in different parts of town, membership in a different ethnic group,** or growing up in a different culture have on perceptions of "normality?"

2.   **Try to imagine a culture in which one of the sexual "deviations" listed in the text is accepted as a normal behavior.** How would our society be different if this deviation were accepted as normal?

3.   **All cultures differ not only in what they actually do in private but in what they say publicly about what they do in private.** Which sexual deviation do you feel is most loudly denounced in public? Which one is most often performed in private?

4.   **Rape is more common in American culture than in many other cultures.** Why? What social factors have affected its occurrence? Do you anticipate that the frequency of rape will increase or decrease over the next ten years? Why? (The rate has remained unchanged for the last 10 years, although the number of attempts has declined.)

■ SUPPLEMENTAL LECTURE

This lecture is a good way to begin the unit on behavior disorders. It accomplishes a couple of useful goals. The first is that it puts behavior disorders into a context that is meaningful and gives the students a way to see unity in what otherwise may be a fragmented discussion of symptoms and behaviors. The second is that it puts the emphasis on the positive by bolstering the concept of mental health. Students will see that mental health and mental illness are neither opposites nor absolutes. They are relative states which coexist in all persons.

The common misconception is that mental illness is a condition that is found in those persons who can no longer cope with the problems they face and need special care to survive. People use various terms which are considered synonymous with it, such as crazy, insane, or irrational (and, no doubt, each of us can think of others). This misconception is completed by the erroneous belief that those who aren't mentally ill, or crazy, are therefore sane, or mentally healthy. So, the thinking goes, you are either mentally ill, and therefore "out of it," or you are mentally healthy. This lecture proposes a different point of view.

MENTAL HEALTH

I.   Introduction

The concepts of mental health and mental illness can be illustrated by a comparison to physical health. It's a good way to do it because no one has a problem admitting to physical ill health-- but they do to mental ill health. Having laid the groundwork by discussing physical health and illness, you should be able to transfer the idea to mental health and illness.

II.   Physical Health

A.   A person's physical health varies from day to day, month to month, and year to year. All will agree to that. One's physical health can be good, bad, or in between and, for most people, it changes with time.

B.   You should illustrate this on the chalkboard as follows. Use a continuum because it is easier to illustrate change when seen on a scale.

PHYSICAL HEALTH

POOR   EXCELLENT
_____

C.   Using the above scale, define the two extremes. A person in excellent health may experience minor problems on occasion, such as a cold or an ingrown toenail, but can manage to take care of these conditions fairly easily and, therefore, maintains him/ herself as a fully functioning person.

A person at the other end of the scale has serious physical problems, and they may be life-threatening. The main criterion is the inability to function at all, or at least, adequately.

D.   Now it should be easy to show that most people are not at either extreme, but somewhere in between. Ask students to locate where they are on the scale at this moment. They will not all be at the same place. Also, it is important to point out that each person moves from one place to another on the scale. They can see that they have moved, some drastically, over the last twelve months.

Ask students where someone would be on the scale if he/she had chronic asthma, ulcers, hardening of the arteries, pneumonia, cancer of the liver, etc. Be sure they see the way in which health changes and varies.

III.   Mental Health

A.   Keep the scale of physical health on the chalkboard as you proceed with this portion of the lecture.

B.   Put the two extremes of mental health on the same scale you used for physical health, as follows:

PHYSICAL HEALTH

POOR   EXCELLENT
_____

MENTAL HEALTH

C.   Mental health varies from day to day, month to month, and year to year. One's mental health can be good, bad, or somewhere in between. It changes over time.

D.   Using the revised scale, define the extremes of mental health. Those at the high end have very few problems that they cannot easily handle. They can manage to handle and resolve problems reasonably well so that they can function adequately and live a relatively happy life.

      A person at the other end of the scale will have great difficulty solving problems and may not be able to handle the stresses of daily life. This person may not function at all or, at least, not well enough to satisfy most psychological and physiological needs.

E.   Now your job is to show that most people are not at one extreme or the other. Ask students to identify where they are on the continuum at this moment. It will become evident that each person is at a different point on the scale. Also, students can readily see that they shift up and down on the scale over time. Ask them to consider the last twelve months from this perspective.

      Now you can ask students to indicate where they think a person would be who hates his/her job and wishes he/she could be doing something else; where would a person be who is unhappy in his/her marriage and is seeking a divorce; if he/she is afraid to leave the house to go to the grocery store; if he/she suspects that aliens will take over the country unless she/he keeps watch, etc. Be sure they can see how one's mental health varies and changes over time.

F.   Just as there are degrees of physical health and physical illness, so there are degrees of mental health and mental illness. Someone with a cold is not as sick as someone with pneumonia--and he/she is not as sick as someone with terminal cancer. However, all are physically ill, just to different degrees. So also, someone with a fear of flying in planes is not as mentally ill as someone who has a fear of all flying insects, and he/she is not as mentally ill as someone who has fear of aliens flying in to take over his brain. However, all are mentally ill, just to different degrees.

IV.   Implications and Applications

      A.   The two concepts, side by side, help to show that:
            1.   Mental illness is a common condition which most people have to a greater or lesser extent.

2. Mental illness is not necessarily severe.

3. Something can be done for mental illness if it is recognized and treated in its early stages, as is the case with physical illness.

4. If left until it is too late, then mental illness, like physical illness, is likely to be difficult, if not impossible, to treat.

B. Help the students to accept the concept of mental illness as a common condition and the importance of early intervention to avoid serious problems.

C. Try to impress students with the fact that, just as serious physical illness is often untreatable and can lead to physical death, mental illness, if it becomes serious, is often untreatable and can lead to irreversible psychological disintegration (death).

■ SUGGESTIONS FOR FURTHER READING

Achenback, T. and C. Edelbrock. "Psychopathology of Childhood." *Annual Review of Psychology* (34) 1984: 227-256.

Alvarez, A. *The Savage God: A Study of Suicide.* Bantam, 1973.

Coleman, J. C. et al. *Abnormal Behavior and Modern Life*, 7th ed. Scott, Foresman, 1984.

Dollard, J. and N. E. Miller. *Personality and Psychotherapy.* McGraw-Hill, 1950.

Goldstein, J. J. and J. O. Palmer. *The Experience of Anxiety: A Casebook.* Oxford, 1963.

Janus, S. S. and C. L. Janus. *The Janus Report on Sexual Behavior.* John Wiley & Sons, Inc., 1993.

Lester, G. and D. Lester. *Suicide: The Gamble With Death.* Prentice-Hall, 1971.

McMahon, F. B. *Abnormal Behavior, Psychology's View.* Prentice-Hall, 1976.

Meyer, R. and Y. Osborne. *Case Studies in Abnormal Behavior.* Allyn and Bacon, 1982.

Parker, B. A. *Mingled Yarn: Chronicle of a Troubled Family.* Yale, 1972.

Rosenhan, D. L. and M. E. Seligman. *Abnormal Psychology.* Norton, 1984.

Schreiber, F. R. *Sybil.* Regency, 1973.

■ FILM SUGGESTIONS

ABNORMAL PSYCHOLOGY: THE PSYCHOSES (1980, Harper and Row, 23 mins.)
   This film tours a schizophrenia ward and interviews patients. The hospital director discusses the role of the hospital.

ANXIETY: THE ENDLESS CRISIS (1975, Indiana University, 59 mins.)
   This film examines a wide range of anxiety-producing situations--from the momentary flashes of anxiety that everyone experiences to extreme anxiety that can lead to death. Two mental health authorities discuss the difference between state anxiety and trait anxiety. The physiological as well as the mental reactions to anxiety are explained.

CASE STUDY OF MULTIPLE PERSONALITY (1973, CRM/McGraw-Hill, 30 mins.)
   This an assemblage of scenes from the film *Three Faces of Eve*; it depicts multiple personality and includes actual interviews.

CHILDHOOD'S END (1982, Filmakers Library, 57 mins.)
   This is a documentary portrait of three suicidal youngsters, one of whom succeeded in killing himself. The film does not try to simplify a complicated phenomenon and leaves a strong impression of the tragedy and waste of this irreversible action.

DEPRESSION: BEATING THE BLUES (1985, Filmakers Library, 28 mins.)
   As this film indicates, unlike normal feelings of being blue which may last for hours or days, true clinical depression can last for weeks and months. The film investigates the latest research on the causes of depression and explores the variety of treatments available. Among the treatments highlighted are chemotherapy, electroconvulsive therapy, and psychotherapy.

DEPRESSION: A STUDY IN ABNORMAL BEHAVIOR (1973, CRM/McGraw-Hill, 26 mins.)
   In this film on abnormal behavior, the viewer follows a young housewife/teacher through the course of a depressive episode. The pattern of abnormal behavior becomes clear through watching her inability to function normally; her husband's attempts to ignore her erratic behavior; his growing awareness that she is disturbed; her suicide threat; his decision to get help; and the process of diagnosis, hospitalization, and treatment.

FINDING OUT: INCEST AND FAMILY SEXUAL ABUSE (1984, Kinetic Films, 25 mins.)
   This film concentrates on the role of the victim's mother in dealing with family sexual abuse. Viewers are shown Robin, a victim since age nine, who talks about the devastating emotional effects of sexual abuse. Her mother tells how she dealt with the disclosure and the subsequent breakup of her marriage.

INCEST: THE FAMILY SECRET (1984, Filmakers Library, 57 mins.)
   As this film indicates, incest is a widespread problem that occurs in all kinds of families. Most commonly, it takes the form of sexual child abuse inflicted by the father on a non-consenting daughter while she is still a child. In this very frank program, adult women talk about the childhood experiences which so traumatized their later lives.

TITTICUT FOLLIES (1971, Zipporah Films, 90 mins.)
>   This is a documentary about the lives of patients in a state mental hospital. It is a controversial film that presents a very stark portrayal of hospital conditions.

SUICIDE - IT DOESN'T HAVE TO HAPPEN (1976, Phoenix/Bfa Films And Video, Inc., 20 mins.)
>   This film presents a dramatization, based on case histories, about a high school teacher who helps a suicidal student.

WHAT IS NORMAL (1990, Coast Community College District Telecourses, 30 mins.)
>   Part of the *Psychology - The Study of Human Behavior Series*, this video explains the distinction between normal and abnormal behavior.

CHAPTER 17

Major Mental Disorders

■ BEHAVIORAL OBJECTIVES

The student should be able to:

1. List and explain the five major characteristics of a psychosis.
2. Define delusion. List and describe the six different types of delusions.
3. Define hallucination and name the most common type.
4. Explain how a brief reactive psychosis differs from other psychoses.
5. Differentiate an organic from a functional psychosis.
6. Describe the following types of organic psychoses:
    a. general paresis
    b. those from lead and mercury poisoning
    c. senile dementia
    d. Alzheimers disease
7. List the three major types of functional psychoses.
8. Describe what a delusional disorder is, including the most common, paranoid psychosis.
9. Generally describe schizophrenia.
10. Distinguish between schizophrenia and a schizotypal personality disorder.
11. List and describe the four major types of schizophrenia.
12. Explain how paranoid delusional disorder (psychosis) and paranoid schizophrenia differ.
13. Describe the roles of the following three areas as causes of schizophrenia:
    a. Environment
        1.   prenatal problems and birth complications
        2.   trauma
        3.   disturbed family environment
        i. double-bind communication
        ii. deviant communication
    b. Heredity
    c. Brain chemistry
        1.   dopamine (include a description of recent studies on dopamine receptors in the brain)
14. Explain how CT, MRI, and PET scans contribute to the study of abnormal brain activity.
15. Explain why the Genain sisters case (Highlight 17-3) supports both genetic and environmental explanations of psychosis. Describe the stress-vulnerability model.
16. State the incidence and characteristics of mood disorders, especially depression, in the general population.
17. Describe the characteristics of depressive disorders. Include a description of dysthymia, cyclothymia, and reactive depression.

18.   Differentiate maternity blues from postpartum depression. Describe what may predict the occurrence of the latter and the best way to treat it.

19.   List and describe the four major mood disorders. As a group, explain how they differ from affective psychoses (include the concept of endogeny).

20.   Explain how major mood disorders differ from dysthymia and cylclothymia.

21.   Describe six possible explanations for the occurrence of depression.

22.   Explain seasonal affective disorder (SAD) and how it can be helped.

23.   Distinguish between the two basic kinds of treatment for psychosis.

24.   Define chemotherapy. List and describe the three classes of drugs used to treat psychopathology.

25.   Discuss the advantages and disadvantages of the use of chemotherapy in the treatment of psychosis. (Include the term tardive dyskinesia in your discussion.)

26.   Describe the risk-benefit controversy for drugs such as Clozaril, Risperdal, and Prozac.

27.   Describe the roles, advantages, and disadvantages of electroconvulsive therapy. Include a discussion of how the ECT debate is resolved.

28.   Describe the past and current uses of psychosurgery in the treatment of psychosis.

29.   Describe the role of hospitalization and partial hospitalization in the treatment of psychological disorders.

30.   Explain what deinstitutionalization is and how community mental health centers have attempted to help in the treatment of mental health.

31.   Discuss how each of the following factors affects suicide rate:
        a.   season
        b.   sex
        c.   age
        d.   income
        e.   marital status

32.   List the emotions which typically precede suicides. Discuss why people try to kill themselves.

33.   Name/identify the eight warning signs of suicide.

34.   List four common characteristics of suicidal thoughts and feelings.

35.   Explain how you can help prevent suicide.

36.   Describe Thomas Szasz's view of mental illness and treatment.

■ DEMONSTRATIONS, DRAMATIZATIONS, AND DISCUSSION

1.   **A number of issues relating to diagnosis, chemotherapy, hospitalization, and patient rights can be addressed by asking the class to consider this hypothetical situation:**

        John has spent much of the last month curled up in a fetal position under the dining room table in his apartment. A worried neighbor called the local county mental health unit. John has been hospitalized on a 72-hour hold for observation.

        There are several questions for discussion:

Who should decide if he should be further hospitalized?

Should he be given drugs, with or without his consent?

When should he be released?

Who should decide: his parents, a psychiatrist, a judge, John alone?

2. **If there is a chapter of the National Association for Mental Health in your area,** volunteer speakers can often be arranged through this organization. Also, interested students may themselves participate as volunteers in out-patient programs or other mental health services.

3. **For some reason, a simple description of the dangers of psychiatric labeling fails to impress many students what a profound impact such labeling can have.** The dramatization described here must be handled with great care and sensitivity, but if it is done well, it may be one of the more memorable sessions of the course. Here is what you can say and do:

Today we have a very special opportunity. After our last meeting a student from this class approached me and said that he had been hospitalized for schizophrenia several years ago. This student has volunteered to share with us his experiences while hospitalized. I told him I thought it was an excellent idea and added a twist of my own. One of the secondary problems often associated with mental hospitalization is the stigma that follows a person afterward. Many people believe that if a person becomes psychotic, that person will be "crazy" for life. To illustrate how complete recovery from schizophrenia is, I'm going to call three people up to the front of the class. One is the student we will be talking to, and the other two don't know I'm going to call on them.

Select three students from the class and call them to the front. (It is best to select three students you know to be stable and adaptable. To avoid gender complications, select all male or all female students. In this example, male students are used.)

In a few moments we're going to do an interesting thing. I want to prove that it is impossible to correctly identify a "former mental patient." To give you something to go on, I'm going to ask each of these people to tell us a little about themselves, their major in school, or their interests.

Have each student give his or her name and speak for one or two minutes. Then ask the class to decide which person they think was hospitalized at one point in his life. Tell them to write their choice. Just as they begin, tell them to stop and cross out anything they have written. Reveal to the class what you have done and emphasize that you selected the students because of their maturity and that you know nothing about their backgrounds. Begin discussion by interviewing the subjects. Given that each knew that <u>he</u> was not the former patient, his perceptions of the other two subjects are usually radically affected. Also note that what subjects choose to say about themselves under these circumstances is usually <u>very</u> safe and <u>very</u> normal. Next interview the rest of the class and discuss how labeling affected their immediate perceptions <u>and</u> their interpretation of the <u>past behavior</u> of each subject. Be sure to point out that, while many were hesitant to choose one of the subjects, most <u>did choose</u> because of the labeling. Finally, be sure to thank the students who participated and ask the class to show their appreciation to them.

4. **The text mentions that there is a case on record of four identical quadruplets all of whom developed schizophrenia.** The odds against this happening are truly staggering. Identical quadruplets occur only once in every sixteen million births, and less than half of them survive to adulthood; only one in a hundred of these is schizophrenic, and the odds against all of them being schizophrenic seem overwhelming. This case, then, could seem to provide evidence for the heritability of schizophrenia. However, you should point out to your students that the quadruplets shared many other things besides their genes. For example, they all shared their mother's uterus where they could have contracted a viral infection or been exposed to some chemical substance. They all had the possibly brain-damaging liability of being born with very low weights. All of them were placed in incubators and spent the first six weeks of their lives in a hospital. They all grew up with constant publicity surrounding their daily activities. Finally, they all shared a father who was known for eccentric and erratic behavior and who remained extremely close to them even into adulthood. For more information, see a report on the twenty-year follow-up on this unusual and interesting case by M. S. Buchsbaum, "The Genain Quadruplets," *Psychology Today,* August 1984.

5. **If there is a mental hospital in your area, arrange to take your students on a tour of the facility.** There will be an office for volunteers in the hospital. They will set it up or direct you to someone who will. Some of the students may wish to become volunteers once they know of the opportunity. Prepare the students beforehand. You should give a thorough briefing, preparing the students for the observation. Discussion, films, or a visit by a volunteer would also help prepare the students so they get the most out of the trip. Otherwise, the students will not know what to look for, and the experience will become a matter of simply feeding their curiosity.

■ ONE-MINUTE MOTIVATORS

1. **Ask students to describe what they think life is like in a mental hospital.** Compare the popular conceptions of a "madhouse" with the real thing.

2. **The popular notion of "split personality" could be explored.** Ask students what it means. What is "split?"

3. **A nervous breakdown is often mentioned when discussing mental illness.** Ask students what has broken down. What "nerves" are affected and where are they? It should lead to a discussion of identifying disorders by symptoms instead of labels.

4. **Students should be asked to recall their most serious occurrence of depression.** Have them write a few sentences describing their mood and behavior. Compare these reports.

■ CLASSROOM EXERCISE

This is an exercise that should help students to appreciate the problems created by using labels to identify the problem behaviors that people have. The persons become identified with the label, and our stereotypes take over. It is difficult for someone who has been labeled with a psychological problem to shake the image no matter how he/she behaves.

PROCEDURE

1. Invite a person unknown to your students to come to class to impersonate a former mental hospital patient. The person needs to be a convincing actor who will feel comfortable in front of the class. It is best to choose someone who has familiarity with a mental hospital--possibly someone who has worked or volunteered in one. Ask the person to talk about life in a mental hospital. Give students the opportunity to ask questions.

2. Prepare your class for the visit. Tell them that this person was diagnosed as paranoid schizophrenic and has spent a couple of brief periods of therapy in a mental hospital. Students should be asked to review the appropriate material in the text and to prepare questions about hospital life. Ask them to be sensitive to the feelings of the "patient."

3. After the speaker has departed, ask the students to discuss his/her behavior. They should look at it from a variety of points of view. Ask them to respond to questions such as those following. You may have other questions which you wish to ask.

    a. What was their impression of this person's behavior?
    b. Did the person show any symptoms of the disorder for which he/she was hospitalized?
    c. Does he/she appear to be "cured" of this disorder?
    d. Did his/her thinking appear to be normal?
    e. Were his/her emotions flat or inappropriate?
    f. Did the students notice any side-effects of medication?
    g. Were there any peculiar or unusual behaviors?

DISCUSSION

After the discussion questions above are completed, tell the students what you did. Now discuss their reactions to this revelation. Also discuss their responses to the above questions. Did labeling influence their reactions and observations?

■ BROADENING OUR CULTURAL HORIZONS

1.   **Depression is much more frequent among females than it is among males.** Why?

2.   **Challenge students to compare the frequency of suicide** in our culture to the frequency in another culture. How would they explain the difference?

3.   **Collect a few clips from *National Geographic*** episodes and ask the class whether the behavior shown would be perceived as "episodes of mental illness" within another culture.

4.   **In many European countries men's restrooms are tended by women.** Discuss the implications this has for any attempt to create a culture-free definition of abnormal behavior.

■ SUPPLEMENTAL LECTURE

An interesting way to present the whole idea of maladaptive behaviors is to present the concept of adjustment as a continuum. The differences among the types of maladjustments, whether they are minor, or more extensive, as in neurosis and psychosis, are matters of degree and not of kind. There are two common threads that can be seen from one end of the continuum to the other. One is anxiety. Anxiety is a constant, but it varies in intensity as one moves along the scale. The other is the use of mechanisms. Small amounts of anxiety require minor mechanisms to give relief, whereas large amounts of anxiety require major mechanisms to help the person survive.

This is not an attempt to explain all neuroses and psychoses. Many factors, both hereditary and environmental, are probably involved. The goal here is to give the students an idea that makes sense and helps them to get a little insight into what is going on in the lives of people who are troubled and unable to cope with the problems they face from day to day.

In preparation for this lecture be sure to review with the class the basic concepts needed to understand what will come next. They need to be familiar with the meaning of anxiety, mechanisms, frustration, and mental health. They should also know how anxiety is aroused and why mechanisms are used.

ADJUSTMENT

I.   Introduction

A.   The notion of adjustment can be useful if we don't make it appear too mechanical--like adjusting a thermostat.

B.   Get help from students to arrive at a working definition. If you used the lecture on mental health given for Chapter 16 of this manual, you already have the basis for this presentation. Well-adjusted people are mentally healthy. The students will volunteer a variety of ideas. Try to steer them into coming up with at least the following characteristics that define adjustment:

1.   how well a person is able to satisfy his/her important needs;
2.   how well a person can get along with others, especially those who disagree with him/her, and those people he/she <u>has</u> to be with: family, co-workers, boss, teachers, classmates, etc.;
3.   how happy and contented a person is.

C.   If you put all that together, you can define adjustment as the ability of the person to get along in society, satisfy his/her needs, and develop his/her capabilities to the fullest extent.

D.   You could picture this concept on the chalkboard by drawing a continuum as follows. It constitutes an adjustment scale:

LOW   HIGH

POORLY   WELL
ADJUSTED   ADJUSTED

Ask student to (privately) mark an X on the scale where they think they are today based on the criteria given above.

II.   Levels of Adjustment

A.   Students should be brought to understand that adjustment is not static. They need to realize that:

1.   No two people are at precisely the same point on the scale at the same time.
2.   Each person moves on the scale, up and down, depending on the circumstances in his/her life. Stress and crises can lower adjustment, so the person may have a tougher time getting along. In good times, the level goes up and it all seems easier.

Students should be made aware that for most of them the toughest tests are still ahead. Can they maintain or improve their present levels of adjustment? Only time will tell! A little discussion will reveal that most of them still have to gain and maintain economic and emotional independence. For some this will be easy; for many it will be stressful, and some will not be able to handle it at all.

If students doubt that they change much, ask them how well they cope with adversity at 7:00 a.m. as opposed to a frustration at 10:00 or noon. Not being able to find his socks at 7:00 a.m. may be a major crisis for someone who feels as if he can slay a dragon by noon.

B.   Those on the high end of the scale are well adjusted; those on the low end are very poorly adjusted. What accounts for a person's place on the scale?

Adjustment is defined as the person's ability to function satisfactorily and satisfy his/her needs. Therefore, the notion of frustration as an obstacle to need satisfaction should be reviewed from previous discussions (Chapter 11). When obstacles stand in the way of satisfying important needs, anxiety can result, especially if the frustrations are chronic.

Anxiety is painful, or at least, uncomfortable, and a person tries to avoid it or get rid of it. Mechanisms are behavior patterns developed to do just that.

The more anxiety a person has, the more need for mechanisms and the greater the mechanisms are. Greater mechanisms take up more time and energy than do minor ones. Therefore, the poorer the person's adjustment is, the greater his/her dependence on mechanisms and the more preoccupying they are.

C.   If we pursue this idea, then we can picture the following continuum. Levels of adjustment on it are identified in relation to the person's ability to adjust, based on the criteria established earlier.

LOW			HIGH
PSYCHOTIC	NEUROTIC	MINOR MALADJUSTMENTS	WELL ADJUSTED

D.   Now ask students (privately, again) to look for the X they marked on the scale a while back. Sometimes they are shocked to see where they put themselves once labels are attached. This is why it is important to ask them to identify themselves on the scale ahead of time.

E.   Now you should remind the students that people move up and down on the scale and that very few are at either extreme. Most are somewhere in the middle--even psychologists!

III.   Definition of Levels of Adjustment

A.   This is where you need to point out that today people are not categorized as neurotic or psychotic. You can remind them of the new classifications (DSM-IV) which take into account a variety of behaviors and don't pigeon-hole people with labels.

B.   Your discussion of the four levels should focus on the following:

1. **Well adjusted**--These people can manage, most of the time, to satisfy their needs and get along with others. They will have some problems but can usually deal with them in a satisfactory way. They seldom need to use mechanisms, and, if they do, they are not major and last only briefly.

2. **Minor maladjustments**--These people have some problems and cannot always deal adequately with them as they arise. They have anxiety and often resort to withdrawal or defense mechanisms to get by.

3. **Neurotic**--These people have high levels of anxiety, and mechanisms occupy a significant part of their time and energy. They will have a great deal of difficulty at work and at home, but can manage to get along to some extent.

4. **Psychotic**--At this level, the mechanisms take on major proportions. Persons here will not be able to function well some or all of the time. Their time and energy are often totally occupied with dealing with anxiety. They may have difficulty maintaining contact with reality. People at this level need to receive some kind of care because they cannot care for themselves during psychotic episodes.

IV. Discussion

A. You need to discuss all aspects of these concepts thoroughly. Students will relate personal experiences with friends or relatives.

B. Students will write very personal and often poignant papers about their experiences with someone in their family if asked to do so. This is a good follow-up assignment.

■ SUGGESTIONS FOR FURTHER READING

American Journal of Psychiatry. 134 (9) 1977. A special issue devoted to the pros and cons of ECT.

Arieti, S. *Understanding and Helping the Schizophrenic.* Basic Books, 1979.

Bassuk, E. L. and S. Gerson. "Deinstitutionalization of Mental Health Services." *Scientific American*, Feb. 1978: 46-53.

Braginsky, B. M., D. Braginsky, and K. Ring. *Methods of Madness: The Mental Hospital as a Last Resort.* Holt, 1969.

Coleman, J. C. *Abnormal Psychology and Modern Life.* Scott, Foresman, 1984.

Goffman, E. *Asylums.* Doubleday, 1961.

Gottesman, I., J. Shields, and D. Hanson. *Schizophrenia: The Epigenetic Puzzle*. Cambridge University Press, 1982.

Green, H. *I Never Promised You a Rose Garden*. New American Library, 1971.

Kesey, K. *One Flew Over the Cuckoo's Nest*. Viking, 1964.

Laing, R. D. *The Politics of Experience*. Ballantine, 1964.

Rosenhan, D. L. "On Being Sane in Insane Places." *Science*, 179, 1973.

Szasz, T. *The Myth of Mental Illness*. Delta, 1967.

-----. *The Manufacture of Madness*. Harper and Row, 1970.

■ FILM SUGGESTIONS

ABNORMAL BEHAVIOR: A MENTAL HOSPITAL (1971, CRM-McGraw Hill, 28 mins.)
>   The purpose of this documentary is to describe the difference between popular myth and the reality of an actual mental hospital and its patients. Included are a series of patient-therapist sessions in which the therapists discuss symptomology, diagnosis, treatment, and general prognosis of their patients.

FULL OF SOUND AND FURY: A FILM ABOUT SCHIZOPHRENIA (1985, Filmakers Library, 54 mins.)
>   What is it like to suffer from schizophrenia? This film explores the lives of three individuals who have been profoundly affected by this elusive mental disorder. For the families of those suffering from schizophrenia, the experience is tragic, and the film presents an interview with the mother of a young man whose torment ultimately drove him to suicide.

MADNESS AND MEDICINE (1977, CRM/McGraw-Hill, 45 mins.)
>   This film explores the mental institution and its patients, the quality of life in the institution, and the patients' feelings about the treatment they receive. The use of chemotherapy, electroshock therapy, and psychosurgery are discussed by both doctors and patients.

THE SILENT EPIDEMIC: ALZHEIMER'S DISEASE (1982, Filmakers Library, 25 mins.)
>   This film describes Alzheimer's Disease and shows the problems raised by its ever-increasing incidence. The film notes that although the disease can be diagnosed, there is still no cure for its degenerative and ultimately fatal course. Also discussed is the issue of whether Alzheimer's patients should be cared for in their homes or in other facilities.

TITICUT FOLLIES (PARTS I AND II) (1969, Grove Press, 84 mins.)
>   This is a revealing exposure of conditions at a Massachusetts hospital for the criminally insane. It is highly recommended as a basis for discussion.

PSYCHOTIC DISORDERS (1990, Coast Community College District Telecourses, 30 mins.)
>   Part of the *Psychology - The Study of Human Behavior Series*, this video discusses schizophrenia, its treatment and possible causes.

CHAPTER 18

Therapies

■ BEHAVIORAL OBJECTIVES

The student should be able to:

1. Define psychotherapy.
2. Describe each of the following approaches to therapy:
   a. individual therapy
   b. group therapy
   c. insight therapy
   d. action therapy
   e. directive therapy
   f. non-directive therapy
   g. time-limited therapy
   h. supportive therapy
3. Evaluate what a person can expect as possible outcomes from psychotherapy.
4. Briefly describe the history of the treatment of psychological problems, including in your description trepanning, demonology, exorcism, ergotism, and Pinel.
5. Explain why the first psychotherapy was developed.
6. List the four basic techniques used in psychoanalysis and explain their purpose.
7. Name and describe the therapy that is frequently used today instead of psychoanalysis. Describe the criticism that helped prompt the switch.
8. Contrast client-centered (humanistic) therapy and psychoanalysis.
9. Describe client-centered therapy including the four conditions that should be maintained for successful therapy.
10. Explain the approach of existential therapy and compare and contrast it with client-centered therapy. Name and generally describe one example of existential therapy.
11. Briefly describe gestalt therapy.
12. Contrast the goal of behavior therapy with the goal of insight therapies.
13. Define behavior modification and state its basic assumption.
14. Describe aversion therapy and explain how it can be used to stop smoking and drinking.
15. Explain the relationship of aversion therapy to classical conditioning. State two problems associated with aversion therapy.
16. Explain how relaxation, reciprocal inhibition, and use of a hierarchy are combined to produce desensitization. State what desensitization is used for and give an example of desensitization therapy or vicarious desensitization therapy. Very briefly describe eye-movement desensitization.
17. List and briefly describe the seven operant principles most frequently used by behavior therapists.
18. Explain how nonreward and time out can be used to bring about extinction of a maladaptive behavior.
19. Describe a token economy including its advantages and possible disadvantages. Include the terms "token" and "target behavior" in your description.

20.   Describe what sets a cognitive therapist apart from other behavior therapists. List and describe four thinking errors which underlie depression and explain what can be done to correct such thinking. Describe the effectiveness of cognitive therapy for depression.

21.   Describe rational-emotive therapy. List the three core ideas which serve as the basis of most irrational beliefs.

22.   Describe the advantages of group therapy.

23.   Briefly describe each of the following group therapies:
       a.   psychodrama
       b.   family therapy
       c.   group awareness training (including sensitivity groups, encounter groups, and large group awareness training)

24.   Discuss the limitations of phone-in psychologists and describe what the APA recommends should be the extent of their activities.

25.   Evaluate the effectiveness of encounter groups and sensitivity groups and include the concept of the therapy placebo effect.

26.   Discuss the effectiveness of psychotherapy. Describe the rate at which doses of therapy help people improve.

27.   List the six goals of psychotherapy, and state the four means used to accomplish the goals.

28.   List and briefly describe the nine points or tips which can help a person when counseling a friend.

29.   Describe how covert sensitization, thought-stopping, and covert reinforcement can be used to reduce unwanted behavior.

30.   Give an example of how you can overcome a common fear or break a bad habit using the steps given for desensitization.

31.   List and describe four indicators that may signal the need for professional psychological help.

32.   List six methods a person can use for finding a therapist.

33.   Describe how one can choose a psychotherapist. Include the concepts of self-help groups and bibliotherapy.

34.   Summarize what is known about the importance of the personal qualities of the therapist and the client for successful therapy.

35.   List the four main cultural barriers to effective counseling discussed by Sue and Sue.

36.   List and explain the six characteristics of culturally skilled counselors.

■ DEMONSTRATIONS, DRAMATIZATIONS, AND DISCUSSION

1.   **Students will undoubtedly find a visit by a clinician interesting in conjunction with the readings in this chapter.** If possible, invite a clinical colleague or clinician in private practice to class. Even if you yourself are a clinician, the inclusion of a person with different viewpoints and experiences will enrich discussion.

2.   **It is not too difficult in the classroom to simulate some basic approaches to psychotherapy.** Ask for a volunteer and begin by asking the student to recount a recent dream. Select an interesting element from the dream and ask the student to free associate to

it. Follow a few of the interesting thoughts through further free association, and make note of any apparent resistances. Point out that you are using psychoanalytic techniques, and then ask the student what he or she would like to talk about next. Shift into a non-directive style and simulate a Rogerian approach. As soon as this approach has been illustrated, begin watching for an irrational assumption in what the student is saying. When you find one, shift to the more confrontative and didactic tone of RET. Again point out what you have done. Finally, return to some topic which has already surfaced and demonstrate the theatrical "here-and-now" approach of Gestalt therapy. For example, ask the student to say something to an empty chair representing a parent, roommate, lover, etc. Next ask the student to sit in the chair and answer as that person, and then to stand up and reply to the imagined person, and so forth. Conclude by reviewing and discussing all the techniques that have been illustrated.

3. **A brief illustration of one or two sensitivity techniques can be interesting. A trust walk is a good choice.** Randomly pair students and instruct them to walk to some point on campus. On the way to the chosen point, one student should be blindfolded while being guided by the second. On the way back, they should reverse roles. For a more dramatic demonstration, have a student stand with several students arranged behind him or her. The student must close his/her eyes and fall backward--to be caught by the group. This takes real trust!

4. **As various therapies are tried, modified, and developed, the possibility of controlling maladaptive behavior increases.** It is possible to foresee a time when such techniques will be perfected to the point where behavioral change, and therefore, behavioral control, will be much easier to accomplish and more certain. Ask the students to consider some questions about this because it would be possible, then, to control not only maladaptive behavior, but any behavior. Is it a good idea to go that far? Can we keep the knowledge for good purposes and keep it out of the hands of manipulators who want to exploit others? Who should decide when and how a therapeutic technique should be used? Who will protect the interests of the mentally ill who could be exploited?

5. **Invite an experienced psychiatrist who has successfully used electroconvulsive shock therapy to class to discuss its use, value, and consequences.** Students should be prepared ahead of time with good questions; otherwise, they tend, on first hearing the specifics of the procedure, to be bothered by what they imagine to be an unpleasant and painful experience since any reference to electric shock has negative connotations. Good preparation can make for a productive class discussion.

6. **If it is possible to find someone who has undergone aversion conditioning at one of the many commercial stop-smoking services,** invite him/her to be a guest speaker. Interview him/her with respect to the effectiveness of the technique, the degree of discomfort experienced, how long the effects lasted, how he/she now feels about the issue of behavior control, etc. A point worth exploring is the cost of the treatment. One could argue that expensive, aversive procedures simply produce strong commitment to a nonsmoking regimen by creating a powerful cognitive dissonance effect, rather than actually conditioning aversions.

7. **To give students experience with the basic elements of systematic desensitization, it can be interesting to guide them through the steps of deep muscle relaxation.** When they are thoroughly relaxed, announce that one of the reasons you wanted them to be relaxed is that in a moment you are going to give a surprise test on behavior modification. At that point, ask students if they were able to notice an increase in tension or anxiety when you announced the test. If they could, tell them they did not pass the item, "surprise quiz announced in class," on a hierarchy of test anxiety, and that they will have to repeat the relaxation exercises! This will allow them to see what actually occurs in systematic desensitization.

8. **For an interesting discussion starter,** have two teams of students prepare a debate reflecting the opposing viewpoints of insight therapists and behavior therapists. Another good topic for debate is the question of whether or not, or under what circumstances, behavior modification techniques should be used in schools, the military, prisons, programs for the mentally retarded, mental hospitals, and other institutional settings.

9. **Students' understanding of systematic desensitization is enhanced when they have an opportunity to experience it.** Another way to provide this experience is to combine Jacobson's traditional relaxation exercise with the construction of a class anxiety hierarchy. Most students seem to have an aversion to tarantulas which can provide a suitable topic for the generation of an imaginary hierarchy. Have class members combine relaxation techniques with visualization of scenes from the hierarchy. If all goes well, some students can be brought to the point of imagining, without obvious discomfort, dozens of tarantulas crawling all over them. (Jacobson's relaxation technique is described in M. Goldfried and G. Davidson, *Clinical Behavior Therapy*, Holt, Rinehart, and Winston, 1976.)

■ ONE-MINUTE MOTIVATORS

1. **Ask students to explain the difference between** a witch doctor, or shaman, and a psychotherapist.

2. **Briefly describe the historical, economic, political, and sociological times of Freud.** If Freud were beginning his career now, how would his theory and therapy be different?

3. **Ask students to keep a "daydream journal" by jotting in the margin of their notes the topic of any daydreams they have.** At the end of a week, ask students to evaluate their daydreams. What are the themes? How frequently do the daydreams occur? What do the dreams say about the student's feelings toward this course or other events in their lives? Do they reveal unconscious desires, as postulated by Freud?

4. **After a few sentences of your lecture, call on a volunteer to restate what you said.** Invite a student who heard your ideas differently to provide her/his view. After three or four attempts to rephrase satisfactorily, it should be clear how important "reflecting" is for really understanding what we are saying to each other.

5. **To focus on the "here-and-now,"** suddenly ask a student what he/she is feeling at the moment. Continue with the lecture. Ask another student. If students have trouble expressing their feelings, use Gestalt techniques to clarify their immediate experience.

6. **Ask students to turn to the person next to them and share "things left unsaid" to someone they care about.** If they could talk to anyone in the world to add closure to the relationship, who would they call? What would they say?

7. **Encourage students to think of five good things that happened today.** If they have been feeling depressed, is this difficult to do? Is it helpful?

8. **Ask students to practice active listening, clarifying, and focusing on feelings.** Students can share the activities of the previous weekend or their feelings about friends, relatives, work, or this class. Students should find that active listening is time consuming, exhausting, and tremendously important. Most of us have not been trained to really listen to each other.

9. **Ask students to think of something they are currently doing that they wish they would not do.** Then pass out a rubber band to each student. Encourage them to zing themselves with the rubber band every time they think about doing that undesirable behavior. Discuss the pros and cons of aversive techniques.

10. **Ask the class to repeat in unison, "I am a valued, competent person."** What are the limits of the "positive thinking" inherent in much cognitive therapy?

11. **As a homework assignment ask each student to identify an irrational fear that he/she has.** He/she should then develop a desensitization plan to overcome the fear. Ask them to try the plan and report to the class.

12. **Students who have pets that do tricks should be asked how the pet was taught** and how the behavior is maintained.

13. **Ask students if they know anyone who has had an intense fear or bad habit and has overcome it.** See if there were any behavioral principles involved in dealing with the problem. If not, discuss how such principles could have been used.

■ CLASSROOM EXERCISES

Exercise 1: A Friend in Need

TO THE INSTRUCTOR:

This is an exercise that ought to be required of every student. Its purpose is to give students first-hand experience in locating mental health services in his/her own area. This could pay big dividends later. Everyone needs at some time to think about getting or helping someone get professional psychological help. In a crisis a person may not have the time or opportunity to do a thorough review of what is available in the area. Being prepared is a great advantage. Students will be surprised, when this project is completed, at the vast number of services available in most communities. There are always many more than people expect there to be.

PROCEDURE

A.   Set up one or more scenarios for the students. An example would be the following. Each scenario could focus on a different type of problem although this one covers quite a few:

>   You have a friend who has a serious adjustment problem. It has reached the point where he/she can no longer do his/her work, is having serious problems with his/her family, is generally miserable and very anxious. Thoughts of suicide recur, and he/she has started drinking heavily. He/she knows you are studying psychology and asks you for some assistance in finding good professional help. The friend indicates that he/she has some money, but is on a limited budget.

B.   Divide the class into groups of three, asking each group to research the resources that would be available in the city and county to help the friend. They should identify specific sources of help and know something about the kind of assistance that would be provided. This means they should visit the facility, talk to personnel there, read brochures, etc. to become well informed. Provide each student with a worksheet. You may want to modify or add to the sample given.

C.   Once the students have completed the research, all groups should report on the same class day. As they give their findings, compile a master list of resources in the area. This could be refined and distributed to the students.

D.   Provide some incentives to the class. Give a reward, such as extra class credit, to the groups who bring in comprehensive lists. Be sure that everyone who tried hard is a winner, not just one or two. Another incentive could be having the students, when the comprehensive list is completed, distribute it to places where it could be used--the college counseling office, local churches and clergy, helping agencies in the local government, etc.

A FRIEND IN NEED: ASSIGNMENT SHEET

TO THE STUDENT:

You have a friend who has a serious adjustment problem. It has reached the point where he/she can no longer do his/her work, is having serious problems with his/her family, is generally miserable and very anxious. Thoughts of suicide recur, and he/she has started to drink heavily. He/she knows you are studying psychology and asks you for some assistance in finding professional help. The friend indicates that he/she has some money, but is on a limited budget.

You and your group are to research the area (extend your search to include the whole county) to find all the possible resources that might help your friend.

On separate sheets, complete the following:

1.   Indicate the resources which you have found. Note where you found out about each and how you checked it out.

2.   State briefly what services your friend could expect from each of the resources, who is eligible for the services, and what the fees might be. This will require a personal visit, a phone call, or, at least, reading some literature provided by the office or agency.

3.   What do you think of the possibilities of your friend getting the kind of help he/she needs, based on what is available in your area? Explain your answer.

Exercise 2: Behavior Self-Modification

TO THE INSTRUCTOR:

This is an exercise that will get students to think about behavior modification techniques. It is a project that can be done in one class period, as it is described here, or could be more elaborate and done over a whole term. Some modification would be needed, but the basic idea is the same whichever way it is done.

Ask the students to form small groups, three per group would be ideal, and work on a plan to change a behavior. Each of the three should have a behavior to change. The group can work on each one. There is an advantage to a group rather than an individual working on the problem because it is more likely to get done if the group works on it. It also gives support to each individual in the planning and executing of the change.

In preparation for this project, you may need to review the basic concepts of operant conditioning to make sure everyone understands them. In particular, go over reinforcement so that they are clear on how it is to be applied.

PROCEDURE

1.   Divide the class into groups of three to design and execute the project.

2.   Distribute the instructions and worksheets for the exercise, and go over them with the students.

3.   Ask students to submit their worksheets and a plan of action for your review.

4.   If you feel this is worthwhile, ask the students to carry out the plan of action, once it has been reviewed and critiqued by you, and to report back to their group and to you on their progress after a specified number of weeks.

BEHAVIOR SELF-MODIFICATION: WORKSHEET

TO THE STUDENT:

In this exercise, you will identify a behavior you want to change, and the group will help you to develop a plan of action to bring this about. You should do the following:

1. Each person in your group should identify a behavior he/she would like to change. Keep it simple. Try something like nail-biting, smoking, a poor study habit, or overeating. You can certainly think of others.

2. Use the outline that follows as a guide for developing your program for change. First you should describe the present situation; then you can work on changes. Keep in mind that you should try to do only what is possible. There is no point in planning what you won't carry out.

I.   The Present Situation

A.   **The problem behavior**: Here you should briefly but clearly state what behavior you wish to change. It should be described exactly as it occurs, indicating frequency, circumstances, and how you feel when doing it.

B.   **The stimulus cues**: These are the stimuli in your environment that have become associated with the behavior you wish to change. An example: smoking while drinking a cup of coffee. If you want to stop smoking, you will have to change that whole behavior pattern because coffee drinking and smoking have become associated. What are all the cues or stimuli that are associated with the undesirable behavior? You should try to identify as many of these as possible. It may be a good idea to do some self-observation, taking notes of the circumstances that surround the behavior you want to change. (If you are doing this assignment over a long period of time, keep a log for several days to be sure you don't miss the significant cues.)

C.   **The reinforcements**: You will need to identify the immediate and delayed reinforcements for the behavior you want to change. Be honest about this, and try to identify what they are. For example, smoking relaxes you and makes you feel good; it looks cool; it gives you something to do with your hands; you can blow neat smoke rings, etc.

II. Changes That You Plan to Make

A.   **The new behavior that you want to develop to replace the old**: Remember, you can't just stop doing something. You need to do something different in its place. An overeater doesn't stop eating, but eats differently! A smoker doesn't stop breathing, but inhales differently! Describe the new behavior. It needs to be attainable.

BEHAVIOR SELF-MODIFICATION WORKSHEET: (page 2)

  B. **New stimulus cues**: Objects or events you plan to associate with the new behavior to help it become established.

  C. **The reinforcements for the new behavior**: These need to be both immediate and long range. Plan specific reinforcements and set specific times when they will be received.

  D. **Behavioral changes**: No behavioral changes occur in a vacuum. The new behavior and the new stimulus cues that are associated with it should constitute a total change in your lifestyle or approach to whatever you are changing. For example, to lose weight or maintain a desired weight you have to change not only how much you eat, but what, when, and where you eat. You also have to change your way of thinking about food. Your new behaviors, reinforcements, etc. have to reflect a total commitment to the new style for it to have a lasting effect.

III. Keep accurate and detailed records to chart your progress. Speak with the instructor about your plan and the progress you are making once you are working on the change.

■ BROADENING OUR CULTURAL HORIZONS

1.   **All societies find some mechanism for facilitating change in others.** Compare and contrast the therapeutic role of witch doctors, folk-medicine practitioners, and religious leaders. What might all these have in common that would help at least some people feel better?

2.   **Research psychotherapy in other cultures.** What is the goal of the therapy? What techniques are used? How effective are they? For example, various drugs, herbs, chemicals, and vitamins are used in the Far East to treat "impotence," which is regarded as a psychological problem in about half the cases in America. [See Shikai, Xu (1990), "Treatment of impotence in traditional Chinese medicine." *Journal of Sex Education and Therapy*, 16(3), 198-200.]

3.   **Sometimes the purpose of therapy is to change a person's behavior,** other times the purpose is to encourage the person to better accept aspects of his/her own behavior. Think about differences between your culture and the culture of your parents (or your children). What behaviors do your parents want you to change? Which behaviors would you want them to better accept? What happens when two cultures or two generations clash in terms of whose behavior is supposed to change? How do the politics of power affect the kinds of changes that therapy encourages and the specific groups who are doing most of the changing.

4.   **Select a single problem such as alcohol abuse or nail biting.** Ask students to interview people from different cultures to find out how they try to deal with these problems. What aversive stimuli might be used? What part do positive and negative rewards play?

■ SUPPLEMENTAL LECTURES

Lecture 1: Personal Adjustment

In this lecture, the perspective is on the positive. The student will have learned, or soon will, that there are no sure cures for mental illness. Most physical illnesses can be diagnosed and treated successfully most of the time. This is particularly true if the condition is treated in its early stages. In the case of mental illnesses, there is not the same assurance that they can be diagnosed and treated successfully. Early identification and treatment can be helpful, but there is no certainty that any therapy will do the job.

Students must be made aware of the devastating consequences of a mental illness. They also need to realize that it can happen to them. Just as no one anticipates an accident, physical injury, or serious physical illness, no one anticipates a mental illness. However, as the physical illnesses come unwanted, so do the mental illnesses. Each student is likely to suffer some mental illness, whether minor or major, at some time in his/her life.

In the light of the certainty of mental illness, a wise person would try to be prepared. Being prepared means doing what is necessary to avoid the likelihood of becoming mentally ill, or, failing that, minimizing the severity of the condition when it comes. However, people are more likely to take precautions to avoid physical illness or injury than they are to avoid mental illness or disability. Also, people are more likely to look for professional help if they have a physical illness than if they have a psychological problem. Often help is not sought from a professional person until the problem is so severe that the person can no longer function adequately. This makes it less likely that treatment will have a satisfactory result.

So, the theme of this lecture is psychological fitness. You can spend a useful class period discussing how to maintain and improve good personal adjustment.

PERSONAL ADJUSTMENT

I. **Introduction**

    A.   Make the comparison between physical health and mental health discussed above.

    B.   Be sure students understand that one can be mentally ill in varying degrees, just as one can be physically ill to a greater or lesser degree. See the lectures for the previous two chapters, which deal with these concepts in some detail.

    C.   Emphasize the importance of maintaining one's mental health and improving it where possible. Be sure that the students understand that most people can be mentally healthier than they are.

II.   Improving One's Personal Adjustment

    A.   People should attempt to achieve self-understanding by the following methods:

        1.   **Accept and tolerate some anxiety;** everyone has some. If people expect it and do not get upset when stress and frustration complicate their lives, they are more likely to deal with the situations adequately.

        2.   **Avoid the excessive use of withdrawal or defense mechanisms.** Some people may try to relieve anxiety through these mechanisms, and it's important to recognize this behavior for what it is and control it, rather than letting it control you. Mechanisms may give short-term relief but usually create more and bigger problems in the long run.

        3.   **Come to understand their motives.** People need to gain insight into what their needs are and how they are seeking to satisfy them. Everyone wants approval, but putting others down to make oneself look better (gain approval) is counterproductive.

B.   People must adjust and alter goals to suit the conditions and circumstances, and take into account what they know about themselves. Goals that are unrealistic lead to frustration, anxiety, and discouragement.

If goals are too high and unattainable, they will cause endless frustration and will be self-defeating. People need to experience success to be encouraged to keep going. Setting goals that are reachable will make people feel successful and want to try for more. A mentally healthy person is constantly reevaluating goals and setting new ones.

On the other hand, goals that are too low will lead to misery and dissatisfaction. People who set low goals feel unfulfilled and cheated. It takes self-confidence and courage to raise one's sights a little higher and work to get there.

C.   People should try to reduce conflict and frustration. Some suggestions for doing this are:

1.   **Learn to postpone satisfaction** for needs that cannot be satisfied immediately. People can plan how to satisfy them better at a future date and avoid frustration and anxiety.

2.   **Develop frustration tolerance.** People should not fret and fuss about things that they cannot attain. Some things will not be attainable. Rather than focusing their thoughts on those and feeling miserable, people should attend to the possible and enjoy their accomplishments and successes.

3.   **Find socially acceptable ways to vent emotions.** Since strong emotions, such as anger, will occur, people need to have ways to express them without doing harm to themselves or others. A person should plan for and have readily accessible ways to express emotions appropriately. Often people tend to simply hold in the emotion, that is, not express it and act as if it didn't exist. This can cause misery for the person and be dangerous if it accumulates and gets out of control.

4.   **Keep busy with useful work.** Besides doing what one has to do, a person should be occupied with interesting and useful activities whenever possible. This could be in one's occupation or as a leisure activity. People have to go out and find success and happiness. It seldom comes to those who wait and hope it will come to them.

D.   Whenever a persistent problem appears, people should seek appropriate help. One can seldom be objective enough to see the situation clearly and take care of it alone. Someone who is not personally or emotionally involved has a better chance of seeing the situation clearly and helping to resolve the problem.

Moreover, professionals should be sought. Advice from well-intentioned, unskilled persons can often lead to disaster and seldom provides the assistance needed to help a person grow and develop fully.

Lecture 2: Who's In Charge Here?

Since nearly everyone has one or more "bad habits" that he/she would like to change, you could spend a productive class session talking with the students about how a behavioral change, using principles of conditioning, could be effectively achieved. It will soon become apparent, in a class discussion, that almost everyone has tried and failed to change a behavior that was troublesome.

The purpose of this lecture is to help students see the importance of secondary reinforcers in human behavior. It is likely that failure or success in changing behavior is due to a large extent on how a person deals with these factors. They are often referred to as cues. Because these cues are associated with the behavior, they trigger the response. Therefore, a smoker is more likely to smoke in the presence of smokers, and an eater is more likely to eat in the presence of food. Smokers and food are cues which initiate or sustain the behavior.

WHO'S IN CHARGE HERE?

I.   **Introduction**

  A.   Review the basic principles of classical and operant conditioning since both are needed to understand this concept.

  B.   Discuss with the students specific examples from their own experience, or from the experiences of people they know well, of how they tried to change bad habits. Talk about the successes and failures and also the successes that later failed. Ask them to speculate on why the successes succeeded and the failures failed. Also, why did some successes eventually turn into failures?

II.   **Primary and Secondary Reinforcement**

  A.   Primary reinforcement is the consequence which initiated the undesirable behavior and maintains it. For any behavioral change to occur, this would have to be identified and eliminated so that extinction of the behavior would be possible. Therefore, this is the first task if a change in behavior is the goal.

  B.   However, it is evident to most people that eliminating the primary reinforcer doesn't always result in extinction of the previously reinforced behavior. Assuming that the diagnosis was accurate and the primary reinforcer was identified, we need to look for an explanation for the resistance to extinction: Why does the earnest dieter have trouble losing weight or the smoker return to the cigarettes?

C. There may be several explanations: One that is certainly going to be a factor is the presence of secondary reinforcers. Most people are not aware that these exist or what they are. Only a careful analysis of one's habits would reveal them. They will be many and varied and may bear very little relationship to the primary reinforcer or the undesirable behavior. For example, a person who likes to sit in his favorite recliner after dinner, sip his coffee, and watch the evening news while smoking a cigarette cannot perform the same ritual after dinner, omitting only the cigarette, and expect to kick the smoking habit. All of these circumstances have become associated (classically conditioned) to the primary reinforcer. The recliner, coffee, and news all are associated with smoking and its satisfaction and so will be strong motivation to continue.

D. A successful program to change a behavior needs to include a study of the reinforcers and all of those factors which have become incidentally associated with the behavior. All of these need to be changed. To lose weight and maintain the loss, a person needs to examine and change all the behaviors related to food. He/she cannot simply eat less or eat smaller portions of fattening foods for a time. A change in one's lifestyle is needed to be successful. This involves a major commitment which most people are unwilling to make.

III. **Discussion**

A. There should be lots of material for discussion in the ideas expressed above. Students should be asked again to think about their failures and how their attempts to change bad habits may have been undermined by secondary reinforcers and unrelated associations of which they were not aware.

B. Suggest to students that they try to keep a personal log relating to a specific behavior. They should keep detailed notes for about a week. They should note the frequency of the behavior, the reason it is performed each time, the possible reinforcement for it, the circumstances surrounding the urge to perform it, and the actual performance of the deed. A log that is detailed will begin to show that there are circumstances and actions that are repeated. It will become evident that certain cues are stimulating the behavior. A plan for behavioral change will need to take those into account.

■ SUGGESTIONS FOR FURTHER READING

Berne, E. *Games People Play*. Grove, 1964.

Binder, V., E. Binder, and B. Rimland. *Modern Therapies*. Prentice-Hall, 1976.

Burton, A. (ed.). *Twelve Therapists*. Jossey-Bass, 1972.

Ellis, A. and R. Harper. *A New Guide to Rational Living*. Prentice-Hall, 1975.

Frankl, V. *Man's Search for Meaning*. Simon and Schuster, 1970.

Freud, S. *General Introduction to Psychoanalysis*. Simon and Schuster, 1969.

London, P. *Behavior Control*. Perennial Library, 1971.

Meyers, R. *The Clinician's Handbook*. Allyn and Bacon, 1983.

Perls, F. *Gestalt Therapy Verbatim*. Real People Press, 1969.

"Psychiatry on the Couch." *Time*. 2 April 1979: 74-82.

Rathus, S. A. and J. S. Nevid. *Behavior Therapy*. Signet, 1978.

Rogers, C. *Client-Centered Therapy*. Houghton Mifflin, 1951.

Ruitenbeck, H. M. *The New Group Therapies*. Avon, 1970.

Tharp, R. and R. Wetzel. *Behavior Modification in the Natural Environment*. Academic, 1969.

Ullman, L. P. and L. Krasner. *Case Studies in Behavior Modification*. Holt, 1965.

Vogler, R. E. and W. R. Bartz. *The Better Way to Drink*. Simon and Shuster, 1982.

Watson, D. and R. Tharp. *Self-Directed Behavior: Self-Modification for Personal Adjustment*. Brooks/Cole, 1981.

Williams, R. L. and J. D. Long. *Toward a Self-Managed Life*. Houghton Mifflin, 1979.

Wolpe, J. *The Practice of Behavior Therapy*. Pergamon Press, 1982.

■ FILM SUGGESTIONS

ACTUALIZATION THROUGH ASSERTION (1976, Research Press, 25 mins.)
    This film illustrates the development of a more assertive style through the use of group techniques.

AUTISTIC CHILD: A BEHAVIORAL APPROACH (1983, CRM, 26 mins.)
    This film portrays what is known about autism, as well as what is unknown, and includes its cause(s). It focuses on the use of behavior modification in teaching autistic children social and verbal skills.

BEHAVIOR MODIFICATION: TEACHING LANGUAGE TO PSYCHOTIC CHILDREN (1969, Prentice-Hall, 42 mins.)
    This film, based on the work of Ivor Lavaas at UCLA, demonstrates reinforcement and stimulus fading techniques used in teaching language skills to psychotic children. Frequent use of graphs and charts

illustrates the effects of the treatment program and rates of improvement.

BEHAVIOR THERAPY: AN INTRODUCTION (1978, Harper and Row, 23 mins.)

This film demonstrates application of contingency management, counter-conditioning, and role playing to a variety of problems, including a violent child, stage fright, and shyness.

CARL ROGERS CONDUCTS AN ENCOUNTER GROUP (1975, Extension Media Center, 70 mins.)

Carl Rogers discusses factors that he believes are important in successful facilitation of a group. Highlights include Rogers in a group setting interacting with individual members.

HARRY: BEHAVIORAL TREATMENT FOR SELF-ABUSE (1980, Research Press, 38 mins.)

The patient shown in this film, Harry, has spent most of his life in institutions, wearing various types of physical restraints. Although he is only mildly retarded, the severity of his self-abuse defeated all attempts to educate him, and past treatment programs had failed to eliminate his unusual behavior and need for physical restraints. The film shows the inauguration of a behavioral treatment program and the use of fading, extinction, time-out, and positive reinforcement in the treatment of Harry.

THE HUMAN POTENTIAL MOVEMENT: JOURNEY TO THE CENTER OF THE SELF (1975, Pennsylvania State University, 18 mins.)

This film focuses on the human potential movement and Dr. William Shutz, founder of the Esalen Institute. There are scenes of encounter group sessions emphasizing techniques for releasing aggression.

PEER-CONDUCTED BEHAVIOR MODIFICATION (1978, Research Press, 24 mins.)

Jeff assaults and provokes his classmates. A program is developed to change Jeff's behavior and that of his peers. The role of peers in shaping and reinforcing deviant behavior and the value of peers as positive behavior modifiers are demonstrated.

THE POWER OF POSITIVE REINFORCEMENT (1978, CRM, 28 mins.)

Behavior modification, with its emphasis on positive reinforcement, is recognized as a powerful tool for managing human performance. This film documents the systematic on-site application of this principle at a 3M plant in California where the result was five million dollars saved through increased worker efficiency. Additionally, the film examines its use in the less traditional settings of Valley Fair Amusement Park in Minnesota, on the defensive line of the Minnesota Vikings, and in the streets of Detroit with the City Sanitation Department.

PSYCHOTHERAPY (1979, CRM/McGraw-Hill, 26 mins.)

This film provides reasons for seeking psychotherapy and clarifies some of the elements crucial to a successful therapeutic experience. Through a series of encounters between patients and their therapists, the film provides an overview of the basic process of therapy and the major elements common to all psychotherapeutic techniques.

RATIONAL EMOTIVE THERAPY (1982, Institute for Rational Emotive Therapy, 29 mins.)

This film overviews "rational emotive therapy" originated by Dr. Albert Ellis in 1955. Interviews with Ellis explain why he rejected traditional therapies and discuss the evolution of RET.

STROKE SEEKING BEHAVIOR: THERAPEUTIC TRAPS AND PITFALLS (1976, APGA, 30 mins.)
Excerpts from group therapy sessions are used to illustrate common stroke-seeking behavior by clients which serves to divert efforts from therapeutic progress. Ways in which counselors are manipulated are illustrated as well as suggestions for ways in which to get clients to change.

THERAPY: WHAT DO YOU WANT ME TO SAY? (1974, CRM/McGraw-Hill, 15 mins.)
This film presents a young woman who has been pressured into seeing a psychologist, and her immediate reactions are hostility and fear. As the film shows, for most young people the stigmas attached to therapy are many. The film attempts to create a climate in which viewers can achieve insights about therapy and the role it can play in troubled lives.

TOKEN ECONOMY: BEHAVIORISM APPLIED (1972, CRM, 23 mins.)
The film begins as B. F. Skinner cites the five classic victims of behavioral mistreatment: old people, orphaned children, prisoners, psychotics, and retardates. He goes on to explain the use of tokens in a program of reinforcement therapy. Finally, to demonstrate Skinner's theories, the film takes the viewer to a facility of the Illinois Department of Mental Health where the program director explains how token economies are practiced.

WHAT IS GESTALT? (1969, Pennsylvania State University, 24 mins.)
This film features a discussion by Fritz Perls and includes an illustration of awareness training.

■ COMPUTER PROGRAMS: *Mind Scope*

Exercise 20, Anxiety Hierarchy

In this exercise students are asked to make a series of paired comparisons of descriptions of different situations that involve snakes, or snake-like stimuli. The different situations are then ordered according to the degree to which the stimuli make the students uncomfortable. The set of stimuli are then reordered according to this hierarchy. This helps illustrate the technique developed by Wolpe in which a phobic client is exposed in a gradual way to the stimuli that provoke terror.

CHAPTER 19

Gender and Sexuality

■ BEHAVIORAL OBJECTIVES

The student should be able to:

1. Differentiate primary from secondary sex characteristics and state (in general) what causes them.
2. Define or describe the following terms or concepts:
   a. gonads
   b. menarche
   c. ovulation
   d. menopause
   e. estrogens
   f. androgens
   g. testosterone
3. List and describe the five dimensions of gender.
4. Explain how a person's gender develops. Include in your discussion a description of these conditions:
   a. androgen insensitivity
   b. hermaphroditism
   c. androgenital syndrome
   d. biological biasing effect
5. Differentiate gender identity from sex role and explain how gender identity is formed.
6. Describe the effects of socialization on sex roles and include a discussion of instrumental and expressive behaviors.
7. Explain the meaning of the term "androgyny" and its relationship to masculinity, femininity, and adaptability.
8. Discuss the differences between males and females in their degree of arousal to erotic stimuli.
9. Explain what a sexual script is and how it relates to sexual behavior.
10. Explain what causes differences in sex drives in males and females.
11. Describe the effects of alcohol, castration, and aging on the sex drive.
12. Discuss the normality and acceptability of masturbation.
13. Define the term sexual orientation. Discuss the combination of influences that appears to produce homosexuality. Characterize the emotional adjustment of homosexuals versus heterosexuals.
14. List in order and briefly describe the four phases of sexual response in men and women.
15. State the two most basic differences in the sexual response styles of men and women.
16. Describe the changes that have taken place in sexual attitudes and behavior in the last 50 years.
17. Explain what is meant by the phrase, "slow death of the double standard."
18. Define acquaintance of "date rape" and discuss its effects.
19. Explain the cause, methods of transmission, and ways of preventing AIDS.

20.   Describe the following sexual problems including the nature, cause, and treatment of each:
      a.   Desire Disorders (hypoactive sexual desire, sexual aversion)
      b.   Arousal Disorders
              1.   *Male erectile disorder*
              2.   *Female sexual arousal disorder*
      c.   Orgasm Disorders
              1.   *Male orgasmic disorder*
              2.   *Female orgasmic disorder*
              3.   *Premature ejaculation*
      d.   Sexual Pain Disorders
              1.   *dyspareunia*
              2.   *vaginismus*
21.   List eight techniques that can be used to encourage effective communication between husbands and wives.
22.   Discuss the cultural limitations of non-sexual touching.

■ DEMONSTRATIONS, DRAMATIZATIONS, AND DISCUSSION

1.   **A high interest class exercise involves having students in small groups discuss their attitudes toward various sexual topics.** Before class, write ten to fifteen of the terms in Chapter 19 on 3 x 5 cards (e.g. masturbation, oral sex, double standard, premarital sex, etc.). Make a separate set of cards for each group. In class, assemble the students in groups of four or five and place a set of cards in front of one member of each group. That person is instructed to randomly draw a card, announce the topic, and then express his or her own attitudes and feelings about the subject. After each person in the group has expressed his/her opinions on the topic, the person next to the one who started the discussion draws a second card which again goes around the group with each person expressing his/her opinions. The exercise continues with each person taking a turn at initiating the discussion. After all the groups have finished, it is useful to conduct a general class discussion on reactions to the exercise. Most students have had few opportunities to share their feelings on these topics with others and usually find the exercise enlightening and valuable.

2.   **Another way to help students explore their attitudes toward various sex-related matters is to give them a sex-topics survey.** You might like to construct your own questionnaire or else adapt the one that appeared in the July 1969 issue of *Psychology Today*. The results of this survey were summarized in the July 1970 issue of the magazine and are usually of great interest to students.

3.   **A topic that usually generates lively discussion is the question of where and how students gained their knowledge of and developed their attitudes toward sexuality.** Studies have indicated that parents are often uncomfortable discussing sex with their children and leave them to gain their information from other sources.

4. **Inviting a representative of a gay rights organization to speak** to the class can give students a new perspective on the issue of homosexuality in our society.

■ ONE-MINUTE MOTIVATORS

1. **Ask students to do the following:**

    List 5 traits of your personality, 5 interests, and 5 behaviors you usually engage in. Then close your eyes and imagine yourself as the other gender. Picture your "self" doing and feeling these same things. If you had been born the other gender, in what ways would your identity be similar or different?

2. **Ask students to complete the following:**

    I feel nurtured when . . .
    I feel angry when . . .
    I feel most attractive when . . .
    I feel most vulnerable when . . .

3. **Carry a purse, wear an earring, man's necktie, man's hat, or some other cross-gender cue to class.** Ask students how their perceptions are affected. How do such objects come to have such powerful gender-linked meanings?

■ CLASSROOM EXERCISE

This exercise is intended to open up discussion on the topic of sexuality. Since students may feel inhibited about sharing their views and knowledge, the Sexual Information Survey can get them into the proper mindset. It also becomes easier to talk about something that has become somewhat impersonal by first responding on paper.

The Sexual Information Survey contains a sampling of facts that are often misunderstood. Students sometimes feel very sophisticated, but have a good deal of misinformation about sex. You may want to add to the list given here. If so, simply type a second page and add it to the questionnaire.

Have the students score their own papers. If the surveys are not signed, you could collect them at the end of the period and report on the next class day, giving students an idea of how informed and misinformed they are as a group. If you use this survey in several classes, you could also get overall statistics for each item to report to the class. However, keep in mind that the survey is intended to be a discussion-starter and a means of letting the students know that they have more to learn about the topic. Its purpose is not simply to show them how uninformed they are.

The correct answers to the items:

1. T	5. F	9. F	13. T	17. T
2. F	6. T	10. F	14. T	18. T
3. T	7. F	11. F	15. F	19. F
4. T	8. T	12. F	16. F	20. T

SEXUAL INFORMATION SURVEY

This survey is intended to measure how much information students have about some topics that will be discussed in the section on human sexuality. You should not sign the survey so your responses will remain anonymous.

Mark each item either true (T) or false (F).

_____ 1. Sex education in school is favored by most parents.

_____ 2. There is clear evidence that the incidence of sex crimes is directly related to the availability of pornographic materials.

_____ 3. Highly educated males are more likely to masturbate than males who have very little education.

_____ 4. American culture is more restrictive regarding sexual activity than most other cultures.

_____ 5. Sexual intercourse is considered proper only in marriage in nearly all cultures.

_____ 6. Impotence in men and frigidity in women usually have no physical cause but are learned behaviors.

_____ 7. Homosexuality is caused by unsatisfactory sexual experiences in the childhood or teen years, according to most recent studies.

_____ 8. Most transsexuals and transvestites are male.

_____ 9. The sex of a child is determined at conception by the genes in the ovum of the female.

_____ 10. It is predicted by most social scientists that marriage will eventually disappear in this country.

_____ 11. A person can expect serious physical and emotional harm from excessive masturbation.

_____ 12. Venereal diseases are usually spread by prostitutes.

_____ 13. Incest taboos are found in some form in all societies.

_____ 14. Sexual arousal can occur without direct stimulation of the erogenous zones.

_____ 15. A person with a small penis is unable to stimulate the most sensitive areas of the vagina.

_____ 16. A vasectomy causes a reduction in sexual desire because male hormones are no longer produced or available.

_____ 17. Sexual desire and response are not affected by a hysterectomy.

_____ 18. A survey of women indicates that about two-thirds of those entering marriage for the first time have had an orgasm.

_____ 19. Frequency of sexual intercourse between married couples increases up to about age thirty-five and then gradually decreases to near zero by about age sixty.

_____ 20. Homosexual women have far fewer sexual partners than do homosexual men.

■ BROADENING OUR CULTURAL HORIZONS

1. **Imagine a society in which one gender is domineering, shrewd, and responsible for the home.** The other gender is team-oriented, cooperative, and the breadwinner. What would the rest of the society be like? What would be the role of the family? Of competition?

2. **Many cultures have special rites of passage into puberty.** A few have circumcision rites—for both males and females. What are the rites of passage into puberty for your culture?

3. **Students can be asked to evaluate a written essay, a work of art, or an accomplishment.** With half the class the creator can be given a female name; with the other half a male name can be used. Quickly collect the data and see if the ratings differ because of the supposed gender of the creator. Would such differences in judgments occur if the work were attributed to a person from a culture very different from ours?

■ SUPPLEMENTAL LECTURE

There is a tendency in American society to stereotype people, put labels on them, and then treat them as if they are all the same. In the area of sexuality, where the term homosexual is used to label persons with a certain sexual orientation, the term is applied equally to all in this group. Those who are labeled in this way are all treated in the same negative manner even though there is a wide range of behaviors.

There is, nevertheless, in our society a wide diversity of sexual orientation and preference. This lecture is a good way to introduce students to this concept. You can expect to find resistance to the idea and a good deal of misunderstanding. Because of the strong feelings about homosexuality, it is difficult for students to see that they themselves behave in ways that could be termed homosexual.

SEXUAL ORIENTATION

I.   Introduction

A.   Begin by defining the term sexuality. Be sure to define it in its broadest terms, which include the quality or state of being sexual and the constitution and life of the person as related to sex.

B.   Make sure that in the definition it is clear that the term refers to more than intimate sexual contact between two people. Rather, it refers to a person's state of being and life style in establishing and maintaining relationships with other people. It is a way of receiving pleasure and enriching one's life.

II.   Sexuality

    A.   Each person relates to many other people sexually. This means that he/she has an interest in establishing or maintaining an intimate relationship with those people and involves sharing something of oneself with them. Most people have a natural desire to do this. The need for love and affection seems universal.

    B.   Have the students examine the way they like to share their interests and with whom they like to do it. It will become evident that many men prefer to drink beer with their male friends, go out dancing with female friends, see a ball game with other males, etc. Women may prefer to shop with other women, go to movies with male friends, eat lunch with female friends, etc.

    C.   The discussion should show that almost everyone enjoys some activities more with members of the same sex and other activities with members of the opposite sex.

    D.   Now move the discussion a step further. With which sex, the same or opposite, does each one prefer spending most of his/her time? It should become evident that there are marked differences. While some will prefer the opposite sex more than their own, many will prefer to spend time with, and they derive pleasure from activities with, like-sexed partners. This should begin to reveal sexual orientation. Discuss what some of these activities are.

    E.   Now ask students to think about their own life styles in regard to sexual orientation. Where would they be on a scale that measures this kind of orientation? Put this scale on the chalkboard, and ask them to identify their spot on it at the present time:

SAME SEX   OPPOSITE SEX

        SAME SEX--place yourself at or near this end only if you prefer to spend most of your time and derive most of your pleasure from activities with members or your own sex.

        OPPOSITE SEX--place yourself at or near this end only if you prefer to spend most of your time and derive most of your pleasure from activities with members of the opposite sex.

Probably most people will find they are not at either extreme, but somewhere in between. That is, they derive pleasure from and like to spend time with members of the opposite sex at times and with their own sex at others. However, most will probably not be in the middle, but will lean in one direction or the other. Some men prefer to spend more time and derive more pleasure from being with women and others with men, and the same is true for women.

III.   Heterosexuality and Homosexuality

A.   Now you can introduce these terms. This is where the fun begins. Students will resist taking this step. Define the terms this way:

HOMOSEXUALITY--preferring to spend more time with and deriving more pleasure from activities with members of one's own sex.

HETEROSEXUALITY--preferring to spend more time with and deriving more pleasure from activities with members of the opposite sex.

B.   You can now put these terms on the orientation scale which you have already drawn on the chalkboard. Now it should look like this:

SAME SEX   OPPOSITE SEX
_____

HOMOSEXUAL   HETEROSEXUAL

C.   Explain what this means. By using a scale that is a continuum, you are illustrating that:

1.   Sexuality varies across the whole span of orientation. There is no such thing as being all homosexual or entirely heterosexual. Most people have some of each orientation.

2.   There is the possibility and likelihood that the orientation can shift or change in either direction over one's lifetime.

D.   Everyone performs heterosexual acts and homosexual acts.

Whenever a person does something that gives pleasure with a member of the opposite sex, it is a heterosexual act, whether it is a date to the movies with a friend, telling an interesting story to one's brother or sister, or having intimate sexual contact.

Whenever a person does something that gives pleasure with a member of the same sex, it is a homosexual act, whether it is having a cup of coffee together, or a beer, going to a ballgame, fixing a car, going shopping, or having intimate sexual contact.

E.   This approach focuses on the behavior rather than on the person. It tells us that we all behave in homosexual and heterosexual ways, and, most of all, it says that neither, in itself, is bad or good.

IV.   Discussion

    A.   Discuss this concept of sexual orientation with the students and compare it with the generally accepted idea that people are one or the other, either all homosexual or all heterosexual.

    B.   Be sure to get the students to discuss the question of values here. Sexual orientation should not be considered good or bad. However, some sexual behaviors may be good or bad, depending on how and when they are done. This is true regardless of the person's sexual orientation--no matter where on the scale he/she is.

■ SUGGESTIONS FOR FURTHER READING

Bach, G. and P. Wyden. *The Intimate Enemy*. Morrow, 1969.

Ellis, A. *The Sensuous Person*. Signet, 1974.

Fisher, S. *Body Consciousness*. Prentice-Hall, 1973.

Hite, S. *The Hite Report*. Macmillan, 1976.

Hunt, M. *Sexual Behavior in the 1970's*. Playboy Press, 1974.

Hyde, J. S. *Understanding Human Sexuality*, 5th ed. McGraw-Hill, 1994.

Janus, S. S. and C. L. Janus. *The Janus Report on Sexual Behavior*. John Wiley & Sons, Inc., 1993.

Kaplan, H. S. *The New Sex Therapy*. Brunner/Mazel, 1974.

Maier, R. *Human Sexuality in Perspective*. Nelson Hall, 1984.

Masters, W. and V. Johnson. *Human Sexual Response*. Little, Brown, 1976.

----. *Human Sexual Inadequacy*. Little, Brown, 1970.

Tavris, C. and C. Offir. *The Longest War: Sex Differences in Perspective*, 2nd ed. Harcourt Brace Jovanovich, 1984.

Wilson, S. et al. *Human Sexuality*. West, 1977.

■ FILM SUGGESTIONS

GENDER AND RELATIONSHIPS (1990, Coast Community College District Telecourses, 30 mins.)
Part of the *Psychology - The Study of Human Behavior Series*, this video explores the complexities of emotional interactions and attachments.

SEX FOR SALE: THE URBAN BATTLEGROUND (1977, CRM, 45 mins.)
This film is a look at the civil, legal, and moral battles currently being fought in most urban centers as prostitution and pornography grow more pervasive. Four mini-reports are included: the damage that commercialized sex is causing to urban centers, the reason pornography is booming, the story of one Detroit neighborhood's battle against prostitution, and a look at one street prostitute's violence-marked life.

SEX ROLE DEVELOPMENT (1974, CRM, 23 mins.)
This film examines the influence that sex roles and stereotypes have on almost every facet of people's lives, the ways they are instilled in successive generations of Americans, and the ways in which some people are currently trying to find better models for human behavior.

THE SEXES: ROLES (1978, Filmakers Library, 28 mins.)
This film surveys the evolution of male-female roles from prehistory to our current industrial age. Judith Bardwick points out the stresses caused by the clash between traditional expectations and new realities while Matina Horner presents her classic studies on women's "fear of success," and sociologist Jean Lipman-Blumen relates how "girls are socialized to destroy their own dreams at an early age."

THE SEXES: WHAT'S THE DIFFERENCE? (1978, Filmakers Library, 28 mins.)
This film addresses the sensitive question, are "male" and "female" traits inborn or are they learned in childhood? Students can observe the research methods of such noted child development experts as Jerome Kagan and Elinor Maccoby as they attempt to isolate biological factors from cultural factors.

SEXUALITY: THE HUMAN HERITAGE (1976, Indiana University, 59 mins.)
This film traces the development of human sexual identity--from the influence of prenatal sex hormones in utero to the external influences of family and society that help to shape our perceptions of what is feminine and what is masculine. In addition, Jerome Kagan discusses how children acquire gender and role identity.

CHAPTER 20

Social Behavior

■ BEHAVIORAL OBJECTIVES

The student should be able to:

1. Define social psychology.
2. Define the following terms:
   - a. culture
   - b. role
   - c. ascribed role
   - d. achieved role
   - e. role conflict
   - f. status
   - g. group structure
   - h. group cohesiveness
   - i. norm
3. Explain how norms are formed using the idea of the autokinetic effect.
4. Define proxemics.
5. List and describe the four basic interpersonal zones and describe the nature of the interactions which occur in each.
6. Define attribution and state the difference between external and internal attribution.
7. Explain how the consistency and distinctiveness of a person's behavior affects his or her attributions.
8. Explain how self-handicapping protects a person who has a fragile self-image.
9. Explain what the fundamental attribution error is.
10. State the needs that appear to be satisfied by affiliation and describe the research indicating humans have a need to affiliate.
11. Describe the social comparison theory.
12. List and describe the factors which affect interpersonal attraction. (Include a description of the similarities and differences in what men and women look for in a date.)
13. Explain self-disclosure and discuss the effects of varying degrees of disclosure on interpersonal relationships.
14. Describe the social exchange theory as it relates to interpersonal relationships.
15. Describe Rubin's studies of romantic love. Discuss the differences between loving and liking and between male and female friendships (including the term mutual absorption and the different love/attachment styles).
16. Define the term evolutionary psychology and describe how it explains the different mating preferences of males and females.
17. State the meaning of social influence.
18. Describe Asch's experiment on conformity.
19. Explain how group sanctions and unanimity affect conformity.
20. Define groupthink and explain how it may contribute to poor decision-making.
21. Describe four ways to prevent groupthink.

22. List and describe the five sources of social power.
23. Describe Milgram's study of obedience.
24. Identify the factors which affect the degree of obedience.
25. Explain how compliance differs from simple conformity.
26. Describe the following methods of compliance:
    a. foot-in-the-door
    b. door-in-the-face
    c. low-ball technique
27. Describe the research that deals with passive compliance and briefly explain how it applies to everyday behavior.
28. Distinguish among assertive behavior, non-assertive behavior, and aggressive behavior.
29. Describe how a person can learn to be more assertive using rehearsal, role-playing, overlearning, and the broken record technique.
30. Explain what a social trap, a collective social trap, and the tragedy of the commons are. Explain how they can be avoided or escaped.

■ DEMONSTRATIONS, DRAMATIZATIONS, AND DISCUSSION

1. **If your classroom can be completely darkened, it is easy to produce the autokinetic effect.** Apply black plastic tape to the lens of a flashlight so that only a pinpoint of light is visible. Darken the room and place the flashlight on any supporting surface so that it faces the class. Tell students that you are going to slowly move the light and that you want them to pay attention to the shape traced by it. Do not move the light but wait three or four minutes for the effect to develop. Then turn on the room lights and ask the class to draw the movement of the light. Those who have not read Chapter 20 will describe its path in detail. Their response can be used as an illustration of suggestion, and, more broadly, of social influence.

2. **A good way to introduce the topic of interpersonal attraction is to ask students to make a list of the five characteristics they look for in their friends.** In other words, what five factors are most important in determining to whom they are attracted. Student lists will typically include attributes such as honesty, sense of humor, openness, and so forth. Compare the lists produced by students to the factors identified by social psychological research: social comparison, propinquity, physical attractiveness, competence, and similarity.

3. **Hall's list of interpersonal space zones relates easily to everyday experience and thus needs little illustration.** Just the same, a few quick dramatizations can be worthwhile. To demonstrate the boundary of intimate distance, select a subject, preferably someone slightly shy. Have this person stand with his or her back to the wall. Then arrange four volunteers in a semi-circle, five or six feet from the subject and facing him or her. Move the semi-circle of people in toward the subject in increments of about six inches. Ask the subject to indicate at what point a noticeable difference in comfort occurs or when he/she feels that his or her personal space is being invaded.

4. **Verbal definitions and discussion of assertive, aggressive, or excessively passive behavior do not necessarily prepare students to make appropriate responses in actual situations.** Modeling each type of behavior can be far more effective. A worthwhile demonstration is to have students role-play assertive, aggressive, and passive responses to various situations. Excellent sample situations, complete with dialogue, can be found in *Your Perfect Right* (6th ed.) by Alberti and Emmons, San Luis Obispo, CA, Impact Press, 1990.

5. **Another way to begin discussion of interpersonal attraction is to divide the class into small groups by sex and ask each group to generate a list of characteristics of the ideal person to date.** After everyone has finished, ask one person from each group to read his/her list to the rest of the class while you write it on the board. This generally elicits a great deal of discussion and debate about the attributes that were chosen. There are usually notable differences in the types of characteristics selected by female groups as opposed to male groups. A class discussion could center on possible explanations for this sex difference in preferred characteristics.

■ ONE-MINUTE MOTIVATORS

1. **Select a person from class to be "King/Queen for the Moment."** Ask students to demonstrate subtle ways they could defer to this person and confirm her/his high status. Ask students to treat this "high status person very well" for the next two days. Ask the "King/Queen" how it felt to be treated royally.

2. **Ask students to violate a social norm.** For example, they could ask to pay more than the asking price for a quart of milk or offer to help pay for a part of someone else's food while waiting in a cafeteria line. How do others react?

3. **If possible, arrange chairs in class very close to each other.** Ask students to move their chairs to make themselves comfortable. Demonstrate different preferences in personal space.

4. **Ask students to turn to the two people sitting adjacent to them and to compliment each person for some behavior they observed during the semester.** The recipient of the compliment is only allowed to say "Thank you." Discuss social reinforcement and social exchange.

5. **Ask students to state whether they are below average, average, or above average in the following ways:** physical attractiveness, friendliness, creativity, athletic ability, sense of humor, height, and weight. Then discuss the concept of social comparison.

6. **Ask students to write the names of people in the class that they didn't know when the class began but now know.** Ask them to swap papers. Does proximity explain whom they have gotten to know this semester? (Include proximity outside class if the students share other classes or live in the same dorm.)

7.   **Put students in pairs.** Ask Person A to establish a specific level of disclosure and for Person B to reciprocate. What are the advantages and disadvantages of reciprocity? How should a person go about changing the level of disclosure in a dialogue?

8.   **Have a "clone" day.** Ask everyone to wear the same color clothes. Discuss how they felt conforming to this suggestion. Can a person conform without giving up her/his own individuality? Did students feel a need to distinguish themselves by their choice of clothing within the color constraint?

■ CLASSROOM EXERCISES

The two exercises outlined in this section should help to get students involved in the discussion of social psychology. They should give students an opportunity to see how the concepts they are studying relate to real-life experiences. Students should be able to see how systematic observations of behavior can give useful results.

The first exercise deals with conformity. Social psychologists tell us that people conform to the norms or rules of a social group only to the extent that they accept the goals of the group and want to attain the objectives the group espouses. This exercise gives students an opportunity to observe and record adherence to a group norm, namely, stopping at a stop sign at a busy intersection.

The second exercise relates to group pressure. Students will themselves be the subjects. Some will be asked a question to which they will respond using their own feelings and judgments while others will be presented with some judgments already made about the same question and then asked to express their estimates. Will the group who see previously made estimates be influenced in their judgments? Try this exercise to find out.

Exercise #1: Conformity

TO THE INSTRUCTOR:

This is a project that can be done individually by each student.

Ask each student to spend an hour at an intersection which has stop signs rather than signal lights. Their task is to observe and record the behavior of the motorists as they reach the stop sign. If it is a four-way stop, the students should be able to collect lots of data.

Students should be given a data sheet to use so they can keep accurate records. It is a good idea to break down the stopping behavior of motorists into all of the likely variations and record each one. The data sheet includes the following:

1. Coming to a full at the stop sign, then slowly moving up to the intersection if visibility is impaired, as is the law;

2. Coming to a full stop, not at the sign, but at the intersection;

3. Rolling to a near stop and moving on;

4. Slowing down, but not stopping, while passing through the intersection;

5. Driving through without slowing down or stopping.

When students return to class with their information, you can ask them to work out the percentages for each of the alternative stopping behaviors. It would also be possible to get a set of percentages for the whole class. See if there are differences in different types of neighborhoods and different times of day.

CONFORMITY: **DATA SHEET**

TO THE STUDENT:

Find an intersection that has stop signs in all four directions. Your task is to observe and record the way motorists behave at the stop signs. You will notice that not all drivers do the same thing. Spend an hour at the location and record all vehicles. Check the appropriate number on the chart using the following criteria. If the intersection is busy, you may need more than one data sheet. Record the motorists' behavior, using the numbers 1 to 5. Observe and record the following five behaviors:

1. Coming to a full stop at the stop sign and then slowly moving up to the intersection if visibility is impaired;
2. Coming to a full stop, not at the sign, but at the intersection;
3. Rolling to a near stop and moving on;
4. Slowing down, but not stopping, while passing through the intersection;
5. Driving through without slowing down or stopping.

TIME OF DAY_____   LOCATION_____

VEHICLE	STOPPING BEHAVIOR					VEHICLE	STOPPING BEHAVIOR				
	1	2	3	4	5		1	2	3	4	5
1						11					
2						12					
3						13					
4						14					
5						15					
6						16					
7						17					
8						18					
9						19					
10						20					

Exercise #2: Group Pressure

TO THE INSTRUCTOR:

This exercise involves a mock student survey. Tell the class that you are cooperating with a campus committee which is surveying a sample of students. Your classes have been chosen to be part of this study. Tell them that you are distributing several survey sheets to speed things up, a couple of which were used in a previous class. Start by passing out four sheets, ask them to read the directions, add their opinions, and pass the sheet on to the next person.

Prepare the sheets to be distributed before the class period. All four sheets should be copies of the STUDENT SURVEY form which follows. Two of them should be blank except for the instructions. The other two should already have five signatures on them, each in different handwriting. Next to the signatures should be the following estimates: $75, $80, $60, $75, $65.

After the sheets have circulated throughout the class, collect them. Find the mean for the first four responses on the two blank sheets and the mean for the first four real responses on the two sheets with fake signatures. See if there is a difference between the influenced and uninfluenced groups.

The purpose of the survey should be revealed to the students. Your discussion should center on group pressure and peer influence. However, students may also want to discuss the ethics of fooling them about the real purpose of the survey.

STUDENT SURVEY

As part of an evaluation of teaching practices, the Administrative Committee on Instructional Policy is conducting a survey of students. In this portion of the survey, your response to the following question is requested.

What do you think is a fair amount for an instructor to require students to spend on books and other materials for a typical college class?

Please write your estimate in dollars, where shown. To authenticate this survey, please write your name in the space provided. Thank you for participating.

NAME   AMOUNT

_____   _____

_____   _____

_____   _____

_____   _____

_____   _____

_____   _____

_____   _____

_____   _____

_____   _____

_____   _____

_____   _____

_____   _____

■ BROADENING OUR CULTURAL HORIZONS

1. **What kinds of role conflicts** do you guess that new immigrants experience?

2. **Do males and females attribute causation of events** in the same ways or different ways? How? Are attributions changing?

3. **Put students in pairs.** Assign each member of a pair one of the following roles:

    a. You come from a culture where cooperation is preferred to individual assertiveness. You solve problems by working as a team.

    b. You come from a culture where people are expected to use power to solve problems. If you don't have power, you are supposed to publicly submit.

    Then ask students to decide which current movie to go to or which local restaurant to go to. Take notes on the processes used to develop or confirm power.

■ SUPPLEMENTAL LECTURE

SOCIAL PSYCHOLOGY--AN INTRODUCTION

I. Introduction

Social psychology has emerged as a distinct area of study in the last half century by a gradual process of defining its subject matter and through the development of a unique research base and terminology. Originally students interested in this area studied psychology and sociology and then combined the two. This resulted in social psychologists who had either a psychological or a sociological orientation, depending on the person's interest and area of study. Today social psychologists have a discipline in their own right.

We can think of psychology as focusing on the individual and sociology as emphasizing the group. Social psychology looks at the relationship between the two: how the individual is affected by the group and the influence of the individual on the group. This individual/group orientation is an oversimplification but is a good place for a new student to begin to look at the discipline. The more complex nature of the subject matter will become apparent as the student progresses.

The relationship could be diagrammed as follows:

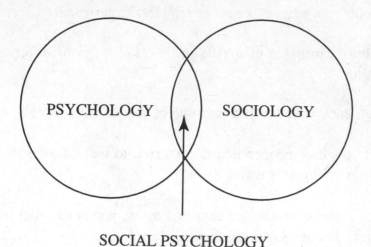

SOCIAL PSYCHOLOGY

The overlapping of the two disciplines created a third. This new discipline has prospered and no longer leans on either of the other two. It has its own terminology and research base on which is being built an exciting field of study that is shedding light on behavior in new ways.

II.   Areas of Study in Social Psychology

The broad areas that social psychologists study give insight into human behavior and the interrelationships that provide the richness of human experience. Psychologists and sociologists provide interesting and important information about behavior through rigorous scientific study, but social psychologists can provide some of the most exciting and relevant data because it is easy to see how their findings are meaningful to our everyday existence. Some of the areas of study are:

A.   Culture--Social psychologists are interested in:

        1.   defining culture,
        2.   seeing how cultures vary and how the differences affect behavior,
        3.   determinants of a culture,
        4.   cultural change.

B.   Social Structure--This is an important area of study. The concern is with how people organize themselves to satisfy their important needs and enrich their lives. Some topics of concern are:

        1.   status and role,
        2.   social class.

C.   Social Groups--Whenever two or more people gather for a purpose, they organize their behavior to achieve common goals. How well the group works and the extent to which the goals are attained depends on several factors. Some concerns of the social psychologists are:

1.   group membership--who is in and who is out,
2.   conformity to group norms,
3.   communication within the group,
4.   structure of a communication system among group members.

D.   Leadership--For a group to function, there has to be a way to move the members toward common goals. Social psychologists are interested in learning how this is done. They study:

1.   types of leadership,
2.   leadership styles,
3.   leadership and social change.

III.   Discussion

A.   Select some outstanding leaders who are familiar to the students. Examine their styles, effectiveness, and contributions to social change.

B.   Discuss the problems in the world today. What kind of leadership is needed to effect needed changes? Do we have it?

C.   As an assignment, ask students to form groups of about ten persons. Assign, or have each group select, a task to plan but not perform. The purpose is to plan a strategy to get the job done, giving assignments to each member. When the students have finished, you can have the class look at how the organization was formed and the various statuses and roles which emerged.

■ SUGGESTIONS FOR FURTHER READING

Aronson, E. *The Social Animal*, 7th ed. Freeman, 1995.

Fensterheim, H. *Don't Say Yes When You Want to Say No*. Dell, 1976.

Freedman, et al. *Social Psychology* (5th ed.). Prentice-Hall, 1985.

Goffman, E. *The Presentation of Self in Everyday Life*. Doubleday, 1959.

Hall, E. T. *The Hidden Dimension*. Doubleday, 1966.

Harvey, J. H. and G. Weary. "Current Issues in Attribution Theory and Research." *Annual Review of Psychology* (35) 1984: 427-460.

Homans, G. C. *Social Behavior: Its Elementary Forms*. Harcourt Brace Jovanovich, 1961.

Hyde, J. S. "Love" in *Understanding Human Sexuality*, 5th ed. McGraw-Hill, 1994.

Kahn, A. S. *Social Psychology*. W. C. Brown, 1984.

Phelps, S. and A. Austin. *The Assertive Woman: New Look*. Impact, 1987.

Rubin, A. *Liking and Loving: An Invitation to Social Psychology*. Holt, 1973.

Zimbardo, P. G. "The Social Disease Called Shyness." *Psychology Today,* May 1975.

■ FILM SUGGESTIONS

CONFORMITY AND INDEPENDENCE (1975, Harper and Row, 26 mins.)
> This film presents a reenactment of the classic conformity studies in social psychology. It begins with a recreation of Sherif's norm formation studies using the autokinetic effect, and then shows several variations of Asch's work on the judgment of line lengths, and concludes with a presentation of Milgram's experiments on obedience to authority.

GROUP DYNAMICS: GROUPTHINK (1973, CRM, 22 mins.)
> In this film, Janis and Kanouse discuss the symptoms of "groupthink" including self-censorship, shared stereotypes of the opposition, and the illusion of invulnerability, and viewers are shown how it influenced such historical events as the Korean War and the Bay of Pigs.

OBEDIENCE (1969, Penn State University, 44 mins.)
> Featured in this film are segments of real subjects in Milgram's original obedience experiment. Subjects are shown expressing considerable distress and discomfort as the authority figure commands them to shock the innocent "victim."

RESPONSIBLE ASSERTION (1978, Research Press, 28 mins.)
> This film examines different styles of behavior through three dramatic scenes in which a graduate student confronts her advisor about the demanding requirements of her assistantship. These scenes demonstrate the different consequences of nonassertive, aggressive, and assertive behaviors. After each scene Dr. Pat Jakubowski comments on the cognitive and behavioral aspects of responsible assertion.

SOCIAL PSYCHOLOGY SERIES (1989, Pennsylvania State University Audio-Visual Services, 30 mins.)
> This eight-part series covers various topics in social psychology, including communication and persuasion, friendship, prejudice, conformity, group decision making and leadership, aggression, and helping and prosocial behavior.

CHAPTER 21

Attitudes, Culture, and Human Relations

■ BEHAVIORAL OBJECTIVES

The student should be able to:

1. Define attitude. Describe the belief, emotional, and action components of an attitude.
2. List, describe, and give examples of six ways in which attitudes are acquired.
3. Explain why people may exhibit discrepancies between attitudes and behavior and how conviction affects attitudes.
4. Briefly describe the following techniques for measuring attitudes:
   a. open-ended interview
   b. social distance scale
   c. attitude scale
5. Differentiate between reference groups and membership groups.
6. Define persuasion.
7. List nine conditions bringing about attitude change.
8. Describe the effects of role playing as a way to change attitudes.
9. Explain cognitive dissonance theory.
10. Indicate the influence of cognitive dissonance on attitude formation.
11. Describe the effect of reward or justification on dissonance.
12. Differentiate between brainwashing and other persuasive techniques.
13. Explain how beliefs may unfreeze, change, and refreeze, and indicate how permanent the attitude changes brought about by brainwashing are.
14. Describe how cults are able to recruit, convert, and retain their members.
15. Define and differentiate prejudice and discrimination.
16. Explain how scapegoating relates to prejudice.
17. Distinguish between personal and group prejudices.
18. Describe the characteristic beliefs (including ethnocentrism and dogmatism) and childhood experiences of the authoritarian personality.
19. Present the major characteristics of social stereotypes and indicate how they may lead to intergroup conflicts. (Include a description of symbolic prejudice.)
20. Explain how status inequalities may lead to the development of stereotypes and how equal-status contact may reduce intergroup tension. Give an example of each situation.
21. Define superordinate goals. (Include an explanation of how they can reduce conflict and hostility.)
22. Explain how a "jigsaw" classroom utilizes superordinate goals and helps reduce prejudice.
23. Discuss the roles of instincts and physiology in terms of aggression.
24. State the frustration-aggression hypothesis, indicating why it may or may not be true.
25. Discuss how frustration, in the form of aversive stimuli, can encourage aggression.

26.   Explain how the weapons effect encourages aggression.
27.   Discuss how the social learning theory explains aggression.
28.   Briefly describe the results of studies on the relationship between aggressive pornography and aggression of males toward females.
29.   Explain how television may serve as a disinhibiting factor.
30.   Present evidence to support the viewpoint that watching television can cause a desensitization to violence.
31.   Explain how it is known that watching television can increase prosocial behavior.
32.   Explain the basic principle of anger control and list five strategies for controlling anger.
33.   Give an example of bystander apathy, and indicate the major factor which determines whether or not help will be given.
34.   Describe four conditions that need to exist before bystanders are likely to give help. (Indicate how the presence of other people can influence apathy.)
35.   Discuss how heightened and empathetic arousal affect helping behavior.
36.   State three ways in which prosocial behavior can be encouraged.
37.   Define the term multiculturalism.
38.   Discuss six ways in which a person can become more tolerant.
39.   Explain how a person can develop cultural awareness.
40.   Explain the basic idea behind sociobiology and evaluate it in terms of is strengths and weaknesses.

■ DEMONSTRATIONS, DRAMATIZATIONS, AND DISCUSSION

1.   **According to dissonance theory,** after one has made an important decision, there is a tendency to seek information which bolsters the choice made and to avoid information which contradicts it (due to the dissonance created). Accordingly, it can be very interesting to interview a student who has recently made a major purchase (an item such as an automobile, stereo, television, etc.). Inquire into the student's information-gathering behavior before the purchase and his or her information exposure after. Typically, people read advertisements for several brands before a purchase but, afterward, only ads for the brand they selected.

2.   **A staged "accident" may be used to dramatize research on the inhibition of prosocial behavior.** During a lecture have an accomplice drop an armload of books outside the classroom door. This should be accompanied by a crashing sound and a pained moan. All this should be out of sight of the class but clearly audible to them. Even if students have already read the discussion of prosocial behavior in the text, the majority will not respond to the "emergency." Follow with a class discussion of student experiences with real emergencies and the inhibiting effects of other bystanders.

3.   **To dramatize the topic of aggression, try beginning this way:** Have students stand in pairs, facing one another. Students are then to play a children's game with which they are probably familiar. One player extends his or her hands, palms down, in front of him/herself; the second player places his or her hands, palms up, touching the palms of the first player. The

object of the game is for the person with his or her hands on the bottom to quickly move one or both hands over the top of the first player's hands in an attempt to slap them with a downward motion. The first player tries to avoid being slapped by moving his/her hands out of the way at the first sign of motion. If the second player is able to slap the first player's hand(s), he or she continues with hands on the bottom. If he/she misses, the players change roles so that the first player tries to slap the hands of the second. (Note: This game has been played by generations of children and poses little risk in class. However, if any student objects, he or she should be excused. Also, it is wise to ask students to remove any large rings they may be wearing.) This game is usually sufficiently frustrating, competitive, and mildly angering to stir up some aggressive feelings in participants. After the game has progressed for a few moments, it becomes interesting to discuss students' reactions and feelings and to ask which views of aggression seemed to relate to their experience.

4. **One of the major problems that occurs in the study of aggression is how to define it.** Although most people seem to know what they mean by the term, when they attempt to define aggression precisely, it becomes less clear. As an example, physical attacks by one individual against another are generally viewed as aggression unless the attacker is in a role in which such behavior is sanctioned (soldier, police officer). Professional football players are seen as aggressive as are used car salesmen. To highlight this problem for your students, you could give them examples of different behaviors and ask them to consider whether or not they constitute aggressive actions. For example, you could include things like someone being an avid gun collector, a married couple having an argument, and a state executioner pulling the switch on an electric chair. Attempting to decide whether each of these reflects aggression usually results in a fairly heated classroom debate and gives students some idea of the problems involved in defining the concept.

■ ONE-MINUTE MOTIVATORS

1. **Bring poster board to class.** On the top write, "Graffiti Board" and tack the board to a wall. Write something on it. Observe and discuss the graffiti that develops over a week or two.

2. **Prior to initiating a class discussion of some controversial topic** (e.g., foreign aid or welfare programs), prepare several students to take a strong but opposing viewpoint to that which appears to prevail when class discussion has begun. Have the dissenters observe and report changes in the class members as the discussion proceeds.

3. **Students should be asked to make two columns on a sheet of paper.** In one column, they should list some "good" prejudices that they personally hold and in the other, list "bad" prejudices that they have. Then discuss with the class what prejudice is and whether there can be "good" and "bad" prejudices.

4. **Take a single social trait, such as aggression, and ask the students to trace it in their family tree to see if there is a hereditary pattern.** Discuss the possibility that such a trait

could be inherited.

■ CLASSROOM EXERCISES

The exercises in this section illustrate several concepts that are important for students to consider. Aggression is a part of everyone's experience and is the subject of the *first exercise*. It is becoming a serious social problem in American society while the causes are not well understood. In the first exercise, students will develop a heightened awareness of violence as a form of aggression and will begin to think about its causes.

The *second exercise* focuses on the concepts of cooperation and competition. Variations of this activity have been done many times, and results generally show that even though cooperation would produce the best results for everyone, competition is most likely to occur when people have a choice, even though the result is less rewarding. It is the Prisoner's Dilemma game and is a rousing and intriguing exercise to do in a class.

Exercise #1: Aggression on Television

TO THE INSTRUCTOR:

Television violence has been a subject of much discussion, and lots of statistics are quoted for its frequency. Through this exercise, students have an opportunity to concentrate on this aspect of TV programming.

PROCEDURE

A.   Divide the class into small groups of three or four persons.

B.   Ask each group to consider the question of violence on television. Each group should develop a definition of violence, and determine what kinds of behavior they would characterize as violent. Both of these should be noted on the student data sheet which is provided at the end of this exercise.

C.   Ask each group to assign members to different shows on television. Each should observe for an hour at a time. By dividing up the day and week, they will be able to sample a variety of times without becoming slaves to the set. They should simply tally the number of violent acts they see for the hour they are viewing.

D.   At the end of a week the students in each group should put their data together, drawing up some statistics for time of day, type of show, etc.

E.   The class discussion should be lively on the day the groups report their findings.

AGGRESSION ON TELEVISION: DATA SHEET

Definition of violence: _____

_____

_____

Some examples of behavior that is evidence of violence on TV:

_____

_____

_____

Make a note of the programs you watched during the week and the number of violent acts you observed.

PROGRAM	DAY	TIME	NUMBER OF VIOLENT ACTS

Exercise #2: The Prisoner's Dilemma

TO THE INSTRUCTOR:

A number of interesting variables may be observed when students play the Prisoner's Dilemma game. Within the groups you will see cooperation, and between the groups there will be competition. The students' meanness to opponents will create cognitive dissonance, which will become evident in their descriptions of those against whom they compete.

The students will attempt to deal with the dissonance by referring to their opponents by derogatory or even subhuman terms. In the column where they are asked to describe the other group, students will often use terms such as "fools," "nerds," "idiots," etc.

PROCEDURE

A.   Divide the class into an even number of small groups. Usually three persons to a group would be sufficient.

B.   The game consists of four rounds of play. Two groups will be paired for each round. Change the pairing for each round.

C.   Supply each group with an instruction and payoff sheet and also a record sheet to keep track of each round.

D.   After the game is over, see how each group did to determine who won and by what strategy-- cooperation or competition.

E.   An interesting aspect of the game may be the type of descriptive terms used about the opponents. You may want to collect the forms and make a list for the students to reflect on during the next class session.

F.   Students should be given an opportunity to discuss how they felt and why they played the way they did.

THE PRISONER'S DILEMMA

Two prisoners, accused of a major jewel theft, are isolated from each other and are being pressured to give evidence against each other. Since there is not enough evidence to hold either one, if they both keep silent (cooperate), they will both go free and can split the booty. However, the prosecutor is offering immunity from prosecution as an inducement for one of them to squeal (compete). The squealer then goes free and keeps the jewels all to himself. If both squeal and testify against each other, then both will go to prison.

INSTRUCTIONS

1. You will play four rounds of this game. On each round, your group will play against one other group.

2. The goal is to win as many points as possible. During each round, your group must decide whether it will cooperate (be silent) or compete (squeal) with the other group.

3. The following table indicates your payoff. Remember that the score you get will depend not only on what your group does, but also on what the other group decides to do.

4. After each round, fill in the requested information on the record sheet.

PAYOFF TABLE

WHEN YOUR GROUP	YOUR PAYOFF IF THE OTHER GROUP	
	COOPERATES	COMPETES
COOPERATES	+10 POINTS	-15 POINTS
COMPETES	+15 POINTS	-5 POINTS

THE PRISONERS'S DILEMMA: RECORD SHEET

DIRECTIONS

A. Select someone in your group to:

1.   Keep a record of your groups' decisions for each round on a piece of paper,

2.   Fill in the information asked for on the chart below. The information should be entered at the end of each round. The description portion should be a group decision to be sure it expresses the feelings of everyone involved.

B.   Once the round has begun, the recorder should write the group decision on a piece of paper as soon as it is made. When the instructor gives the signal, both groups should reveal their decision at the same time.

C.   At the end of each round, the recorder should enter on the chart:

1.   The decision of the group--to cooperate or compete;

2.   The number of points won or lost in that round;

3.   Two or three words that describe the members of the opposing group.

D.   After the fourth round, the recorder should enter the total number of points earned. Remember to subtract the negative points from the positive ones. It is possible to end up with a negative score.

ROUND	COOPERATE OR COMPETE	POINTS + OR -	DESCRIPTION OF OTHER GROUP
1			
2			
3			
5			

TOTAL POINTS _____

■ BROADENING OUR CULTURAL HORIZONS

1. **Describe the "traditions" of your home,** including favorite holidays, dinner and bedtime rituals, preferred formal language and slang, value and use of money, views toward sex, attitudes toward grandparents, religious values, etc.

2. **Make a list of twenty different cultural groups.** Who would you: Exclude from your country? Leave alone but not want face-to-face contact with? Tolerate face-to-face contact with? Enjoy having as an acquaintance? Enjoy becoming close friends with? Admit to marriage within your family? Marry yourself?

3. **What are your feelings about affirmative action hiring?** In what ways does a more culturally diverse set of employees add to the quality of the decisions made by a company?

4. **Prejudice and discrimination can take place based on age.** Imagine that a person has a brain tumor and goes to a physician for treatment. What kind of treatment would you recommend if the person is age 40? Would the treatment be different if the person is 75?

5. **Many people have suggested that "economic warfare" should be used during international disputes instead of traditional weapons.** Why? What principle of group interaction does this reflect?

6. **Some cultures encourage more prosocial behavior than others.** Does your family stress helping others? Does your general culture suggest that people should go out of their way to help others? Research a culture where strangers are expected to help each other.

■ SUPPLEMENTAL LECTURE

PROPAGANDA

I. **Introduction**

    A. Review the material on attitudes and how they are formed. Propaganda is a way that attitudes may be created, maintained, and changed.

    B. Propaganda is defined as a deliberate attempt to influence the attitudes of others. It may be directed at changing attitudes, creating them, or confirming them. The propagandist has a purpose which is being served best by others' acquiescence.

    C. Since education is also an important way to form and change attitudes, discuss the difference between education and propaganda.

II.   **How does the propagandist do it?**

A.   Devices used by the propagandist include:

1.   *Loaded words*--Certain words are most likely to evoke predictable responses. By using them selectively, one can create an image which is appealing and which tends to produce a suspension of judgment. If a person is branded a "liberal" among conservatively-inclined people, a negative attitude develops without any critical examination. Students should be asked to contribute examples from their experience.

2.   *Suggestion*--Uncritical acceptance of a statement is what the propagandist is looking for. A person's perception can be altered if the right suggestions are made. Some politicians try to sway voters by suggesting they are in some way like John F. Kennedy, an assassinated president. The term "communist-leaning" applied to someone may raise suspicion. In the 1960's and 70's being referred to as a "college student" would raise the hackles of many Americans.

3.   *Need satisfaction*--Where known needs exist or where a particular need is difficult to satisfy, a propagandist can use the opportunity to form or develop attitudes. Fear of a common enemy, whether it is the Russians or rapists, can be used to manipulate attitudes.

4.   *Need arousal*--Where no need exists, one can be aroused. Senator Joseph McCarthy did that with his attacks on "communists" in the army and government in the 1950's. People went along with his contention that America was being undermined from within and allowed him and his committee to do untold harm to lives and reputations.

B.   You can generate a good class discussion by asking the students to think about how advertisers use the same techniques to gain uncritical acceptance of their products. Who can forget the ads for toothpaste, mouthwash, and deodorants whose messages stress the need to avoid the fear of "being close." Fear of rejection is a powerful motive to change behavior.

III.   **Discussion**

A.   Discuss with the students how these techniques are used in times of emergency. How did the government muster up the support needed to fight World War II? Why didn't it work as well in the Vietnam War?

B.   What are the propagandists doing today? Examine politics, business, religion, and other areas such as environmental concerns. See if students can identify some techniques being used.

■ SUGGESTIONS FOR FURTHER READING

Allport, G. *The Nature of Prejudice*. Doubleday, 1958.

Aronson, E. *The Social Animal*. Freeman, 1980.

Baron, R. A. and D. Byrne. *Social Psychology: Understanding Human Interaction*, 7th ed. Allyn and Bacon, 1994.

Baum A., J. D. Fisher, and J. E. Singer. *Social Psychology*. Random House, 1985.

Cohen, A. *Attitude Change and Social Influence*. Basic Books, 1964.

Cooper, J. and R. T. Croyle. "Attitudes and Attitude Change." *Annual Review of Psychology* (35) 1984: 395-426.

Festinger, L., H. W. Riecken, and S. Schachter. *When Prophecy Fails*. University of Minnesota Press, 1956.

Festinger, L. *A Theory of Cognitive Dissonance*. Stanford University Press, 1957.

Himmelfarb, S. and A. H. Eagly. *Readings in Attitude Change*. Wiley, 1974.

Siegel, M. "Crime and Violence in America." *American Psychologist* (38) 1983: 1267-1273.

Zimbardo, P. G. and E. B. Ebbesen. *Influencing Attitudes and Changing Behavior*. Addison-Wesley, 1977.

■ FILM SUGGESTIONS

EYE OF THE STORM (1970, ABC, 25 mins.)
    This very dramatic and effective film shows the experiment on prejudice performed by grade school teacher Jane Elliot in which children's eye color becomes the basis for discrimination against them.

FEAR AND PRESENT DANGER (1981, Indiana University, 55 mins.)
    This film examines the growing fear of crime among Americans. Private citizens, believing self-protection is the answer, are taking up weapons and barring doors as never before. The program also explores the sources of the fear and the variety of responses to it--from learning to use small arms for self-defense to organizing protection groups like the Guardian Angels.

PREJUDICE: CAUSES, CONSEQUENCES, CURES (1974, CRM, 24 mins.)
    This film focuses on research findings that have implications for dealing with prejudice against women and specific racial, national, and ethnic groups. It explores some of the dangers of stereotypes and how they are perpetuated by the media, social distance, and socialization; the psychological effects on the victims of prejudice; the influence of consciousness-raising groups, and the effects of cooperative contact.

UNDERSTANDING AGGRESSION (Prentice-Hall, 29 mins.)
    This film analyzes aggression in terms of social learning theory and discusses avenues for controlling it.

■ COMPUTER PROGRAMS: *Mind Scope*

Exercise 17, Social Dilemma

Psychologists have devised various artificial situations to determine how people make choices when the outcomes of those choices depend on the actions of other people. One such situation is the well-known "prisoner's dilemma." Social dilemmas such as the prisoner's dilemma take many forms. In this exercise students are exposed to one such simulated dilemma. (See Classroom Exercise #2 of this chapter for another version of this game.)

CHAPTER 22

Applied Psychology

■ BEHAVIORAL OBJECTIVES

The student should be able to:

1. Define the term applied psychology.
2. Describe the work of a community psychologist.
3. List some areas of interest of industrial/organizational psychology and engineering psychology.
4. Describe the typical activities of the engineering psychologist.
5. Describe the activities of personnel psychologists by defining or describing the following areas:
   - a. job analysis
   - b. biodata
   - c. vocational interest test
   - d. aptitude test
   - e. assessment center
6. Differentiate scientific management styles (Theory X) from human relations approaches (Theory Y) to management including work efficiency and psychological efficiency. Include the terms participative management, management by objectives, and quality circles.
7. List six factors which seem to contribute the most to job satisfaction.
8. Explain the purpose and results of job enrichment.
9. Explain the goals of environmental psychology.
10. Describe how people exhibit territoriality.
11. Discuss the results of animal experiments on the effects of overcrowding, and state the possible implications for humans.
12. Differentiate between crowding and density. Discuss the concept of attentional overload.
13. List and describe four ways people can be encouraged to preserve the environment.
14. Explain how architectural psychology can be used to solve environmental problems.
15. Describe the goals of educational psychology. Differentiate direct instruction from open teaching in your answer.
16. Describe the activities and interests of a consumer psychologist.
17. Discuss the psychology of law and identify topics of special interest.
18. Explain the ways in which a sports psychologist might contribute to peak performance by an athlete.
19. Define the terms motor skill and motor program. List and explain six rules that can aid skill learning.
20. List and explain ten ways to improve communication skills.
21. List and describe six ways to be a good listener.
22. Describe several major human factors concerns that will have an impact on the success of future space missions and habitats.

■ DEMONSTRATIONS, DRAMATIZATIONS, AND DISCUSSION

1. **Even when classroom seats are not assigned, there is a strong tendency for students to select a particular spot at the beginning of the semester and to occupy that place for the rest of the term.** While most of them are not conscious of their territorial behavior, they can be made aware of it by being forced to sit somewhere else. At the beginning of class, simply tell the students that you want everyone to sit in a different seat for that day. Instruct the people who typically sit in the back to come up to the front and vice versa. Ask those who usually sit on the left hand side of the room to move to the right and so forth. Then proceed with the class as usual. It won't be long before you begin to notice marked changes in the students' behavior. Normally talkative students will seem subdued; those who often ask questions will be quiet; the mood of the entire class will seem altered. Stop at this point and ask the students how they feel--they generally report feeling quite anxious and uncomfortable. This effect is particularly pronounced if it is toward the end of the semester and they have had plenty of time to get used to their seats. (You may even find it necessary to allow them to return to their usual places.) You might like to conclude the demonstration with a discussion of whether human territoriality is innate or learned.

2. **Students could be asked to play the role of an engineering psychologist and redesign the classroom.** It might be useful to begin with their initial perceptions of the environment--is it seen as a friendly place or cold and forbidding? Is it spacious or crowded? Cluttered or neat? What features contribute to these impressions? Then ask them to come up with modifications in the design of the room that would make it a more comfortable and/or effective learning environment. Have them consider ambient conditions that might readily be altered like lighting, noise level, and temperature as well as the more permanent architectural features like walls, floor, ceiling height, and windows. Occasionally, students will suggest practical and reasonable ideas that can actually be implemented.

3. **As the text notes, there is little doubt that teachers can greatly affect student interest, motivation, and creativity.** You might like to begin a discussion of teaching styles by asking students to describe instructors that they have had who they feel have contributed the most to their educational experience. What characteristics did these instructors possess that enabled them to be so effective? Did these instructors use a direct instruction method, or did they tend more toward an open teaching style?

4. **Relatively few psychological problems have manifested themselves among space crew members thus far; however, an analysis of the situation suggests that in the future, more, rather than fewer, psychological problems will arise.** This is because, in future missions, the reward/cost ratios will reverse themselves. That is, in the early missions, the psychological and physical costs to the astronauts were quite high, but so were the rewards. However, as space flight becomes increasingly routine and the number of individuals to visit space increases, the external rewards to astronauts will undoubtedly diminish more rapidly than their costs. Therefore, as the extrinsic rewards for space flight wane, it should become increasingly important to select candidates on the basis of positive psychological

characteristics. You could ask your students to generate a list of attributes that they think the successful astronaut of the future will need to possess. For more information on this subject, see R. L. Helmreich, "Applying Psychology in Outer Space," *American Psychologist*, April 1983: 445-450.

5.   **Geographers have studied cognitive representation of the physical environment for centuries, but it is only recently that psychologists have become interested in cognitive maps and how they influence behavior.** Maps are, by nature, distortions of physical space, and it is thought that these errors reveal important information about the values and interests of the map-maker. Accordingly, it might be interesting to ask your students to draw a map of their college campus. After they are finished, students can compare maps with one another or you might provide actual copies of a map of the campus. Are there certain landmarks that were included on most students' maps? Were certain parts of the campus over-represented or more detailed than others (e.g. campus center, gym, library)? Were there any major aspects of the campus environment that were completely omitted from some students' maps? Do the students agree that a map such as this provides a measure of what is important to them? For an interesting look at how maps reveal what different societies consider important, see B. Nimri Aziz "Maps and the Mind," *Human Nature*, August 1978.

■ ONE-MINUTE MOTIVATORS

1.   **Ask students to answer this question:** If you wanted to take a series of interest and aptitude inventories, to what specific area of the campus would you go? Who would you talk to?

2.   **Hold class in a very small area.** Try to lecture as usual. Act a bit surprised when students act restless, uncomfortable, or frustrated. Discuss how it would feel to live in a very densely packed home.

3.   **Spend five minutes attempting to overload the class with sensory stimulation.** You can ask another instructor to class and introduce your double or triple lecture by saying, "Studies have shown the brain can process twice as much information as it normally processes. Accordingly, Doctor ____ and I will lecture simultaneously. Take notes as well as you can."

4.   **Hold class in a large open space—a large auditorium, field bleachers, the parking lot.** Make certain that everyone is as spread out as possible. After about fifteen minutes ask students to move in closer. Briefly discuss feelings experienced when distant versus when crowded.

■ CLASSROOM EXERCISE

What Do Psychologists Do?

TO THE INSTRUCTOR:

Students have many misconceptions about what psychologists do once they receive their basic education. They also have some erroneous ideas about what it takes to become a practicing psychologist. A beginning course may whet their appetites and make psychology seem like a glamorous career to pursue. Every instructor has experienced students who, after the introductory course, decide to follow a career in psychology. A realistic appraisal of what it takes to become a qualified practitioner and a look at the work done by psychologists may help students to make a better decision regarding the next step in their education.

There are five suggestions here, any one of which could help students. Which you do will depend on time and resources. However, some activity along this line would pay dividends.

1. If you are at a university or college with a graduate program in psychology, invite faculty and/or graduate students to participate in a panel discussion. Try to get as wide a variety of backgrounds and interests as possible to reflect the diversity in the field. Have the students prepare questions ahead of time so that the time will be spent in a productive, non-repetitive discussion.

2. A second type of panel which, though harder to put together, may be most rewarding is to invite a group of practicing psychologists from the community. You should look for persons in school systems, mental health clinics, industry, advertising, social services, research institutes, etc. Speakers should be asked to identify their area of interest and specialization, the kind of work they do, the education required to do the work, the salary range, the career advancement opportunities, etc. Allow students to ask questions. Some questions should have been preplanned to be sure pertinent information is elicited.

3. Provide students with an up-to-date list of careers in psychology such as that put out by the American Psychological Association. Ask them to select an area they might be interested in pursuing or that they want to know more about. Send the students to the library, career placement center, or counseling office to gather information on that particular career. They should look for educational requirements, type of work done, salary range, and career advancement opportunities. Students should submit a written report and also report on interesting aspects of their findings to the class.

4. Since most students will not be psychologists, a different approach might be interesting to pursue. Ask students to identify their career goals. Since many will be vague about this, you may have to do some work to get every student to settle on some specific area that is, at least, of interest to them.

Now your task is to convince the students that psychologists work in their area of interest either directly or indirectly. For example, if someone says he/she wants a career in business, you can help them discover that there are psychologists in industry, advertising, personnel selection and training, etc.

Once the students have settled on a career choice and identified a psychological service that is provided to people in that field, have them research what the psychologist does. The idea is that they should discover what psychological services they can expect from a psychologist once they enter their career.

It may be possible for students with common career goals to work together on this project. Written papers should be submitted and an oral report given to the class.

5.   Send some or all of the students to interview some persons who work in psychological careers. Questions should be developed by the class as a whole, and the interviewees should be carefully selected.

■ BROADENING OUR CULTURAL HORIZONS

1.   **Within what kind of society would Taylor's Theory X be most common?** A capitalist, a socialist, or a communist society? Why?

2.   **Research managerial techniques.** What are the advantages and disadvantages of the Japanese management style?

3.   **How might a person's view of the world be affected** by living in a dense and crowded urban environment?

4.   **In some cultures, marriages are arranged by relatives rather than being based on romantic attraction.** Such marriages are just as likely to last as marriages formed by choice. Why would this be?

5.   **Make a list of all the aggression cues used by different groups of people.** Spend some time researching gangs that may be active in your area. What cues do they use to indicate power and to trigger aggression?

■ SUPPLEMENTAL LECTURE

Students are always interested in human factors engineering and engineering psychology. They may not be aware of the value or importance of the person in the person-machine relationship. It is easy to show how the psychologist can contribute to machine design and operation to improve efficiency. It is harder to convince students that it is important to do so.

THE PERSON AND THE MACHINE

I.   Introduction

    A.   Discuss what engineers do in designing machinery and equipment to do a specific kind of work. Also remind the class that the psychologist is concerned with the behavior of the person.

    B.   The engineering psychologist is concerned with both. He/she is interested in the person first, however. He/she will be concerned not only about the efficiency of the operator of the machine but also about his/her welfare. Therefore, the engineering psychologist will be involved in designing the machine and in training the operator.

    C.   The training of engineering psychologists will include both engineering and psychology. It is a long and rigorous program. As a result, experts in this area are scarce, and salaries are high.

II.   The Person and the Machine

    A.   Students should be aware that today it is easy to manufacture equipment, machinery, etc. in many ways. The psychologist helps to produce a machine that serves the needs of the person rather than the other way around.

    B.   Use some examples. Students can tell stories of work experiences they have had. You can bring in some of your own.

        1.   A common textbook example is the cockpit of a jumbo-jet aircraft. The pilot must make many (and correct) decisions and often must do it in a hurry. Design of the instrument panels and controls involves a great deal of study of human behavior. Reaction time and perception are two of the many factors that need to be considered. When a plane crashes due to "pilot error," what does that mean?

        2.   It is amusing to see the student reactions and arguments to the following example. Ask them to consider the standard traditional car. It has its power source in front (engine) and is propelled from the rear (rear-end driven cars). This requires machinery to connect the engine to the rear axle. Logic would

dictate that the power source should be where its effect is going to be, at the rear end. Why, then, is the engine in front? Suggest that in the horse and buggy days the power source was in front. Then, of course, that was the best place for it. It was easier for the horse to pull than to push the buggy.

Now the car does not need the power source where the horse was. But that's where it is! Think about the human factors. The driver had to sit behind the horse, and now the driver sits behind the engine. This means his/her view is obstructed, and it is harder to gauge distance to nearby objects such as curbs and small children. A psychologist, if he/she were designing the car would put the engine out of the way so the driver could see better and have an easier job of navigating the vehicle.

3.   Again, the example of the car! When driving the horse, the driver held onto the reins which meant that the hands were held up in front of him/her all the time while driving. Now the steering wheel is held in the same way. It is held in a position which is inefficient and fatiguing. An engineering psychologist would not design the steering apparatus this way. The psychologist would minimize stress--he/she would find ways to rest the arms to avoid fatigue and to increase control.

III.   Discussion

A.   You could go on with the analogy to make the point, but perhaps the above two examples would do. Ask the students to think of ways to design the car to make it suit the person better. Ask them to brainstorm with all the interesting and wild ideas they can think of.

B.   Discuss why cars have not been made more efficient, practical, and "user-friendly" long ago since we have had the technology and understanding to do so.

■ SUGGESTIONS FOR FURTHER READING

Altman, I. *The Environment and Social Behavior: Privacy, Personal Space, Territoriality and Crowding.* Brooks/Cole, 1975.

Baron, R. A. *Understanding Human Relations: A Practical Guide to People at Work,* 2nd ed. Allyn and Bacon, 1991.

Bolles, R. N. *What Color is Your Parachute.* Ten Speed Press, 1979.

Evans, G. W. *Environmental Stress.* Cambridge University Press, 1982.

Levine, C. "Making City Spaces Lovable Places." *Psychology Today* June 1984.

McCormick, E. J. *Human Factors in Engineering and Design*. McGraw-Hill, 1976.

Milgram, S. "The Experience of Living in Cities." *Science* (167) 1970: 1461-1468.

Poindexter, J. "Shaping the Consumer." *Psychology Today* May 1983.

Postman, N. and C. Weingartner. *Teaching as a Subversive Activity*. Delta, 1969.

Rice, B. "Why Am I in This Job." *Psychology Today* January 1985.

■ FILM SUGGESTIONS

THE BRONSWICK AFFAIR (1980, CRM, 24 mins.)
   Just how much do the media and advertising affect consumer purchasing? This film explores the concept of the self-fulfilling prophecy and shows how a manager's expectation alone can influence a worker's performance. The Pygmalian Effect is presented through a combination of live action and animation to illustrate both the theory and practical application of the phenomenon.

BUILDING MORE EFFECTIVE TEAMS (1978, Indiana University, 26 mins.)
   This film discusses the use of behavioral science findings in dealing with the problems of different organizations. Highlights include group sessions in which managers deal with particular problems.

THE CITY AND THE SELF (Time-Life Films, 52 mins.)
   This is an examination of urban settings based on the theories and research of Stanley Milgram. The film illustrates the ways in which city dwellers perceive their environments.

JOBS: HOW THE BROTHER FEELS (1975, CRM/McGraw-Hill, 27 mins.)
   This film, in the setting of an encounter group, discusses the problems and attitudes of the hard-core unemployed.

LIFELINES: A CAREER PROFILE STUDY (1981, Document Associates, 26 mins.)
   In order to be fully satisfied and productive at work, a person must understand the forces that shape his or her career and make it grow. Using illustrations from three actual case histories, the film explores Schein's concept of "career anchors," patterns by which individuals discover what they are good at and what they would like to do for the rest of their lives.

APPENDIX A

The Cloze Inventory*

The Cloze Inventory is an easily administered test of reading comprehension. It, too, can be used to identify students who are likely to experience reading problems which may impair their performance. In addition to being easy to create, score, and administer, it uses samples of the text to test students. It therefore has high face validity with respect to the psychology course. The Cloze Inventory can be administered to an entire class as a diagnostic reading test or to individual students who seem to be having comprehension problems.

To construct a Cloze Test, begin by selecting from the text a sample about 250 to 500 words in length. The sample should be of typical difficulty. That is, it should not be from highly technical discussions such as the brain and behavior or the section on classical conditioning.

The next step is to delete every fifth word from the selection, replacing it with an underlined blank of standard length (10 typewriter spaces). Start your deletions with the seventh word in the first sentence. Type the sample and duplicate it for administration to students.

Instructions for the Test The Cloze Test can be administered in class or it can be given to students for completion before the next class meeting. The instructions should read as follows:

> The object of this short exercise is to see if your reading ability is likely to aid or hinder your comprehension of the textbook for this course. The results of this exercise may prove valuable to you as you make plans for the course.
>
> The exercise below was made by taking every fifth word out of sentences from your textbook. A blank was left where a word was taken out. As you read the material, try to write in each blank the word you think was left out. Try to fill every blank as accurately as you can.
>
> Try to get clues for guessing the correct words from the information surrounding the blanks.
>
> The length of the blank does <u>not</u> indicate the length of the word. Remember, use only <u>one</u> word per blank. Do not be afraid to guess. But do try to complete the story so it makes sense and is like the original from which it was taken.

* Taylor, W. "Cloze Procedure: A New Tool for Measuring Readability." <u>Journalism Quarterly</u> (30) 1953: 415-433.

Scoring the Test Scoring can be done easily by students in class or at home. Ask students to turn to the page in the text from which the sample was taken. Have them count the number of correct answers. A percentage score can then be obtained by dividing the correct responses by the total number of blanks and multiplying by 100.

Implications Most students should get 40 to 60 percent correct. Those who score above 60 percent correct should have no difficulty understanding the textbook. Those who score between 50 and 60 percent correct may want to consider purchasing the student Study Guide or the Mastery Study Guide (if not already assigned). A study guide or tutorial help is strongly recommended for those who score below 50 percent correct. Students scoring below 35 percent are likely to find the course quite difficult and may require special attention, tutoring, or a concurrent reading course. In some cases, low-scoring students may be best advised to take psychology at a later date after their vocabulary and reading comprehension have improved.

The criteria described here are, at best, rough estimates. As general guidelines, however, they serve well to identify student reading comprehension problems. The Cloze procedure can be very helpful to instructors who, like the author, work with a heterogeneous student population. The procedure has merit even when students are not asked to reveal their scores because it gives them a way of judging their chances of success in the course. Most students seem to appreciate the feedback the Cloze provides.

APPENDIX B

Cognitive Diagnostic Test

Charles Croll and Linda Kovacs have developed a reading inventory for use with their own students. Professors Croll and Kovacs have graciously allowed adaptation and reproduction of the inventory in this manual. The *Cognitive Diagnostic Test* is an open-book test based on Chapter 8 of the text. In the inventory, students are asked to answer 30 questions by consulting specific sections of the chapter. Since the inventory is open-book, memory and study skills have little or no effect on scores. The inventory, therefore, gives a direct indication of reading strengths or weaknesses. (The inventory and answer key are reproduced at the end of this discussion to facilitate duplication.)

Interpretation The *Cognitive Diagnostic Test* measures six important subskills. These are: vocabulary, classification, graph reading, analogies, recognition of main ideas, and cause-effect reasoning. These subskills, in turn, fall into three broad categories of cognitive ability: translation, interpretation, and application. Translation is the ability to change information into a different form. Interpretation is the ability to discover relationships among facts, definitions, and ideas. Application is the ability to solve lifelike problems that require the identification of an issue and the selection and use of appropriate information or skills. As you can see on the Diagnostic Sheet at the end of the inventory, test scores can be broken down to identify specific problem areas in reading skills.

Using the Test If a student is struggling with course work, the *Cognitive Diagnostic Test* can help you judge whether the difficulty is due to a lack of study or problems with reading comprehension. When reading skills are the primary problem, the diagnostic aspect of the inventory can serve as a basis for improving the student's skills. For example, a student might need work on vocabulary, graph reading, and ability to identify main ideas. When study skills appear to be at fault, a review of Chapter 8, the Application in Chapter 1, and the student's present study habits is in order.

Answer Key The correct answers for the Cognitive Diagnostic Test are listed below:

1.	d	8.	c	15.	c	22.	d	29.	e
2.	c	9.	b	16.	b	23.	e	30.	d
3.	c	10.	a	17.	d	24.	e		
4.	d	11.	c	18.	c	25.	e		
5.	d	12.	e	19.	b	26.	c		
6.	b	13.	b	20.	a	27.	c		
7.	a	14.	b	21.	c	28.	a		

Cognitive Diagnostic Test

Name _____

DIRECTIONS: This is an open book test, so please refer to your text. Read each test item carefully.

1. The third paragraph on page 236 begins, "Short-term memory acts..." The word <u>trivia</u> as it is used in this paragraph means:

   a. signs   d. unimportant details
   b. outcomes   e. small amounts
   c. ordinary feelings

2. Within the next-to-last paragraph preceding the *Learning Check* on page 237 under the section, "Dual Memory", the word <u>analogy</u> is used to mean:

   a. final analysis   d. brain area
   b. reverse situation   e. usual order of events
   c. corresponding example

3. On page 238 in the last sentence of the first paragraph under the heading "Long Term Memory—Where the Past Lives," the word <u>vivid</u> is used to mean:

   a. frightening   d. different
   b. forgotten   e. comical
   c. lifelike

4. On page 249 the paragraph under the heading "Cue-Dependent Forgetting" begins, "Often, memories appear..." The word <u>retrieve</u> as it is used in this paragraph means:

   a. renew   b. consider   c. transfer   d. recover   e. apply

5. The first line of the second paragraph under the heading "Order Effects" on page 250 begins "Retroactive interference is . . ." The word <u>demonstrated</u> as it is used in this sentence means:

   a. interrupted   d. shown
   b. decreased   e. prevented
   c. managed

DIRECTIONS: Read the explanation of the diagrams below. Use it as a guide for labeling the diagrams which follow.

EXAMPLE 1

1. Books

2. Novels

3. Chapter

EXAMPLE 2

1. Books

2. Dictionaries

3. Encyclopedias

EXAMPLE 1: In example 1, the concept "books" is the largest category and includes both novels and chapters. "Novels" is the next largest category and includes chapters. "Chapters" is the smallest category. Both books and novels have chapters.

EXAMPLE 2: In example 2, the concept "books" is the largest category and includes both dictionaries and encyclopedias. "Dictionaries" and "encyclopedias" are the next largest categories. Because neither encyclopedia nor dictionary includes the other, they are separate and equal sub-categories.

Label the following diagrams by choosing a correct term for each number. Darken the corresponding letter after the numbers on your answer sheet.

6-8.

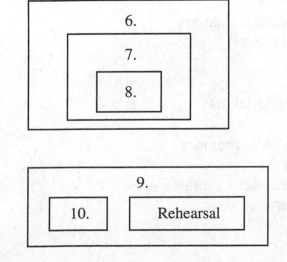

6.

7.

8.

a. recognition
b. memory measures
c. limited cues
d. proactive inhibition

9-10.

9.

10.   Rehearsal

a. coding
b. aids to retention
c. retroactive inhibition
d. proactive inhibition

11. Based on Figure 8-11, page 246, it can be said that as distance decreases, reaction time

a. increases   d. approaches 17%
b. stays the same   e. reaches zero
c. decreases

12. Based on figure 8-12 on page 248, the least amount of forgetting occurs between:

a.   0 to 20 minutes   d.   9 hours to 6 days
b.   20 minutes to 1 hour   e.   6 days to 31 days
c.   1 hour to 9 hours

13. Based on Figure 8-15, page 250, as the hours after learning increase, the difference between the percent remembered when asleep and the percent remembered when awake:

a.   decreases   d.   approaches 0
b.   increases   e.   increases, then decreases
c.   stays the same

14. Old is to new as:

a.   short term memory is to long term memory
b.   proactive interference is to retroactive interference
c.   suppression is to repression
d.   repression is to suppression
e.   retroactive interference is to proactive interference

15. Essay exam is to multiple choice exam as recall is to:

a. relearning   d. eidetic imagery
b. recoding   e. savings
c. recognition

16. Electroconvulsive shock is to consolidation as:

a.   long term memory is to short term memory
b.   head injury is to memory loss
c.   proactive interference is to retroactive interference
d.   eidetic imagery is to internal imagery
e.   encoding is to disuse

17.   On page 239, a section begins "Constructing Memories." The main idea of the paragraph that starts this section is:

   a.   Short-term memories do not involve coding of information.
   b.   Most subjects cannot accurately estimate the speed of cars prior to a crash.
   c.   The amount of time between an event and a later test for memory of the event can be an important factor in long-term memory recall.
   d.   Long-term memories are altered by later factors which were not part of the original experience.
   e.   Repeated information tends to function eventually as the mind's way of building an encyclopedic storehouse of knowledge.

18.   The first paragraph under "Forgetting" on page 247 begins with "Generally speaking, most . . ." The main idea of this paragraph and the next is:

   a.   Ebbinghaus showed that cramming can be helpful to the memorizing process.
   b.   Cramming is a good technique only if you haven't learned enough in the first place.
   c.   As a review technique before a test, cramming can counteract the immediate drop in the forgetting curve.
   d.   The forgetting curve starts off with a slow decline.
   e.   You should wait various amounts of time before testing yourself on text material in order to determine your rate of forgetting on the forgetting curve.

19.   On page 249 the paragraph under the heading "Cue-Dependent Forgetting" begins with "Often memories appear..." The main idea of this paragraph is found in the sentence beginning:

   a.   "Often memories appear"   d.   "However, if you"
   b.   "This situation indicates"   e.   "The presence of"
   c.   "You know the"

20.   The main idea of the paragraph on page 250 beginning with "The sleeping college. . ." after the heading "Order Effects" is:

   a.   Interference can be held to a minimum if one avoids new learning between a final study session and an exam.
   b.   When retroactive interference is held to a minimum, new learning can result much more quickly and efficiently.
   c.   One can improve new learning by avoiding old learning that is similar to the new learning.
   d.   Evidence suggests that one should avoid learning material from all classes at the same time.
   e.   Memory can be improved if one watches T.V. after studying.

21. On page 253, the main idea of the paragraph beginning, "Recent memories are..." is:

    a.   Memory is unaffected by ECS.
    b.   ECS given after an accident causes memory loss.
    c.   Interference has less effect after consolidation.
    d.   Sleeping immediately after studying impairs memory.
    e.   Interference prevents forgetting.

22. Recall ceases to be recall and becomes recognition if (refer to pages 243-244):

    a.   an essay exam is given.
    b.   no information is given after the initial learning task is completed.
    c.   important facts and information are reproduced without specific cues or stimuli.
    d.   the type of memory measure gives cues to help the person remember what was learned.
    e.   one small recollection is remembered.

23. Eidetic imagery may have little value if (refer to pages 245-246):

    a.   less than 30 seconds are allowed to pass between viewing a picture and being tested on details of the picture.
    b.   the person tested has shown no savings score.
    c.   a person has no better long term memory than the average person.
    d.   the person being tested has no previous experience in using eidetic imagery.
    e.   the person using eidetic imagery also has unlimited memory for internal visual images.

24. Herman Ebbinghaus found that (refer to pages 247-248):

    a.   nonsense syllables are easier to learn than words.
    b.   reviewing has little effect on memory.
    c.   he was a poor subject for memory studies.
    d.   nonsense syllables are forgotten slowly at first.
    e.   initial forgetting is quite rapid.

25. Retroactive interference would never be a problem if (refer to pages 250-251):

    a.   no prior learning were ever tested before new learning occurred.
    b.   interference theory is totally accurate in what it predicts.
    c.   new learning were never retested.
    d.   new learning showed a savings score.
    e.   no new learning ever followed old learning.

26. A rat given ECS will remember an earlier painful shock if (refer to pages 253-254):

    a. ECS reverses the consolidation process.
    b. sleep follows the earlier shock and the ECS.
    c. consolidation is completed before the ECS is given.
    d. the ECS stimulates long-term memories stored in the hippocampus.
    e. ECS destroys interfering memories undergoing consolidation at the same time.

27. A prisoner has been held in solitary confinement with no outside communication or information for 30 years. She has just been released and decides to learn about microcomputers. Which concept in the chapter would most likely explain her ability to learn and retain information about microcomputers without a great deal of interference?

    a. Priming   d. Repression
    b. Retroactive interference   e. Retrograde amnesia
    c. Proactive interference

28. Several years ago Juanita learned Morse Code in approximately 8 hours. She never had an opportunity to use this new knowledge. Now she would like to teach the code to another person, so she must first relearn the code. Which of the following is most likely to happen?

    a. It will probably take her less than 8 hours to master the code.
    b. It will probably take her more than 8 hours to master the code.
    c. She will be unable to master the code well due to the aging process.
    d. She will probably remember the code in its entirety within the first twenty minutes of relearning it.
    e. She will have eidetic images stored in long-term memory, and the flashbulb memory effect will periodically enable her to recall large parts of the code.

29. Which test of memory would be best to use if you were trying to determine how a person codes and organizes her/his long-term memories?

    a. True/False test   d. Objective, short answer test
    b. Multiple choice test   e. Essay test
    c. Fill-in-the-blank test

30.   Tabitha is studying biology but not getting good results. Below is a description of
      her class and study routines.   Read and analyze them.   Then choose the best
      recommendation for change:

      Tabitha has her biology class from 9:00-10:00 a.m. From 10:00 a.m. to
      noon each day she relaxes with friends and has lunch. From noon to 1:00
      p.m. she has French, and from 1:00-2:00 p.m. she has sociology. She
      studies biology for a total of two hours each afternoon from 2:00-4:00 p.m.

      Tabitha should change her study habits by:

      a.   decreasing her study time to three half-hour sessions falling between
           2:00-4:00 p.m.
      b.   increasing her study time to four hours by studying from 2:00-6:00
           p.m. each day.
      c.   studying biology from 10:00-11:00 a.m. and again from 2:00-4:00
           p.m. in solid blocks so she won't be distracted.
      d.   studying biology from 8:30-9:00 a.m., 10:00-10:30 a.m., and then
           from 2:30-3:00 p.m. and 3:30-4:00 p.m.
      e.   increasing her study time to eight hours every other day, distributing
           the time in four two-hour blocks from 7:00-9:00 a.m., 10:00-12 noon,
           2:00-4:00 p.m., and 6:00-8:00 p.m.

DIAGNOSTIC TEST

Name_____

This reading inventory consisted of seven sections as follows:

	Type of Question	Skill Tested	Number Missed
1. Questions 1-5	Vocabulary	Translation	_____
2. Questions 6-10	Classification	Translation	_____

TRANSLATION SCORE = Total % you missed on q. 1-10 _____

3. Questions 11-13	Graph Reading	Translation and Interpretation	_____
4. Question 14-16	Analogies	Interpretation	_____
5. Questions 17-21	Main Idea	Interpretation	_____
6. Questions 22-26	Cause and Effect	Interpretation	_____

INTERPRETATION SCORE = Total % you missed on q. 11-26 _____

7. Questions 27-30	Cause and Effect	Application	_____

APPLICATION SCORE = Total % you missed on q. 27-30 _____

TRANSLATION is the ability to change information into different forms.

INTERPRETATION is the ability to discover relationships among facts, definitions, or ideas.

APPLICATION is the ability to solve lifelike problems that require identification of the issue, plus selection and use of appropriate information and skills.

APPENDIX C

Leading Productive Discussions

1. One essential ingredient of productive discussion (over which instructors have little control) is the degree of preparation students bring to class. If students have not read the material to be discussed, no amount of skill on the instructor's part is likely to produce an effective interchange. If a sizable portion of the students in a particular class do not seem to be keeping up with reading assignments, it might be wise to schedule a short quiz on days when you plan to devote class time to discussion. If the quiz is brief and "painless," students will then be ready and eager to discuss what they have learned.

2. It is frequently useful to set the stage for discussion with an overview of the topics to be addressed. In the case of an enthusiastic and usually well-prepared class, this can serve as an alternative to the quiz strategy described above.

3. Numerous specific questions are often essential to maintain high content quality and to keep a discussion moving. It is usually best to begin an extended discussion with a long list of questions or issues in hand. The Behavioral Objectives can be useful for generating questions.

4. If possible, try to phrase questions so that they cannot be answered "yes" or "no." Also avoid questions that call for a straight factual answer. Remember that the goal is discussion, not rote recall of the text. Even if the question or issue at hand is fairly factual, questions should be stated in a way that encourages elaboration.

   If students feel that what they say must be "right," they are often very hesitant to say anything at all. Try to use phrases like, "How did you feel about," "Do you agree with," "What do you find attractive or unattractive about," "Do you see any problems with," "What might happen if," "Who has had an experience that relates to," and so forth. Once discussion is underway, it is relatively easy to shift to more challenging questions or issues, but at first it is important not to intimidate students.

5. Don't worry about getting to another question or topic if the group is interested, and the discussion is informative. However, as soon as the quality of contributions begins to decline (i.e. they become redundant or irrelevant), change immediately to a new question or issue. This type of movement is what distinguishes a sparkling classroom discussion from the sort of session that students and instructors may perceive as a waste of time. It also makes clear to the students that the instructor is providing structure and leadership.

6.   It is wise to avoid revealing your own position early in the discussion of a particular topic or issue. This allows you to play devil's advocate, and it avoids closing off expression of divergent viewpoints. Eventually students will want to know what <u>you</u> think, but save this for a summary statement and then move on to the next question. Specific misinformation can and should be corrected immediately. Beyond this, however, be sure to make a clear distinction between your opinions and more factual information.

7.   Try to make your interest in students visible and liberally compliment interesting and informative contributions. If the initial participants in a discussion are treated in a reinforcing manner, others are more likely to join in. Try to make it "safe" to participate. If you strongly disagree, say so, but try to do it in a non-threatening way. Often you need only say, "I'm not sure I agree with that. Who can think of a reason why?" Then another student will correct the first. In this way you can avoid being the sole dispenser of disagreement or disapproval.

8.   Don't allow one or two individuals to monopolize the discussion—even if they are articulate and what they say is interesting. Strive to involve as many students as possible. This can often be done by simply saying, "(S)he says...Let's get another viewpoint." If no one volunteers, ask another student, "What do you think?" Or say, "Who agrees (or disagrees with (student's name)?" or, "Has anyone had a similar (or different) experience?" It is not unreasonable, of course, to return to particularly articulate students after others have had a chance to participate.

9.   Try to ensure that the entire group can hear questions and responses. Whenever possible, try to prevent comments from becoming a conversation between you and an individual student. In larger classes a student who cannot be heard can be handled in several ways:

     (a) Restate for the class what the student has asked or said and call for a response.

     (b) Compliment the student on an interesting contribution and ask her or him to face the class and repeat it for others to hear.

     (c) Walk to the far side of the class as the student speaks so that his or her voice must be raised and directed at the class.

10. It is generally a good idea to move around the classroom during a discussion. Also make a point of establishing eye contact with students in each section of the classroom once every few minutes. Sometimes, looking expectantly at students in a particular area can be as effective as a direct question for prompting a response. Remember, too, that posture and gestures can influence classroom atmosphere. If you approach students, sit or lean on front desks, etc., a casual tone is set. Standing at a greater distance or behind a lectern or desk imparts a more formal

quality.   By effectively manipulating such cues, you can communicate your intentions (lecture or discussion) to students. This can be more effective than saying, "Now let's discuss...," (which is often as ineffective as saying, "Be spontaneous"). If you simply begin, students will follow your lead.

11.   When working with large classes, or when performing demonstrations that preclude participation by the entire class, choose one or two students and have them come to the front of the class.   In this way, other students will identify with the participants and will feel involved.   Also, your interaction with the surrogate participants will add a dimension of spontaneity that will make the class more interesting for you as well as for the students.

APPENDIX D

Helpful Resources for Teaching Introductory Psychology

■ TACTICS, RESOURCES, DEMONSTRATIONS

American Psychological Association

The Psychology Teacher's Resource Book: First Course, 3rd ed. Washington, D.C.: APA, 1979.

Program on the Teaching of Psychology in the Secondary School: Final Report. Washington, D.C.: APA, 1970.

Teaching of Psychology Newsletter. A Publication of Division 2 of the APA.

Activities Handbook for the Teaching of Psychology. Washington, D.C.: APA, Vol 1, 1981; Vol 2, 1988.

Library Use: A Handbook for Psychology. Washington, D.C.: APA, 1983.

Directory of Teaching Innovations in Psychology. Washington, D.C.: APA, 1975.

Benjamin, Jr., L. L., R. S. Daniel, and C. L. Brewer. *Handbook for Teaching Introductory Psychology*. Hillsdale, N.J.: Lawrence Erlbaum, 1985.

Boneau, C. A., S. E. Golann, and M. M. Johnson. *A Career in Psychology*, revised edition. Washington, D.C.: APA, 1971.

Brown, C. L. "Maintaining Student Interest." *Improving College and University Teaching* (13) 1965: 224-225.

Cahn, S. M. "The Art of Teaching: The Essentials for Classroom Success." *American Educator*, Fall 1982: 36-39.

Eble, K. E. *The Craft of Teaching: A Guide to Mastering the Professor's Art*. San Francisco: Jossey-Bass, 1976.

----. *The Aims of College Teaching*. San Francisco: Jossey-Bass, 1983.

Erickson, S. C. *The Essence of Good Teaching*. San Francisco: Jossey-Bass, 1984.

Fuhrmann, B. S. and A. F Grasha. *A Practical Handbood for College Teachers*. Boston: Little, Brown and Co., 1983.

Gardner, R. M. *Exercises for General Psychology*. Minneapolis: Burgess, 1980.

Gleitman, H. "Introducing Psychology." *American Psychologist* (39) 1984: 421-427.

Gronlund, N. E. *Stating Behavioral Objectives for Classroom Instruction*. New York: Macmillan, 1970.

----. *Individualizing Classroom Instruction*. New York: Macmillan, 1974.

Hoover, K. *College Teaching Today*. Boston: Allyn-Bacon, 1980.

Johnson, J. M. and H. S. Pennypacker. "A Behavioral Approach to Teaching." *American Psychologist* (26) 1971: 219-244.

Johnson, K. R. and R. S. Ruskin. *Behavioral Instruction*. Washington, D.C.: APA, 1977.

Jung, J. and J. H. Bailey. *Contemporary Psychology Experiments: Adaptations for Laboratory*, 2nd ed. New York: Wiley, 1976.

Kaufman, H. *Introduction to the Study of Human Behavior*. Philadelphia: Saunders, 1968.

Keller, F. S. "Goodbye Teacher..." *Journal of Applied Behavior Analysis* (1) 1968: 79-89.

Lowman, J. *Mastering the Techniques of Teaching*. San Francisco: Jossey-Bass, 1984.

Lunneborg, P. W. *Why Study Psychology?* Monterey, CA: Brooks-Cole, 1981.

MacLeod, R. B. "The Teaching of Psychology." *American Psychologist* (26) 1971: 245-249.

Matthews, J. R., A. M. Rogers, and C. J. Scheirer. "Selected Resources for College Teachers of Psychology." *Teaching of Psychology* (13) February 1986: 3-7.

McKeachie, W. J. *Teaching Tips: A Guidebook for the Beginning College Teacher*, 9th ed. Lexington, MA: Heath, 1994.

Pophane, W. J. and E. L. Baker. *Planning an Instruction Sequence*. Englewood Cliffs, NJ: Prentice-Hall, 1970.

Radford, J. and D. Rose (eds.). *The Teaching of Psychology*. New York: Wiley, 1980.

Sarbin, T. R. and W. C. Coe. *The Student Psychologist's Handbook: A Guide to Sources*. New York: Harper and Row, 1969.

Singer, B. A. "A practical annotated bibliography on college teaching and the teaching of psychology." *JSAS Catalog of Selected Documents in Psychology* (3) 1973: 34-35.

Turner, R. H. "Dithering Devices in the Classroom." *American Psychologist* (21) 1965: 957-963.

Walker, E. L. and W. J. McKeachie. *Some Thoughts About Teaching the Beginning Course in Psychology*. Belmont, CA: Brooks-Cole, 1967.

Woods, P. (ed.). *Sourcebook on the Teaching of Psychology*. Roanoke, VA: Virginia Scholars' Press, 1980.

■ READERS

Atkinson, R. C. (ed.). *Psychology in Progress: Readings from Scientific American*. San Francisco: Freeman.

Cohen, I. S. (ed.). *Perspectives on Psychology: Introductory Readings*. New York: Praeger.

CRM Books. *Readings in Psychology Today*. Del Mar, CA: CRM.

Doyle, K. O. (ed.). *Interaction: Readings in Human Psychology*. Lexington, MA: Heath.

Dushkin Publishing Group. *Annual Edition Readings in Psychology*. Guilford, CN: Dushkin, yearly.

Eble, K. E. (ed.). *New Directions for Teaching and Learning*. San Francisco: Jossey-Bass.

Janis, I. L. (ed.). *Current Trends in Psychology: Readings from American Scientist*. Los Altos, CA: William Kaufmann.

McGee, M. (ed.). *Introduction to Psychology: Reader*. St. Paul: West.

Merbaum, M. and G. Strickland (eds.). *Search for Human Understanding*, 2nd ed. New York: Holt, Rinehart, and Winston.

Milgram, S. (ed.) *Psychology in Today's World*. Boston: Educational Associates/Little, Brown and Co.

Rubinstein, J. and B. D. Slife (eds.). *Taking Sides: Clashing Views on Controversial Psychological Issues*. Guilford, CN: Dushkin.

APPENDIX E

Film Sources

ABC-TV--American Broadcasting Co.
1330 Avenue of the Americas
New York, NY 10019

Access Network
295 Midpark Way SE
Calgary, Alberta, CANADA T2X 2A8

Aims Media, Inc.
6901 Woodley Ave.
Van Nuys, CA 91406

Ambrose Video Publishing
Exclusive Distributors of
Time Life Video
381 Park Ave. S.
Suite 1601
New York, NY 10016

American Association for Counseling and
Development
5999 Stevenson Ave.
Alexandria, VA 22304

Barr Films
12801 Schabarum Ave.
P.O. Box 7878
Irwindale, CA 91107

Carousel Films
260 Fifth Ave.
Room 705
New York, NY 10001

Cinema Guild
1697 Broadway
New York, NY 10019

Cinema 16 Film Library
196 W. Houston St.
New York, NY 10014

Coast District Telecourses
11460 Warner Ave.
Fountain Valley, CA 92708

Coronet Films and Video
108 Wilmot Rd.
Deerfield, IL 60015

CRM McGraw-Hill
P.O. Box 641
Del Mar, CA 92014-9988

CTV Television Network Ltd.
42 Charles St. East
Toronto, Ontario, CANADA M4Y 1T4

Educational Dimensions Group
P.O. Box 126
Stamford, CT 06904

Encyclopedia Britannica Educational Corp.
310 So. Michigan Ave.
Chicago, IL 60604

Extension Media Center
University of California
2176 Shattuck Ave.
Berkeley, CA 94704

Federal Mogul Service
P.O. Box 1966
Detroit, MI 48235

Filmakers Library, Inc.
124 E. 40th St.
New York, NY 10016

Films for the Humanities
P.O. Box 2053
Princeton, NJ 08540-2053

Films Incorporated
5547 N. Ravenswood
Chicago, IL 60640-1199

Harcourt Brace Jovanovich, Inc.
1250 Sixth Ave.
San Diego, CA 92101

HarperCollins
10 E. 53rd St.
New York, NY 10022

Houghton Mifflin Co.
One Beacon St.
Boston, MA 02108

Indiana University
Media and Teaching Resources Center
Bloomington, IN 47405-5901

Institute For Rational Emotive Therapy
(See Pennsylvania State University)

International Film Bureau
332 S. Michigan Ave.
Chicago, IL 60604

John Wiley and Sons, Inc.
Educational Services Department
605 Third Ave.
New York, NY 10158-0012

Karol Media
350 N. Pennsylvania Ave.
Wilkes Barre, PA 18773-7600

McGraw-Hill Films
674 Via DE La Valle
P.O. Box 641
Del Mar, CA 92014

Motivational Media
12001 Ventura Place #202
Studio City, CA 91604

National Film Board of Canada
Indiana University Audio-Visual Center
Bloomington, IN 47405

New York University Film Library
26 Washington Place
New York, NY 10003

Pennsylvania State University
Psychological Cinema Register
Audio-Visual Services
University Park, PA 16803

Phoenix/Bfa Films and Video, Inc.
468 Park Ave. South
New York, NY 10016

Psychological Cinema Register
(see Pennsylvania State University)

Psychological Films
Distribution Center
110 N. Wheeler
Orange, CA 92669

Pyramid Film & Video
Cornell University
Audio-Visual Resource Center
8 Research Park
Ithaca, NY 14850

Research Press
Box 3170
Champaign, IL 61826

San Diego State College
5402 College Ave.
Sand Diego, CA 92115

Time Life Films
(see Ambrose Video Publishing)

University of Illinois
Film and Video Center
1325 S. Oak St.
Champaign, IL 61820

University of Minnesota
University Film and Video
1313 Fifth St. SE
Suite 108
Minneapolis, MN 55414

APPENDIX F: Crossword Puzzles

CHAPTER ONE

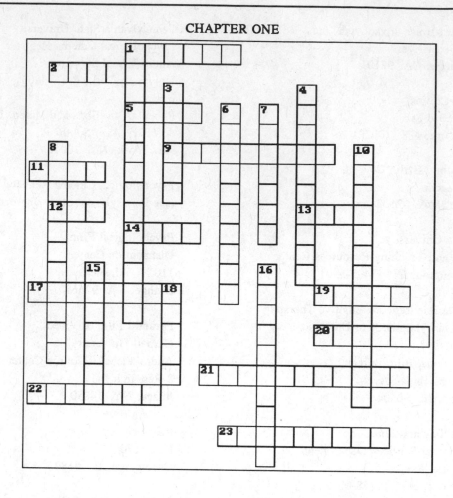

ACROSS

1. Russian scientist who studied conditioning.
2. Founder of functionalism.
5. Author of your text.
9. Type of thoughts or information gained through observation.
11. The accuracy score of graphologists.
12. American Psychological Association.
13. Recommended reading and study technique.
14. First step of the LISAN plan.
17. The human ability to make choices.
19. Founder of psychoanalysis.
20. Challenged the ideas of the functionalists.
21. _____ thoughts are below the level of awareness.
22. Last of the four goals of psychology.
23. Modern approach concerned with mental processes.

DOWN

1. Freudian approach to therapy.
3. Animals may serve as _____ to provide data on behavior.
4. Approach developed by Rogers and Maslow.
6. Approach requiring careful measurement.
7. Best known modern behaviorist.
8. School of thought that focuses on the conditioned response.
10. "Looking inward."
15. School of thought founded by Wertheimer; means "whole."
16. Scientific study of human and animal behavior.
18. Listening and note-taking.

CHAPTER TWO

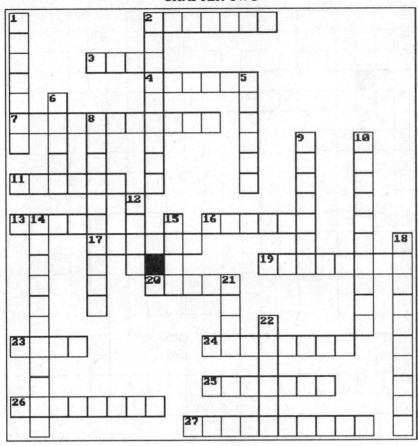

ACROSS

2. Group that does not receive independent variable.
3. Observer ___; should be minimized.
4. Research ____ should be considered when designing experiments.
7. Existence of a consistent relationship between variables.
11. Haphazard and without definite pattern.
13. Experimental or control ____.
16. Portion of a population.
17. Did first in-depth study of accidental frontal lobotomy.
19. Can be self-fulfilling.
20. Can be single or double.
23. The mathematical wonder horse.
24. Any experimental condition that can change.
25. Para_____; not truly scientific.
26. Correlation designated by +1.00.
27. A scientific technique that maximizes control.

DOWN

1. Michael ____; impaled his head on a rod and survived with no major personality changes.
2. Investigation of one subject's behavior.
5. Method using polling techniques.
6. Did field experiment in aiding behavior.
8. Peptides linked to pain control.
9. Inactive substance given in place of a drug.
10. Type of variable to be excluded.
12. Indicates a weak or non-existent relationship.
14. Reproducing an experiment.
15. Method of gathering data.
18. Predicted outcome of an experiment.
21. Collected by experimenters.
22. Straight-line relationship.

CHAPTER THREE

ACROSS

1.   A brain peptide.
6.   Body of a nerve cell.
7.   Glands whose secretions pass directly into the bloodstream.
9.   _____ callosum; connects the two hemispheres.
11. Two of these make the cerebrum.
15. Individual nerve cell.
17. A bundle of neurons.
20. Controls vital life functions.
22. Lobe that receives auditory input.
26. Microscopic space between neurons.
28. Controls consciousness.
30. Carries messages to and from sense organs and skeletal muscles.
31. Regulates muscular coordination.

DOWN

2.   Chemical substance that crosses the synapse.
3.   Electrically charged molecules.
4.   Central nervous system.
5.   Sector of cerebral cortex.
8.   Chemical secreted by endocrine glands.
10. Branching projections of neurons.
12. Brain structure related to emotion and memory.
13. Type of speech disturbance.
14. Building block of living organisms.
16. A neural transmission that bypasses the brain.
18. Fatty layer that covers some axons.
19. _____ neurons; carry commands to muscles and glands.
21. System divided into sympathetic and parasympathetic.
23. Love that is primary visual area.
24. "Switching station" for sensory messages.
25. Gland that regulates metabolism.
27. Long, thin fiber that carries electrical impulses.
29. Spinal ____; brain-body connector.

CHAPTER FOUR

ACROSS

3. Response to stimulation of sensory receptors.
5. Area of retina that provides sharpest vision.
7. Structure that focuses images on retina.
9. Property that classifies color.
10. Threshold or limit.
12. Colored circular muscle of the eye.
13. Sensed by buds.
16. Corresponds to sensed loudness.
17. Degree of energy of light waves.
18. Visible external part of ear.
20. Caused by fatigue of visual system.
23. Clear outer membrane covering the eyeball.
25. Snail-shaped organ of hearing.
27. Studied activity of cells in visual cortex.
28. Pertaining to skin senses.
29. Number of sound waves per second.
30. Visual receptors producing black and white vision.
31. _____ vision; loss of peripheral vision.

DOWN

1. Detectable change in a stimulus.
2. Visual receptors that detect color.
3. Pureness of a color.
4. Minimum amount of energy.
6. The act of smelling.
8. Tympanic membrane.
11. _____ senses; related to balance or equilibrium.
14. Photosensitive lining at the back of the eye.
15. ____ canals; fluid-filled tubes that affect balance.
19. ____ and key theory; explanation of the process of smelling.
21. Test for color blindness.
22. Studied sensory thresholds.
24. The smallest possible "package" of light energy.
26. Psychological experience of high or low tones.

CHAPTER FIVE

ACROSS

2. ____ perception; ability to see three-dimensional space.
4. Process of meaningfully organizing sensation.
7. Perceptual tendency to complete figures.
8. Nearness in time or space.
12. Scientific study of the extranormal.
15. Studied psi events.
17. Depth cue that occurs when one object partially blocks another.
18. ____ illusion; perceptual error caused by apparent distance.
19. ____ phenomena seem to defy scientific laws.
20. Simultaneous inward turning of eyes as they focus on nearby objects.
22. Mental state caused by experience, motives, context, or suggestion.
24. ____ disparity; most basic source of depth perception.
25. Found that people focus longer on unusual elements than on familiar ones.
26. ____ attention; priority given to some

messages.
27. Studied depth perception in remote tribes.

DOWN

1. Changes in the shape of lens in order to focus.
3. Form of ESP in which thoughts are transferred from sender to receiver.
5. Illusion in which lengths of lines are compared.
6. A clue in depth perception.
9. ____ room; challenges perceptual habits of an observer.
10. Pertaining to the function of one eye.
11. Form of ESP in which objects or events are perceived without aid of normal sensory system.
13. Pictorial ____; aids in depth perception.
14. Decrease in response to repeated presentation of a stimulus.
16. Orienting toward or focusing on some stimulus.
21. Extrasensory Perception.
23. ____ constancy; perceived size remains even when retinal image changes.

CHAPTER SIX

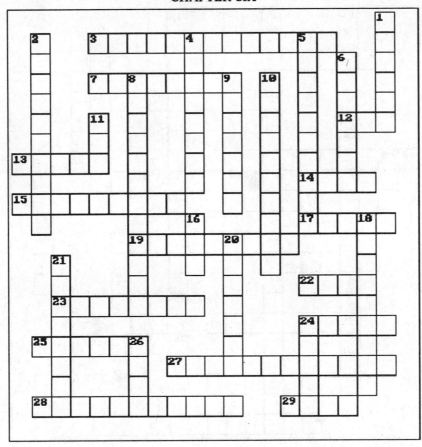

ACROSS

3. Awareness.
7. State of increased susceptibility to suggestion.
12. Altered states of consciousness.
13. Occurs during REM stage of sleep.
14. Sleep stages without dreams.
15. Mild hallucinogen.
17. Opposes current drug regulation.
19. Ability to adapt to increasing amounts of a drug.
22. _____ waves; brain activity during waking state.
23. Natural drug with stimulant properties.
24. _____ waves; brain activity during relaxed state.
25. Patterns of sleep activity.
27. Substance that distorts reality.
28. Drug that lowers activity of central nervous system.
29. Found that dreams reflect everyday events.

DOWN

1. _____ jerk; reflex muscle contraction when falling asleep.
2. Dream in which one feels fully conscious.
4. Common sleep disorder.
5. Substances that cause excitation of the central nervous system.
6. Drug used as stimulant and local anesthetic.
8. Substance capable of altering perception and sensation.
9. Freud used these to interpret dreams.
10. Can be physical, psychological, or both.
11. Sleep stage involving dreaming.
16. Brainwave machine.
18. Studied effects of smoking.
20. America's favorite depressant.
21. Natural stimulant found in tobacco.
24. An interruption in breathing.
26. Crib death.

CHAPTER SEVEN

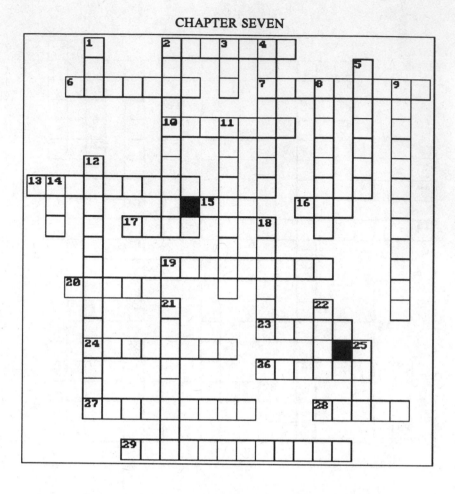

ACROSS

2. Stated the principle of prepotency.
6. Type of conditioning dependent on consequences.
7. Prevention of an unpleasant stimulus.
10. Reinforcing successive approximations.
13. Patterns of partial reinforcement.
15. Skinner ___; conditioning chamber
16. Computer Assisted Instruction.
17. Repetition and memorization.
19. _____ map; internal representation of spatial relationships.
20. _____ and practice; simplest computerized instruction.
23. Secondary reinforcer that can be exchanged for a primary reinforcer.
24. Imitating the behavior of another.
26. A simple innate behavior.
27. Combination of classical and operant conditioning.
28. Variable _____; schedule that produces high response rates.

29. Punishment involving lost privileges, e. g.

DOWN

1. Fixed Action Pattern.
2. Reduces the probability of the recurrence of a response
3. Cognitive ___; part of Tolman's findings.
4. Occurs when a single reinforcer maintains a series of responses.
5. Researched observational learning.
8. Period of time between reinforcements.
9. Process of learning by association.
11. Relating to a frequent response.
12. Any stimulus that increases frequency of a response.
14. Conditioned Emotional Response.
18. Learning that is not apparent until reinforcement occurs.
21. Studied the effects of TV on Canadian children.
22. Used by Pavlov as neutral stimulus.
25. Sign over the door to go out.

CHAPTER EIGHT

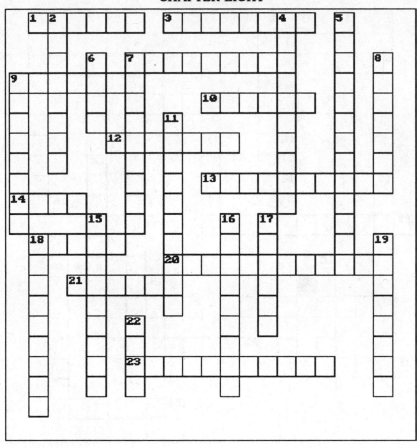

ACROSS

1. Capacity for storing and recovering information.
3. ____ memory; permanent memory storage.
7. Keeps a short-term memory alive.
9. Product of LTM.
10. A memory trace.
12. _____ imagery; photographic memory.
13. Researched memory using nonsense syllables.
14. A mental image or representation.
18. _____ memory; procedural memory.
20. Proactive or retroactive.
21. ____-memories; false memories.
23. Brain structure involved in memory transfer.

DOWN

2. Changing information into a storable form.
4. A measure of memory for prior learning.
5. Process by which memories are made permanent.
6. ____ memory; ability to learn specific information.
7. Extracting stored information from memory.
8. Measure of time of relearning.
9. ____ memory; a mental dictionary.
11. Barring unwanted memories from consciousness.
15. ____ memory; a lasting image frozen in memory.
16. Techniques that assist remembering.
17. Questioned permanence of long-term memory.
18. ____ memory; has capacity of 7 +/- 2 items.
19. Neurosurgeon who researched long-term memory.
22. Sounds held in sensory memory.

CHAPTER NINE

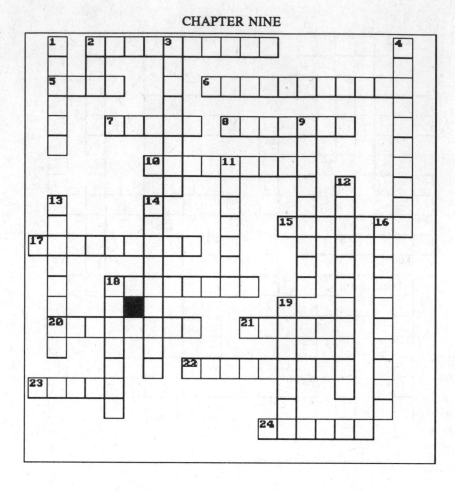

ACROSS

2.   ____ intelligence; sophisticated computer programs.
5.   Transformation ____; implicit or unspoken linguistic standard.
6.   Subjective or personal meaning.
7.   Conversed with Washoe.
8.   A set of rules for making sounds into words and words into sentences.
10.   Process of thinking.
15.   A characteristic of creativity.
17.   Smallest meaningful units in a language.
18.   Generalized ideas.
20.   Changing information into storable forms.
21.   Stands for an object or idea.
22.   ____ thinking; another term for creativity.
23.   Multiple-____ problem; used to test for insight.
24.   Study of word order.

DOWN

1.   The ____ task; naming colors and colored words to test interference.
2.   American Sign Language.
3.   Tendency to repeat wrong solutions.
4.   Characterized by divergent thinking.
9.   Assumptions brought to a problem.
11.   Sudden reorganization of the elements of a problem.
12.   Ability to see a variety of solutions to a problem.
13.   The basic sounds of a language.
14.   Study of meanings in language.
16.   ____ thinking; directed toward a single correct solution.
18.   Discussed transformational rules of grammar.
19.   Mental ____; mind pictures.

CHAPTER TEN

ACROSS

1.   Eating disorder characterized by binging.
7.   Autonomic Nervous System.
8.   ____-needs; Maslow's actualization motives.
11.   ____ effect; illustrates non-homeostatic quality of the sex drive.
12.   Hormone that activates the body in emotional arousal.
13.   The polygraph is wrongly believed to detect ____.
15.   Steady state of physiological equilibrium.
18.   Focus of the Triangular Theory.
19.   ____ motives; those based on learned psychological needs.
23.   A branch of the ANS.
25.   Opponent-____ theory; deals with aftereffect of strong emotion.
26.   Its root means "to move."

DOWN

1.   First two levels of Maslow's hierarchy.
2.   Schacter says we ___ our emotional arousal.
3.   Process of initiating, directing, and sustaining behavior.
4.   Theory that says emotional feelings follow bodily arousal.
5.   ____ Feedback hypothesis.
6.   ____ motives; those based on biological needs.
9.   Need for ____; desire to have impact on or control over others.
10.   With Dodson, studied performance and levels of arousal.
14.   Whatever satisfies a need.
16.   Proportion of fat that bodies seek to maintain.
17.   Process of ascribing behavior to various causes.
19.   Most widely recognized expression of emotion.
20.   Activates behavior.
21.   Female sex hormone.
22.   Kind of love based solely on physical attraction.
24.   The ANS causes the body to ___ to emotional arousal.

CHAPTER ELEVEN

ACROSS

1.   Mechanisms give relief from _____ .
5.   Behavioral _____ factors; increase likelihood of illness and death.
6.   Stage three of the GAS.
8.   Results from blocking of goal-directed behavior.
12. Stage one of the GAS.
13. Said "to be totally without stress is to be dead."
15. Occurs when one must work near capacity for a long period.
16. Person who bears the blame for others.
17. Type of personality unusually resistant to stress.
19. Return to earlier behavior patterns.
21. The GAS has three of these.

DOWN

1.   Being attracted to and repelled by the same goal.
2.   The competitive and striving personality.
3.   Frustration is often met first with a more vigorous effort and a more varied _____ .
4.   Mental state caused by incompatible motives.
7.   Three hundred is a _____ score on the SRRS.
9.   Explaining away one's shortcomings to avoid responsibility.
10. Occurs when one must adjust or adapt to the environment.
11. General Adaptation Syndrome
14. Life Change Units.
18. Refusing to recognize a problem.
20. Social Readjustment Rating Scale.

CHAPTER TWELVE

ACROSS

3. Understanding that volume remains the same in spite of a change in shape.
7. Effects of environment.
8. ___ reflex; startle response in infants.
11. Newborn.
12. Researched the concept of concrete operational thought.
13. Reproduction from a single cell.
15. Transmission of characteristics through genes.
18. Stage of moral development characterized by a desire to conform.
19. Early stage in speech development.
20. Promoted natural childbirth.
21. Two-word sentence stage of speech.
23. Analysis of amniotic fluid for genetic anomaly.
24. Could be "gentle" or "prepared."
25. Modification of existing ideas.

DOWN

1. Hereditary unit.
2. ___ operations; period when thinking can be based on abstract principles.
4. Using existing thought patterns in new situations.
5. Science that deals with improvement of a species.
6. ___ development; area of Kohlberg's research.
9. Threadlike structure that carries genes.
10. Orderly emergence of personal characteristics.
14. Believed that moral values are learned.
16. ___ anxiety; distress displayed when parents leave.
17. Fetal Alcohol Syndrome.
22. Person between infancy and adolescence.

CHAPTER THIRTEEN

ACROSS

1. "Womb to tomb."
3. Craving for unnatural foods.
5. A hospital for the terminally ill.
6. Skill that must be acquired for optimal development.
8. Distinguished between a child's feelings and behavior.
9. Sometimes called "smotherlove."
11. Considered a turbulent time for many in our culture.
14. Believes that many parents hurry their children's development.
16. Intimacy is forming bonds of ____ and friendship.
17. Theorist who outlined psychosocial crises.
19. Self-imposed starvation.
21. ____ speech; one of the two most common speech problems.
22. Fear that one will ____ makes it more likely to occur.
23. Cessation of female menstrual cycles.

25 Erikson's crisis of young adulthood.

DOWN

2. Parenting style that is overly restrictive and lacking in warmth.
4. Freezing a person's body just after death.
5. Characterized by short attention span and restlessness.
7. Prejudice based on age.
10. Time of rapid growth and hormonal changes.
12. May result when parents have a high level of stress and frustration.
13. Studied parenting styles.
14. Lack of bladder control.
15. Inability to read with understanding.
18. Activity ____; adjustment to aging requiring social involvement.
20. Severe disorder involving mutism, tantrums, and other problems.
24. Near Death Experience.

CHAPTER FOURTEEN

ACROSS

1. Standardized measures of ability.
2. Founder of modern intelligence testing.
7. General Intelligence.
8. Retardation associated with poverty.
10. Associated race and IQ.
13. Testing for this factor involves language- and/or symbol-oriented tasks.
16. Global capacity to deal with the environment.
17. Phenylketonuria.
18. Measuring what a test claims to measure.
19. Instrument that can be given to more than one person at a time.
20. An index of intellectual ability.
21. Retardation caused by physiological or genetic factors.
23. Twins conceived from two separate eggs.
24. An indication of mental ability as determined by the Stanford-Binet.

DOWN

1. Developed the Stanford-Binet.
3. Retarded persons with an IQ ranging from 50 to 70.
4. Retarded person with an exceptional talent in a very narrow area.
5. A bell-shaped mathematical construct.
6. Refers to a person's physical age.
9. Mental capacity significantly below average.
11. Process of making a test valid and reliable.
12. Intelligence measured by a person's standing relative to age group.
14. Yielding similar results on retesting.
15. Nonverbal measure of intelligence.
22. Culture-____; not disadvantaging certain groups.

CHAPTER FIFTEEN

ACROSS

1. Personality testing involving direct observation.
3. An outgoing person.
7. Basic ____; occurs when people feel alone in a hostile world.
8. Displacing sexual energies to socially acceptable activities.
9. Branch of psychology emphasizing free will.
12. ___ effect; favorable impression from unrelated details.
14. Developer of the TAT.
15. An enduring way of thinking, feeling, or behaving.
16. In Freudian terms, getting "stuck" in an early developmental stage.
19. A well known trait theorist.
21. Freudian conscious controller of behavior.
22. Allport's traits that are the building blocks of personality.
24. Oral, anal, phallic, and genital.
26. Anticipation that a response will lead to reinforcement.

27. Basic, pervasive personality trait.
28. One's ____ are strongly affected by temperament.

DOWN

2. Becoming like an admired adult.
4. _____ complex; boy's attraction to his mother.
5. Thematic Apperception Test.
6. Roger's theory centers on the concept of self.
8. Perception of one's own personality traits.
10. Rating ____; more objective technique than the interview.
11. Developed the 16PF.
13. First of Freud's stages.
17. The person one would like to be.
18. Believed we can move toward, away from, or against others.
20. Category of individuals who have a number of traits in common.
23. Minnesota Multiphasic Personality Inventory.
25. This makes up the structure of personality according to behaviorists.

CHAPTER SIXTEEN

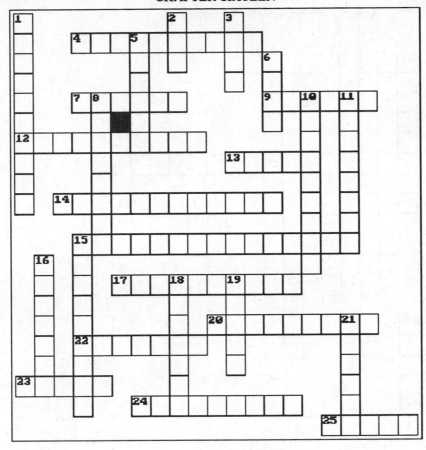

ACROSS

4. Exaggeration of sadness and despondency.
7. Sex with blood relatives.
9. Intense and unrealistic fear.
12. Feeling driven to repeat an action.
13. Taking flight by a loss of memory.
14. Type of disorders including amnesia, fugue, and multiple personality.
15. Another term for mental illness.
17. Disorders characterized by physical complaints or disabilities.
20. Sexual arousal associated with inanimate objects.
22. Disorders with clear physiological or genetic causes.
23. _____ disorder; involves intense anxiety and fear of loss of control.
24. Desire to view the genitals of others.
25. _____ anesthesia, loss of feeling in the hand.

DOWN

1. Type of personality that is in conflict with society.
2. Diagnostic and Statistical Manual of Mental Disorders.
3. Disorders involving disturbances in emotions.
5. Believes mental illness is the result of faulty self-image.
6. Sexual act of brutality or aggression.
8. Problem involving excessive anxiety without loss of contact with reality.
10. Recurring irrational or disturbing thoughts.
11. Legal term for serious mental illness.
15. One who has withdrawn from reality and suffers from personality disorganization
16. Loss of memory for past events.
18. Feeling of apprehensive uneasiness.
19. Founder of psychoanalysis.
21. _____ sadism, gaining pleasure by inflicting pain during the sex act.

CHAPTER SEVENTEEN

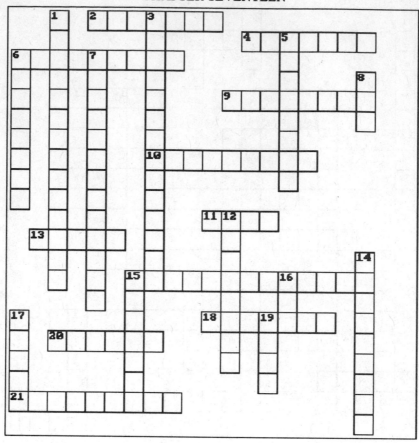

ACROSS

2. Psycho_____; prefrontal lobotomy, for example.
4. Mood disorder involving swings between mania and depression.
6. False beliefs held against all contrary evidence.
9. Neurotransmitter found in the brain.
10. Severe disturbance involving a break with reality.
11. ____ affect; showing almost no signs of emotion.
13. Stress-vulnerability ____; attributes psychosis to an interaction of stress and heredity.
15. Psychological treatment for behavior disorders.
18. Therapies that include chemotherapy, ECT, and psychosurgery.
20. Symptom of catatonia.
21. Type of disorder involving mutism and waxy flexibility of the body.

DOWN

1. Sensations that have no basis in reality.
3. Organic psychosis caused by syphilis.
5. Psychotic state characterized by delusions of persecution.
6. Senile _____; a form of organic psychosis.
7. Psychosis characterized by withdrawal from reality.
8. Positron Emission Tomography.
12. Disconnecting frontal lobes surgically.
14. _____ disorder; moderate depression that lasts for two years or more.
15. Produces colored images of brain areas and their activities.
16. Electroconvulsive Therapy.
17. Extremely elated, hyperactive, and energetic.
19. ____-psychotic; a major tranquilizer, for example.

CHAPTER EIGHTEEN

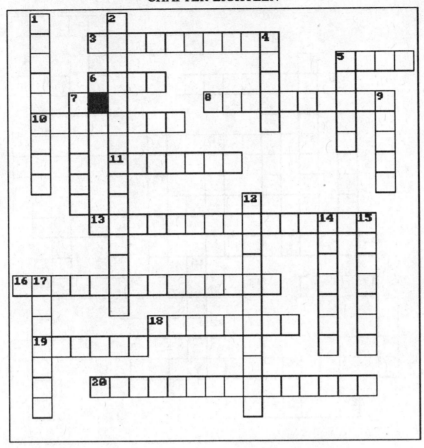

ACROSS

3. Avoidance of certain topics during therapy.
5. ____ association; saying whatever comes to mind.
6. Believes that negative thoughts underlie depression.
8. Suppressing a response through discomfort.
10. Generalization of aversion conditioning.
11. Removing an individual from a reinforcing situation.
13. Therapy in which clients abandon self-defeating behavior.
16. Freudian approach to therapy.
18. Therapy in which a negative response is associated with an undesirable habit.
19. Pioneer in classical conditioning.
20. Behavior modification and cognitive, for example.

DOWN

1. Therapy focusing on thoughts as well as behavior.
2. Repeated exposure to a feared stimulus.
4. Developer of RET.
5. Founder of psychoanalysis.
7. ____ therapy; husband, wife, and children working as a group to solve problems.
9. ____ economy; system of rewards.
12. Groups that gently enlarge awareness of self and others.
14. Therapy that strives for deeper understanding of thoughts, emotions, and behavior.
15. Taking another's point of view.
17. Reinforcing successive approximations of a behavior.

CHAPTER NINETEEN

ACROSS

1. Studied females exposed prenatally to androgens.
2. Female sex organs that produce eggs.
5. State of being sexual.
8. Release of sexual excitement.
9. Female sex hormones.
13. Time when menstrual periods end.
14. Sexual ___; determine when, where, and with whom we express sexual feelings.
15. Male sexual hormones.
17. Observed Tchambuli sex role behavior.
19. Male hormone responsible for secondary sexual characteristics.
23. Sensate ____; treatment for retarded ejaculation.
24. ____ rape; sexual assault by an acquaintance.
25. Surveyed women concerning orgasm.
26. Condition of having both male and female traits.
27. Second phase of sexual response, according to Masters and Johnson.

DOWN

1. Gynecologist who studied sexual intercourse.
2. Release of eggs from the ovaries.
3. State of being male or female.
4. Chemical substances secreted by endocrine glands.
6. Release of sperm and seminal fluid during orgasm.
7. Inability to produce or maintain an erection.
10. Testes in male and ovaries in female.
11. Learned behavior that fits social expectations for males and females.
12. Glands that are the source of sperm.
16. Listed ten ways to avoid intimacy and communication.
18. Glands that supply additional sex hormones; located above the kidneys.
20. Should be expressed in a healthy relationship.
21. Acquired Immune Deficiency Syndrome.
22. Sexually Transmitted Diseases.

CHAPTER TWENTY

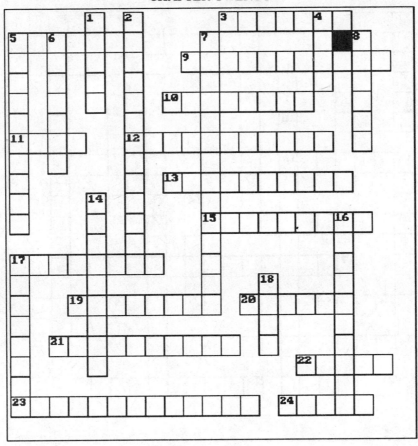

ACROSS

3. Did studies on obedience.
5. Ongoing pattern passed from one generation to the next.
9. Consequence of moderate self-disclosure.
10. ____ power; based on respect for a person or group.
11. Expected behavior pattern linked with a particular social position.
12. Process of ascribing behavior to various causes.
13. Situation in which present rewards lead to undesirable aftereffects.
15. Milgram's subject.
17. ____ roles; those not under the individual's control.
19. Can be personal, social, or public.
20. ____ comparison; judging oneself by comparison with others.
21. Basis for most voluntary social relationships.
22. Researched "groupthink" in government.
23. Making a large request to get a smaller one.
24. Means of influence in a social group.

DOWN

1. Developed "liking" and "love" scales.
2. Invisible spatial envelope.
4. Studied conformity.
5. Yielding to pressures for uniformity.
6. Making larger demands after getting an initial commitment.
7. Baring private thoughts and feelings.
8. Position in a group.
14. To associate with other people.
16. Agreeing to the request of another.
17. ____ role; one that is attained voluntarily.
18. Accepted social rule for behavior.

CHAPTER TWENTY-ONE

ACROSS

1. Predisposition toward a particular social stimulus.
3. Institutionalized prejudice based on race.
6. Studied social apathy.
7. Sociobiologists believe that social traits are passed on through one's ____.
8. Any deliberate attempt to change attitudes.
11. ____ control; techniques for controlling aggressive impulses.
12. Habitual redirection of aggression toward some person or group.
15. A negative attitude held against members of a particular group.
17. Theory that combines learning principles with cognitive processes.
18. ____ winter; possible effect of international aggression.
19. Groups using high pressure indoctrination techniques.
20. Theory that maintains that social behavior has roots in heredity.
21. Harvard zoologist and sociobiologist.
22. Inaccurate or oversimplified images of particular social groups.

DOWN

1. Bystander ____; failure to give help in a crisis.
2. Open-ended ____; technique for measuring attitudes.
4. Any response intended to harm another.
5. Studied inter-group conflict.
6. Cognitive ____; an imbalance between thoughts and behavior.
9. ____ classroom; emphasizes cooperation rather than competition.
10. Behavior toward others based on prejudice.
11. Distinguished between personal and group prejudice.
13. Type of contact that may reduce prejudice.
14. Worked with 3 ACROSS.
16. Strong feeling about an issue.

CHAPTER TWENTY-TWO

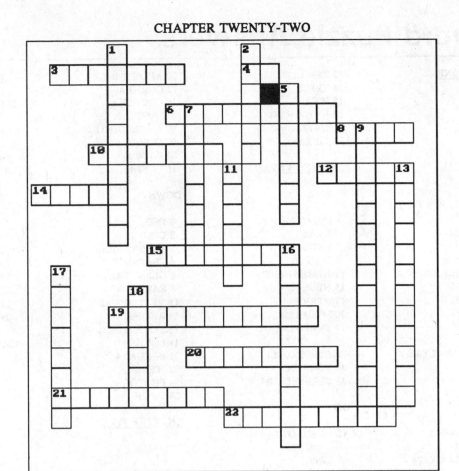

ACROSS

3. Based on the assumption that workers must be goaded and guided.
4. Industrial/organizational psychology.
6. _____ research; studies consumer behavior.
8. _____ teaching; emphasizes active teacher/student discussion.
10. Detailed biographical information about a job applicant.
12. Can be fantasy, realistic, or tentative.
14. Studied the effects of scents.
15. Flexible working hours.
19. Determination of skills and knowledge needed to succeed at a job.
20. Overpopulation.
21. Mental health professional specializing in adjustment problems.
22. Time of high productivity and acceptance by co-workers.

DOWN

1. _____ counselors; match people with jobs.
2. _____ instruction; information presented by lecture and demonstration.
5. Quality _____; in business, voluntary discussion groups that meet regularly.
7. Type of test that rates a person's potential to learn tasks or skills.
9. Intense concentration, detachment, and feeling unusual power, in athletes.
11. _____ psychologists; seek to understand and improve athletic performance.
13. Can be social or psychological.
16. Work _____; maximum output at lowest cost.
17. Producing an immediate and obvious effect.
18. Studied emergency survival techniques.

APPENDIX G

Crossword Puzzle Answers

CHAPTER ONE

ACROSS

1 PAVLOV
2 JAMES
5 COON
10 EMPIRICAL
11 ZERO
12 APA
13 SQ3R
14 LEAD
17 FREEWILL
19 FREUD
20 WATSON
21 UNCONSCIOUS
22 CONTROL
23 COGNITIVE

DOWN

1 PSYCHOANALYSIS
3 MODELS
4 HUMANISTIC
6 SCIENTIFIC
7 SKINNER
8 INTROSPECTION
9 BEHAVIORISM
15 GESTALT
16 PSYCHOLOGY
18 LISAN

CHAPTER TWO

ACROSS

2 CONTROL
3 BIAS
4 ETHICS
7 CORRELATION
11 RANDOM
13 GROUP
16 SAMPLE
17 HARLOW
19 PROPHECY
20 BLIND
23 HANS
24 VARIABLE
25 SCIENCE
26 POSITIVE
27 EXPERIMENT

DOWN

1 MELNICK
2 CASESTUDY
5 SURVEY
6 BRYAN
8 ENDORPHINS
9 PLACEBO
10 EXTRANEOUS

12 ZERO
14 REPLICATION
15 POLL
18 HYPOTHESIS
21 DATA
22 LINEAR

CHAPTER THREE

ACROSS

1 ENDORPHIN
6 SOMA
7 ENDOCRINE
9 CORPUS
11 HEMISPHERE
15 NEURON
17 NERVE
20 MEDULLA
22 TEMPORAL
26 SYNAPSE
28 CEREBRUM
30 SOMATIC
31 CEREBELLUM

DOWN

2 NEUROTRANSMIT-
   TER
3 IONS
4 CNS
5 LOBE
8 HORMONE
10 DENDRITE
12 HIPPOCAMPUS
13 APHASIA
14 CELL
16 REFLEXARC
18 MYELIN
19 MOTOR
21 AUTONOMIC
23 OCCIPITAL
24 THALAMUS
25 THYROID
27 AXON
29 CORD

CHAPTER FOUR

ACROSS

3 SENSATION
5 FOVEA
7 LENS
9 HUE
10 LIMEN
12 IRIS
13 TASTE
16 AMPLITUDE
17 BRIGHTNESS
18 PINNA

20 AFTERIMAGE
23 CORNEA
25 COCHLEA
27 HUBEL
28 SOMESTHETIC
29 FREQUENCY
30 RODS
31 TUNNEL

DOWN

1 JND
2 CONES
3 SATURATION
4 THRESHOLD
6 OLFACTION
8 EARDRUM
11 VESTIBULAR
14 RETINA
15 SEMICIRCULAR
19 LOCK
21 ISHIHARA
22 WEBER
24 PHOTON
26 PITCH

CHAPTER FIVE

ACROSS

2 DEPTH
4 PERCEPTION
7 CLOSURE
8 CONTIGUITY
12 PARAPSYCHOLOGY
15 RHINE
17 OVERLAP
18 MOON
19 PSI
20 CONVERGENCE
22 EXPECTANCY
24 RETINAL
25 LOFTUS
26 SELECTIVE
27 HUDSON

DOWN

1 ACCOMMODATION
3 TELEPATHY
5 MULLERLYER
6 TEXTURE
9 AMES
10 MONOCULAR
11 CLAIRVOYANCE
13 CUES
14 HABITUATION
16 ATTENTION
21 ESP
23 SIZE

CHAPTER SIX

ACROSS

3 CONSCIOUSNESS
7 HYPNOSIS
12 ASC
13 DREAM
14 NREM
15 MARIJUANA
17 SZASZ
19 TOLERANCE
22 BETA
23 CAFFEINE
24 ALPHA
25 STAGES
27 HALLUCINOGEN
28 DEPRESSANTS
29 HALL

DOWN

1 HYPNIC
2 LUCIDDREAM
4 INSOMNIA
5 STIMULANTS
6 COCAINE
8 PSYCHOACTIVE
9 SYMBOLS
10 DEPENDENCE
11 REM
16 EEG
18 SCHACHTER
20 ALCOHOL
21 NICOTINE
24 APNEA
26 SIDS

CHAPTER SEVEN

ACROSS

2 PREMACK
6 OPERANT
7 AVOIDANCE
10 SHAPING
13 SCHEDULES
15 BOX
16 CAI
17 ROTE
19 COGNITIVE
20 DRILL
23 TOKEN
24 MODELING
26 REFLEX
27 TWOFACTOR
28 RATIO
29 RESPONSECOST

DOWN (CH. 7)

1 FAP
2 PUNISHMENT
3 MAP
4 CHAINING
5 BANDURA
8 INTERVAL
9 CONDITIONING
11 PREPOTENT
12 REINFORCEMENT
14 CER
18 LATENT
21 WILLIAMS
22 BELL
25 EXIT

CHAPTER EIGHT

ACROSS

1 MEMORY
3 LONGTERM
7 REHEARSAL
9 STORAGE
10 ENGRAM
12 EIDETIC
13 EBBINGHAUS
14 ICON
18 SKILL
20 INTERFERENCE
21 PSEUDO
23 HIPPOCAMPUS

DOWN

2 ENCODING
4 RELEARNING
5 CONSOLIDATION
6 FACT
7 RETRIEVAL
8 SAVINGS
9 SEMANTIC
11 REPRESSION
15 FLASHBULB
16 MNEMONICS
17 LOFTUS
18 SHORTTERM
19 PENFIELD
22 ECHO

CHAPTER NINE

ACROSS

2 ARTIFICIAL
5 RULE
6 CONNOTATIVE
7 FOUTS
8 GRAMMAR
10 COGNITION
15 FLUENCY
17 MORPHEMES
18 CONCEPTS
20 ENCODING
21 SYMBOL
22 DIVERGENT
23 STICK

24 SYNTAX

DOWN

1 STROOP
2 ASL
3 FIXATION
4 CREATIVITY
9 MENTALSET
11 INSIGHT
12 FLEXIBILITY
13 PHONEMES
14 SEMANTICS
16 CONVERGENT
18 CHOMSKY
19 IMAGERY

CHAPTER TEN

ACROSS

1 BULIMIA
7 ANS
8 META
11 COOLIDGE
12 ADRENALINE
13 LIES
15 HOMEOSTASIS
18 LOVE
19 SECONDARY
23 SYMPATHETIC
25 PROCESS
26 EMOTIONS

DOWN

1 BASICNEEDS
2 LABEL
3 MOTIVATION
4 JAMESLANGE
5 FACIAL
6 PRIMARY
9 POWER
10 YERKES
14 GOAL
16 SETPOINT
17 ATTRIBUTION
19 SMILE
20 DRIVE
21 ESTROGEN
22 FATUOUS
24 REACT

CHAPTER ELEVEN

ACROSS

1 ANXIETY
5 RISK
6 EXHAUSTION
8 FRUSTRATION
12 ALARM
13 SELYE
15 PRESSURE
16 SCAPEGOAT
17 HARDY
19 REGRESSION
21 STAGE

DOWN

1 APPROACH-
  AVOIDANCE
2 TYPEA
3 RESPONSE
4 CONFLICT
7 HIGH
9 RATIONALIZATION
10 STRESS
11 GAS
14 LCU
18 DENIAL
20 SRRS

CHAPTER TWELVE

ACROSS

3 CONSERVATION
7 NURTURE
8 MORO
11 NEONATE
12 CROLL
13 CLONING
15 HEREDITY
18 CONVENTIONAL
19 BABBLING
20 LAMAZE
21 TELEGRAPHIC
23 AMNIOCENTESIS
24 BIRTH
25 ACCOMMODATION

DOWN

1 GENE
2 FORMAL
4 ASSIMILATION
5 EUGENICS
6 MORAL
9 CHROMOSOME
10 MATURATION
14 KOHLBERG
16 SEPARATION
17 FAS
22 CHILD

CHAPTER THIRTEEN

ACROSS

1 LIFESPAN
3 PICA
5 HOSPICE
6 TASK
8 GINOTT
9 OVERPROTECTION
11 ADOLESCENCE
14 ELKIND
16 LOVE
17 ERIKSON
19 ANOREXIA
21 DELAYED
22 STUTTER
23 MENOPAUSE
25 INTIMACY

DOWN

2 AUTHORITARIAN
4 CRYONICS
5 HYPERACTIVITY
7 AGEISM
10 PUBERTY
12 CHILDABUSE
13 BAUMRIND
14 ENURESIS
15 DYSLEXIA
18 THEORY
20 AUTISM
24 NDE

CHAPTER FOURTEEN

ACROSS

1 TESTS
2 BINET
7 GFACTOR
8 FAMILIAL
10 JENSEN
13 VERBAL
16 INTELLIGENCE
17 PKU
18 VALIDITY
19 GROUPTEST
20 IQ
21 ORGANIC
23 FRATERNAL
24 MENTALAGE

DOWN

1 TERMAN
3 EDUCABLE
4 SAVANT
5 NORMALCURVE
6 CA
9 RETARDATION
11 STANDARDIZATION
12 DEVIATIONIQ
14 RELIABILITY
15 PERFORMANCE
22 FAIR

CHAPTER FIFTEEN

ACROSS

1 SITUATIONAL
3 EXTROVERT
7 ANXIETY
8 SUBLIMATION
9 HUMANISTIC
12 HALO
14 MURRAY
15 TRAIT
16 FIXATION
19 ALLPORT
21 EGO
22 CENTRAL
24 STAGES
26 EXPECTANCY
27 CARDINAL
28 EMOTIONS

DOWN (CH. 15)

2 IDENTIFICATION
4 OEDIPUS
5 TAT
6 SELF
8 SELFCONCEPT
10 SCALE
11 CATTELL
13 ORAL
17 IDEALSELF
18 HORNEY
20 TYPE
23 MMPI
25 HABIT

CHAPTER SIXTEEN

ACROSS

4 DEPRESSION
7 INCEST
9 PHOBIA
12 COMPULSION
13 FUGUE
14 DISSOCIATIVE
15 PSYCHOPATHO-
   LOGY
17 SOMATOFORM
20 FETISHISM
22 ORGANIC
23 PANIC
24 VOYEURISM
25 GLOVE

DOWN

1 ANTISOCIAL
2 DSM
3 MOOD
5 ROGERS
6 RAPE
8 NEUROSIS
10 OBSESSION
11 INSANITY
15 PSYCHOTIC
16 AMNESIA
18 ANXIETY
19 FREUD
21 SEXUAL

CHAPTER SEVENTEEN

ACROSS

2 SURGERY
4 BIPOLAR
6 DELUSIONS
9 DOPAMINE
10 PSYCHOSIS
11 FLAT
13 MODEL
15 PSYCHOTHERAPY
18 SOMATIC
20 MUTISM
21 CATATONIC

DOWN

1 HALLUCINATIONS
3 GENERALPARESIS
5 PARANOIA
6 DEMENTIA
7 SCHIZOPHRENIA
8 PET
12 LOBOTOMY
14 DYSTHYMIC
15 PETSCAN
16 ECT
17 MANIC
19 ANTI

CHAPTER EIGHTEEN

ACROSS

3 RESISTANCE
5 FREE
6 BECK
8 PUNISHMENT
10 TRANSFER
11 TIMEOUT
13 RATIONALEMOTIVE
16 PSYCHOANALYSIS
18 AVERSION
19 PAVLOV
20 BEHAVIORTHERAPY

DOWN

1 COGNITIVE
2 DESENSITIZATION
4 ELLIS
5 FREUD
7 FAMILY
9 TOKEN
12 SENSITIVITY
14 INSIGHT
15 EMPATHY
17 SHAPING

CHAPTER NINETEEN

ACROSS

1 MONEY
2 OVARIES
5 SEXUALITY
8 ORGASM
9 ESTROGENS
13 MENOPAUSE
14 SCRIPTS
15 ANDROGENS
17 MEAD
19 TESTOSTERONE
23 FOCUS
24 DATE
25 HITE
26 ANDROGYNY
27 PLATEAU

DOWN

1 MASTERS
2 OVULATION
3 GENDER

4 HORMONES
6 EJACULATION
7 IMPOTENCE
10 GONADS
11 SEXROLES
12 TESTES
16 STRONG
18 ADRENAL
20 EMOTION
21 AIDS
22 STD

CHAPTER TWENTY

ACROSS

3 MILGRAM
5 CULTURE
9 RECIPROCITY
10 REFERENT
11 ROLE
12 ATTRIBUTION
13 SOCIALTRAP
15 OBEDIENCE
17 ASCRIBED
19 DISTANCE
20 SOCIAL
21 ATTRACTION
22 JANIS
23 DOORINTHEFACE
24 POWER

DOWN

1 RUBIN
2 PERSONALSPACE
4 ASCH
5 CONFORMITY
6 LOWBALL
7 SELFDISCLOSURE
8 STATUS
14 AFFILIATE
16 COMPLIANCE
17 ACHIEVED
18 NORM

CHAPTER TWENTY-ONE

ACROSS

1 ATTITUDE
3 RACISM
6 DARLEY
7 GENES
8 PERSUASION
11 ANGER
12 SCAPEGOATING
15 PREJUDICE
17 SOCIALLEARNING
18 NUCLEAR
19 CULTS
20 SOCIOBIOLOGY
21 WILSON
22 STEREOTYPES

DOWN

1 APATHY
2 INTERVIEW
4 AGGRESSION
5 SHERIF
6 DISSONANCE
9 JIGSAW
10 DISCRIMINATION
11 ALLPORT
13 EQUALSTATUS
14 LATANE
16 CONVICTION

CHAPTER TWENTY-TWO

ACROSS

3 THEORYX
4 IO
6 MARKETING
8 OPEN
10 BIODATA
12 STAGE
14 BARON
15 FLEXTIME
19 JOBANALYSIS
20 CROWDING
21 COUNSELOR
22 MIDCAREER

DOWN

1 VOCATIONAL
2 DIRECT
5 CIRCLES
7 APTITUDE
9 PEAKPERFORM-
   ANCE
11 SPORTS
13 ENVIRONMENTS
16 EFFICIENCY
17 FEEDBACK
18 LOFTUS

APPENDIX H:

Transparencies to Accompany Introduction to Psychology, Seventh Edition
by Dennis Coon

Chapter 20

Chapter 21

Appendix B